AF753836

OECD Business and Finance Outlook 2016

BETTER POLICIES FOR BETTER LIVES

Please cite this publication as:
OECD (2016), *OECD Business and Finance Outlook 2016*, OECD Publishing, Paris.
http://dx.doi.org/10.1787/9789264257573-en

ISBN 978-92-64-25756-6 (print)
ISBN 978-92-64-25757-3 (PDF)

Photo credits: © iStockphoto.com/OttoKrause.

Corrigenda to OECD publications may be found on line at: *www.oecd.org/about/publishing/corrigenda.htm.*

Foreword

This is the second edition of the OECD Business and Finance Outlook, *an annual publication that presents unique data and analysis that looks at what might affect and change, both favourably and unfavourably, tomorrow's world of business, finance and investment. This year's edition focuses on "doing business in a fragmented world". Using analysis from a wide range of perspectives, the report addresses past over-investment in certain industrial sectors, the reversal of the commodity supercycle and the implications of low interest rates for corporate and institutional investors. It provides a new look at large observed differences in productivity performance across firms and at the profitability of clean energy projects. Different aspects of the business environment are addressed, including fiscal incentives for R&D innovation; foreign bribery regimes; and investment treaties. The publication also analyses life expectancy around retirement age across different socio-economic groups and its implications for both social justice and the sustainability of pension systems.*

The Outlook is complemented by a sister publication, the OECD Business and Finance Scoreboard 2016. *The Scoreboard contains indicators and data that support analysis of developments in the financial markets and corporate sector.*

The 2016 OECD Business and Finance Outlook *is the joint work of staff of the OECD Directorate for Financial and Enterprise Affairs. It has benefited from contributions from national government delegates and other parts of the OECD Secretariat. Chapter 3 was co-authored by staff of the OECD Centre for Tax Policy and Administration and the OECD Directorate for Science, Technology and Innovation.*

Table of contents

Tables

Figures

Acronyms and abbreviations

ABS	Asset-backed security
ACWI	All Country World Index
ADV	Advanced economies
ALM	Asset-liability management
ATSs	Alternative trading systems
BATS	Bats Global Markets
BEPS	Base erosion and profit shifting
BIT	Bilateral investment treaty
BMD4	4th edition of the *OECD Benchmark Definition of Foreign Direct Investment*
BNEF	Bloomberg New Energy Finance
BO	Buyout
BoP	Balance of payment
BRIICS	Brazil, Russia, India, Indonesia, China, and South Africa
CAPEX	Company sales and capital expenditure
CAPM	Capital asset pricing model
CCGT	Combined-cycle gas turbine
CCP	Centralised clearing counter-party
CDB	China Development Bank
CEO	Chief executive officer
CETA	Comprehensive economic and trade agreement
CHX	Chicago Stock Exchange (CHX)
CIP	Covered interest parity
CITR	Corporate income tax rate
CMU	Capital market union
CO_2	Carbon dioxide
COD	Cost of debt
COE	Cost of equity
COK	Cost of capital
COP21	21st Conference of the Parties to the UNFCCC in December 2015 in Paris
CPI	Consumer Price Index
CPM	Canadian Pension Mortality
CSRC	China Securities and Regulatory Commission
CTA	Commodity trading advisor
DB	Defined benefit pension plans
DC	Defined contribution pension plans
DTD	Distance-to-default
EA	Age at which the individual began accumulating savings
EBITDA	Earnings before interest, taxes, depreciation and amortisation

ECB	European Central Bank
ECT	Energy charter treaty
EECA	Eastern Europe and Central Asia
EIOPA	European Insurance and Occupational Pensions Authority
EKF	*Eksport Kredit Fonden* (Denmark's export credit agency)
EME	emerging market economy
EMEA	Europe, Middle-East and Africa
EMIR	European market infrastructure reform act
EPS	Earnings per share
ESMA	European Securities and Markets Authority
ETF	Exchange traded fund
EU	European Union
FAFT	Financial Action Task Force
FCF	Free cash flow
FDI	Foreign direct investment
FED	United States Federal Reserve Board
FET	Fair and equitable treatment
FINRA	Financial Industry Regulatory Authority
FOI	Freedom of Investment
FSB	Financial Stability Board
FVS	Future value of savings
G20	Group of 20 (Argentina, Australia, Brazil, Canada, China, France, Germany, India, Indonesia, Italy, Japan, Mexico, Russia, Saudi Arabia, South Africa, Korea, Turkey, the United Kingdom, United States and the European Union)
GARCH	Generalized Auto Regressive Conditional Heteroskedasticity
GBI	Government bond index
GDP	Gross domestic product
GHG	Greenhouse gas
GICS	Global Industry Classification Standard
GSIB	Globally systemically important banks
GVC	Global value chains
GW	Gigawatt
HF	Hedge fund
HFRI	Hedge fund research index
HFT	High-frequency trading
HQLA	High-quality liquid assets
HTF	High-frequency trading
IBI	International business investment
IBO	*Emissions Obligataires par Offre au Public* [Order Book for Retail Bonds (ORB)]
IC	Insurance company
ICMA	International Capital Markets Association
ICSID	International Centre for Settlement of Investment Disputes
ICT	Information and communications technology
IEA	International Energy Agency
IG	Investment grade
INDC	Intended nationally determined contribution
IP	Intellectual property

IPO	Initial public offering
ISCED	International Standard Classification of Education
ISCO	International Standard Classification of Occupations
ISDS	Investor-state dispute settlement
ITF	International Transport Forum
KBC	Knowledge based capital
KfW	Kreditanstalt für Wiederaufbau
LCOE	Levelised cost of electricity
LCR	Local-content requirement
LCRs	Liquidity coverage ratio
LPF	Large pension funds
LSE	London Stock Exchange
M&A	Mergers and acquisitions
MBS	Mortgage-backed securities
MCAP	Market cap to GDP as an equity bullishness valuation metric
MDB	Multilateral development bank
MENA	Middle East and North Africa
MF	Mutual fund
MFT	Multilateral trading facilities
MiFID	Markets in Financial Instruments Directive (in the European Union)
MLA	Mutual legal assistance
MLP	Master limited partnerships
MMF	Money market funds
MNE	Multi-national enterprises
MPC	Marginal propensity to consume
MPS	Marginal propensity to save
MSCI	Morgan Stanley Composite Index
MTF	Multilateral trading facilities
MWh	Megawatt hour
NAFTA	North American Free Trade Agreement
NAIC	National Association of Insurance Commissioners
NASDAQ	National Association of Securities Dealers Automated Quotations
NAV	Net asset value
NDF	Non-deliverable forward
NEA	Nuclear Energy Agency
NMS	National Market System (in the United States)
NPL	Non-performing loans
NPV	Net present value
NSFR	Net stable funding ratio
NT	National treatment
NYSE	New York Stock Exchange
OECD	Organisation for Economic Co-operation and Development
OPEC	Organization of Petroleum Exporting Countries
ORB	Order Book for Retail Bonds [*Emissions Obligataires par Offre au Public* (IBO)]
OTC	Over-the-counter
P2P	Peer-to-peer
PE	Private equity

PF	Pension fund
PFI	Policy Framework for Investment (OECD)
PMR	Product market regulation
PP	Private placement
PPP	Public-private partnership
PPRF	Public Pension Reserve Funds
PV	Photovoltaic
QE	Quantitative easing
R&D	Research and development
RA	Retirement age
RD&D	Research, development and demonstration
REIT	Real estate investment trusts
ROE	Return on equity
RPP	Registered pension plans
SDC	Small distributed capacity
S-I	Saving and investment
SME	Small and medium sized enterprises
SOE	State-owned enterprise
SPE	Special purpose entity
SPO	Secondary public offering
SSDS	State-to-state dispute settlement
STAN database	OECD Structural Analysis Database
STEM	Science, technology, engineering and mathematics
SWF	Sovereign wealth fund
TPP	Trans-Pacific Partnership
TTIP	Transatlantic Trade and Investment Partnership
TTP	Transpacific Partnership
UCITS	Undertakings for collective investment in transferable securities
UIC	Ultimate investing country
UNCITRAL	United Nations Commission on International Trade Law
UNEP	United Nations Environment Programme
UNFCCC	United Nations Framework Convention on Climate Change
US SEC	US Securities and Exchange Commission (US SEC)
VA	Value-added
VC	Venture capital
WGB	OECD Working Group on Bribery in International Business Transactions
WTO	World Trade Organization

ISO country and currency abbreviations

Country		Currency	
Australia	AUS	Australian dollar	ASD
Brazil	BRA	Brazilian real	BRL
China, People's Republic of	CHN	Yuan renminbi	CNY
Chinese Taipei	TWN	Taiwan new dollar	TWD
Colombia	COL	Colombian peso	COP
Euro area	EMU	Euro	EUR
India	IND	Indian rupee	INR
Indonesia	IDN	Rupiah	IDR
Japan	JPN	Yen	JPY
Korea	KOR	Won	KRW
Russian Federation	RUS	Russian rubble	RUB
Singapore	SGP	Singapore dollar	SGD
South Africa	ZAF	Rand	ZAR
United Kingdom	GBR	Pound	GBP
United States	USA	Dollar	USD

Editorial

More than seven years have passed since the onset of the global crisis and the global economy has yet to recover its pre-crisis levels of growth. Two major headwinds pose serious challenges: the sluggishness of the growth of investment; and issues relating to the re-regulation of banks and non-performing loans which still persist in many regions. The implementation of structural reforms is paramount in dealing with these challenges and ultimately realigning the global policy and business environments.

In this context, the business sector has been unable to contribute adequately to global growth and development. This year's Business and Finance Outlook focuses on "fragmentation" as a unifying theme when exploring the multiple causes for the sub-par recovery from the crisis: the heterogeneous economic systems, policies, rules, laws and industry practices that create perverse incentives and block business efficiency and productivity growth. Fragmentation manifests itself at all levels and acts as a blocking force to economic progress.

The effects of the global financial crisis have also shaken up the corporate world and fragmented the industrial sector. The companies which have come out of the crisis with more dynamic productivity growth followed similar financial strategies, and thus, left behind their industrial peers that were unable to develop new products or to restructure quickly and in financially prudent ways. The structure of corporate finance and the ability to use the market for corporate control are crucial factors in this process.

Overall, there is a need to implement new structural policy initiatives to stimulate investment and productivity growth. These include, among others, encouraging more openness to new and innovative ideas – such as "clever" fiscal support for business research and development; and more openness to markets – both between countries and within them, where rules and regulations often block the entry to new markets. Corporate restructuring through mergers and acquisitions has also proven to be a positive force in an excess capacity environment, and equity is more conducive to a longer-term focus than is debt.

Fragmentation, which blocks efficiency and productivity, is found at many different levels. For example, stock exchanges are important in funding business investment since they not only facilitate raising new capital, but add to the attractiveness of such funding by providing it with liquidity. Yet fragmentation arising from the proliferation of trading venues, including between lit and unlit exchanges, will require regulatory initiatives in order to maintain a level playing field among investors.

Fragmentation also blocks progress in the renewable energy power sector, which is critical in dealing with post-COP21 commitments to limit global warming. While there is plenty of money waiting on the sidelines to be invested, many of the issues that must be addressed in order to move this capital into profitable projects relate more to the framework conditions surrounding the power sector than to financial engineering.

Pension funds and insurance companies also need to deal with their own set of fragmentation issues for example, in the differences in life expectancy as well as the retirement age across different socio-economic groups. The rules governing access to pensions and retirement savings must be designed carefully to avoid discriminating against lower socio-economic groups.

Different laws and legal regimes across countries also fragment the economic environment by treating similar activities differently. One of these is foreign bribery, where differences in both penalties and their enforcement across jurisdictions create very different economic incentives to resort to bribery. It is often profitable to bribe even when there is a 100% chance of detection.

A further example is investment treaties, which must be interpreted by arbitration tribunals. These tribunals establish rules that modify corporate law and governance arrangements and create different classes of shareholders with different sets of rights. The current interpretation of many treaties allows covered shareholders to recover losses resulting from company damages incurred by host government actions. This, in turn, creates incentives that may affect companies, shareholders, creditors and capital markets.

This second Business and Finance Outlook assesses fragmentation issues from the fresh perspective of microdata on companies, markets, regulations and laws. If we want to see a return to stronger and more sustainable growth, we need to put these pieces back together in a more harmonious way.

Angel Gurría
OECD Secretary-General

Executive summary

The theme of this year's *OECD Business and Finance Outlook* is fragmentation: the inconsistent structures, policies, rules, laws and industry practices that appear to be blocking business efficiency and productivity growth. It manifests itself at all levels of the global economy, from the global macro-economy to sectoral and micro-economic issues to legal ones.

Fragmentation in the global economy: financial markets and productivity

The global economy is caught between two major headwinds: the reversal of the investment-heavy commodity supercycle; and "L-shaped" recovery in advanced economies caused by the aftermath of the financial crisis and the interaction of re-regulation with low and negative interest rates. Normalisation of interest rates and a sustainable recovery of asset prices is shown to depend on which global scenario emerges: an "inflation first" set of policies favoured by central banks, and avoidance of a "creative destruction" phase to deal with over-investment and excess capacity in certain sectors and countries; or "productivity first" policies that bring about structural adjustment more quickly.

The best scenario would be one in which the low aggregate productivity growth of the post-crisis period improves. Company and sector value-added data of more than 11 000 of the world's largest listed non-financial and non-real-estate companies, taken from 20 different industry sectors, are used to analyse productivity performance at the firm level and to suggest priorities to improve it. The contribution to productivity growth of these companies is very narrowly based within each sector, indicating slow diffusion of gains across the economy. Best performance is encouraged by certain company financial decisions with respect to capital expenditure, sales, dividend and buy-back policies, research and development expensing, debt-versus-equity, and merger and acquisition activity.

Fragmentation at sectoral and micro-economic levels

Research and development (R&D) is one of the most important contributors to productivity growth and its diffusion. Accordingly, public policy has an important role in promoting it. Fiscal incentives, including tax policies, should be directed at specific barriers, impediments or synergies to facilitate the desired level of investment in R&D and innovations. Any tax incentives need to be considered in the context of the country's general tax policies, its broader innovation policy mix and its other R&D policies. More R&D activity in one country does not necessarily result in an overall increase in global innovation if it is simply shifted from another country.

Structural changes in the stock exchange industry have included fragmentation of the stock market resulting from an increase in stock exchange-like trading venues, such as alternative trading systems and multilateral trading facilities, and a split between dark (non-displayed) and lit (displayed) trading. Based on firm-level data, statistics are provided for the relative distribution of stock trading across different trading venues as well as for different trading characteristics, such as order size, company focus and the total volumes of dark and lit trading.

One important sector in which market fragmentation needs to be addressed is clean energy. Scaling-up investment in renewable electricity is critical for reducing greenhouse gas emissions from the power sector, and is therefore important for implementing the 2015 Paris Agreement on climate change. Despite increasing cost-competitiveness, overall investment in renewables projects remains constrained by policy and market obstacles. These hinder development of a sufficient pipeline of bankable projects and affect the risk-return profile of renewable electricity projects.

Finally, differences in life expectancy around retirement age across different socio-economic groups raise issues for the insurance industry and pension funds as well as for public policy. Evidence from selected OECD countries based on measures of education, income and occupation shows that those in higher socio-economic groups live longer than those in lower socio-economic groups and these differences may be increasing over time. This makes it more challenging for pension funds and insurance companies to manage longevity risk. However, it also presents an opportunity to better tailor retirement solutions to the needs of different segments of society. Policy makers need to ensure that rules governing access to pensions and retirement savings do not put those in lower socio-economic groups at a disadvantage.

Fragmentation of legal frameworks across countries

Variations in laws and legal regimes across countries unnecessarily fragment the economic environment by treating similar activities differently. One area where this is an issue is foreign bribery. In many jurisdictions sanctions are weak and foreign bribery may be an attractive investment. In others, foreign bribery is subject to strong penalties, although some of these are not backed up by effective enforcement. This patchwork of incentives and disincentives is explored using simulations of "net present value" for "investments in foreign bribery" under assumptions of both certainty and uncertainty. The simulations show that fines for bribery are set too low in many jurisdictions.

A second area where legal frameworks fragment the environment is investment treaties. These are concluded between two or more governments and typically offer covered foreign investors protection for their investments from host government conduct in violation of the treaty, such as expropriation without compensation, discrimination or treatment that is not "fair and equitable". The unique combination of rules applied under many investment treaties, which includes rules about the types of loss recoverable by shareholders covered by treaties and about the availability of damages for covered investors in claims against governments, creates different classes of shareholders with different sets of rights. This may be undesirable since it can allow covered shareholders to strip assets from the company to the detriment of company creditors and other shareholders.

Key findings and conclusions

Monetary ease has reached its limits in terms of stimulating most of the global economy. The key to better performance is structural reform across a broad range of policy domains in order to reduce fragmentation that hinders business performance and productivity. This will encourage needed investment in growing industries, such as renewable electricity, as the commodity supercycle reverses, while stimulating innovation and diffusion of its benefits to regenerate productivity growth after too many years of stagnation.

Overview: Doing business in a fragmented world

It is seven years since the global crisis and despite easy monetary policy, financial regulatory reform, and G20 resolutions favouring structural measures, the world economy is not making a lot of progress. Indeed, responses to the crisis seem mainly to have stopped banks from failing and then pushed the many aspects of the crisis around between regions – currently taking the form of excess capacity in emerging markets. Productivity growth raises income per head, allows companies to pay better wages and raises demand to help eliminate excess capacity and improve employment. However, this element is missing in the global corporate sector. The theme of this year's *Business and Finance Outlook* is fragmentation: the inconsistent structures, policies, rules, laws and industry practices that appear to be blocking business efficiency and productivity growth.

A world economy beset by two major headwinds

The broadest fragmentation in the world economy concerns two very different approaches to economic organisation that are now butting up against each other: advanced economies run with more open markets; and emerging economies where the role of the state plays a central role. Emerging economies built up savings rapidly and state-owned enterprises have played a key role in driving investment in the supercycle sectors (energy, materials, utilities, capital goods and industrials) that has led to excess capacity and high debt levels. Fragmentation is also reflected in financial reform, which has focused mainly on banks, opening the way for the products of other financial sectors to fill gaps and respond to countries' attempts to use unconventional policies to help their own regions, sometimes at the expense of others.

Following the financial crisis, the world economy is now beset by two major headwinds:

- the reversal of the commodity supercycle, with investment now falling led by the excess capacity sectors; and
- the L-shaped recovery in the advanced economies resulting from deleveraging as banks continue to struggle with non-performing loans in many parts of the world while new financial regulations are imposed.

The interaction between these two forces is taken up in the opening Chapter 1. Central banks have stepped in to deal with the lack of growth because other policies have not dealt with these structural problems at their source. Quantitative easing and low-interest-rate monetary policy can do little to correct over-investment in global industrial sectors. This has led to innovative responses and new and building forms of liquidity and leverage risks. At this point, such policies may be harming the prospect of a sustainable recovery.

- Regulatory reform has focused on banks that are being forced to hold minimum amounts of high quality liquid assets while raising capital, before non-performing loans on bank balance sheets have been properly dealt with. The combination of low and negative interest rates with rules that force banks to hold the very assets to which they apply hurts bank profitability. Nor do negative interest rates lead to predictable effects on exchange rate transmission mechanisms to help growth and counter deflation. This is because other countries are changing monetary policy too and altering the way they manage their currencies to ensure maximum advantage to their own citizens, contrary to the collective interest.
- Zero (or worse, negative) interest rates imply a zero time value for money and encourage short-termism by investors, whereas innovation and productivity growth requires the financing of long-term risk taking in capital expenditure and its financing. These policies are creating incentives that lead investors in new directions that interact with banking in different ways, and where the solvency and liquidity characteristics of products are untested. Very low rates have created a demand for a kind of portfolio "barbell" in institutional investment: large asset allocations to both i) private equity and low-cost exchange-traded funds (ETFs) at one end; and ii) capital market risk assets, based on leverage, that pay higher short-term cash yields (e.g. hedge and absolute return funds, etc.) at the other end. In between is an allocation to equities, cash and bonds within which further herding of investors into concentrated positions is found: into high-yield non-investment grade bonds; and into equities that focus on providing strong dividends and buybacks.

The reversal of the supercycle emanating from emerging economies is arguably an even stronger headwind than the L-shape recovery in advanced economies. Excess investment is always accompanied with financial consequences where borrowing is a factor, and there is little doubt that non-performing loans are building up in emerging economies and energy sectors more generally. The size of the impact of the supercycle reversal is easy to underestimate. At its recent peak, some 40% of corporate investment in the global economy was carried out in just two sectors, energy and materials, and its full influence goes well beyond these two driving forces. Investment is now flat in advanced economies and is declining in emerging markets (see the blue segments of the columns in Figure 1.17 in Chapter 1).

Dividends and buybacks have been rising in advanced economies since the crisis and have reached about 60% of what companies spend on investment. Advanced economy companies could raise this investment very easily without any need for external finance – but they do not do this. Investors resist companies that want to use earnings to invest for the long term, and they demand cash-like returns that are better than those available in actual cash and investment grade bond markets. This works against companies wanting to take on long-run projects needed to promote innovation and productivity – they would be punished by investors for doing so. This is a direct result of attributing a zero time value to money via low interest rates.

The return on equity in emerging markets is far below its cost, a sure reflection of excess capacity (in sectors like steel, energy, resources, cement, glass, chemicals, automobiles and the like). Investment is still running at double the rate in advanced economies (around 10% of net sales). But it is capital-widening investment in the main, using existing technology, often as a part of global value chains. The value added of these companies per employee has also not risen (the company productivity problem which is discussed in detail in Chapter 2).

"Inflation first" policies will delay a sustainable lift-off in rates

Policies need to restore "animal spirits" in the company sector by dealing with the global misallocation of resources and excess capacity and by creating incentives for long-term risk taking. When "animal spirits" recover to the point where "true" risk assets are desired in the company sector, and investors are willing to forego short-term income for long-term capital gain, there will be a significant asset allocation shift. Capital will move from cash returns and leveraged instruments to "growth" investments simultaneously within and across all asset classes. This lift-off would lead to the end of secular stagnation. But how could this happen?

In the event that inflation comes first – say because unconventional monetary policy in advanced economies and credit expansion in emerging markets are not supported by measures to deal with structural problems – the outlook would not be too encouraging. Central banks would be obliged to lift interest rates in response to inflation, while growth of capital-widening investment using existing technology in the near term would raise global supply without lifting productivity growth. This is what happened in some emerging economies in response to the 2008 crisis. Any success would be short-lived now, just as it was then. The "creative destruction" phase needed on the supply side would not happen: i.e. just as some policies after the crisis worsened the excess capacity problems and increased debt, the lack of structural adjustment now and the actual emergence of inflation would ultimately cause the "lift off" in interest rates to turn into a two-step process.

Near zero interest rates allow companies to carry excess debt, to borrow cheaply to carry out buybacks and to engage in unproductive investments that are based on a distorted cost of capital while waiting for the tide of aggregate demand to rise. The global output gap will never close in a sustainable manner while the outstanding stock of unproductive and misallocated investment remains in place. Rising interest rates under an "inflation first" scenario would risk another financial crisis. The need for shedding excess capacity and debt would once more become a priority. If a healthy "creative destruction" phase ensued, because rates were not once again cut to zero and structural policies were implemented in advanced and emerging economies on the scale required, then the scene would then be set for more sustainable growth and normalised interest rates later on.

A "productivity first" corporate scenario

Rather than inflation first, it would be desirable to have a productivity first scenario. Such a scenario is not encouraged at all by making the time value of money zero – monetary policy is not the instrument needed at this point in time. But what policies would actually address the productivity problem in the company sector? To answer this question, better knowledge of what is happening to productivity in the corporate world is required. This is the subject taken up in Chapter 2.

By studying 11 000 (non-financial and non-real estate) companies in an OECD database (representing a large proportion of world GDP), some very interesting facts emerge about those companies that have succeeded and those that have failed since the crisis. These facts point the way to policies that might actually work. Prior to the crisis, there was a group of high-productivity level companies (sometimes referred to as being on the "frontier"), and a very long string of low-productivity level companies that appeared not to be sharing in technology and growth. The crisis shook up everything and led to two distinct groups of high-productivity companies in the post-2008 period: those in the high-level productivity group that remained there, but whose growth in productivity has been negative (i.e. they are losing their shine); and, at the other extreme, a separate group that succeeded in achieving rapid productivity growth. In between these two groups sits the majority of companies with both lower productivity levels and only moderate growth.

The group exhibiting both high levels of productivity and high growth shows all the signs of having been through a creative destruction phase: shedding businesses and locations that are not working in the tougher post-crisis environment while acquiring others that are more synergistic with their goals. However, there are simply not nearly enough of these companies.

The financial decisions that the more dynamic creative destruction companies took in order to succeed had four key interrelated corporate finance characteristics:

- They expensed much more on research and development (R&D) than other companies, which in turn requires risk taking and a long-term focus critical to the innovation process.
- They did not increase borrowing compared to equity in the post-crisis period (while those that did were in the low productivity groups). Equity is for the long term and success or failure is reflected in its price, whereas debt must be serviced and the inability to do so in the short-run will lead to bankruptcy.
- They had a buffer of free cash flow; i.e. their operating cash flow was in excess of that needed for capital expenditure. Such companies can maintain a focus on long-term goals in the face of short-term disruptions.
- They used mergers and acquisitions (M&A – buying and selling business segments) to rationalise what they were doing in the tougher, more competitive post-crisis environment.

Having identified these key characteristics of companies that succeed, it is critical to fashion policies that foster them in a broader range of companies.

Some policy implications

With respect to R&D: R&D expensing can be encouraged by fiscal incentives and funding for basic research – provided the policies are well targeted. The issue of designing tax incentives for R&D that are consistent with broader tax policy efficiency is taken up in Chapter 3.

With respect to equity finance instead of debt: Policies here include inter alia the removal of tax incentives that favour debt over equity; the simplification of equity listing rules that increase costs relative to private equity; and equity market reforms that encourage initial public offerings and improve trust. An examination of stock market fragmentation into lit and dark trading (where the latter reduce transparency, create distrust and impede price discovery) is taken up in Chapter 4.

With respect to improving free cash flow: The best way to enhance this key requirement in a broader range of companies is to make it easier for them to access new markets for their core products and to adopt policies that minimise their costs (flexible labour contracts, more open cross-border and internal trade and investment regimes, access to cheaper external funding and fiscal incentives). Open trade and investment regimes between countries are particularly important, not only for market access, but also to ensure policies directed at supporting specific sectors do not inadvertently fracture global value chains which add to costs for other downstream companies hurting their cash flow (see

Chapter 5). Financial reforms need to be cognisant of their impact on the availability and cost of external financing (both debt and equity), and regulations and tax rules should not inhibit cheaper non-traditional sources of funds (angel investors, crowdfunding, peer-to-peer lending and distributed ledger innovations in payments technology). Fiscal support has a direct impact on cash flow but needs to be well targeted, e.g. where R&D is concerned, firms need a lot of upfront cash given the asymmetric information that exists between young firms and their potential investors (again, see Chapter 3).

With respect to M&A activity: Breaking down cultural and regulatory barriers to cross-border M&A, consistent with allowing entry and facilitating a genuine open market for corporate control, is needed. Efficiency-enhancing measures include better co-operation between competition agencies when considering cross-border deals to speed up the M&A process, to minimise costs and to reduce inconsistent criteria. Eliminating the culture of "national champions" whereby governments support incumbent firms when they face challenges from new (particularly foreign) entrants is also an important requirement.

The role of expenditure and tax incentives for R&D

Fiscal incentives for R&D are discussed in Chapter 3. Government support for business R&D seeks to encourage firms to invest in knowledge which can result in innovations that transform markets and industries and result in benefits to society. Most often, support is provided to firms with the intention of correcting market failure, such as difficulties appropriating the returns to investment in R&D and difficulties in finding external finance, in particular for small or young firms.

Fiscal incentives should be directed at specific barriers, impediments or synergies to facilitate the desired innovation and uses within each country and region. Public policy must recognise the heterogeneity of the markets and individual actors involved in developing and using new innovations, as well as the heterogeneity of alternative fiscal incentives and their design. The latter is particularly important in achieving R&D objectives: firms might easily restructure to meet age criteria for benefits, re-label expenditure that would have occurred anyway as R&D, or apply for a patent simply because it is required to qualify for an incentive measure.

Governments have many different fiscal incentives to encourage R&D, and tax incentives are an increasingly important element of the funding for business R&D. Thirty out of the thirty four OECD countries use tax incentives for R&D of some kind. The most widely used types of tax incentives include tax credits or favourable tax deductions for R&D expenditures, but other types are focused on income from certain R&D activities (such as royalties), on certain types of R&D financing and are, in some cases, provided directly to R&D researchers.

Most countries providing R&D tax incentives focus on reducing costs and encouraging increased expenditures on R&D. This can take the form of credits against income and/or payroll taxes for expenditures on wages and/or capital investments for R&D. It can also take the form of accelerated depreciation, allowing recovery of the investment faster than the underlying economic depreciation of the long-lived asset; or enhanced depreciation, where taxpayers can recover more than 100% of R&D expenditure costs.

Effectiveness requires specific circumstances of companies and the nature of activities to be taken into account. Income tax measures are most beneficial to companies that already have income, whereas such benefits can be lost if younger R&D companies experience prolonged periods without any taxable income. Direct measures that reduce costs and enhance cash-flow are more suitable for liquidity-constrained firms because they need upfront funds (including contracts, grants, and awards). Exemptions for payroll tax and/or withholding tax for qualified R&D workers also provide immediate relief, while wealth tax exemptions for angel investors can help to attract upfront funds for start-ups. The type of R&D in question also warrants consideration. OECD studies show that longer-term research activity may be better served by direct subsidies whereas tax schemes are more effective for short-term applied research.

An increasing number of countries have adopted, or are considering adopting, income-based tax incentives, often in addition to their expenditure-based incentives. These provide for lower tax rates on future income from investments in R&D and an increased after-tax rate of return to those investments. Assets are highly mobile, however, allowing both assets, and future income from them, to be located away from the activity that generated the assets and income. This is often in low-tax jurisdictions to reduce their corporate tax liabilities, which erodes tax revenues in the countries where the R&D investments were actually made.

To avoid harmful tax practices, preferential tax regimes for R&D should be consistent with a "nexus" approach, as established as a minimum standard in the G20-OECD Base Erosion and Profit Shifting (BEPS) project. This uses expenditure as a proxy for real activity and allows taxpayers to benefit from the preferential regime only to the extent that the taxpayers themselves incurred the qualifying expenditures that gave rise to the income generated by the R&D investment.

The role of the stock exchange

Regulatory reforms and developments in information and communication technology have increased competition between different types of stock trading venues. The result is fragmentation in two dimensions. First, the extensive fragmentation of trading between stock exchange venues and off-exchange venues, such as Alternative Trading Systems and Multilateral Trading Facilities. Second, there is an increased fragmentation between dark (non-displayed) trading and lit (displayed) trading. These issues are analysed in Chapter 4.

Fragmentation in both dimensions is now very significant. In 2015, two-thirds of all stock trading in the United States took place on 11 different exchanges and the remaining 33% on numerous off-exchange venues. Of all trading, 42% was in the form of dark trading, of which about one-fifth was carried out on exchanges. In the European Union, around 50% of all trading takes place on exchanges and the rest on off-exchange venues. The amount of dark trading in Europe varies across countries from 35-48% of all trading.

Off-exchange and dark trading have often been seen as a way for investors to reduce the market impact that could occur if they placed large orders on a stock exchange. However, a detailed analysis of trading data for the United States indicates that average order size does not differ significantly between off-exchange venues and traditional exchanges. Nor does fragmentation seem to have affected the distribution of trading in large and small company stocks, which appears to be fairly similar across countries whether or not it occurs within concentrated or fragmented markets. Since 2000, trading in the largest decile of listed companies has accounted for 70-90% of all trading, both in the United States and Japan.

The main concerns with respect to increased off-exchange and dark trading are the quality of the price discovery process, the fairness of markets, and the level playing field among investors. This is more pronounced in an era of increased high-frequency and algorithmic trading. Investors typically have access to pre-trade information about buying and selling interests (lit trading). Transactions where pre-trade information is not available, often referred to as dark trading, can adversely impact the price discovery process to the detriment of some investors.

These developments may have undermined trust in the equity market which, as noted earlier, is the preferred vehicle for long-term investment and innovation. Recent enforcement action against some dark pools has opened up a discussion about the rationale for existing differences in regulatory regimes between trading venues that seem to serve similar functions. Looking ahead, it is likely that regulatory initiatives in both Europe and the United States will come to focus on regulatory convergence between exchange and off-exchange venues, to ensure a level playing field and improve price discovery. It remains to be seen what effect such reforms will have on stock market fragmentation in the future.

A case study of fragmentation and the clean energy sector

In many ways, the clean energy sector presents an excellent case study of many issues discussed in the first four chapters of this *Outlook*: the sector is at times constrained by access to bank credit; there are elements of excess capacity from emerging markets (for example, manufacturing of solar photovoltaic panels in 2010-13); for some firms the return on equity has fallen versus the cost of equity; and the industry operates in fractured domestic and international markets. Yet despite these obstacles, an increase in the scale and pace of investment and its financing for renewable electricity generation is necessary to successfully implement the 2015 Paris Agreement concluded by the 21st Conference of the Parties (COP21) of the United Nations Framework Convention on Climate Change (UNFCCC). The case of market fragmentation and policy misalignment in clean energy investment and financing is taken up in Chapter 5.

Investment in renewable energy has rebounded somewhat recently (to an all-time high of USD 286 billion in 2015) with growth centred mainly on China. In the tougher post-crisis environment it has done so by significant innovation in its financing model coupled with policy support for renewable energy. The tougher economic environment has seen the traditional providers of equity funds for renewable energy (typically the balance sheets of utilities and corporate project developers) almost halve their share of commitments over the past five years. In its place new ownership and financing models have emerged. Most notably, institutional investors with long-term liabilities to manage have recognised the infrastructure asset class (both debt and equity) as a source of inflation-linked, long-term and stable cash flow.

In essence, a strategy has emerged to recycle capital from the balance sheets of traditional funding institutions. By buying into projects and/or refinancing existing projects, institutional investors free up debt and equity capital in construction and operating-stage renewable electricity projects. Banks, private equity funds, project developers and utilities can then redeploy the proceeds into the development and construction of new projects. Closed-end funds and real-estate investment trusts (REITS) have played an important role in this respect for some time. More recently in the United States, utilities and other corporate entities have sponsored "yieldcos", essentially selling renewable energy assets (e.g. wind and solar power generation) to the publicly-traded yieldco entities which pay significant dividends to their shareholders.

While innovative funding abounds, and technology costs for renewable electricity are falling fast, the most basic problem is the limited nature of the pipeline of bankable projects. There are both policy and market obstacles that significantly diminish investment opportunities and/or the risk-return profile of renewable electricity projects. The absence of carbon pricing mechanisms and other sufficiently ambitious and coherent climate mitigation policies is a well-known and critical issue, as is the historical instability of specific incentives for renewables such as feed-in tariffs. But the misalignment of broader policies and regulations with respect to climate goals can also hinder investment in renewable electricity. Misalignment can occur across the general investment environment, such as in areas of investment policy, attitudes of competition authorities, electricity market design, internal and external trade, and financial market policies.

Trade and investment policies that are inconsistent with climate change goals can create barriers to cross-border trade and investment in renewable electricity generation. The increasing use of local-content requirements (LCRs) attached to solar photovoltaic and wind energy incentive schemes since 2008 threatens to fragment, rather than optimise, global renewable electricity value chains. With the best intentions in mind, policy makers believe that supporting the local manufacture of a renewable technology through LCRs helps employment when, in fact, failure to use cheaper intermediate inputs raises costs and reduces employment in much larger downstream activities (such as power plant project development). Other outstanding trade and investment barriers in solar photovoltaic and wind energy sectors include trade remedies and divergent national technical standards.

Fragmentation in electricity markets and networks, including in the development of transmission and distribution infrastructure, can favour fossil-fuel incumbency in the power sector and increase the cost of further integration of renewables. Factors include insufficient cross-border interconnection of transmission networks, which limits the flexibility of electricity systems and hinders integration of renewables, and heterogeneous design of capacity mechanisms with insufficient regional planning.

To unlock investment in renewable electricity, policy makers need to consider options to address existing obstacles to investment, especially concerning existing fragmentation in electricity markets and policy misalignments with climate change goals. Dissemination of research on these issues is needed to help policy makers address key policy priorities to overcome barriers to renewable energy investment and financing.

Fragmentation and the pension and insurance sector

Life expectancy increases have been putting pressure on pension systems to provide adequate and sustainable incomes in retirement: individuals are not necessarily working longer and may be spending more years in retirement. This alone poses a challenge to pension funds and annuity providers who must manage longevity risk. The issue of longevity and its interaction with very low interest rates affecting the solvency of pension and insurance companies was taken up in last year's *Business and Finance Outlook*. This year, Chapter 6 looks at the issue of fragmentation in the longevity of different social groups.

Significant differences in life expectancy across socio-economic groups, as measured by education, income and occupation, mean that the challenge of ensuring sufficient income in retirement cannot only be assessed "on average". Chapter 6 also assesses the implications of this fragmentation for pensions and annuity markets and for public policy.

Not only are there differences in current levels of mortality and life expectancy, but evidence is growing that there are also differences in the rate at which mortality and life expectancy are improving over time across socio-economic groups. In many countries, those in higher socio-economic groups have benefited from larger improvements in mortality and life expectancy over the last few decades than those in the lower socio-economic groups.

As a result of these differences, two individuals of different socio-economic groups, retiring at the same age, can expect very different lengths of retirement. Policy makers need to be aware of these differences to ensure that rules governing the access to pensions and retirement savings do not put those in lower socio-economic groups at a disadvantage. Policies encouraging people to work longer, following the average increases in life expectancy may disproportionately put individuals in lower socio-economic groups who would be working longer, but not necessarily living longer, at a disadvantage. In addition, pension pay-out rules may have unintended consequences to the total pension payments that individuals in lower socio-economic groups can expect to receive.

These differences present challenges for pension funds and insurance companies in measuring and managing longevity risk. The demographic mix of pensioners and insured populations will influence the actual longevity improvements that they experience. Unpredictable changes in demographics lead to higher uncertainty about the future life expectancy of these populations. Furthermore, adverse selection in annuity markets (longer-lived cohorts tend to buy them) implies a higher cost of mitigating the longevity risk of beneficiaries. While lower cost index-based hedges could present a solution to this problem, there is uncertainty about the efficacy of these instruments due to the differences in mortality trends across socio-economic groups. This presents a barrier to their widespread use.

Nevertheless, these differences also present opportunities to serve society's financial needs for retirement through increased market segmentation. Different segments of the population have different needs with respect to financing their retirement. Product innovation should adapt better to meet these diverse needs. Enhanced annuities, for example, have emerged as a solution to provide higher annuity incomes to more disadvantaged groups with lower life expectancies. Other types of products could be structured to provide unique solutions for different segments of society.

There is scope for public policy to help. More accurate and timely mortality data by socio-economic group would facilitate the measurement and management of the longevity risk exposure of pension funds and annuity providers. Product innovation to meet the various needs of different market segments should be encouraged and facilitated so long as the risks arising from these products are managed appropriately. Finally, policy makers need to be aware of differences in mortality rates to ensure that rules on how overall access to funds earmarked for retirement are governed do not put lower socio-economic groups at a disadvantage. This may occur because policies defined "on average" may be regressive.

Variations in legal frameworks that fragment the business environment

While there are many reasons for variations in legal regimes, varying laws or legally constituted institutional arrangements across the global economy, these can in some cases unnecessarily fragment the economic environment by treating similar activities differently. Taxation and labour market regulations are two of the most obvious examples.

Two chapters in this *Outlook* examine areas which receive much less attention but are nevertheless important. Variations in enforcement regimes for the Anti-Bribery Convention provide one example of fragmentation of the economic environment, even though the origin is not really economic, and this is taken up in Chapter 7. Many investment treaties, as interpreted by arbitration tribunals, establish a unique combination of rules that can result in fragmentation of companies and corporate governance on key issues. These aspects are addressed in Chapter 8.

Foreign bribery: Variations in enforcement regimes across the 41 Parties to the Anti-Bribery Convention provide an interesting example of how different laws and enforcement regimes affect the profitability of bribery – if it is profitable, firms will bribe. These variations arise from the failure of many countries to combine strong sanctions with active enforcement of anti-bribery laws. This creates a situation where in many jurisdictions with weak sanctions, foreign bribery can be an attractive "investment". In other jurisdictions, foreign bribery is subject to strong penalties, although some of these penalties exist on paper only because they are not backed up by effective enforcement.

Fragmentation across jurisdictions is documented in the chapter by simulations of returns on investments in foreign bribery for Parties to the Convention. These are based on cash flows from a real-world bribery scheme. For each Party that has a maximum sanction for foreign bribery, this maximum sanction is applied to the cash flow analysis to calculate a net present value for the investment in the bribery scheme. The results show that, because sanctions are weak in many jurisdictions, companies would still have an interest in investing in the bribery scheme, even if they knew with certainty that they would be caught at the end of the scheme.

Simulations under an uncertainty scenario, where a firm faces at least some probability of getting caught and sanctioned for bribery in each year of the scheme, also demonstrate great variations of incentives across countries. This implies that an appropriate balance between enforcement effort and levels of sanctions needs to be found in order to establish an effective system of deterrence.

Another way to discourage bribery would be to create an effective system of confiscation, that is, the deprivation of property by a competent authority such as a court. This would make disincentives to bribery more powerful, but in many cases the Parties to the Convention lack the necessary expertise and legal infrastructure to establish such systems.

An essential element of any regime that involves extremely high sanctions is to ensure that they are proportionate to the offence and arrived at through due process. Prosecutors and judges must be committed to justice and avoid overreach. In order to defend fundamental values of law such as non-discrimination, transparency and predictability, tools for disciplining discretion need to be in place for both judges and prosecutors.

Investment treaties: This chapter examines some consequences of investment treaties that typically offer covered foreign investors protection from certain host government conduct such as expropriation, discrimination or treatment that is not "fair and equitable". Such treaty protection is not available to domestic shareholders or foreign shareholders not covered by the treaties. These treaties are concluded between two or more governments and include both stand-alone investment treaties and investment chapters in broader trade and investment agreements (e.g. the North American Free Trade Agreement or the Trans-Pacific Partnership).

Over 3 000 investment treaties have been signed. Claims against governments by covered investors under treaties are normally subject to resolution by arbitration by tribunals. At least 70 investment claims against governments were filed last year, many against developed countries, far outstripping the 14 requests for consultations at the WTO. As of 2012, the average claim in publicly-available resolved cases reportedly exceeded USD 620 million, almost doubling from five years earlier. Some individual awards can run much higher, but successful claimants generally receive far less than the claimed amount.

As interpreted in these arbitration proceedings, many treaties effectively establish rules that significantly modify widely-applied corporate law and corporate governance principles and can result in fragmentation of companies. They effectively create different classes of shareholder with different rights. The interpretations that create these differences include: i) the acceptance of claims by covered shareholders for losses incurred by companies in which they own shares (claims for "reflective" loss, typically loss in the value of shares as a result of injury to "their" company); and ii) the general availability of damages, including lost profits, as a remedy for government misconduct in breach of a treaty, subject to adequate proof.

In contrast to these treaty interpretations, claims for damages for reflective losses are generally barred under national corporate law and other systems of law. The injured company, not its shareholders, owns the claim for redress and recovers any damages. Shareholders that invest in a company are generally accordingly not permitted to seek recovery of reflective loss suffered due to a corporate loss.

The rules under many treaties as outlined above can allow covered shareholders to strip assets from the company to the detriment of company creditors and other shareholders. This is likely to affect the availability, pricing and other conditions of debt and equity financing for investment that is subject to regulatory risk. Providing greater rights to covered foreign shareholders than those of non-covered domestic shareholders creates incentives that are likely to affect the ratio of foreign and domestic share ownership over time. The unique rules can also fragment corporate governance because they shift power on key issues from the centralised corporate boards of directors to covered shareholders. Governments and others are now carefully analysing and evaluating these likely impacts as part of their investment treaty policies going forward. They are developing new approaches to address different aspect of the issues that arise.

Chapter 1

The financial markets outlook

The global economy is caught between two major headwinds: the reversal of the investment-heavy commodity supercycle; and the "L-shaped" recovery in advanced economies caused by the aftermath of the financial crisis and the interaction of re-regulation with low and negative interest rates. The zero and even negative time value given to money is having perverse effects. Investors are being herded into concentrated and less liquid positions which work against long-term value creation and productivity growth. Normalisation of interest rates and a sustainable recovery of asset prices is shown to depend on which global scenario emerges: an "inflation first" set of policies favoured by central banks, and avoidance of a "creative destruction" phase to deal with over-investment and excess capacity in certain sectors and countries; or "productivity first" policies that bring about structural adjustment more quickly. The scenario most likely to emerge is one of continued monetary ease and choppy and sometimes volatile markets. Equities are least overvalued but cannot rise sustainably on monetary policy alone. Longer-run negative valuation adjustments are implied for some of the other most severely overvalued asset classes.

Main findings

- The world is caught between two structural headwinds: a) the reversal of the commodity supercycle and the related (and often underestimated) energy and materials company investment on which growth came to depend; and b) the aftermath of the global financial crisis with re-regulation contributing to a continuation of the L-shaped recovery in advanced economies, and low and negative interest rates hurting bank returns and introducing distortions in investment portfolios.
- The supercycle headwind was caused by massive over-investment in the BRIICS, especially the People's Republic of China, and the sector misallocation of resources globally resulting from it. The return on equity, less the cost of capital, is negative in the key supercycle sectors in emerging economies and this has spilled into other sectors globally. Despite a bounce related to recent Chinese policy, commodity prices are low and the Baltic Dry Index was at an all-time low in early 2016. This will take years to set right.
- Some regions (unlike the United States) have not been able to deal with non-performing loans by taking them off bank balance sheets; and bank exposure to energy assets is a problem. Both issues are reinforcing the L-shaped recovery. Negative interest rates interact with regulatory measures that force banks to hold high quality liquid assets. Bank distance-to-default (DTD) measures are declining again.
- The low and sometimes negative interest rates imply a zero or negative time value of money which is causing investor responses that portend problems for the future. Investors are being herded into concentrated trades with poor liquidity. A kind of barbell has developed with alternative assets: with private equity (because they specialise in managing long-term risk premiums) and exchange-traded funds (because their fees are low and easier access to illiquid assets can be obtained with promises of daily liquidity) at one end; and products which generate absolute cash-like returns based on leverage at the other end. In between is an allocation to equities and bonds within which further herding of investors into concentrated positions is found: in high-yield non-investment grade bonds; and in equities that focus on providing strong dividends and buybacks (instead of investment).
- Cross-border divestment (apparent in mergers and acquisition activity) concentrated in emerging economies accelerated after the crisis. To this weakened longer-term trend component was added portfolio outflow pressure at the turn of the year when US tightening came into view, resulting in exchange rate pressures (temporarily abated in March with the softer Federal Reserve tone).
- Normally markets have a way of forcing required policy adjustments. But because emerging countries are less market oriented, pressures arising from resource misallocation are also relayed elsewhere. Emerging countries (and notably China) have increased market restrictions and Chinese equity prices are distorted by policy actions.
- Corporate borrowing is concentrated in the supercycle sectors (especially energy, materials and capital goods) which are particularly exposed to falling commodity prices.

- The impact of normalisation or "lift-off" in interest rates will depend on whether this occurs as an "inflation first" scenario with more monetary ease and emerging economy investment spending (which raises global supply further), or as part of a "productivity first" strategy led by structural policy. With the former, central banks would be obliged to lift interest rates in response to inflation before the "creative destruction" phase to deal with excess capacity, as happened in 2009. The "lift-off" in interest rates would turn into a two-step process.
- If a healthy "creative destruction" phase ensued, as higher interest rates confronted companies with a realistic cost of capital and structural policies were implemented, then the scene would be set for more sustainable growth and normalised interest rates later on. The required structural policies to lift productivity that might actually work, based on evidence from the analysis of financial decisions of companies that succeeded following the crisis, are set out.
- If monetary policy continues to try to do the heavy lifting without global structural reform, then choppy and sometimes volatile markets with little sustainable rise in asset valuations will be the result. Equity is the least overvalued asset class, but even here a sustained rally would be unlikely unless productivity growth accelerates – it cannot be based on monetary policy alone.

Introduction

Seven years of extremely easy monetary policy has not restored the investment and productivity growth needed to raise income per head, real wages, demand and growth. This policy was originally designed to stabilise the financial system and support economic recovery, but somehow has slipped into trying to compensate for the absence of the other policies that are needed. Monetary policy is now trying to deal with issues that are not wholly "nominal" in their origins.

The world economy, which has seen poor growth and no sign of inflation since the global crisis, is facing two major headwinds:

- The reversal of the commodity supercycle based on over-investment which has led to excess capacity in emerging economies; and
- The L-shaped recovery in the advanced economies resulting from deleveraging, as banks struggle to deal with non-performing loans in some parts of the world while new financial regulations are imposed.

Central banks have stepped in because other policies have not dealt with these structural problems at their source. However, quantitative easing and low-interest-rate monetary policy can do little to correct over-investment in global industrial sectors. At this point, the unintended consequences of such policy may be harming the prospect of sustainable recovery.

- Zero rates imply a zero time value for money and can encourage short-termism, whereas innovation and productivity growth require long-term risk taking in capital spending and its financing.
- Low and negative interest rates may combine with regulatory factors to hurt banks in some advanced economies.
- These policies have also created incentives for investors that may lead to problems for the future. Very low rates have created a demand for a kind of portfolio "barbell" in the

world of institutional investors: large asset allocations to both i) private equity and low-cost exchange-traded funds (ETFs) giving easy exposure to less liquid assets at one end; and ii) capital market risk assets, based on leverage, that pay higher short-term cash yields (e.g. hedge and absolute return funds) at the other end. In between is an allocation to equities and bonds within which further herding of investors into concentrated positions is found: in high-yield non-investment grade bonds; and in equities that focus on providing strong dividends and buybacks.

This chapter is concerned with analysing these issues and presenting a financial outlook based on the research within this, and some of the other chapters, in this publication.

Headwind 1: The reversal of the commodity supercycle

The prolonged boom and subsequent collapse of energy and commodity prices is related to the reversal of the so-called "supercycle". The development strategy in emerging economies based on saving, state-driven investment and exporting to advanced economies was never going to be sustainable. This is because: the group became too big for all to follow the "Asian Tigers" model; and investment-led-growth using existing technology within the lower-value-added parts of the global supply chain does not enhance company productivity growth.[1] Figure 1.1 shows national saving by major countries and regions in the global economy. Saving declines in 2015 and national investment follows, more-or-less, exactly the same pattern. Prior to the 2000s, emerging market national saving and investment was around 20% of the world economy total and it then rose to over 50% by 2015 – in the space of a single decade. By far the greater part of the rise in saving and investment in the world economy is attributable to emerging market economies (EMEs) and to China in particular, although Europe also rose. At the start of the 2000s, China was responsible for around 5% of the total and subsequently this rose to be over 30%, far in excess of the United States or Europe, both at around 20% each. State-owned enterprises (SOEs) and banks were heavily involved in the process within EMEs, so market discipline was largely absent in the allocation of resources.

Figure 1.1. **Emerging economies drive recent surge in gross national saving and investment, 1995-2015**

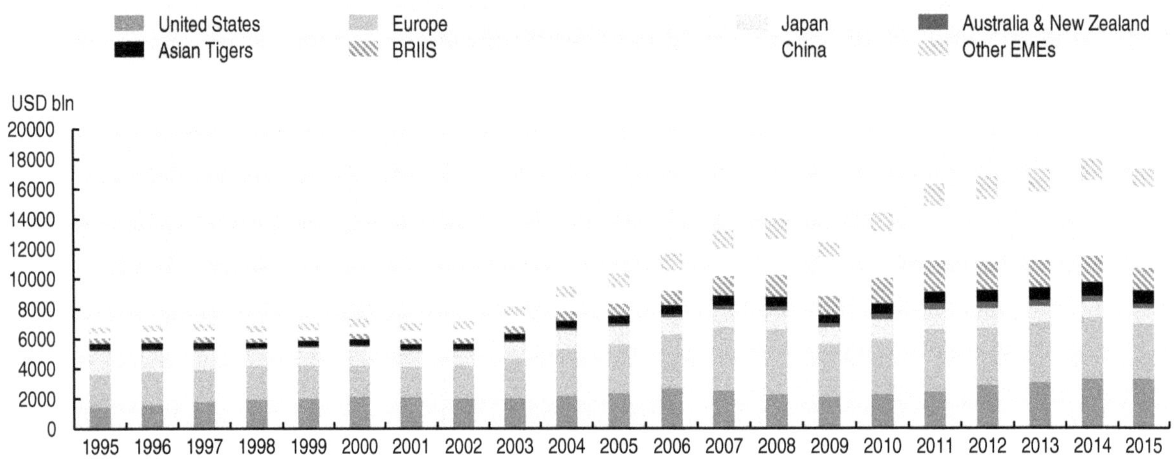

Note: Europe refers to the European Union, Norway and Switzerland.
Source: OECD calculations, IMF World Economic Outlook Database.

StatLink http://dx.doi.org/10.1787/888933362112

This strategy in countries often poor in natural resources stimulated investment in the energy, materials and industrials sectors on an unprecedented scale. This growth led to over-investment in these sectors; and this began reversing in 2015. The extent of the importance of this reversal in global growth is easy to underestimate.

Figure 1.2 shows a long time series of key commodity prices and the Baltic Dry Index (an index of the US dollars paid per day to hire four categories of ships[2] over 23 shipping routes). This presents a price snapshot of how over-investment works. Demand picks up due to state-driven investment and growth, commodity and shipping shortages abound and prices rise sharply. This rise in price stimulates strong investment in commodities and ships.[3] Supply in the end becomes too great in relation to demand (contributing to low inflation), and resource prices then fall. This leaves past investments stranded with financial consequences for the companies that borrowed – which for China has been estimated to be around 230% of GDP – and then capital expenditure declines relative to depreciation and a reversal begins.

Figure 1.2. **Commodity prices and the Baltic Dry Index, 1980-2016**

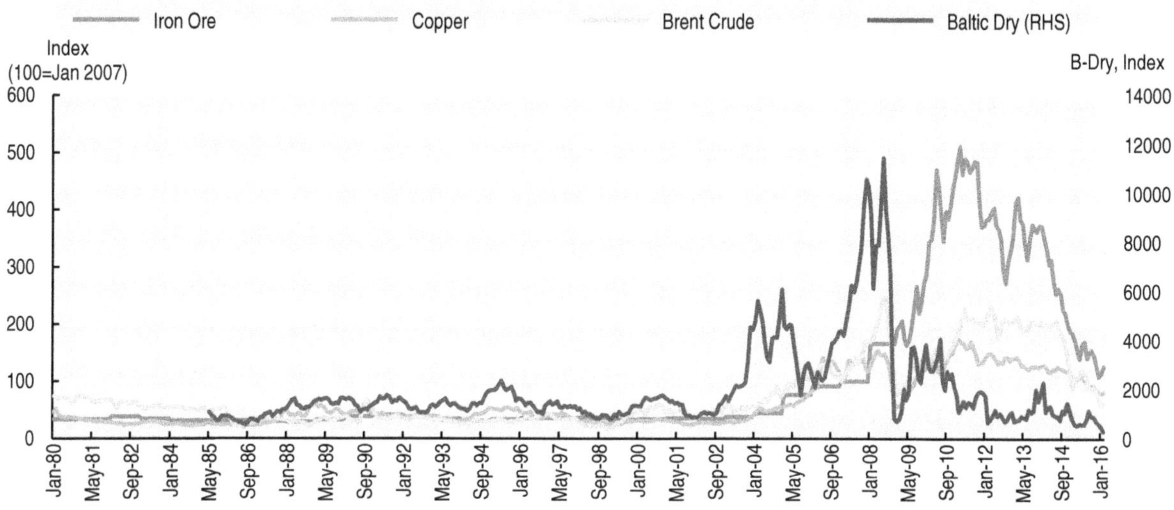

Source: OECD calculations, Thomson Reuters Datastream.

StatLink http://dx.doi.org/10.1787/888933362120

The so-called "hog cycle" in farming has occurred on a global scale. Unlike swine that can be slaughtered, however, investment in energy, commodities, related services and infrastructure are long-term in nature and may take years to be built and years to be run down via depreciation. Investing on the assumption of a supercycle that turns out not to be sustainable gives rise to over-investment in the affected sectors with negative consequences for future investment and for dealing with past liabilities.

This current period of weakening investment has also coincided with the stronger US dollar since 2012 (as the US economy has been improving vis-à-vis other countries in the past few years). In addition to weakening fundamentals, movement in the dollar is a swing factor that can drive turning points in commodity prices: since commodities are priced in dollars, a stronger dollar acts to reduce commodity demand from the non-dollar-block countries (e.g. prices rise in yen and euro which can reduce demand from from places like Japan and Europe); conversely, commodity prices tend to rise when the dollar falls.

The commodity currencies are recognisable as those dropping the most sharply in Figure 1.3. Commodity-based countries have little choice but to allow the exchange rate to move down as a shock absorber for the negative impact on their terms of trade. The dollar block currencies (China and the Asian Tigers) in the higher part of the chart have been relatively stable versus the dollar and commodity prices are less affected by currency shifts for this group. Between these sit the yen and the euro, whose movements versus the dollar are swing factors affecting commodity demand. These currencies depreciated in 2013 and 2014, respectively, as their quantitative easing (QE) policies came into effect, reinforcing the influence of weak fundamentals on commodity prices. Subsequently these depreciations stalled out in 2015, and in 2016 the yen has begun to rise versus the dollar, contributing to the early 2016 bounce in commodity prices.

Figure 1.3. **Exchange rates: The supercycle reversal breaks the pack, 2011-16**

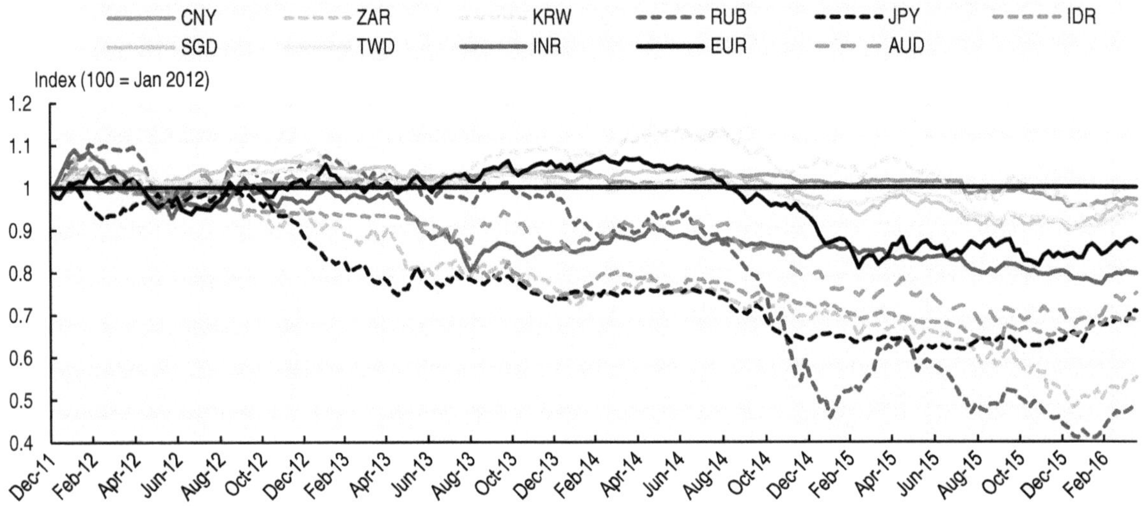

Note: Exchange rates are expressed in US dollar per national currency.
Source: OECD calculations, Thomson Reuters Datastream.

StatLink http://dx.doi.org/10.1787/888933362136

It's big: the unusual global dependence on energy and materials investment

The sheer scale of national saving and investment in the BRIICS led to the build-up of excess capacity in many sectors. During the global financial crisis of 2008, some of these countries responded by further accelerating investment and borrowing, and hence saw little loss of momentum in growth compared to the advanced economies. This caused excess capacity and indebtedness to build up even further in the supercycle sectors. This investment was not limited to EME energy and resources. The high price of oil and gas brought in new players in North America, and energy investment advanced on a global scale, and derived demand from supercyle sectors spread to related industries (utilities, capital goods, transport, etc.).

Figure 1.4 shows the rates of growth of capital expenditure in the nine broadest non-financial and non-real estate Global Industry Classification Standard sectors for advanced economies and EMEs using a sample of 11 000 of the world's largest companies. After the tech bust came the supercycle mania. Capital expenditure in the energy and materials sectors grew strongly in EMEs, reaching rates of 34%, and 46% p.a., respectively, by 2007 – much faster than in advanced economies (at 23% and 28% in 2007).[4]

Figure 1.4. **Capital expenditure by sector in advanced and emerging economies, 2003-15**

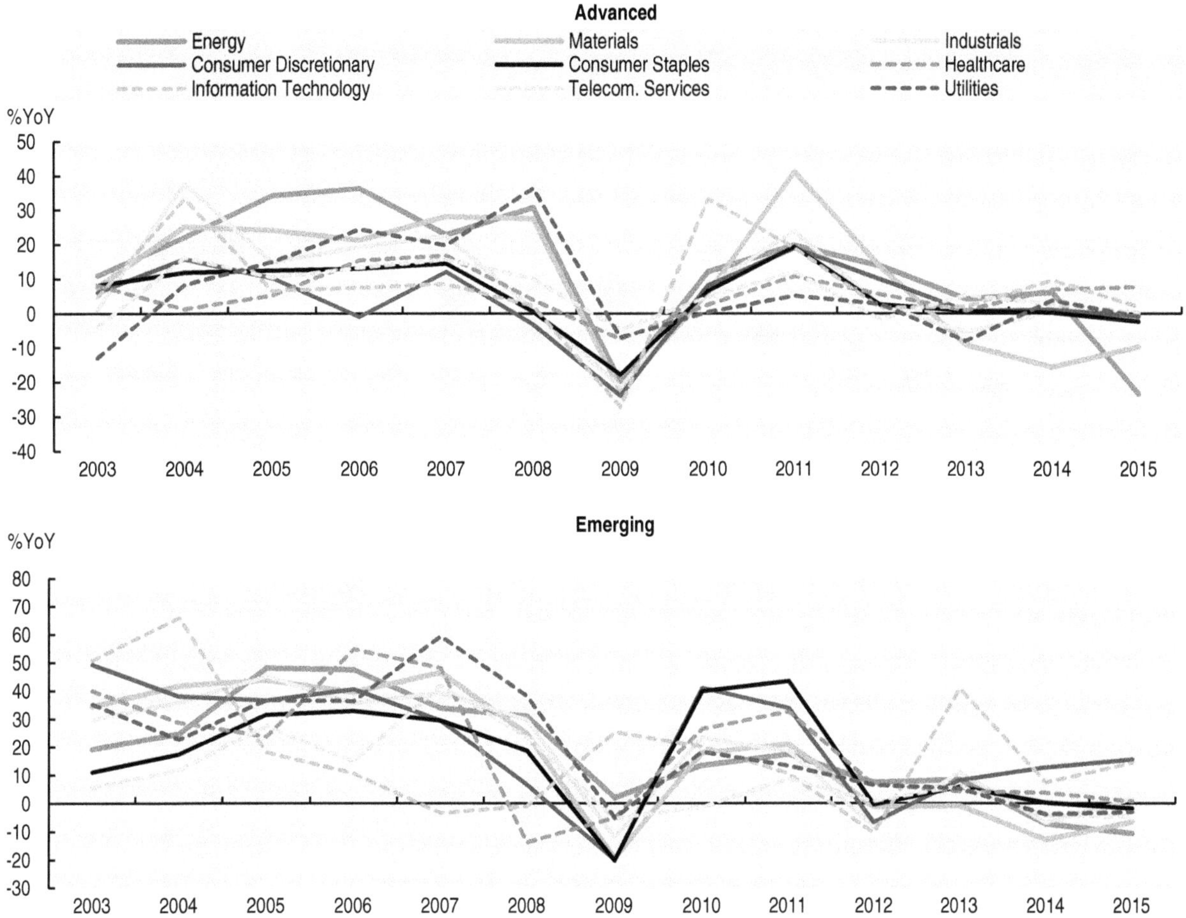

Source: OECD calculations, Bloomberg.

StatLink http://dx.doi.org/10.1787/888933362144

It is seldom appreciated just how important these two sectors became as a share of global (non-financial and non-real estate) capital expenditure by companies shown in Figure 1.5. In the sample of 11 000 companies these percentage shares peaked around 2013-14. By 2014, the energy and materials sectors together constituted 40% of global listed-company capital expenditure across all sectors (excluding banking and real estate). If related industrials and utilities are added, this rises to a 60% share.

Energy is a vast sector consisting of oil, gas, drilling, oil and gas equipment and services, exploration, refining, storage, transportation, coal and consumable fuels. Materials also cover widespread industries that are major inputs to the industrialisation of EMEs including: chemicals, fertilisers, industrial gases, construction materials, metal and glass containers, paper packaging, aluminium, diversified materials and mining, gold, precious metals and minerals, forest products and paper products.

The slowdown and reversal of such a major part of investment has become and will remain a major headwind to world economic growth going forward. Capital spending in these three sectors has moved into negative growth in EMEs since 2014. This is compounded by similar weakness induced in advanced economies.

Figure 1.5. **Global capital expenditure by sector, 2002-15**

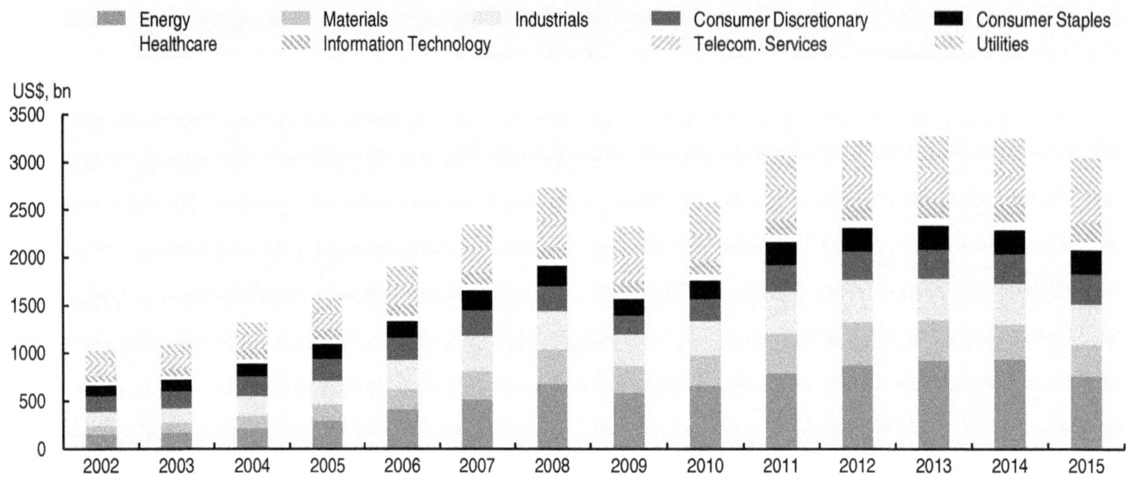

Source: OECD calculations, Bloomberg.

StatLink http://dx.doi.org/10.1787/888933362150

Monetary policy does not address this problem of sector misallocation

A snapshot of the over-investment problem in certain sectors in EMEs is compared with advanced economies in Figure 1.6, using the same scale for easy comparison.[5] If the return on equity (ROE) less the cost of capital (COK) is low or negative there is an indication of over-investment: the ROE is less than the weighted cost of external finance for the company. The sectors are ranked according to the ROE-COK in 2015. The charts in the worst categories (the two top panels) for emerging economies suggest that the sectors most prone to excess capacity are precisely those where investment was strongest in the pre-crisis period and most of which are associated with the supercycle, notably: materials, energy, software and services, utilities, consumer services (including investment in hotels, resorts, casinos, etc.), capital goods, transport, retailing and technology hardware and equipment.[6] The reversal of the supercycle has also affected interrelated advanced economy ROEs (shown in the four bottom panels), and notably also in the energy, materials and utilities sectors. It is striking, however, that outside of these three sectors advanced country returns (where open economy market disciplines operate) are on average better than in the emerging world. The presence of excess capacity in certain sectors of the world economy cannot be addressed by a one-size-fits-all monetary policy.

Restructuring high-saving emerging market economies will not happen quickly

Restructuring high-saving emerging economies towards being more consumer-oriented societies cannot happen quickly. Restructuring takes time and, in any case, large emerging market companies are biased towards a structurally low wages share. Such companies in the sample used in this study have an average wages share in company value added of just 39%, compared to an average of 64% in advanced economy companies. Raising wages to rectify this imbalance will cause the ROEs shown earlier to decline much further, which in turn will make it difficult for the companies to service their substantial debt. Rising wages will also cause inflation and would require monetary policy to tighten. All of these pressures would be disruptive. This means that, like Japan in previous decades, rectifying global imbalances – even if countries were to be supportive of a change in policy direction – would have to take some considerable time.

Figure 1.6. **Sector investment misallocation: ROE-COK in emerging versus advanced economies, 2002-15**

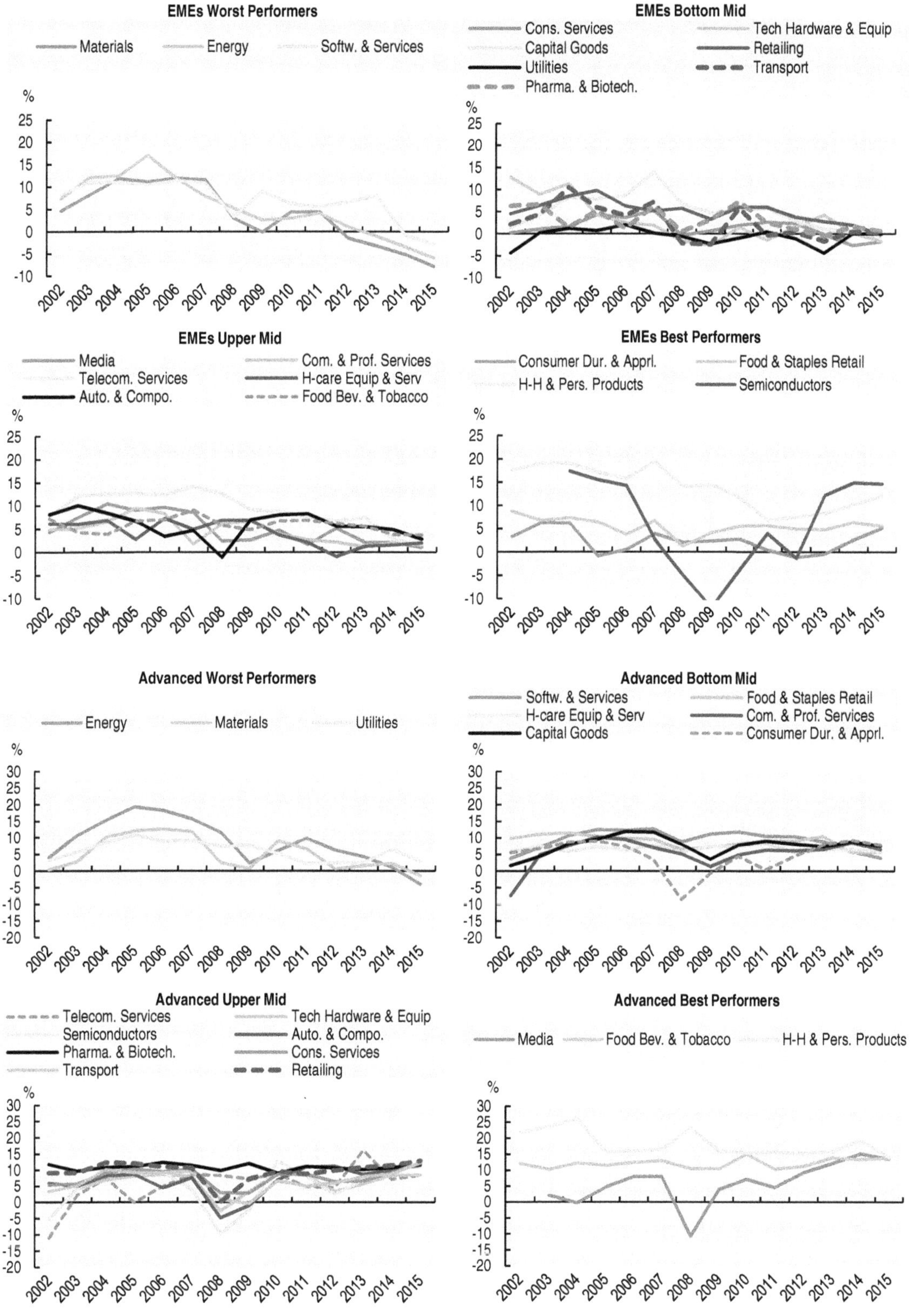

Note: ROE: return on equity; COK: cost of capital.
Source: OECD calculations, Bloomberg.

StatLink http://dx.doi.org/10.1787/888933362162

Headwind 2: The L-shaped recovery in advanced economies due to the aftermath of, and responses to, the financial crisis

The financial crisis of 2008 was the first phase of the collision in mega-trends that policy makers are still trying to deal with. This led to unconventional monetary policy and a move to zero (and now negative) rates in many countries to avoid a collapse of the world financial system. This has been followed by new rules to re-regulate the banking system. Deleveraging associated with these new capital and liquidity rules, together with the size of current and prospective non-performing loans, have become the prime contributors to the L-shaped recovery in many advanced economies. This has always been expected by financial market analysts who argued that bank ROEs would fall sharply, particularly for banks involved with capital market products.[7] But this has been the intention of re-regulation: i.e. policy makers aiming to have a smaller, safer and more consolidated banking system where higher risks are priced appropriately. Banks have pushed back hard against these reforms.[8]

Figure 1.7 shows the Basel III capital requirements in the top panel and the simple leverage ratio long argued by the OECD to be the preferred binding measure in the bottom

Figure 1.7. **Deleveraging and the capital rules: GSIBs, 2006-16**

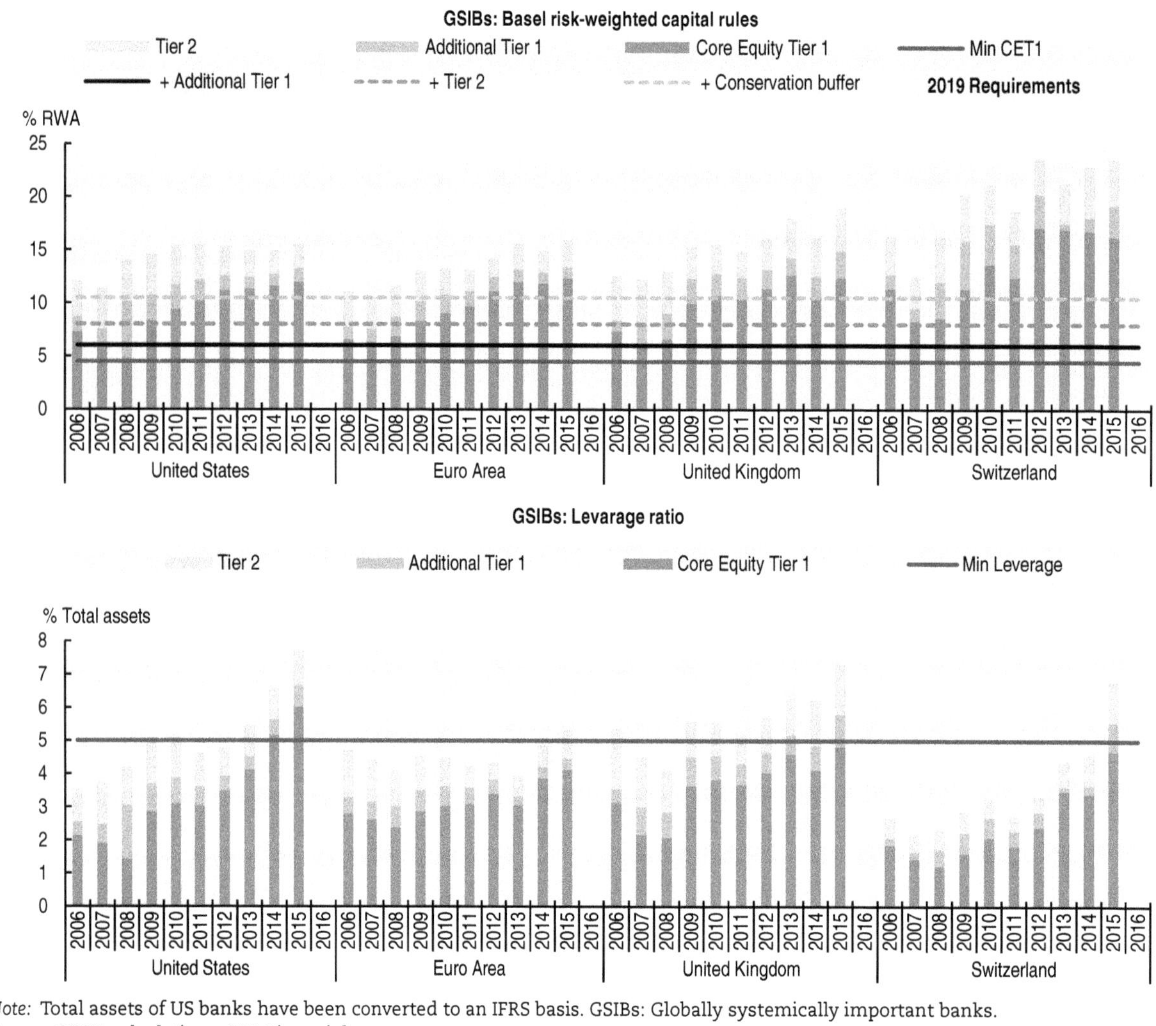

Note: Total assets of US banks have been converted to an IFRS basis. GSIBs: Globally systemically important banks.
Source: OECD calculations, SNL Financials.

StatLink http://dx.doi.org/10.1787/888933362171

panel.[9] The rise in the ratio of core tier 1 (T1) equity to total assets in all of the jurisdictions shown in blue reflects the deleveraging pressure on economies. All banks in all countries appear to satisfy the Basel rules, and have done so for some time. The total loss absorbing capacity (TLAC) extension of Basel III for globally systemically important banks (GSIBs) was also examined. This work (not reported) found that only a handful of such banks would be required to issue more long-term unsecured debt for potential bail-in purposes.

If the Basel risk-weighted rules were the binding constraint on banking then the L-shape recovery should be lifting, as it has done in the United States. But this is not the case. The OECD recommendation that banks should have core equity equal to 5% of their total un-weighted assets has only been surpassed in the United States. Bad loans have not been dealt with in Europe and this makes it more difficult (with the continual slow bleeding of non-performing loan write-offs) to finish raising capital and to begin lending. For other non-GSIBs, which are very important in lending and economic growth, lack of T1 equity is most apparent in Europe and the United Kingdom, but not the United States and Switzerland. The United States and Switzerland are parts of the world where economic growth is reflecting less of the L-shape pattern that is more prevalent elsewhere.

Figure 1.8. **Deleveraging and the capital rules: Other non-GSIB banks, 2006-16**

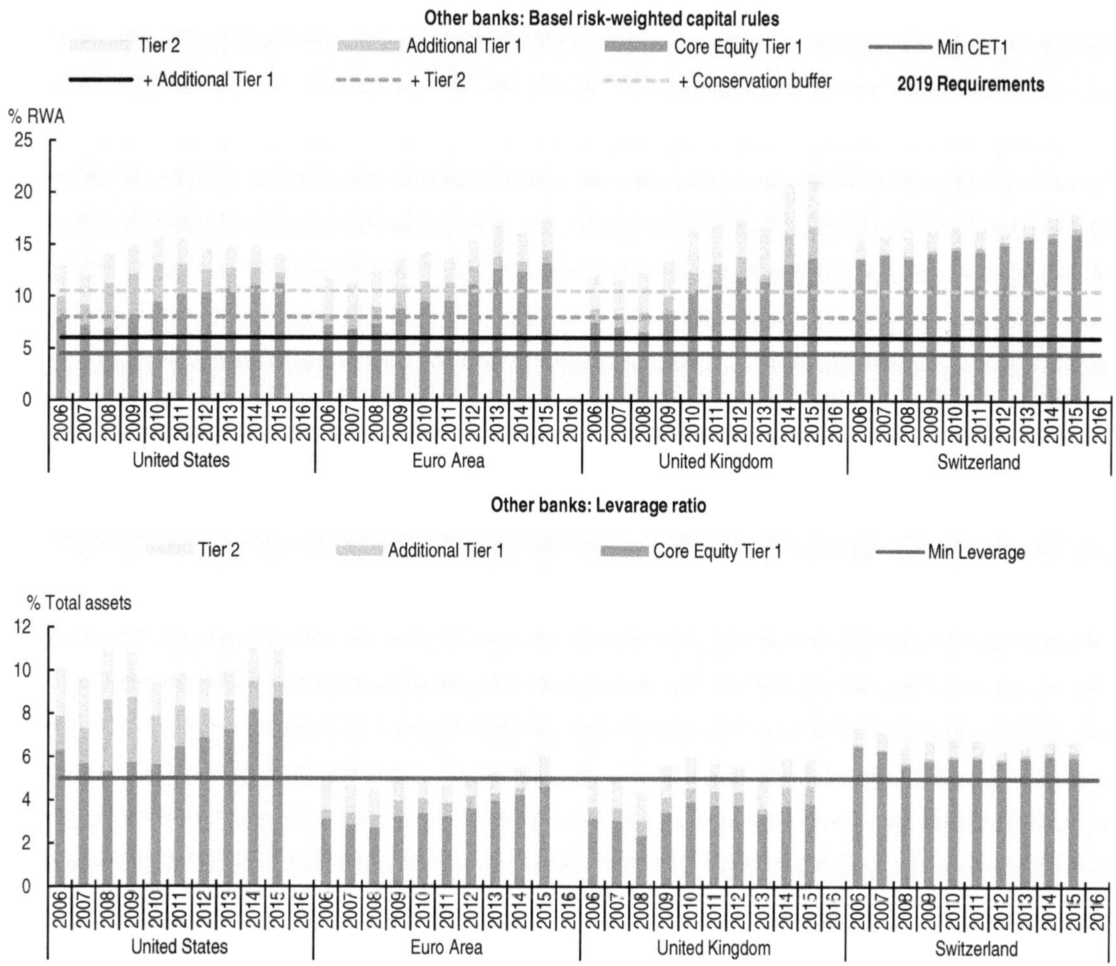

Note: Total assets of US banks have been converted to an IFRS basis. GSIBs: Globally systemically important banks.
Source: OECD calculations, SNL Financials.

StatLink http://dx.doi.org/10.1787/888933362185

Having prevented a collapse of the global financial system in 2008, unconventional monetary policy continues and may now become counterproductive with:

- negative rates hurting banks
- investment decisions being distorted (discussed in detail below)
- weak banks and companies being kept alive and non-performing loans (NPLs) not being addressed (delaying the "creative destruction" phase required to restore productivity growth).

The negative interest rates problem

Europe and Japan are growing too slowly and a number of central banks have imposed negative interest rates (the ECB and the central banks of Switzerland, Denmark, Sweden, and Japan). The theory is that this will force banks to do something else other than deposit cash with the central bank, i.e. to lend to the real economy, and it may also help to weaken the exchange rate. While it is always hard to know what would have happened without negative rates, this policy certainly does not appear to be helping a great deal at this stage.

High Quality Liquid Assets (HQLA) are supposed to be at 70% of the ultimate Basel III requirement of the Liquidity Coverage Ratio (LCR) rule from January 2016, and this rises to 100% by 2019. HQLA consist mainly of central bank reserves and sovereign bonds (and a few high-grade corporate bonds and equities). QE has forced up the amount of central bank reserves in bank portfolios (now carrying negative rates) and bond rates in most jurisdictions are also very low or negative. It is hard to see how paying banks a negative return on forced holdings helps the economy through the banking channel.[10] In an environment of weak demand for credit, banks have to offset the negative return on HQLA via higher rates or increased fees for their clients, thereby exacerbating the already weak demand for loans.

The distance-to-default of banks

As if these problems were not enough, it must also be noted that many banks across all regions are also exposed to the fall in oil prices and the potential defaults of borrowers, which could add to the NPL problems noted in Box 1.1. The DTD of banks is falling once more (shown in standard deviations from the default point in Figure 1.10).[11]

Box 1.1. **Hypothetical illustration of the impact of negative interest rates on banks**

A stylised example is shown in Figure 1.9. Hypothetical overheads, the loan loss ratio, deposit costs and the leverage ratio are as shown in the chart. HQLA are at 12% of total assets (TA).[1] The two lines show the ROE and interest rate trade-off arithmetic. In the steeper solid grey line the loan rate is considered over a range from 1.5% to 5%, while the rate on HQLA is held constant at -1% per year. In this case only the highest lending rates for banks allow for a positive ROE, i.e. lending rates at greater than 4%. But even at 5% the ROE of 6% would be below the cost of capital. The problem of course is that overheads, deposit funding and loan loss provisions are always there as costs (in the example shown, banks have to make 3.9% on their assets just to break even).

Negative rates on HQLA and weak loan demand work against banks being able to make reasonable returns. In the flatter blue solid line the bank's loan rate is held at the high 4% (e.g. the US prime rate is 3.5% and European rates are typically much lower), while the rate on HQLA starts at minus 1.5% and rises to plus 2% (rising 50 basis points at each interval). Paying more on deposits clearly helps: if -0.5% is paid the ROE breaks even (the bank does not lose money). At a positive return of 1% on HQLA the bank achieves 3.3% and 2%

Box 1.1. **Hypothetical illustration of the impact of negative interest rates on banks** *(cont.)*

allows an ROE of 5.5% to be earned. Fees are excluded from the calculation but everywhere these are rising (on ATM withdrawals, especially-out-of-network, on overdrafts and for many services) as banks pass on this adverse combination of the LCR and negative interest rates in an environment of weak loan demand.[2]

Of course the assumption of a loan loss rate of only 1% of TA does not apply to many of the banks in Europe. The 1% of assets would be roughly equivalent to 2% of loans, and this is a gross under-estimate in the case of Europe: the European Parliament recently reported a much higher NPL range based on European Banking Authority (EBA) numbers versus gross loans (e.g. 2.5% for the United Kingdom, 4.2% for France, 6.8% for Spain, 16.9% for Italy, 18.5% for Portugal, 20.6% for Ireland and over 40% for Greece).[3] NPLs much higher than 1% of total assets would push all of the curves of Figure 1.9 into negative territory and such banks would need to be resolved to restore the chance of better growth. The use of public money to establish a "bad bank" to deal with NPLs has been constrained by Brussels regulations concerning state aid.

Figure 1.9 also shows the impact of reducing the LCR from 12% to 6%. This acts to offset the impact of negative interest rates and pushes up ROEs as banks would act to minimise their exposures. The regulation may have a good long-term rationale, but it is interacting with negative interest rates in a manner harming the role of banks in promoting recovery. The message would seem to be that negative rates should be removed as quickly as practicable or the LCR reduced and/or the regulatory timetable extended.

1. In a sample of large global banks operating in all major jurisdictions, these assets appear to be higher in the United States (around 15% excluding custody/clearing banks) but lower in European banks (12%) where negative rates apply. This ratio is set to move higher with full implementation. The calibration here based on 12% of total liabilities is roughly consistent with an ECB (2013) conceptual calculation.
2. At a recent OECD meeting the Austrian central bank presented econometric evidence for Europe that showed a systematic negative impact on bank profitability – reported here with permission from the author. See Redak (2016).
3. See European Parliament (2016).

Figure 1.9. **Hypothetical bank return on equity trade-offs with negative rate assumptions**

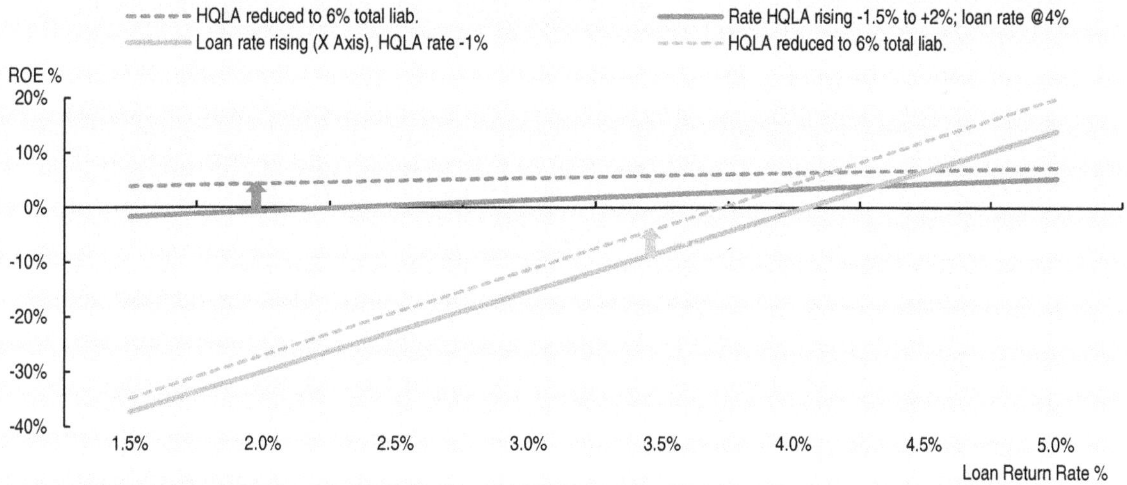

Note: High quality liquid assets (HQLA) = 12% of total assets; O/heads = 1.5% of total assets; Loan loss = 1% of total assets; Leverage ratio = 6%; Deposit rate = 1%.
Source: OECD calculations.

StatLink http://dx.doi.org/10.1787/888933362196

The average DTD of banks has fallen most in Asia and Latin America. In Asia (where the supercycle reversal is most prevalent) the DTD is back to levels last seen in 2010. In Latin America (also a large resources area) the DTD is at levels last seen in 2009. US banks appear to be the strongest at this point. Nevertheless the situation bears watching closely.

Figure 1.10. **Average distance-to-default (DTD) for large banks, 1998-2016**

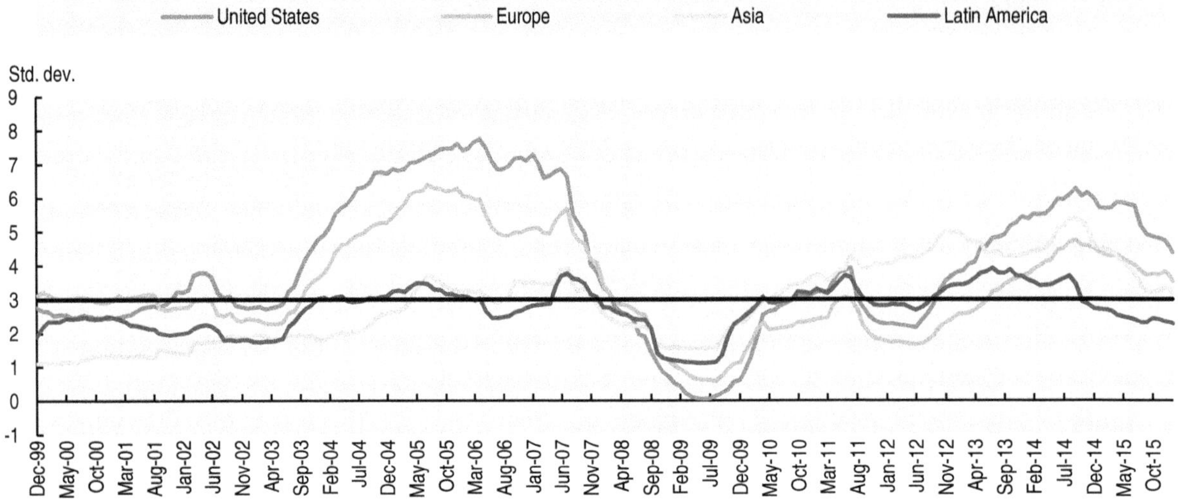

Note: Europe refers to the European Union, Norway and Switzerland. The horizontal 3-standard-deviation line represents a minimal level of "safety" based on calibration from previous crises.
Source: OECD calculations, Bloomberg.

StatLink http://dx.doi.org/10.1787/888933362209

Quantitative easing, negative interest rates and foreign exchange markets

One argument favouring negative interest rates noted earlier might be the hope for a monetary policy transmission mechanism to depreciate the exchange rate. However, the current environment is one where private sector portfolio reactions have become very unpredictable.

Japan announced negative rates in January 2016 and the yen surprisingly rose sharply against the weaker US dollar (see Figure 1.3). In interconnected financial markets (and nowhere is this more the case than in foreign exchange) there are too many moving parts. Negative interest rates may lead to a powerful carry trade, essentially borrowing yen at negative rates and buying the dollar outright. A central bank might buy JGBs in its reserves and swap them into dollar assets. But if the trend in the dollar turns to depreciation, these structures are unwound and can reinforce appreciation of the negative interest rate currency.

Other influences on currencies are simply more important than interest rates: notably economic growth and, more recently, the change by Chinese authorities to manage the currency versus a basket. The Federal Reserve changed its tone at the start of 2016 and appears to have become more worried about the impact on the United States of a reversal of the supercycle in the global economy. This caused the dollar to fall, commodity prices to bounce and flows into emerging economies to stabilise and improve a little. Since the exchange rate is the price of one currency in terms of another it stands to reason that QE could, other things given, lead to depreciation. Hence QE policies in Europe and Japan (implemented to support the economy) could do so via exchange rate depreciation. However, this would not necessarily happen in the changed policy environment of 2016 following the announcement of the Chinese to manage the renminbi versus a currency basket. The depreciation of a large currency would cause the Chinese currency basket to rally and may lead to Chinese responses (discussed in the next section). In the case of the yen market, sources suggest that uncovered investors hurt by the rise in the yen are bringing their investments back home (leading to further upward currency pressure) and some foreign exchange reserves managers have been unwinding carry trade structures.

Emerging markets responses to the reversal of the supercycle and the L-shaped recovery, with a focus on China

Underlying real structural problems in emerging economies will continue to affect the business and finance outlook until they are dealt with via reforms affecting the openness of trade and investment, and which promote a greater role for domestic demand and the services sectors. It was noted earlier that this may be a long time in coming due to the low wages share in EME companies and the difficulty of dealing with over-investment issues.

The problem of net outflows from emerging markets

Advanced economy companies have been taking notice of the apparent sharp decline in the ROEs of emerging economy companies compared to their cost of equity by reducing net mergers and acquisitions (M&A) inflows (a key element of foreign direct investment). In the years prior to the crisis, inflows of foreign direct investment had helped underpin exchange rate strength and the need for exchange market intervention to resist upward pressure – particularly in China where foreign exchange reserves built up strongly. Cross-border M&A into emerging economies rose in both gross and net terms up to 2008 and then dipped sharply in 2009 in response to the crisis (Figure 1.11). Cross-border divestment with respect to developing economies, which had anyway begun rising prior to the crisis, accelerated sharply in 2010. This divestment has meant that net inward M&A has not recovered to pre-crisis levels.

Figure 1.11. **Net inward mergers and acquisitions in emerging economies, 1996-2015**

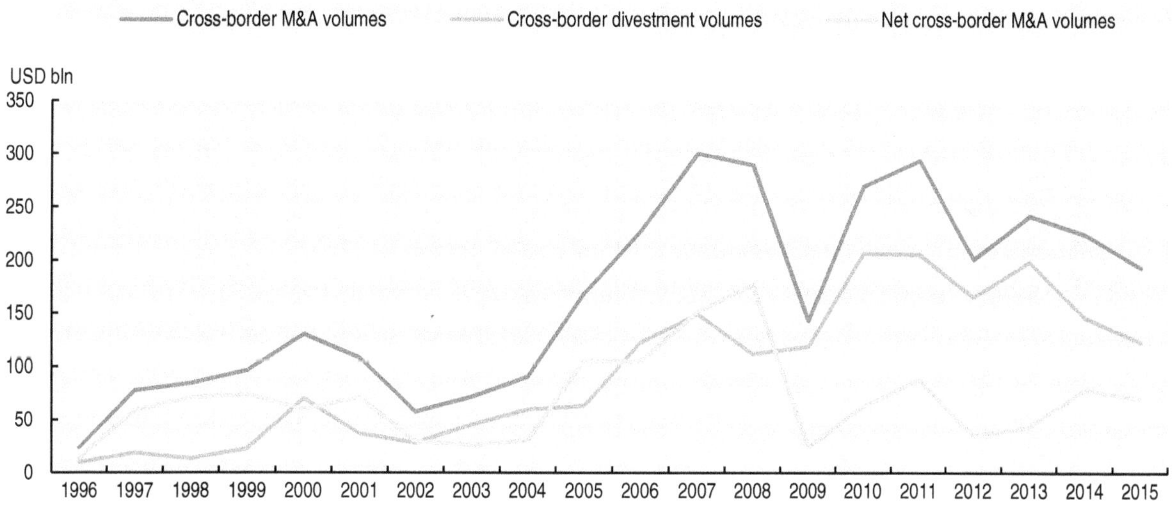

Source: OECD calculations, Dealogic M&A Analytics database.

StatLink http://dx.doi.org/10.1787/888933362216

Portfolio outflows and exchange rate pressure reversal in EMEs

As the net inward M&A "underpinning" demand for emerging assets declined in a structural sense, cross-border portfolio outflows actually accelerated from some countries in 2015 due to fear of portfolio losses (overvalued supercycle assets and currency translation losses) as the expectation of Federal Reserve tightening and resulting exchange rate pressures mounted. Figure 1.12 shows indexes of international reserves since the supercycle reversal began (equal to 100 in January 2012). Countries losing reserves (where the index in the chart begins to turn downwards) are in large part associated with portfolio outflows and attempts to resist a fall of the currency (for example: China, Turkey, Russia, and Argentina).

Figure 1.12. **International reserves in emerging economies, 2012-16**

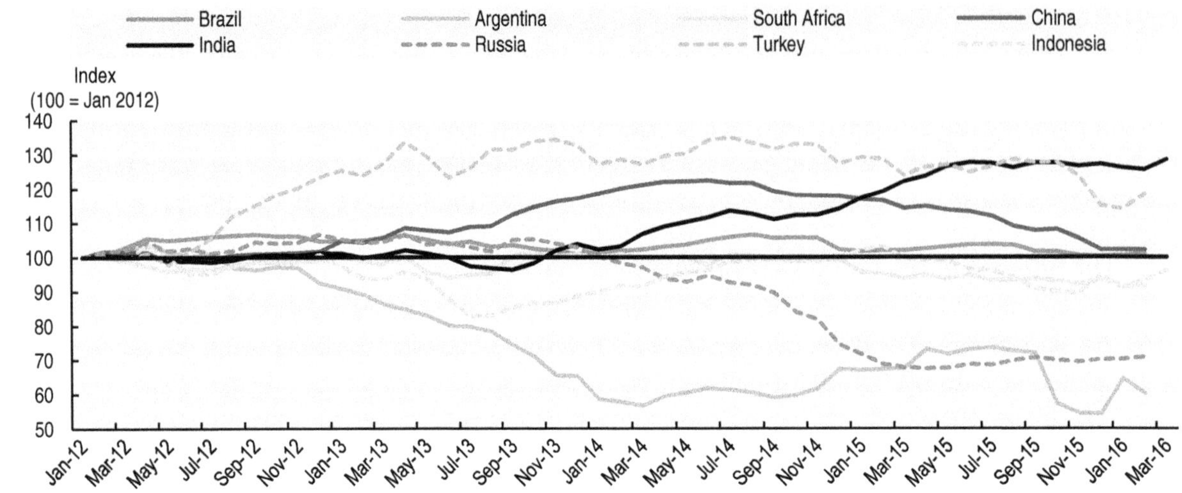

Source: OECD calculations, Thomson Reuters Datastream.

StatLink http://dx.doi.org/10.1787/888933362222

These stabilised in early 2016 as the Federal Reserve commentary about tightening was perceived in markets to be more "dovish". Market sources suggest this calmed concerns and actually helped to increase the portfolio demand for emerging assets in March 2016. This could yet prove to be premature.

The Chinese foreign exchange market

In China the non-deliverable forward (NDF) market operates mostly in Hong Kong, China.[12] An offshore renminbi market developed after the crisis because of dollar shortages: the market was encouraged by the authorities, and an overnight interbank market and a fledgling market of longer duration securities ("dim sum" bonds and similar instruments) developed. This market is traded and the renminbi is fully convertible offshore. The idea was that importers could find dollars in the offshore traded market.

Unfortunately, a number of events in China came together to cause selling in its financial markets and outflow pressure on the foreign exchange market in 2015 and early 2016. These events included:

- The end of the supercycle and falling company investment due to declining returns on equity versus the cost of capital.
- Extreme equity market overvaluation and volatility.[13]
- A crackdown on corruption amongst the elite.
- A move to liberalise the foreign exchange market including convertibility of the renminbi (stimulated by the desire to enter the IMF SDR basket) which could see the currency fall further (investors want to get out at better levels).

These factors resulted in a desire by residents and companies to try to get money out via Hong Kong, China – this would normally have led to market arbitrage as the offshore rate diverges from the onshore one, and the renminbi would fall more quickly. China did not want this to happen and so market intelligence suggests it intervened in the market – both the official onshore market and the offshore spot and NDF market.

The targeted exchange rate is now a basket of currencies and not just the US dollar. China carries out its offshore intervention by using private financial institutions that participate in those offshore markets and trade on behalf of China. To help stem the pressure, China has imposed various additional controls on outflows in the last couple of months of 2015. These include:

- Suspending the right of onshore foreign banks to participate in the offshore market (DBS, Standard Chartered, and Deutsche Bank).
- Limiting the amounts individuals and companies can transfer.
- Insisting on more screening by banks to ensure that amounts above USD 50 000 are genuinely for the purposes of importing goods into China.
- Suspending the structural reform process related to the currency.

At the same time that it is imposing outflow controls, China is liberalising measures affecting capital inflows (to try to offset the outflow pressure). In particular, it has abolished bond investment quotas on qualified foreign institutional investors (including insurance companies, pension funds, commercial banks, endowment funds, and mutual funds). The strategy has led to increased volatility: the spread between the onshore and offshore markets is large at times and reserve loss has been quite significant. On 12 January 2016, their intervention in the offshore market completely drained renminbi in the (relatively small) market and pushed the overnight rate to over 60%.

Complicating quantitative easing strategies in Europe and Japan

The announcement in December 2015 that policy is now focused on a basket of currencies and less so on the US dollar will enable the authorities to decouple monetary policy from the US tightening process – should that process continue in 2016.[14] With regard to other major currencies this approach complicates things. For example, if the European Central Bank (ECB) or the Bank of Japan (BoJ) used QE in 2016 and beyond, the currency might behave very differently compared to the period prior to the new Chinese exchange rate management regime. Whereas QE might have affected the exchange rate in the direction of depreciation prior to 2016, under the new regime the *ex ante* pressure to appreciate the basket will lead to a Chinese policy response to manage the basket. There appear to be two choices in this respect: the renminbi could be depreciated versus the dollar to stabilise the basket; or the Chinese could intervene in the cross rates (e.g. sell dollars to buy yen or euro to offset the quantitative easing policy effects). The latter approach has advantages in the near term, since China has large corporate debts in US dollars and HK dollars. Some of the outflows early in the year have been Chinese corporates repaying these foreign currency debts, so that depreciating the renminbi versus the dollar before this is done makes less sense.

The Chinese stock market

In the stock market, wealthy individuals and companies would like to sell some of their stock and transfer money to the Hong Kong, China market before exchange rates deteriorate further. To prevent confidence being dented by a collapse in prices, the authorities have been using official funds to prop up the Shanghai stock market. This, together with cross-border controls, has led to huge discrepancies between the prices of the same stocks listed in both Shanghai and Hong Kong, China in the same currency. The median of the daily stock price divergence of 69 such companies, shown in Figure 1.13, is volatile, and there has always been a risk premium for the Chinese listings. These premiums took a severe jump upwards in 2015 (from a 25% median premium to 75%) with considerable differences amongst the stocks included.

Figure 1.13. **Shanghai and Hong Kong, China price ratio for 69 dual-listed stocks, 2012-16**

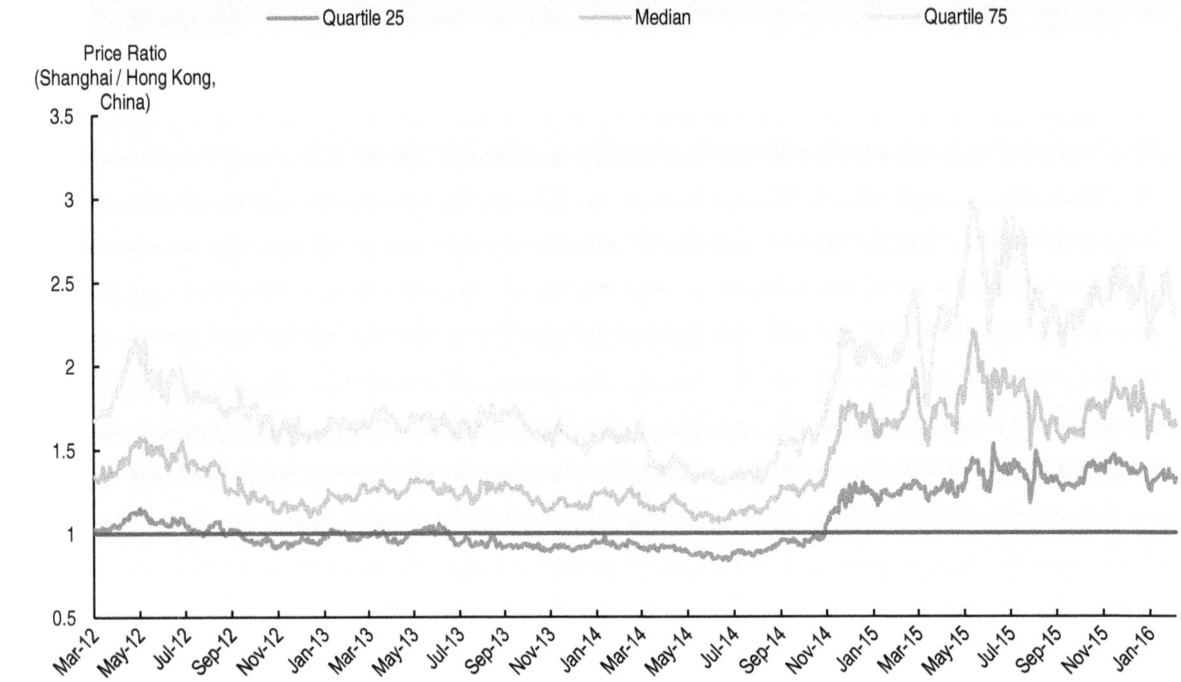

Source: OECD calculations, Bloomberg.

StatLink http://dx.doi.org/10.1787/888933362232

China monetary policy and spending responses

China has responded to the sharp slowing in the economy via credit and fiscal expansion (in the areas of housing and infrastructure). Fixed asset investment is still running at over 10% p.a. (double the stated GDP growth so that it is rising as a share of GDP). While China's medium-term plan is to move towards a greater consumption and services-driven growth model, bold structural reforms are likely to be delayed due to the slowdown: the internationalisation of the renminbi has already been halted somewhat; key internal prices remain distorted (e.g. as in Figure 1.13); and Chinese industrial policy, which heavily involves the role of the state, has contributed to global excess capacity (particularly in energy, steel, other materials sectors, construction and solar photovoltaic, and automobiles) and will take time to move to a different modus operandi.[15]

Dealing with excess capacity sectors requires a "creative destruction" phase: closing down old industries and then building new ones guided by market signals and with a lesser role of the state. But major reform now would risk slowing the economy further. Faced with this challenge, the People's Bank of China (PBOC) is stepping in (as central banks are also doing in the United States, Japan and Europe).

As international reserves have fallen, domestic credit expansion and liquidity policies have been turned on via reduced bank reserve ratios, interest rate cuts and other measures.[16]

The China Development Bank (CDB) is continuing to play an important role in debt-funded public spending in 2016, and has accelerated lending versus 2015. The focus for 2016 is on shantytown redevelopment (RMB 950 billion, up 26% from last year), and a continuation of lending to railways (RMB 100 billion), water conservation (RMB 65 billion) and industrial upgrading (RMB 180 billion). The PBOC has loaned significant sums to the China Development Bank via the relending facility for these projects in recent years, creating claims on the CDB. These are equivalent to claims on the government. Market sources suggest the PBOC could lend out claims on the CDB to other banks in worse shape (for a spread) improving their liquidity since they could use the CDB claim for collateral for their own borrowing. The money supply and domestic credit growth shown in Figure 1.14 is accelerating.

Figure 1.14. **M2, international reserves and domestic credit in China, 2000-16**

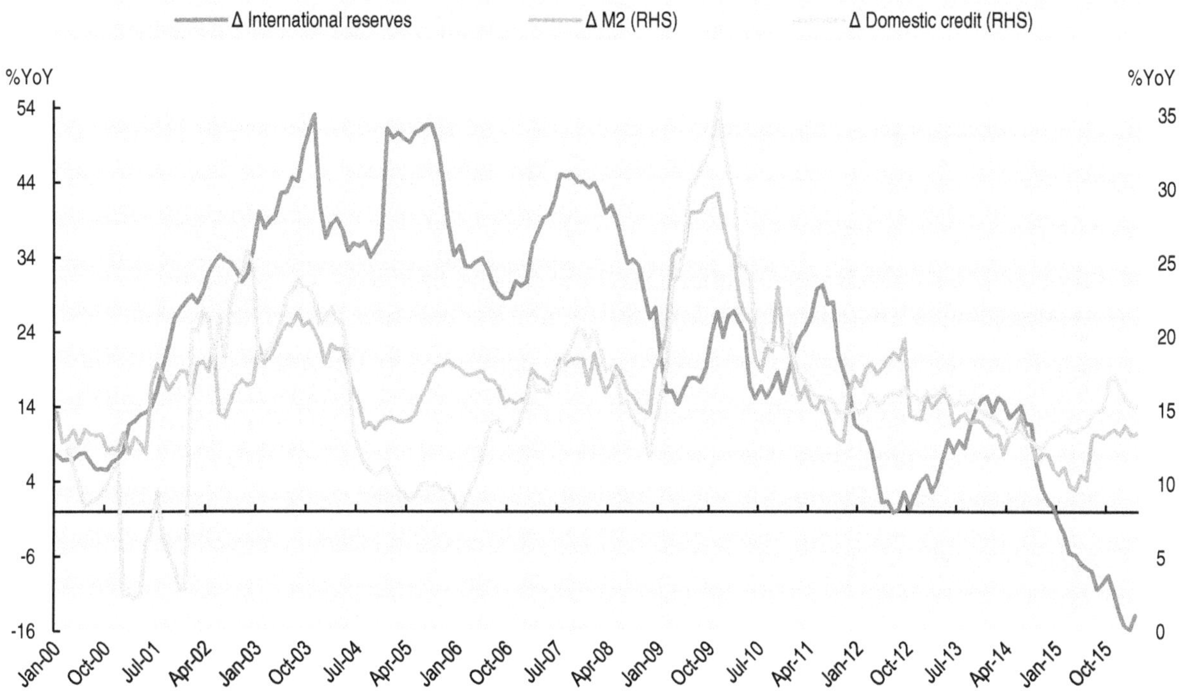

Source: OECD calculations, Thomson Reuters Datastream.

StatLink http://dx.doi.org/10.1787/888933362241

The problem with these approaches is that structural reform has not yet been carried through and will likely take a long time. This may mean that policies in response to the current crisis will not be sufficiently different from 2009, which exacerbated the excess capacity situation and worsened credit problems in China.

Other emerging market economies' responses

Other emerging markets have also eased monetary policy by cutting interest rates to ensure that they do not lose competitiveness (e.g. India, Indonesia, Chinese Taipei, Turkey and Hungary). Singapore, which manages its currency versus an effective exchange rate basket, set the appreciation band to zero in April (from a previous undisclosed rising appreciation band). Some countries have also stepped up the extent to which they use capital flow measures. OECD research suggests that these measures are quite closely linked with reducing pressure on foreign reserves in the exchange rate management process, but are not particularly efficient at affecting variables associated with financial stability when macro-prudential explanations are offered for their use.[17]

Perverse incentives for investors created by monetary policy

Investors have been herded into concentrated trades, many of which are illiquid, and recent volatility reflects periodic attempts to exit them – particularly when there is any hint of a withdrawal of the monetary policy "morphine" to which they have become addicted. Financial fragility means that central banks will embark upon the normalisation of interest rates only very slowly and the outlook for the next year or two in financial markets is one of choppiness about trend modest returns, with persistent risks of extreme volatility.

Markets have had a way of forcing required policy adjustments in non-performing economies, forcing them to deal with problems like inflation, fiscal deficits and external crises. The problem here, however, is that over-investment and falling returns are located in countries that are less market oriented – this interference with markets relays pressure elsewhere. This is playing out with advanced-economy central banks taking on the results of intersecting global and domestic issues, while the reaction of some key emerging economies has been to move even further away from market forces.

Quantitative easing and low-interest-rate monetary policy can do little to correct over-investment in global industrial sectors and may be combining with regulatory factors to hurt banks in some advanced economies. These policies have also created incentives for investors that may portend problems for the future. Very low rates have created a demand for a kind of portfolio barbell: to match large allocations to private equity and low-cost exchange-traded funds (ETFs) at one end, with a greater demand for capital market risk assets based on leverage that pay higher short-term carry/cash flows (e.g. hedge and absolute return funds, etc.) at the other end.[18] In between is an allocation to equities and bonds within which further herding of investors into concentrated positions is found: in high-yield non-investment grade bonds; and in equities that focus on providing strong dividends and buybacks.

Barbell of private equity and exchange-traded funds versus cash generating funds

Private equity has been one of the main ways that investors have responded to the low-interest-rate and low-growth environment. A "time premium" has been given to private equity funds because they specialise in realising long-term risk premiums. One problem with mutual fund managers is that fees are high while cash rates are very low. This has led to the strong growth of ETFs which give exposure to assets of the investor's choice for very low fees. ETFs allow investors to gain exposure to higher-return but less liquid underlying assets, while the ETF shares promise daily liquidity.[19] In Figure 1.15, the alternative assets shown have risen since the crisis to an amount equal to 23% of the size of pension fund and insurance company assets,[20] with private equity and ETFs making up 13 percentage points of this.

Hedge funds and real estate investment funds tracked by the OECD are equivalent to 10% of institutional investor funds under management. Hedge funds promise absolute returns benchmarked against cash. Real estate investment funds pay higher yields. Underlying assets may, however, be more illiquid than clients would expect in a strong redemption demand situation.

Private equity valuations have been stellar (driven by inflows) and they may be rich when compared to what underlying investments might deliver in the current slow growth environment. This is one of the most illiquid asset classes and it is not clear how investors would fare if redemption demand strengthened. Similar comments apply to closed-end ETFs.

Figure 1.15. **Alternative assets and pension and insurance company funds under management, 2002-15**

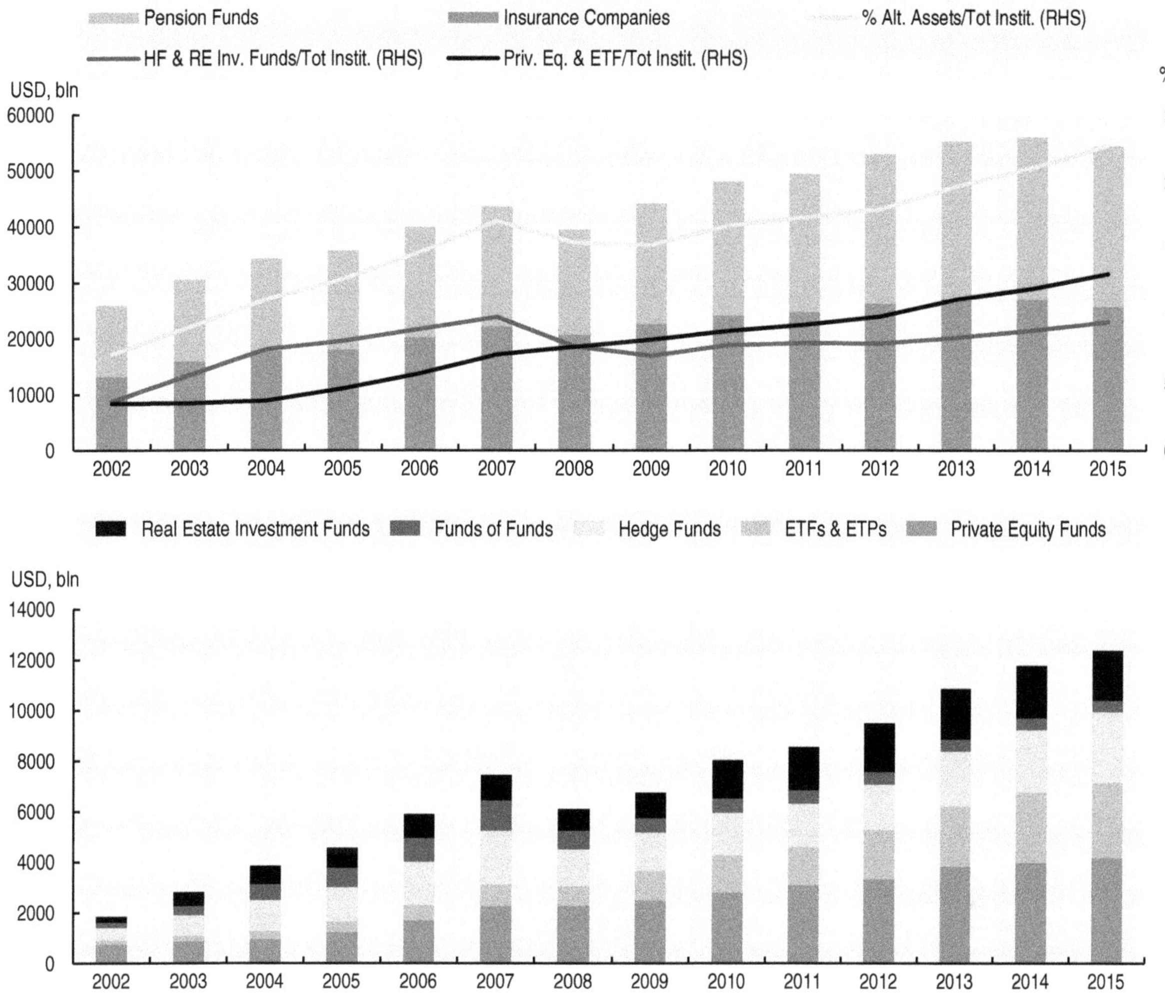

Note: 2015 estimates for pension funds, insurance companies and real estate funds' total assets.

Source: FSB Global Shadow Banking Monitoring Report 2015, 2016 Preqin Global Private Equity Report, 2016 ETFGI monthly newsletter, BarclayHedge.

StatLink http://dx.doi.org/10.1787/888933362256

These products offer daily liquidity while often referencing illiquid underlying securities. In the period of high market volatility in August 2015 strong selling from closed-end funds such as ETFs was a factor. With ETFs there are two market levels – that for the traded ETF shares, where the normal buying and selling just transfers the underlying securities without selling them on the open market, and the market for the underlying basket of securities. In August 2015 the discounts (to the underlying basket) to get out of ETFs were steep. When one-way selling emerges, the ETF providers are supposed to redeem ETF shares to arbitrage the difference between the ETF value and the underlying stocks and bonds. In August, the providers did not on average redeem ETF shares and sell the underlying. They apparently judged that selling the underlying illiquid securities would not have resulted in arbitrage profit, raising the question of what would happen in a more sustained crisis without monetary policy "morphine".

The transformation of traditional bond and equity holdings

In between the barbell of alternative assets sits equity and fixed income. These, too, have shifted with consequences for future economic performance. Figure 1.16 is drawn from the OECD database of all corporate bonds. The top panel shows the annual issuance of all bonds, 11 ratings of non-investment grade C to BB+, and 10 ratings of investment grade BBB- to AAA.

Figure 1.16. **Corporate bond issuance and declining quality, 2000-15**

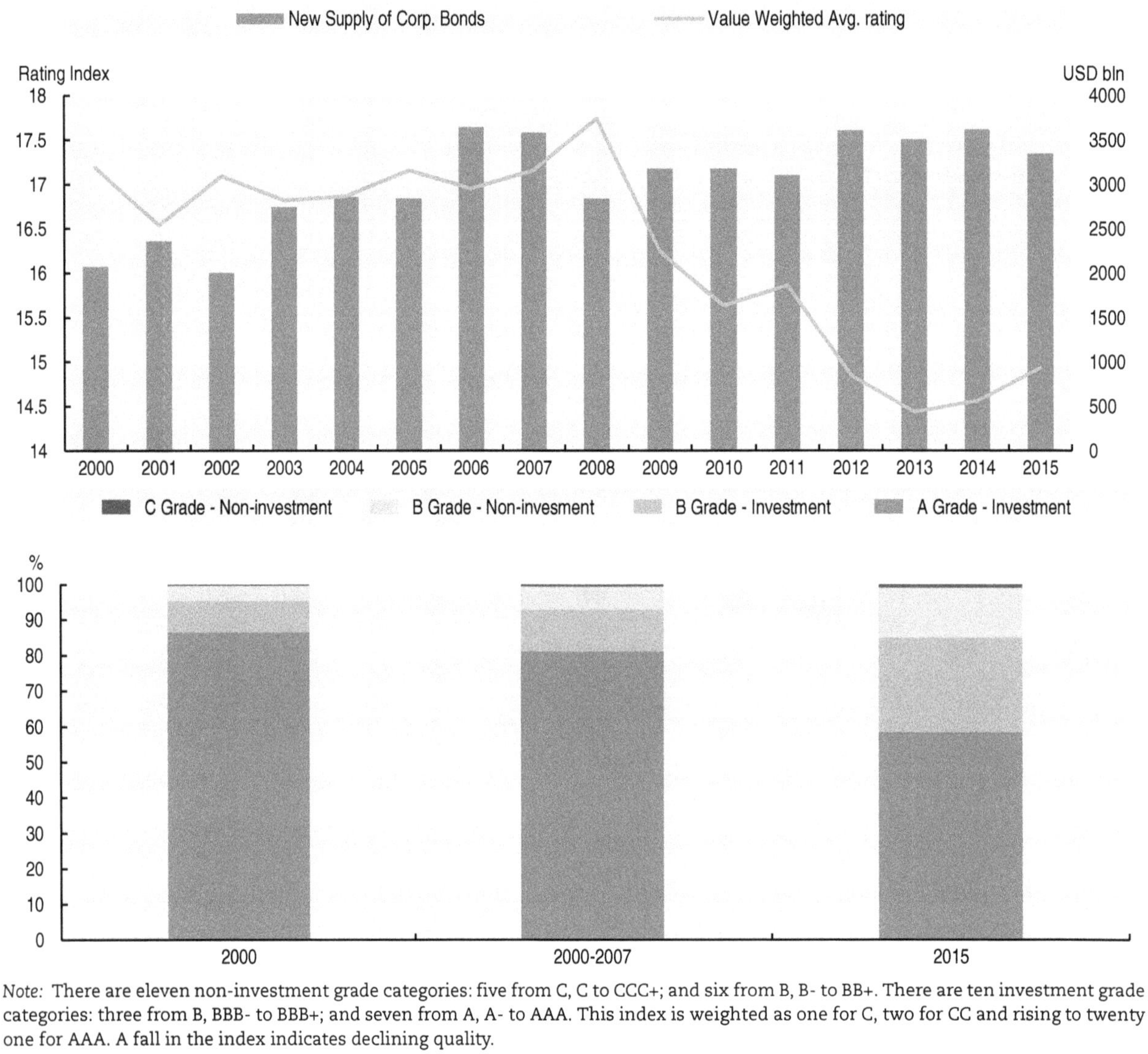

Note: There are eleven non-investment grade categories: five from C, C to CCC+; and six from B, B- to BB+. There are ten investment grade categories: three from B, BBB- to BBB+; and seven from A, A- to AAA. This index is weighted as one for C, two for CC and rising to twenty one for AAA. A fall in the index indicates declining quality.

Source: OECD calculations, Thomson Reuters, Bloomberg.

StatLink http://dx.doi.org/10.1787/888933362266

An index is constructed weighted by the rating (see the note to Figure 1.16) showing a sharp 20% decline from 2008 when unconventional monetary policies began. In the bottom panel it can be seen that from around 14% of all issuance in 2000, non-investment grade bonds and low quality investment grade bonds rose to 42% of the total issuance by 2015.

These issuance trends respond to the demand for investors caused by low-interest-rate policies. High-yield debt is much more susceptible to liquidity squeezes than listed equity.

Rollover risk is rising, and more asset class flight from local corporate emerging market debt is likely to be coming. There has been a superhighway into high-yield emerging market debt on the way in, but it is not a dual carriageway, and the market could evaporate if faced with a desire on the part of investors to get out at some point in the future. The primary markets for junk bonds have already begun to close, and the secondary markets may well follow.

Flat capital spending and the demand for dividends and buybacks

The OECD has examined in great detail the investment and financial behaviour of 11 000 of the world's biggest listed companies across 75 economies. Figure 1.17 shows a summary picture of their corporate finance activity (expressed as a share of net sales). Company operating cash flow and net borrowing, shown in the lines, fund the elements in the bars: i.e. capital expenditure, dividends and buybacks and other net accumulation of assets. The return on equity (ROE) less its cost (COE) is also shown (using the right-hand axis).[21] If the ROE less the COE is low or negative, investors would prefer not to have their earnings retained for capital expenditure and instead returned to them as cash for reallocation to consumption or other investments (including the leveraged alternative investments referred to earlier).

Figure 1.17. **Return on equity (ROE), capital costs and interest rates, 2002-15**

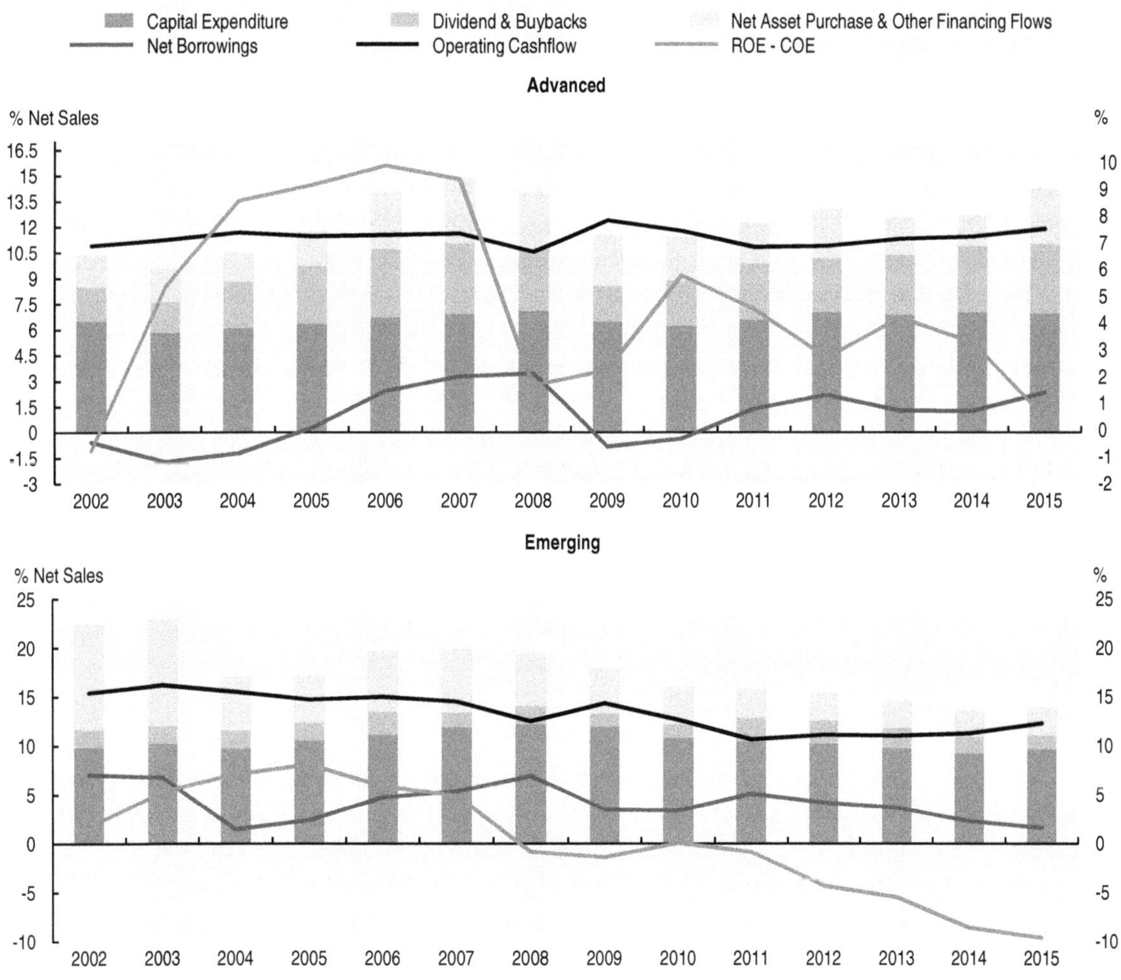

Source: OECD calculations, Bloomberg.

StatLink http://dx.doi.org/10.1787/888933362275

Some observations are worth noting:

- Capital expenditure of companies as a share of net sales has been flat in advanced economy companies since 2008. While not shown in Figure 1.17, the value added of these companies per employee has also not risen (the productivity problem which is discussed in detail in Chapter 2).
- Dividends and buybacks have been rising in advanced economies since the crisis and have reached about 60% of what companies spend on investment. Advanced economy companies could raise this investment very easily without any need for external finance – but they do not do this. Investors resist companies that want to use earnings to invest for the long term, and they demand cash-like returns that are better than those available in actual cash and investment grade bond markets. This works against companies wanting to take on long-run projects needed to promote innovation and productivity – they would be punished by investors for doing so. This is a direct result of attributing a zero time value to money via low interest rates.
- Dividends and buybacks are less in emerging markets due to the state-driven investment process. The return on equity in emerging markets is far below its cost, a sure reflection of excess capacity (in sectors like steel, energy, other materials, automobiles and the like). Investment is still running at double the rate in advanced economies (around 10% of net sales). But it is capital-widening investment in the main, using existing technology, often as a part of global value chains. As in advanced economies, productivity is not rising in emerging market companies.

Concentrated sector borrowing

A counterpart of the world becoming more dependent on energy and materials sector investment in the 2000s, has been a sharp increase in borrowing concentrated in these two sectors. In the OECD 11 000 company database, energy sector debt issuance on average tripled in both advanced and emerging economies in the post- versus the pre-crisis period (Figure 1.18). The materials sector debt issuance doubled in advanced economies and rose by an even more impressive four times in EMEs. Of the total debt of USD 3.1 trillion issued by emerging market companies in the post-crisis period, 40% resides in the energy and materials sectors. Of the total debt of USD 16.8 trillion issued by advanced economy companies in the post-crisis period, 23% resides in the energy and materials sectors.

Debt issued by emerging economy companies is not well diversified across sectors. Of the companies studied, 77% of the debt issued comes from just five of the 20 sectors considered. These sectors are precisely those that are most subject to falling commodity prices and the risk of company defaults. Falling commodity prices and debt concentrated in these sectors is likely to add financial headwinds to growth: there are always financial consequences to over-investment.

The "lift-off" issue for monetary policy in advanced economies

Policy needs to restore "animal spirits" in the company sector by dealing with the global misallocation of resources and excess capacity and by creating incentives for long-term risk taking. When "animal spirits" recover to the point where "true" risk assets are desired in the company sector, and investors are willing to forego short-term income for long-term capital gain, there will be a significant asset allocation shift. Capital will move from cash return and leveraged instruments to growth investments simultaneously within and across all asset classes. This "lift-off" would lead to the end of secular stagnation. But how could this happen?

Figure 1.18. **Long-term debt issuance by companies, pre-crisis versus post-crisis**

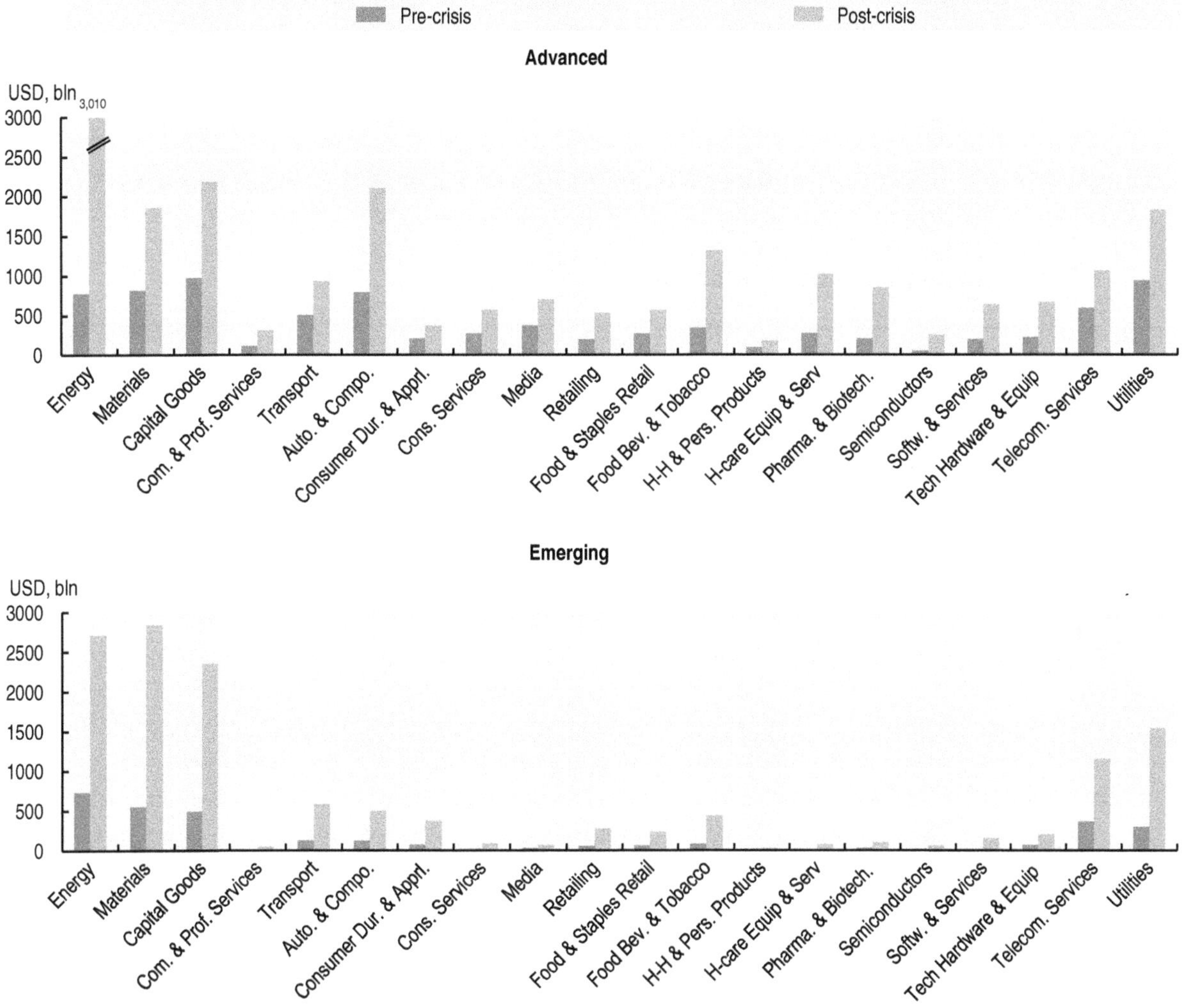

Note: Pre-crisis: 2002-07; post-crisis: 2008-15.
Source: OECD calculations, Bloomberg.

StatLink http://dx.doi.org/10.1787/888933362281

"Inflation first" policies will delay a sustainable "lift-off" in rates

In the unlikely event that inflation comes first – say because unconventional monetary policy in advanced economies and credit expansion in emerging markets are not supported by measures to deal with structural problems – the outlook would not be too encouraging. Central banks would be obliged to lift interest rates in response to inflation, while growth of capital-widening investment using existing technology in the near term would raise global supply without lifting productivity growth. This is what happened in some emerging economies in response to the 2008 crisis. Any success would be short-lived now just as it was then. The needed "creative destruction" phase on the supply side would not happen. Just as some policies after the crisis worsened the excess capacity problems and increased debt, the lack of structural adjustment now and the actual emergence of inflation would ultimately cause the lift-off in interest rates to turn into a two-step process.

Near zero interest rates allow companies to carry excess debt, to borrow cheaply, to carry out buybacks and to engage in unproductive investments that are based on a distorted cost of capital while waiting for the tide of aggregate demand to rise. The global output gap will never close in a sustainable manner while the outstanding stock of unproductive and misallocated investment remains in place. Rising interest rates under an "inflation first" scenario would risk another financial crisis. The need for shedding excess capacity and debt would once more become a priority. If a healthy "creative destruction" phase ensued, as higher interest rates confronted companies with a realistic cost of capital and as structural policies were implemented in advanced and emerging economies on the scale required, then the scene would then be set to have more sustainable growth and normalised interest rates later on.

A "productivity first" corporate scenario

Rather than inflation first, it would be desirable to have a productivity first scenario. Such a scenario is not encouraged at all by making the time value of money zero – monetary policy is not the instrument needed at this point in time. But what policies would actually address the productivity problem in the company sector? To answer this question requires better knowledge of what is happening in the corporate world. In studying the 11 000 (non-financial and non-real estate) companies in the next chapter, some very interesting facts emerge about those that have succeeded and those that have failed since the crisis. These facts point the way to policies that might actually work.

Prior to the crisis, there was a group of high-productivity level companies (sometimes referred to as being on the "frontier"), and a very long string of low-productivity level companies that appeared not to be sharing in technology and growth.[22] The crisis shook up everything and led to two distinct groups of high-productivity companies in the post-2008 period: those in the high-level productivity group that remained there, but whose growth in productivity has been *negative* (i.e. they are losing their shine); and, at the other extreme, a separate group that has had *rapid* productivity growth. In between these two groups sits the majority of companies with both lower productivity levels and only moderate growth.

The group exhibiting both high levels of productivity and high growth shows all the signs of having been through a "creative destruction" phase: shedding businesses and locations that are not working in the tougher post-crisis environment while acquiring others that are more synergistic with their goals. However, there are simply not nearly enough of these companies.

The following productivity chapter looks at the financial decisions that those dynamic "creative destruction" companies took to succeed in the post-crisis environment – focusing only on those where true one-way causality could be established. These companies had four key interrelated corporate finance characteristics that investors need to take note of:

- They expensed much more on research and development (R&D) than other companies, which in turn requires risk taking and a long-term focus critical to the innovation process.
- They did not increase borrowing compared to equity in the post-crisis period (while those that did were in the low productivity groups). An equity focus enabled the successful firms to focus on longer-term goals instead of altering their business model to try to generate more short-term cash to meet debt obligations.
- These same high-productivity companies had a buffer of free cash flow: i.e. their operating cash flow was in excess of that needed for capital expenditure. Such companies can maintain a focus on long-term goals in the face of short-term disruptions.
- Those that succeeded used M&A (buying and selling business segments) to rationalise what they were doing in the tougher more competitive post-crisis environment.

Looking through the lens of what companies need to benefit from these four success factors, the following sets of policies discussed in more detail in the next chapter, if implemented, would create an environment where investors could become more optimistic and would permit interest rates to rise without negative consequences for markets:

- *With respect to R&D:* improved R&D fiscal incentives (the issue of designing tax incentives for R&D that are consistent with broader tax policy efficiency is taken up in full in Chapter 3).
- *With respect to equity finance instead of debt:* the removal of tax incentives that favour debt over equity and the simplification of equity listing rules that increase costs relative to private equity. Other equity market reforms that encourage initial public offerings are also considered (see also Chapters 3 and 4).
- *With respect to increased free cash flow:* crucial for a strong uplift of "animal spirits" are: more open trade and investment regimes between countries; breaking down competitive barriers to entry often granted by government rules and regulations; more flexible labour market rules to allow companies to manage their cash flow when setbacks occur; recapitalising banks, dealing with their NPL problems and getting the nexus right between regulations and negative interest rates; and encouraging lower-cost non-bank finance.
- *With respect to M&A activity:* breaking down cultural and regulatory barriers to cross-border M&A.

The near-term financial markets outlook

Unfortunately structural reform on the scale required is unlikely in the near term. This means that "creative destruction" and a "lift-off" in rates is postponed. Central banks are most likely to continue with low interest rates and the quantitative easing approach. It is not the best environment to be raising interest rates and yet low rates delay the "creative destruction" phase.

It is difficult to convince governments that the only choice is incremental-but-persistent "creative destruction" when they are faced with unemployment – particularly in more rigid, less market-oriented economies. Adding to the current stock of debt and supporting the current "portfolio shift" towards illiquid securities and herding into crowded trades that favour higher yields (even when leverage is required) does nothing to bring us closer to a bull market "lift-off" in interest rates. It does increase the probability of a scenario where another setback in growth and markets will be required to bring about the right mix of policy later on.

Some near-term financial implications are:

- The zero or negative time value of money will continue to work against long-term risk taking in the real economy (as opposed to financial risk taking via leveraged speculation).
- The delay in the ending of unconventional monetary policy will lead to further easing in emerging markets and related exchange rates distortions.
- Exchange rate battles will continue: net negative terms of trade shocks will remain in play for commodity exporters encouraging them to ease monetary policy and lower exchange rates. As other countries will not want to lose competitiveness, they too will bias their own monetary policy in the same direction (and possibly blunting positive terms-of-trade shocks for commodity-importing countries that succeed in keeping their exchange rate lower).
- Renewed emerging market portfolio outflows if Federal Reserve confidence in tightening resumes, may lead other emerging markets to follow China and impose cross-border controls. This would be to enable them to keep monetary policy easier than otherwise

and to decouple from any United States tightening – particularly those that are losing the most reserves.

- The tendency for weakening currencies versus the dollar and easier monetary policy outside of the United States will likely mean United States policy too will err on the side of a drawn out tightening cycle. With no clear policy direction, choppy markets will remain.
- Stress in high-yield energy company debt including outside of emerging markets.
- Slow growth and exposure to the energy sector will continue to put pressure on bank stocks for those that do not have enough capital (in the simple leverage ratio sense).

This choppy and uncertain market environment will, at some point, require resolution. If the markets decide (incorrectly) that monetary ease is a solution to real structural problems, then an unsustainable rally is certainly always feasible. But financial markets will have to behave in a way that forces structural policies and required "creative destruction" in the end. In the long-run this cannot be bullish for securities.

Figure 1.19 shows selected financial prices over the supercycle period from January 1998 to the present.

Figure 1.19. **The evolution of selected financial prices, 1998-2030**

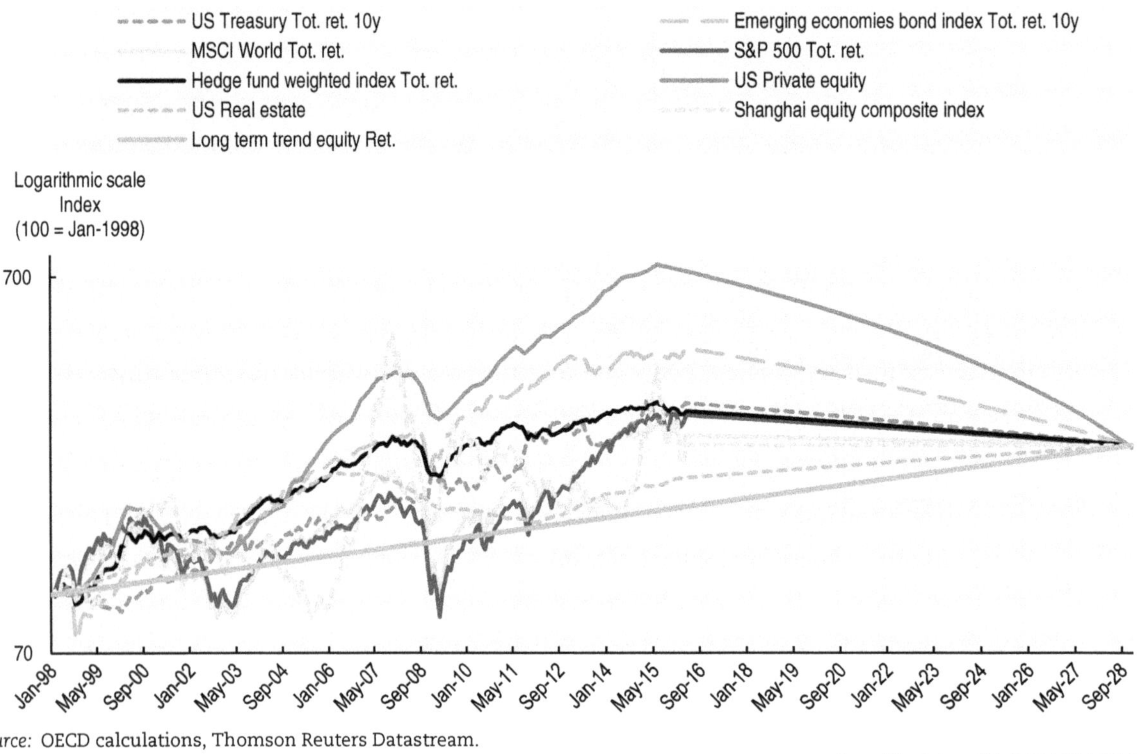

Source: OECD calculations, Thomson Reuters Datastream.

StatLink http://dx.doi.org/10.1787/888933362297

The thick grey trend line is based on a portfolio of 50% equity and 50% 10-year bonds in the United States using the average return for the past 96 years of data. The real return is 2.6% over that long period and, allowing for 1% inflation going forward, implies a 3.6% nominal return – this return is pushed out 15 years to 2030. All financial prices are currently well above this trend-line due to the world-wide monetary ease response to excess capacity and the lack of structural adjustment. Equity markets are the least out of line. Unfortunately most of the other markets are far less liquid than listed equities. There is likely to be illiquidity-related volatility in some of these markets. This volatility will be greater if markets, in the end, have to force structural adjustment and it would be much less with a "productivity first" scenario.

The equity market in 2015 had been discounting a very negative scenario for the global economy and then corrected. Figure 1.20 shows an OECD indicator of equity market valuation. While it is unfair to compare the market value of listed stocks in an individual economy to that country's GDP as a valuation tool, since with global value chains earnings may come from any part of the world, this cannot be a problem for all stock exchanges together when compared to world GDP. In late 2014 and the first half of 2015, global equity markets together reached levels which have previously been associated with corrections. In the second half of 2015 and early 2016, the correction in equity markets brought values back into line with the historical valuation average. The markets appeared to stabilise at this level, and then began to rally again without moving into the "cheap" region. It is inconceivable that the market can sustainably rally on easy monetary policy alone. World GDP led by productivity will need to move up with the equity market – this will require the structural policies discussed in this and following chapters.

Figure 1.20. **Global market capitalisation versus world GDP, 1999-2016**

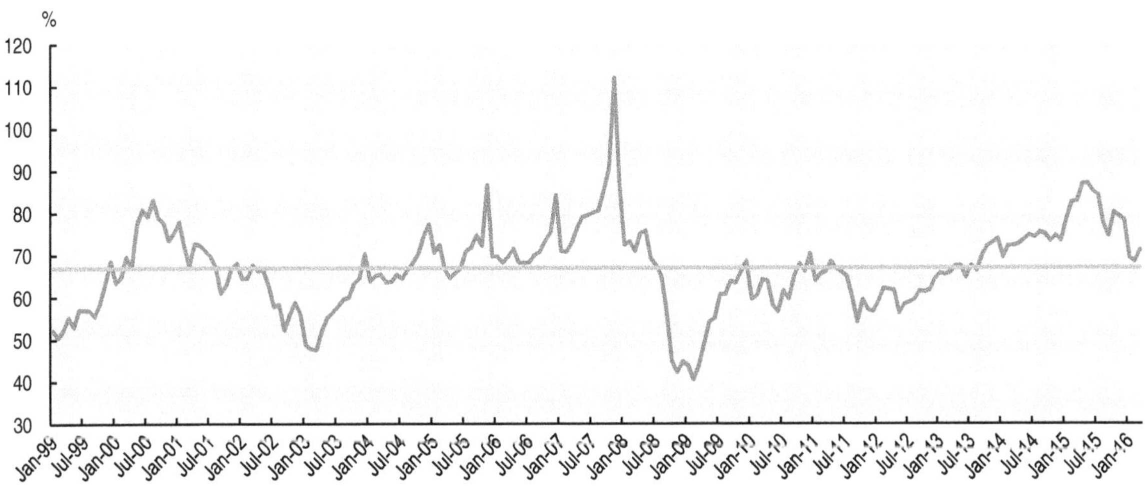

Source: OECD calculations, World Federation of Stock Exchanges, Thomson Reuters Datastream.

StatLink http://dx.doi.org/10.1787/888933362300

Notes

1. This theme is developed in full in OECD (2015a).
2. Handy Size (15 000-35 000 tonnes); Supramax (45 000-59 000 tonnes), Panamax (60 000-80 000 tonnes) and Capesize (100 000 tonnes). Capesize carry about 62% of the trade.
3. Large numbers of ships were built on the basis of the needs of the supercycle, and many of these now lie idle.
4. Figures for capital expenditure include depreciation. The sectors where capital expenditure is well in excess of depreciation include the supercycle-related sectors: energy, materials, utilities, and capital goods and transport.
5. See data appendix of Chapter 2 for definitions.

6. The European Chamber of Commerce (2016) publishes estimates of excess capacity in eight severely affected sectors: steel, aluminium, cement, chemicals, refining, flat glass, shipbuilding, and paper and paper board.

7. See McKinsey and Company (2011) who predicted that ROEs would fall from 20% pre-crisis to 7% post crisis, roughly in line with their cost of equity.

8. See Warren (2105), for example.

9. See Blundell-Wignall and Atkinson (2010) for example.

10. In order to minimise this disincentive, Japan has introduced a 3-tier system whereby most of the bank reserves held at the central bank still receive a small positive interest rate and the increased portion of reserves due to QE continues to have a zero interest rate. Japanese banks have already met the 100% ultimate LCR requirement.

11. See Blundell-Wignall and Roulet (2013) for a definition of the DTD. The horizontal 3-standard-deviation line is shown because, historically, banks with a DTD above 3 prior to a crisis managed not to default.

12. These markets arise when currencies are not convertible and/or where extreme capital flow measures are used – they trade in US dollars as a parallel market.

13. Wealthy individuals, according to market intelligence, have participated in syndicates that ramp up equity markets and then sell to less sophisticated investors as they are drawn into the market.

14. The weights at the time of writing are US dollar 26.4%, euro 21.4%, Japanese yen 14.7%, HK dollar 6.6%, Australian dollar 6.3%, Malaysian Ringgit 4.7%, rouble 4.4%, sterling 3.9%, Singapore dollar 3.8%, Thai Bart 3.3%, Canadian dollar, 2.5%, Swiss franc 1.5% and NZ $ 0.7%.

15. This process led to duplication and excess capacity in the supercycle sectors discussed elsewhere in this Outlook. Political connections are important, and once local champions become too big to fail exit strategies become problematic. Historically, an unintended adverse consequence is that companies listed on the New York Stock exchange with better technologies have been forced into bankruptcy while local companies supported by local banks have not: e.g. in photovoltaic cells, massive over capacity resulted in Suntech and LDK (both listed in the United States) going bust. See Chen, Tain-Jy (2015).

16. Domestic credit growth is M2 growth minus reserves growth in Figure 1.14.

17. See OECD (2015a).

18. Supposedly less correlated with bonds and equities, though rarely so in practice.

19. The underlying assets may be illiquid and are not traded while a market is made in real time for the shares of the ETF. Zero fees are handled by securities lending.

20. These data are collected separately. While pension and insurance companies hold much of it, these are not taken from institutional investor asset allocations.

21. The cost of equity is the trend earnings growth for the company plus its dividend yield.

22. OECD (2015b) corroborates these results.

References

Blundell-Wignall, A. and Paul Atkinson (2010), "Thinking beyond Basel III: Necessary Solutions for Capital and Liquidity", *OECD Journal: Financial Market Trends*, Vol. 2010/1, *http://dx.doi.org/10.1787/fmt-2010-5km7k9tpcjmn*.

Blundell-Wignall, A. and Caroline Roulet (2013), "Business models of banks, leverage and the distance-to-default", *OECD Journal: Financial Market Trends*, Vol. 2012/2, *http://dx.doi.org/10.1787/fmt-2012-5k4bxlxbd646*.

Blundell-Wignall, A. and C. Roulet (2015), "Evaluating capital flow management measures used as macro-prudential tools", *OECD Journal Financial Trends*, Vol. 2015/2, *http://dx.doi.org/10.1787/fmt-2015-5jm0p44dlq6f*.

Chen, Tain-Jy (2015), "The Development of China's Solar Photovoltaic Industry: Why Industrial Policy Failed", *Cambridge Journal of Economics*, March.

European Central Bank (2013), "Liquidity Regulation and Monetary Policy Implementation", *ECB Monthly Bulletin*, April.

European Chamber (2016), *Overcapacity in China: An Impediment to the Party's Reform Agenda*, European Chamber of Commerce, China.

European Parliament (2016), *Non-Performing Loans in the Banking Union: Stocktaking and Challenges*, Brussels.

IMF (2015), "Managing Capital Outflows-Further Operational Considerations", *Staff Report for the IMF Executive Board*.

McKinsey and Company (2011), *Global Corporate and Investment Banking: an Agenda for Change*.

OECD (2015a) *OECD Business and Finance Outlook 2015*, OECD Publishing, Paris, *http://dx.doi.org/10.1787/9789264234291-en*.

OECD (2015b), *The Future of Productivity*, OECD Publishing, Paris, *http://dx.doi.org/10.1787/9789264248533-en*.

Redak, V. (2016), "The Impact of Low and Negative Interest Rates on Bank Profitability and Business Models", *Presentation to the OECD Committee on Financial Markets* (available from the author on request).

Warren, D.R. (2015), "Developments in Banking Law", *Review of Banking and Financial Law*, Vol. 34. (pp 439-450, section V, on "Congress's Rollback of the Dodd-Frank Swaps Push-Out Rule").

Chapter 2

Corporate finance and productivity

One of the puzzles of the post-crisis period is low observed aggregate productivity growth. This chapter dissects the problem using the company and sector value-added data of more than 11 000 of the world's largest listed non-financial and non-real-estate companies, taken from 20 different industry sectors of the Global Industry Classification Standard. The contribution to productivity growth of these companies is very narrowly based within each sector. This chapter explores why productivity growth is fragmented, i.e. highly varied across enterprises. It considers what distinguishes "more" from "less" productive companies and examines the effect of different company financial decisions with respect to capital expenditure, sales, dividend and buy-back policies, research and development expensing, debt-versus-equity, and merger and acquisition activity.

The statistical data for Israel are supplied by and under the responsibility of the relevant Israeli authorities. The use of such data by the OECD is without prejudice to the status of the Golan Heights, East Jerusalem and Israeli settlements in the West Bank under the terms of international law.

Main findings

- When 11 000 large global companies are sorted by weighted productivity growth into deciles within 20 Global Industry Classification Standard (GICS) sectors, fragmentation is apparent. Prior to the crisis, there was a single group of high-productivity-level companies (incumbents) grouped from various sectors in advanced economies, some of whom were beginning to experience declining growth rates. There was a very long tail of low-growth and low-productivity-level companies outside of this cutting edge group. In emerging market economies, growth was much stronger than for advanced economies but the level of productivity much lower.
- The crisis seems to have shaken things up in advanced economies. A second group of companies emerged with strong dynamic growth and rising productivity levels, reflecting a competitive challenge to the pre-crisis incumbent group: sometimes from incumbents who adopted new financial strategies and moved into the growth group and sometimes from entirely new companies. There is a large amount of company "persistence" within and between these two groups. In the post-crisis period, productivity growth in emerging economy companies has collapsed.
- In advanced economies, research and development spending is concentrated mainly in pharmaceuticals and biotechnology, and in the main digital economy sectors. It is much lower in emerging market economies. Between the pre- and post-crisis periods, research and development was, on average, cut in those companies staying in the incumbent group, but appears to have been a key factor in those that transitioned to the high-growth group.
- Changes in favour of more debt financing in the post-crisis period is more prevalent in the incumbent (negative productivity growth) companies with falling free cash flow. High-growth companies had higher levels of debt but did not increase it in the post-crisis period and instead focused on maintaining high levels of free cash flow and favouring equity as an external source of finance. Productivity growth and innovation involve risk taking and require a longer-term perspective for which equity capital and free cash flow (as a buffer for unforeseen short-term disruptions) is more suited. Weaker firms with poor cash flow might borrow excessively in order to be able to compete with more successful firms in carrying out mergers and acquisitions, paying dividends and carrying out buybacks, achieving their tax objectives, or defending against takeover. This undermines their ability to have a longer-term focus.
- In 2002-15, there was an average of 1 650 merger and acquisition deals per annum, or around 15% of the 11 000 companies in the sample. When merger and acquisition data are matched with the company names in this sample, they are found to be heavily concentrated in those companies that transitioned to higher growth. Mergers and acquisitions appears to be a surprisingly net positive mechanism for rationalising a business and promoting productivity growth.
- Stock prices reflect expected future earnings and benefit from productivity growth, and hence may shed some light on the efficacy of the four corporate strategies: higher research

and development, a greater equity (versus debt) focus, higher free cash flow and more mergers and acquisitions activity to rationalise business models. The strategies seem quite powerful in helping companies raise share prices and transition to the strong productivity growth group in the tougher post-crisis period. In this latter period strong equity performance continues in portfolios based on the four identified business strategies.

- At present the world is characterised by excess supply capacities, and it is critical to rationalise industries and to boost productivity growth in non-excess-capacity areas as quickly as possible. Low interest rates do not to address this problem of fragmentation holding back sustainable productivity growth. Policies that help companies lock in the four key corporate finance factors associated with improving productivity growth are identified, and Chapter 3 discusses tax incentives for research and development in detail.

Introduction

One of the puzzles of the post-crisis period is low observed aggregate productivity growth.[1] This chapter dissects the problem using company and sector value added data of more than 11 000 of the world's largest listed non-financial/non-real-estate companies. The contribution to productivity growth of these companies is very narrowly based within each sector; productivity growth is fragmented and the reason for this may go to the heart of the macro economist's puzzle.

The OECD Economics Department and the Science, Technology and Innovation, and Financial and Enterprise Affairs Directorates have been using micro company data to explore various puzzles in economics relating to stagnation, investment and productivity (OECD, 2015a and 2015b). One of the key insights of *The Future of Productivity* (OECD, 2015a) was that companies in the manufacturing and service sectors appear to have only a small number of "frontier firms" that do very well in productivity growth, but since the crisis the spill-overs to non-frontier firms has slowed down.[2] Indeed, firms at the global productivity frontier are four to five times more productive than non-frontier firms that are not catching up. OECD work on the future of productivity examines a number of influences of trade (global value chains), the international mobility of skilled labour, upscaling by lagging firms, and other influences on spillovers and adoption. This previous work looks at the issue from the perspective of diffusion of technical progress and related policies. It does not look at the companion set of issues of the financial characteristics of successful companies resulting from strategic decisions taken in the Boardroom. This chapter looks at company productivity data and links it to the financial processes of firms.

Companies in 20 different industry sectors of the Global Industry Classification Standard (GICS)[3] are reviewed to explore the financial characteristics that might distinguish "more" and "less" productive companies (see Annex 2.A1). The focus is on global sectors because with global value chains (GVCs). As discussed in the *OECD Business and Finance Outlook 2015*, these companies operate across national borders. This chapter looks at the fragmented nature of productivity growth rates and levels and the interface of these with company financial decisions with respect to capital expenditure, sales, dividend and buy-back policies, research and development (R&D) expensing, debt versus equity, free cash flow and merger and acquisition (M&A) activity.

Most productive firms

As the focus is on explaining poor aggregate productivity performance through a micro-economic lens, the productivity of a company (value added per employee) is defined by its contribution to sector productivity growth. Value added is calculated for each firm as employee compensation plus earnings before interest, tax, depreciation and amortisation (EBITDA), divided by the number of company employees). The period of study covers 2002 to 2015, and it is broken into two key sub-periods: 2002 to 2007 (pre-crisis) and 2008 to 2015 (post-crisis).

Box 2.1. **Decomposing productivity in multinational enterprises where merger and acquisition activity dominates**

Compositional changes at the firm's micro level are well known drivers of aggregate productivity changes. Following individual firms over time decomposition studies usually involves four broad components: the entry of new firms, the exit of old firms, productivity changes in survivors and the reallocation of market shares amongst survivors.[1] Entrants are usually interpreted as new firms that take up a market share from zero, while exiting firms decrease their market share to zero. Dynamics also come into play. Allocative efficiency might predict that the most productive firms attract more labour and the rising weight of these firms would raise sector productivity growth.[2] There are however two further factors: when entry takes the form of the divestment of assets from an existing conglomerate; and when exit takes the form of M&A (the absorption of an existing company).

Multinational enterprises in the 20 sectors considered in this study, which are a very large component of the world economy, have an even more complex measurement problem because of corporate financial activity. A conglomerate in multiple regions may divest part of its business, creating a new company during the data measurement period. Including the "new" company alongside the existing company (now reduced in value-added size), notwithstanding the complications of different time periods for starting and ending the weighting process (M&A does not conveniently occur at the end of standard reporting periods), is essential to avoid spurious underestimation of sector productivity. Similarly, if an important new company emerges in the comparison period (not divested but listing from private equity, e.g. a Facebook) then excluding it may also understate productivity of the sector. On the other hand, if two companies merge, and the acquired company disappears, then double counting would emerge if attempts were made to keep the old company somehow in the weighting procedure. Finally, if a company does go bankrupt in the comparison period and its assets are not sold to another firm, then it is wise to exclude the company due to the extreme outlying nature of its (negative) productivity growth. Controlling for M&A and divestments is an intractable accounting exercise, not least because there is no way to estimate the value added of the acquired or divested firm in its new configuration. Nevertheless, it is the view of the present authors that these financial transactions have a substantial effect on the productivity of sectors considered in this study – a process quite different from technical change and innovation of a given firm. Mergers may increase efficiency where synergies are important. However, they may also result in more market power and an increase in rent-seeking behaviour. Reducing competition in this way may be negative for sector productivity growth – particularly if it reduces openness to ideas, and access to domestic and foreign markets.

1. See Baily et al. (1992), Foster et al. (2001), and Griliches et al. (1995). Aghion et al. (2004) show that entry by foreign firms is a strong driver of productivity growth in UK manufacturing.
2. See for example Olley and Pakes (1996) and Melitz et al. (2012).

The average compound growth rate of productivity for each company is calculated for the full period under consideration (the interest is in sustained performance), and this number is multiplied by the company's share of the total value added of the (non-financial, non-real-estate) GICS industry sector within which it sits.[4] This weighting of compound growth also helps to focus on companies that matter the most.[5] This weighted productivity growth is then used to rank companies by decile for the firms within each GICS industry sector. The characteristics of the companies from the lowest to the highest weighted productivity growth by sector are then examined and discussed.

The productivity shake-up of incumbents in the post-crisis period

A broad summary of the picture that emerges is shown in Figure 2.1. The productivity levels by decile shown in the top panel are calculated as follows: the companies in each sector ranked in the above manner are then weighted by their value added shares within and between sectors (the sector decile averages are shown in Figure 2.2). The corresponding

Figure 2.1. **Company productivity levels and growth rates: Averages combining the decile rankings by sector, pre-crisis versus post-crisis**

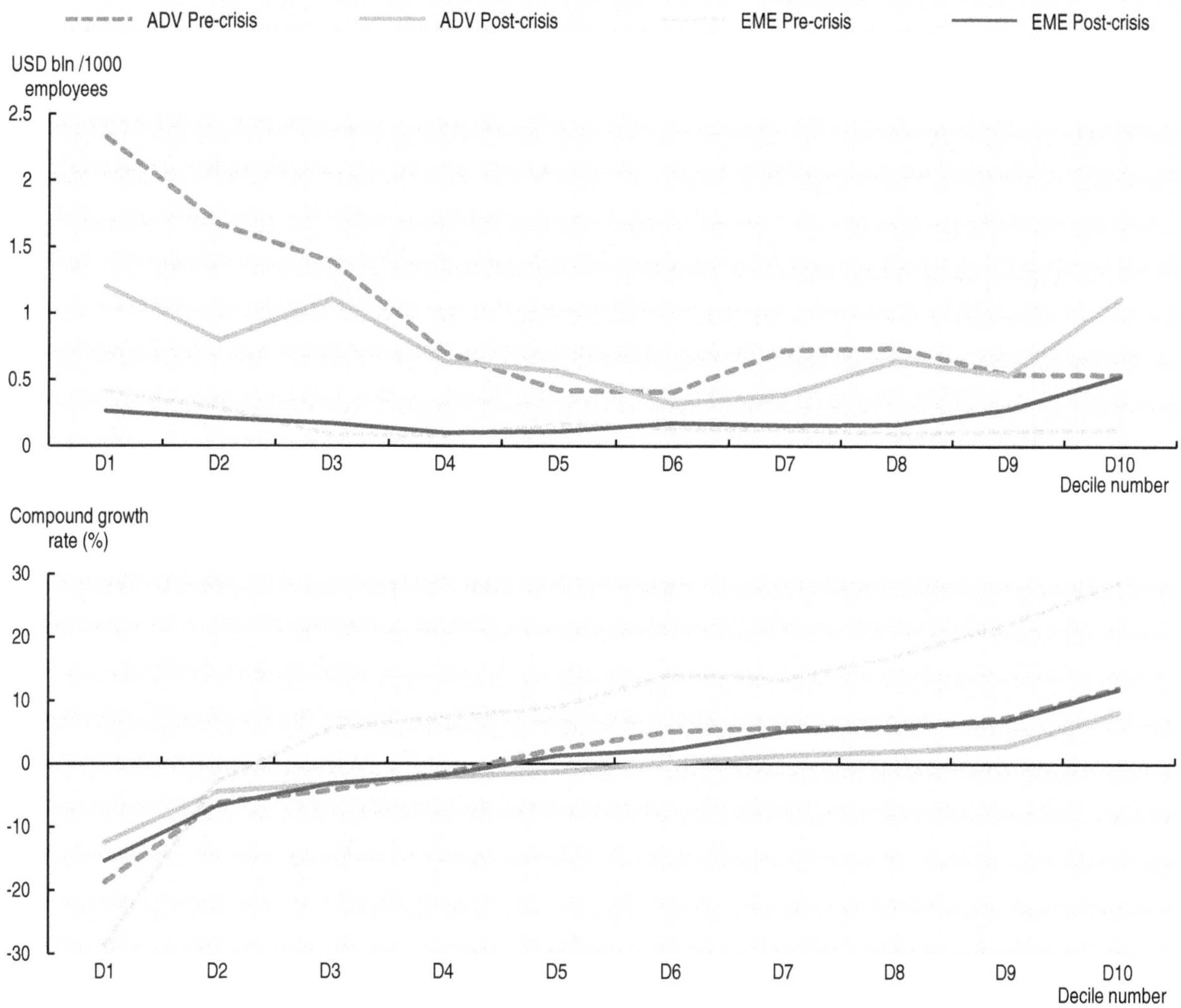

Note: Company productivity growth rates, weighted by the company's share of value added within its own sector, are ordered within each sector and separated into deciles. The figures shown are the average productivity levels and (compound) growth rates of the companies in each decile, weighted by value added across sectors. The geometric Törnqvist weighting procedure is used for the periods 2002-07 (pre-crisis) and 2008-15 (post-crisis) within each sector. The energy sector is excluded from the averages shown here due to the extreme volatility in oil and gas prices.

ADV: advanced economies; EME: emerging economies.

Source: OECD calculations, Bloomberg.

StatLink http://dx.doi.org/10.1787/888933362311

Figure 2.2. **Productivity by sector: Advanced economy companies, post-crisis**

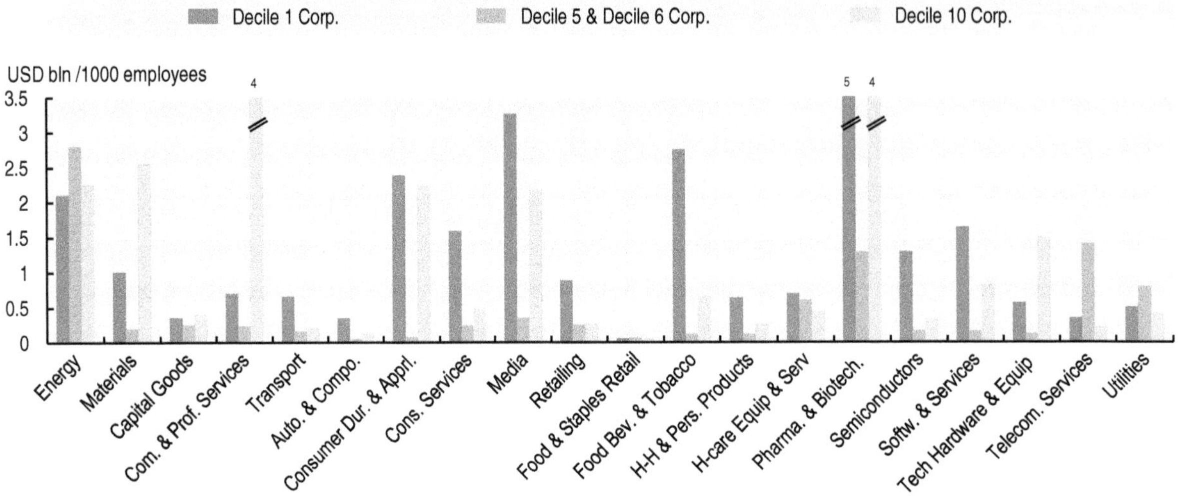

Note: The figures shown are the weighted average productivity levels using geometric Törnqvist weighting procedure over the 2008-15 period within each sector.
Source: OECD calculations, Bloomberg.

StatLink http://dx.doi.org/10.1787/888933362322

productivity growth rate averages by decile are shown in the bottom panel. Decile 1 (D1) is the lowest-weighted-productivity growth from the 20 sectors, which turns out to be very negative, and decile 10 (D10) consists of the highest-weighted productivity growth companies from each sector; and so on for the deciles in between. These data are shown for advanced and emerging economies before and after the crisis.

Main observations are:

- Productivity growth based on company data (bottom panel) has fallen most sharply in the post-crisis period for emerging market economies. Growth has also fallen in advanced economies (though less so).
- In the pre-crisis period there was a group of high productivity level (but negative growth) firms in advanced economies (particularly D1). This group, henceforth referred to as incumbent, was "shaken up" by the crisis which led to a much tougher financial environment. Firms that remained in this group after the crisis lost significant ground with the level of productivity falling (top panel). Some, however, joined a more dynamic group of companies taking productivity-enhancing business and financial decisions in the D10 category. This tilting upwards of the curve has resulted in a pronounced "smile" pattern in the level of productivity across all the deciles, in contrast to the pre-crisis period.
- Between these two groups (especially the D4-D9 growth range) sit the majority of firms that have lower productivity levels and moderately negative or slightly positive productivity growth. They are not growing fast enough per employee to catch up to the high-growth D10 group.
- Emerging market productivity level curves by definition lie well below those of advanced economies.[6] For the most part these companies have made little progress in catching up between the pre- and post-crisis periods. Only the high-growth D10 companies that took sound financial decisions (see below) made a strong improvement.

Productivity at the sector level: advanced economies

Figure 2.2 shows a simplified summary of the GICS industry sectors productivity levels used in Figure 2.1. The D1 weighted-productivity level is shown on the left, D10 on the right and the D5 to D6 average in the middle for the advanced economies in the post-crisis period. Some noteworthy features include:

- Consistent with the post-crisis line in Figure 2.1, there is a tendency in most (though not all) sectors for the D1 and D10 companies to have higher productivity levels than the middle ranked companies.
- Pharmaceuticals and biotechnology companies are very R&D intensive, and have very high productivity levels.
- Energy, materials and (to a lesser extent) utilities are high capital/labour ratio sectors and tend to have high labour productivity levels as a consequence.
- Most sectors are benefitting from the digital economy, but particularly: commercial and professional services; media; semiconductors; software and services; and technology hardware and equipment. These all appear to have higher relative productivity.

The food, beverages and tobacco sector (particularly incumbent D1 companies) also appears to be very efficient. Other sectors appear to have more moderate levels of efficiency, particularly "old economy" sectors like capital goods, transport, automobiles and food and staples retailing.

Productivity at the sector level: Emerging market economies

It is of course no surprise that emerging market economies must have a lot lower productivity levels that those of advanced economies (see the vertical scales) – otherwise they would be classed as advanced economies. On average, productivity in emerging market economies (Figure 2.3) is about one-fifth of that of advanced economies.

Figure 2.3. **Productivity by sector: Emerging economy companies, post-crisis**

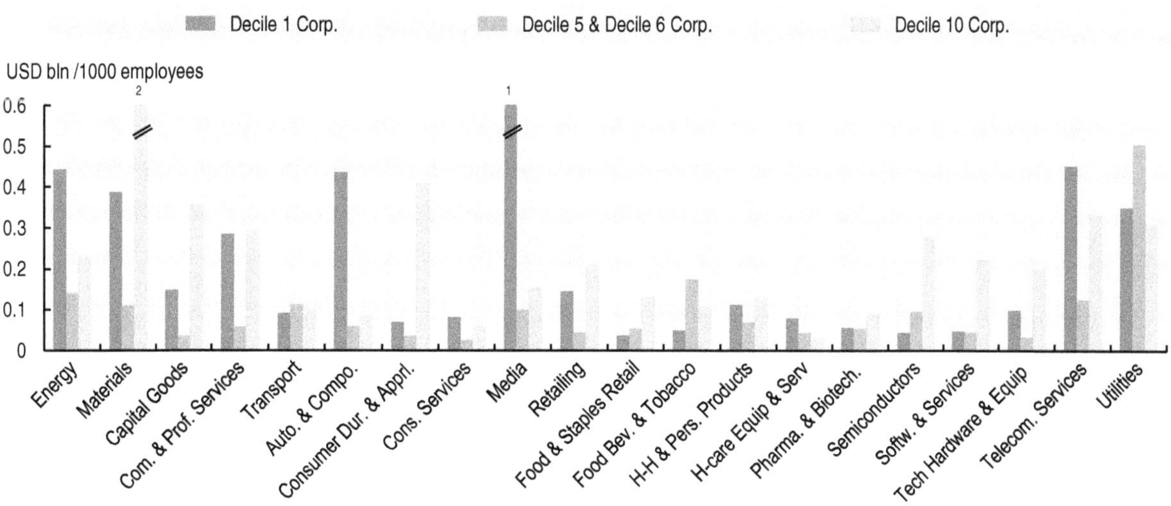

Note: The figures shown are the weighted average productivity levels using geometric Tornqvist weighting procedure over the 2008-15 period within each sector.
Source: OECD calculations, Bloomberg.

StatLink http://dx.doi.org/10.1787/888933362335

Productivity levels are mostly (though not always) relatively highest in the D1 and/or D10 companies. The main lagging emerging country sectors appear to be in the areas of: transport; consumer services; retailing; food and staples retailing; food beverages and tobacco; household and personal products; healthcare equipment; and pharmaceuticals and biotechnology.

The fragmentation pattern lies at the heart of the productivity puzzle

The fragmentation of productivity and its growth across the deciles may lie at the heart of the puzzle concerning the absence of productivity growth at the aggregate macro level. The major question facing investors and policy makers alike is what is driving this fragmented pattern and what is blocking the vast number of companies (that stay in the incumbent declining group or within the poor-productivity-level and moderate-growth middle groups) from catching up in the post-crisis tougher economic environment. It is evident that they are blocked when the persistence of companies in the pre-crisis and post-crisis periods is compared. A large percentage of these companies persist within their deciles between the two periods and, if they move, it is often from one to the other but much less often between sectors.

Persistence within deciles and movement between deciles, pre-crisis and post-crisis, in advanced economy companies

The top panel of Figure 2.4 shows all advanced economy sectors where the companies ranked by their weighted sector productivity growth in the 2002-07 pre-crisis period ended up in the 2008-15 post-crisis period.[7]

About 25% of the pre-crisis D1 companies (the blue line) remained in D1, while 20% of them transitioned to the high-growth D10 group. Some D1 companies also moved to the groups just adjacent to either of the two frontier groups, but relatively few transitioned to the large number of companies in the middle group of low productivity levels (D3 to D8). About 73% of the D1 firms remained at or near to D1 or moved to D9 or D10. Similarly, 24% of the high-growth D10 companies in the pre-crisis period (shown in the green line) managed to stay in D10, while 25% (by taking poor strategic decisions) moved to D1. About 77% of the D10 group managed to remain at or just adjacent to either end (the two high-level productivity groups). Such patterns in the incumbent and high-growth groups give rise to the "smile" shape of the two persistence lines. It is worth noting that the companies in the incumbent and high-growth groups, while too many to name, include many of the largest and most famous corporate names in the world.

In contrast, it seems to be more difficult for the companies in the middle group (D3 to D8 shown as the averages of that group by the grey line) to penetrate either of the incumbent or high-growth groups. This results in the inverted curve also shown in the top panel of Figure 2.4. These firms, for whatever reason, appear to be blocked in terms of innovations, finance and/or market access. This persistence suggests that companies that remain at the top of the productivity league tables are by no means random.

The sector detail consistent with these patterns is shown in the bottom panel of Figure 2.4. The column on the left for each sector consists of the D1 companies that stayed in that group between the two periods. The right hand column consists of those high-growth D10 companies that stayed in D10 between the two periods. The middle column consists of the average persistence of those in the large middle group (including all

Figure 2.4. **Persistence of contributions to sector productivity growth in advanced economy companies, pre-crisis and post-crisis**

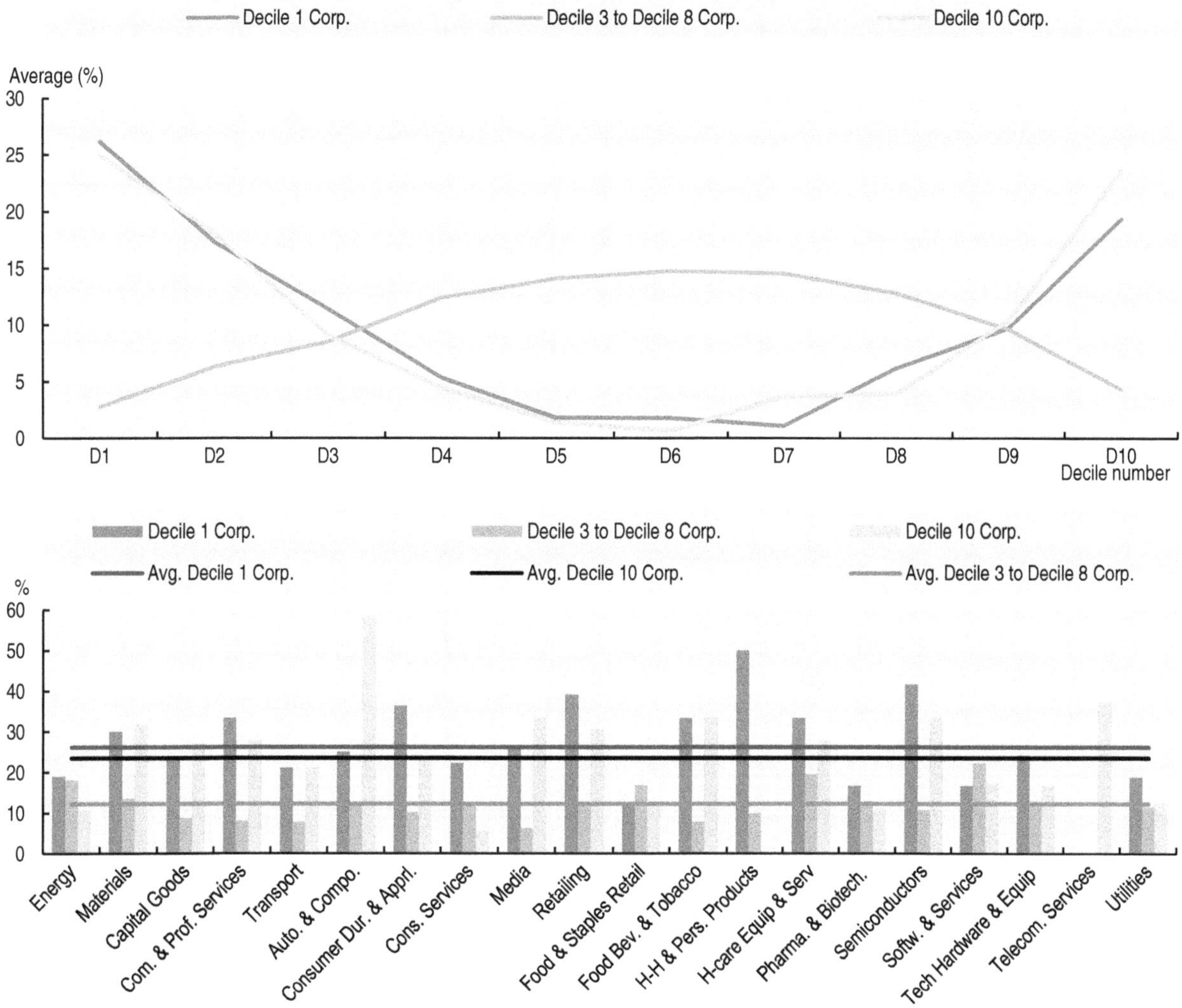

Note: Pre-crisis: 2002-07; post-crisis: 2008-15.
Source: OECD calculations, Bloomberg.

StatLink http://dx.doi.org/10.1787/888933362348

companies in D3 to D8). Average persistence is high in the D1 and/or D10 firms in most sectors as shown by the two upper horizontal lines (but particularly in: materials; commercial and professional services; automobiles and components; consumer durables and apparel; media; retailing; food beverages and tobacco; semiconductors; and telecommunication services). The average persistence is lower in the middle group (the lower horizontal line) and companies tend to move around within the D3 to D8 deciles without penetrating the higher productivity groups.

Persistence within deciles and movement between deciles in emerging market economy companies, pre-crisis and post-crisis

The persistence between the pre-crisis and post-crisis periods for emerging economies shown in the upper panel of Figure 2.5 is somewhat different to advanced economies. There is slightly less persistence of D1 companies (about 20% stay in D1), and a similar 18%

Figure 2.5. **Persistence of contributions to sector productivity growth in emerging economy companies, pre-crisis and post-crisis**

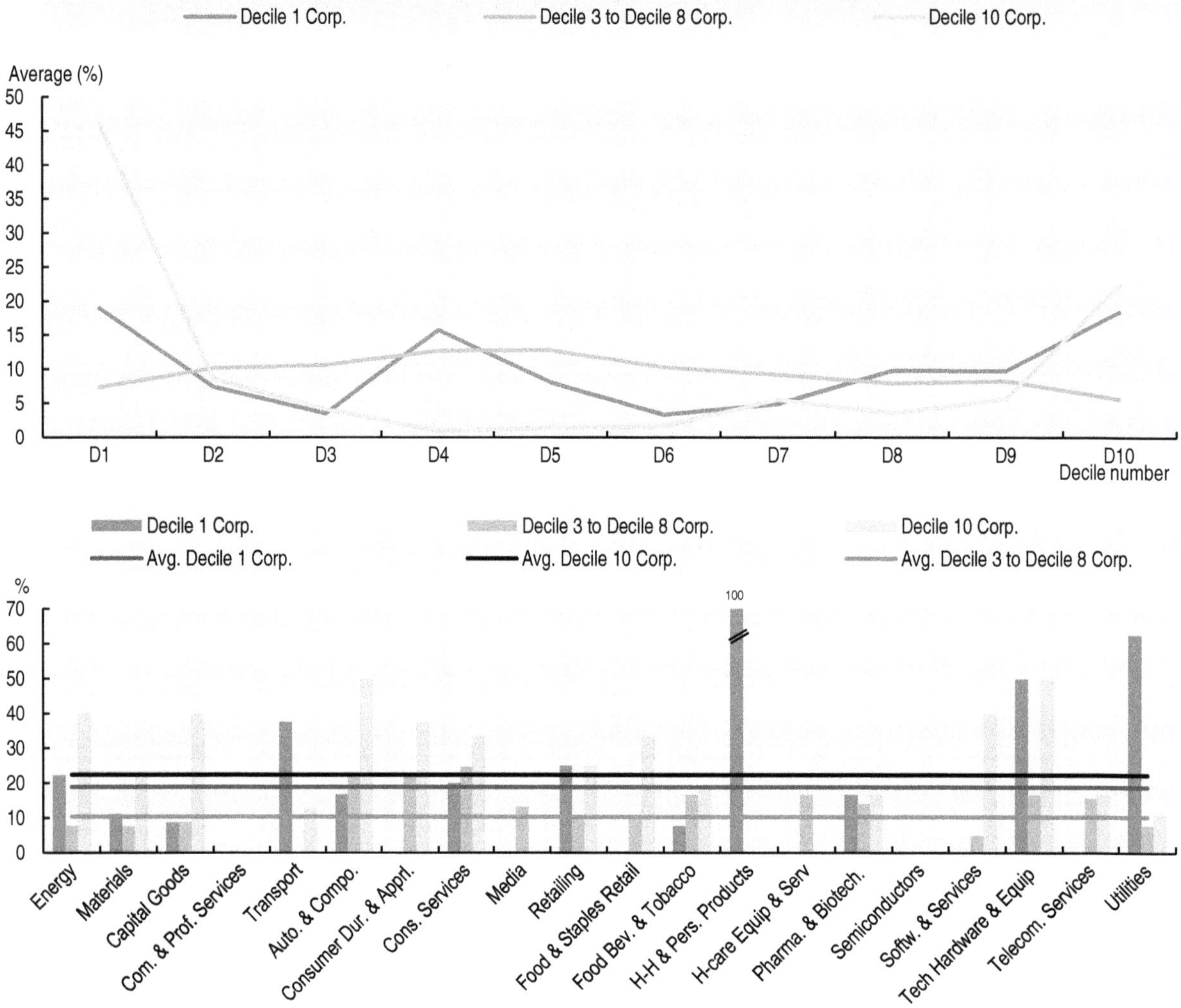

Note: Pre-crisis: 2002-07; post-crisis: 2008-15.
Source: OECD calculations, Bloomberg.

StatLink http://dx.doi.org/10.1787/888933362359

managed to transition to the fast growth D10 group in the post-crisis period. Persistence within the D10 group is roughly the same as advanced countries at 23%, but a very large 46% transitioned away from the high-growth to the negative-growth D1 group. The large middle group (including all companies in D3 to D8) has a slightly flatter profile than in advanced economies (a little more entered D1).

The emerging economy sector detail for persistence is shown in the bottom panel of Figure 2.5. The D10 companies have highest persistence at around 23% on average in 2008-15 versus the pre-crisis period (the highest horizontal line). Persistence is particularly high in energy, capital goods, transport, automobiles and components, consumer durables and apparel, consumer services, food and staples retailing, household and personal services, software and services, technology hardware and equipment, and utilities.

Financial characteristics of companies that do well in fragmented productivity groups

In Box 2.2 the financial characteristics of the 11 000 companies are tested in a simple causality exercise. Unambiguous causality from the financial variable to the growth rate of productivity (and not the other way around) was found for just four variables:

- the growth of R&D per employee in the company (companies that do more R&D have better productivity growth)
- the debt-to-equity ratio in first differences (firms that borrow more relative to equity are associated with subsequent weaker productivity growth)
- free cash flow per employee (operating cash flow of the company minus its capital expenditure improving is associated strongly with subsequent productivity growth)
- the value of M&A per employee for the company (companies that do more M&A on average have better productivity growth later on).

For all of the other variables shown either two-way or reverse causality (from productivity to the variable) was found to be present.

Box 2.2. Granger causality tests: Company productivity and the characteristics of their financial data

Table 2.1 shows Granger causality tests for company productivity data versus some of the key financial aspects of the 11 000 companies from 2002 to 2015. This will help to identify variables that characterise the most successful and least successful companies. Two lags are used and variables are included in their stationary form after unit root tests.

Table 2.1. Granger causality tests: Company productivity and financial data

Granger causality results using 2 Year lags: Hypothesis variable in the left column does not cause the variable in the row

Annual non-financial company data from 2002 to 2015. The dependent variable is the annual percent change in value added per employee.

	Value Added Per Employee (%YoY)	Net Sales Per Employee (%YoY)	Capital Expenditure Per Employee (%YoY)	Dividends and Buybacks Per Employee (%YoY)	R&D Expenditure Per Employee (%YoY)	Free Cash Flow Per Employee (%YoY)	Δ Debt to Enterprise Value Ratio	Δ ROE	Value of M&A Deals Per Employee
Net Sales Per Employee (%YoY)	No reject	-	-	-	-	-	-	-	-
Capital Expenditure Per Employee (%YoY)	Reject***	-	-	-	-	-	-	-	-
Dividends and Buybacks Per Employee (%YoY)	No reject	-	-	-	-	-	-	-	-
R&D Expenditure Per Employee (%YoY)	Reject*	-	-	-	-	-	-	-	-
Free Cash Flow Per Employee (%YoY)	Reject***	-	-	-	-	-	-	-	-
Δ Debt to Enterprise Value Ratio	Reject*	-	-	-	-	-	-	-	-
Δ ROE	Reject***	-	-	-	-	-	-	-	-
Value of M&A Deals Per Employee	Reject***	-	-	-	-	-	-	-	-
Value Added Per Employee (%YoY)	-	Reject***	Reject***	Reject***	No reject	No reject	No reject	Reject***	No reject

Source: OECD calculations, Bloomberg.

The null hypothesis is that the variable considered in the left-hand column does not cause the variable in the row. A large number of variables were tested in a regression model and seven variables were selected as potentially causal versus company productivity. The results are discussed in the rest of this chapter focusing on the nature of the financial characteristics of companies identified in this technical analysis. Given the fragmented and concentrated characteristics of company productivity in the global sectors, the focus is on the different financial aspects of firms at either end of the spectrum (the D1 and D10 companies) and that larger group of poorly performing countries in the middle deciles (including all companies from D3 to D8).

R&D spending as a driver of productivity growth

Fundamental R&D is an important driver of technical progress and product innovation and this comes through in the above causality tests. It will be recalled from the earlier discussion that the D1 incumbent companies with high productivity before the crisis saw these levels fall with negative growth in the post-crisis period (i.e. those that took poor financial decisions and remained in D1 and were joined by others also failing to adapt to the post-crisis environment). This is also reflected in R&D spending per employee in Figure 2.6. The R&D curve behaves in the same way as shown in Figure 2.1 for value added per head (falling in levels in the D1 to D3 range in the post-crisis period grey line and rising in the higher deciles).

Figure 2.6. **R&D per employee: Averages combining the decile rankings by sector, pre-crisis versus post-crisis**

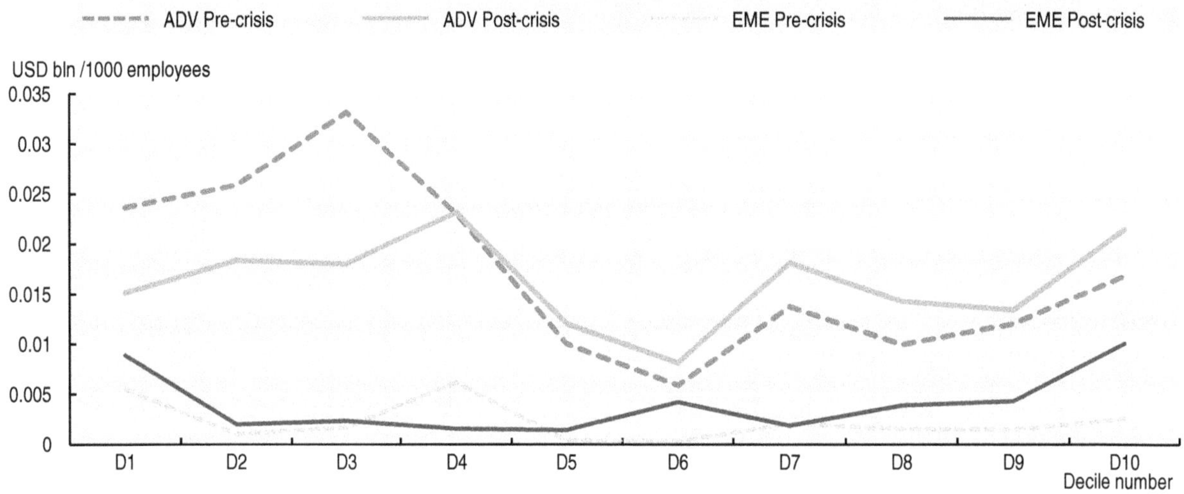

Note: The figures shown are the weighted average R&D expenditure per 1000 employees using the geometric Törnqvist weighting procedure for the periods 2002-07 (pre-crisis) and 2008-15 (post-crisis) within each sector.
ADV: advanced economies; EME: emerging economies.
Source: OECD calculations, Bloomberg.

StatLink http://dx.doi.org/10.1787/888933362362

In *The Future of Productivity*, which focuses on technology and its diffusion, R&D plays a critical role but it is found to be narrowly based in frontier firms. That observation appears to be confirmed in this study of large companies in the global sectors for advanced economies in the post-crisis period shown in the top panel of Figure 2.7. R&D per employee is the highest in pharmaceuticals and biotechnology, and semiconductors, followed by the other digital economy sectors: software and services, and technology hardware and equipment. R&D also occurs in other sectors, but is much smaller in comparison. However, it should be borne in mind that R&D, and the scientists and researchers that carry it out, can be purchased through financial transactions, as noted in the discussion around Box 2.1. The image of a company with a clever team innovating on a production frontier is appealing, but is impossible to separate from the M&A activity of firms in the continual evolution of deal making. Innovating companies and their researchers may survive, but in the new form of larger companies as a part of the process of controlling the sources of productivity growth in R&D teams, patents, trademarks and market share. This issue of M&A activity is taken up further below.

In emerging economies, shown in the bottom panel of Figure 2.7, R&D per employee is a lot smaller compared to advanced economies across all sectors (note the lower left hand scale). R&D is relatively high in the same sectors found to be dominant in advanced economies, but it is also significant in some of the "older" industries on the left side of Figure 2.7: energy, materials, capital goods, automobiles and components, and consumer durables and apparel. R&D is also important in emerging country utilities.

Figure 2.7. **R&D per employee by sector, post-crisis**

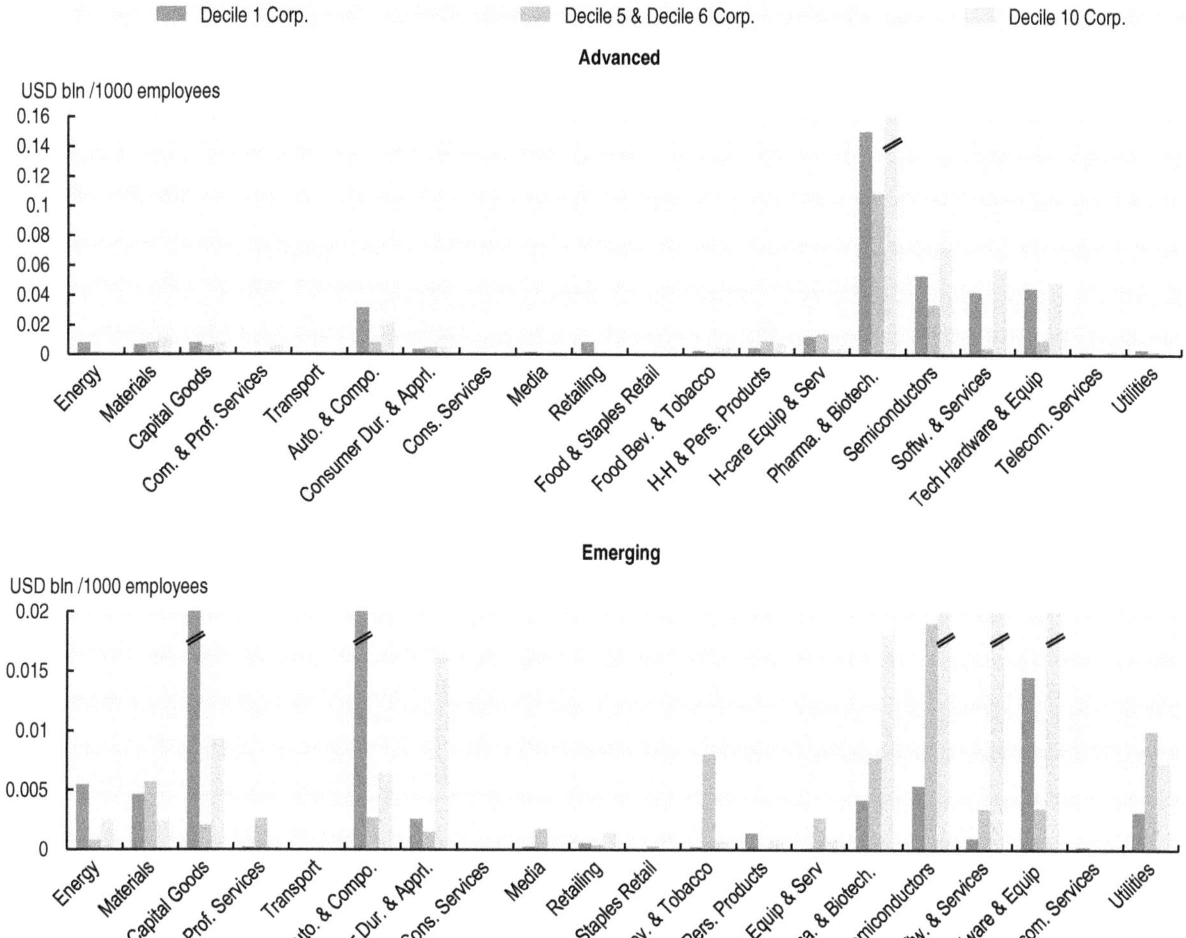

Note: The figures shown are the weighted average R&D expenditure per 1000 employees using the geometric Törnqvist weighting procedure for the period 2008-15 within each sector.
Source: OECD calculations, Bloomberg.

StatLink http://dx.doi.org/10.1787/888933362372

According to the causality tests, it is growth in R&D per employee value that boosts productivity growth. These effects are, on average, strong in advanced economies, as shown in the illustration in the top panel of Figure 2.8: post-crisis on the left side and pre-crisis on the right. Emerging economy companies are shown in the bottom panels. The positive relationship in both periods is suggestive of the idea that sustained increases in R&D are associated with better productivity growth. The high decile productivity growth

Figure 2.8. **R&D per employee and productivity compound growths, pre-crisis and post-crisis**

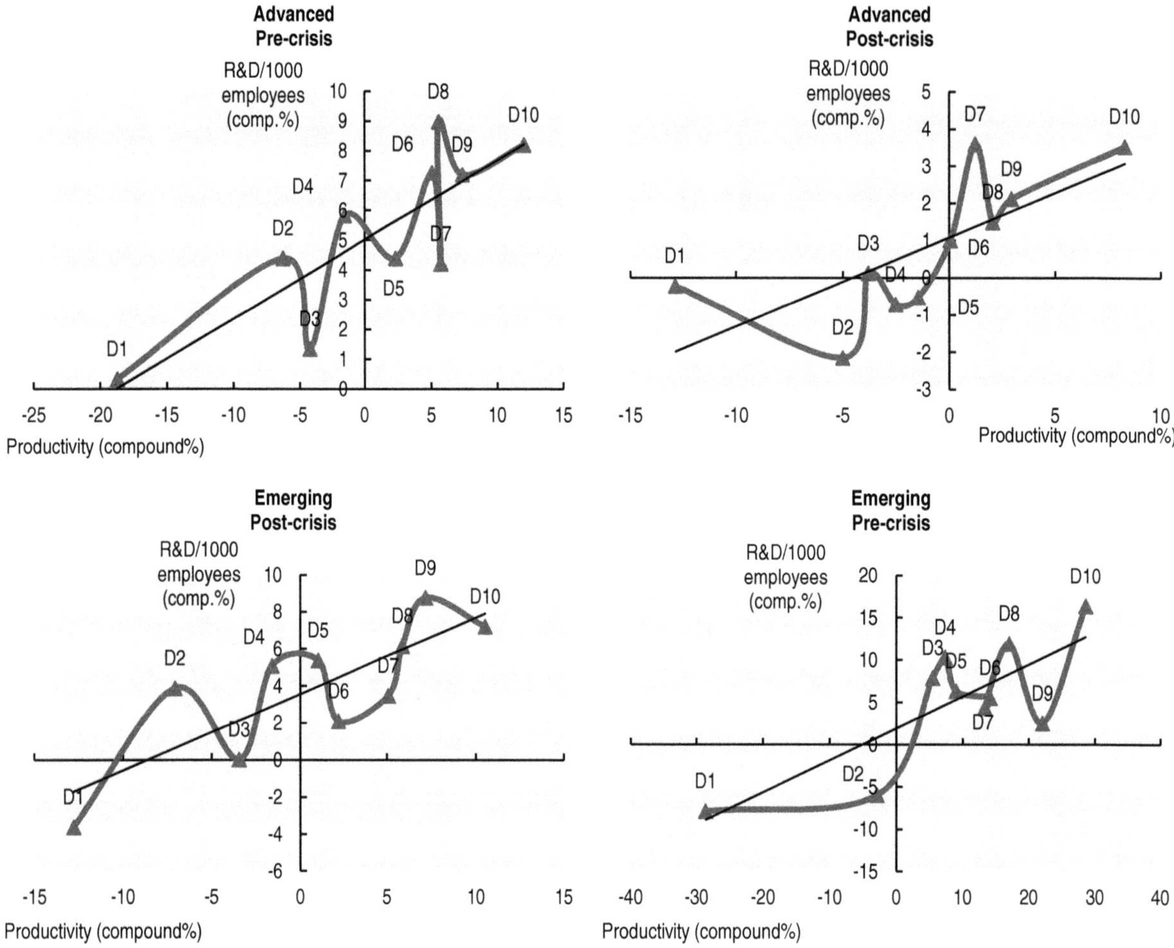

Note: Pre-crisis: 2002-07; post-crisis: 2008-15.
Source: OECD calculations, Bloomberg.

StatLink http://dx.doi.org/10.1787/888933362382

companies also grow R&D more quickly in both periods, but the R&D growth is much less in the post-crisis period (as shown by the different scales on the vertical axis). This slow-down is associated with the slower productivity growth.

Debt-versus-equity and free cash flow as productivity drivers

A company's equity capital is its share capital, plus retained earnings and minus treasury stock.[8] Equity capital is of particular importance for innovative investment and productivity growth due to its longer-term nature and the ability to absorb pressures on the company when strategies fail. For example, returns to shareholders can be reduced or increased depending on the success of the company's strategy. Equity capital cannot be withdrawn, and shareholders are last in the queue for income (and for the return of capital in the event of a resolution), behind creditors, employees' remuneration and tax obligations. None of this is true for debt. A rising debt-to-equity ratio comes about because companies are borrowing more relative to their ability to raise equity capital including via retained earnings, or because they are reducing equity through buybacks.

Productivity growth depends in part on the outcome of research, innovation and product development, all of which require longer-term risk taking for which equity capital is well suited. While debt can play an important role in the early stages of some long-term investments (like certain infrastructure projects) – a rising debt ratio is likely to be associated with taking advantage of distorting tax regimes which favour debt and a general shortening of the investment horizon. If the company has a lack of productivity enhancing projects in the boardroom, then it makes sense to give cash back to shareholders so that they can reallocate it to companies with innovative ideas. But this would not necessarily raise the debt ratio – cash can be used both to retire debt and to reward shareholders as well. Weaker companies borrow more (encouraged in the post-crisis period by low interest rates) to:

- Carry out M&A deals (either trying to rationalise and improve or for rent-seeking market share objectives).
- Pay dividends and carry out buybacks to boost the share price artificially (often to keep up with competitors with better cash flow).
- Substitute debt for equity for tax reasons, or as a takeover defence.

Debt must be serviced and the company is forced towards shorter-term cash-generating activities and away from long-term risk taking. Figure 2.9 shows the debt-to-equity ratio by weighted productivity growth deciles (D1 to D10) for advanced countries before and after the crisis in the top panel. The main shift is a significant rise in debt in the low productivity growth deciles (D1 to D4) and no change at the top. These latter stronger productivity growing companies have similar debt/equity ratios on average compared to the pre-crisis period, but more ability to service it than the weaker firms. They have not increased their debt in the post-crisis period. The weaker negative productivity growth companies are increasing their levels of debt and have less ability to pay.[9] The high productivity growth companies also have better cash flow.

Free cash flow (FCF) is the money a company has left over after carrying out the expenditure needed to maintain or expand its asset base shown in the bottom panel of Figure 2.9. In many ways FCF is an indicator of the resilience of a company. In advanced economies, the FCF curves slope upwards to the right in both the pre- and post-crisis periods. In other words, the higher productivity growth companies always exhibit better FCF. Strikingly, the crisis has led to a severe hit to FCF for the companies between the two high productivity groups D1 and D10. Weaker firms with poor cash flow might borrow excessively in order to be able to compete with more successful firms in carrying out mergers and acquisitions, paying dividends and carrying out buybacks, achieving their tax objectives, or defending against takeover. Servicing higher debt levels is a drain on cash flow, which will deteriorate further if interest rates rise. This undermines their ability to have a longer-term focus. The high-productivity companies have stronger FCF as a buffer and can maintain a focus on long-term goals in the face of shorter-term disruptions. Companies with high FCF typically have strong corporate governance, have penetrated new markets and use technology and flexible labour market contracts to contain costs and in general do not manipulate earnings.[10]

In emerging economies, the debt picture is somewhat different with both higher productivity level groups (D1 and D10) borrowing more. The FCF curves slope downwards to the right in both the pre- and post-crisis periods. In other words, the higher productivity growth companies seem to exhibit worse FCF, possibly due to rising real wages as prices are held down by the presence of excess capacity.

Figure 2.9. **Debt-to-capital ratios and free cash flow per employee in advanced economy companies by decile, pre-crisis versus post-crisis**

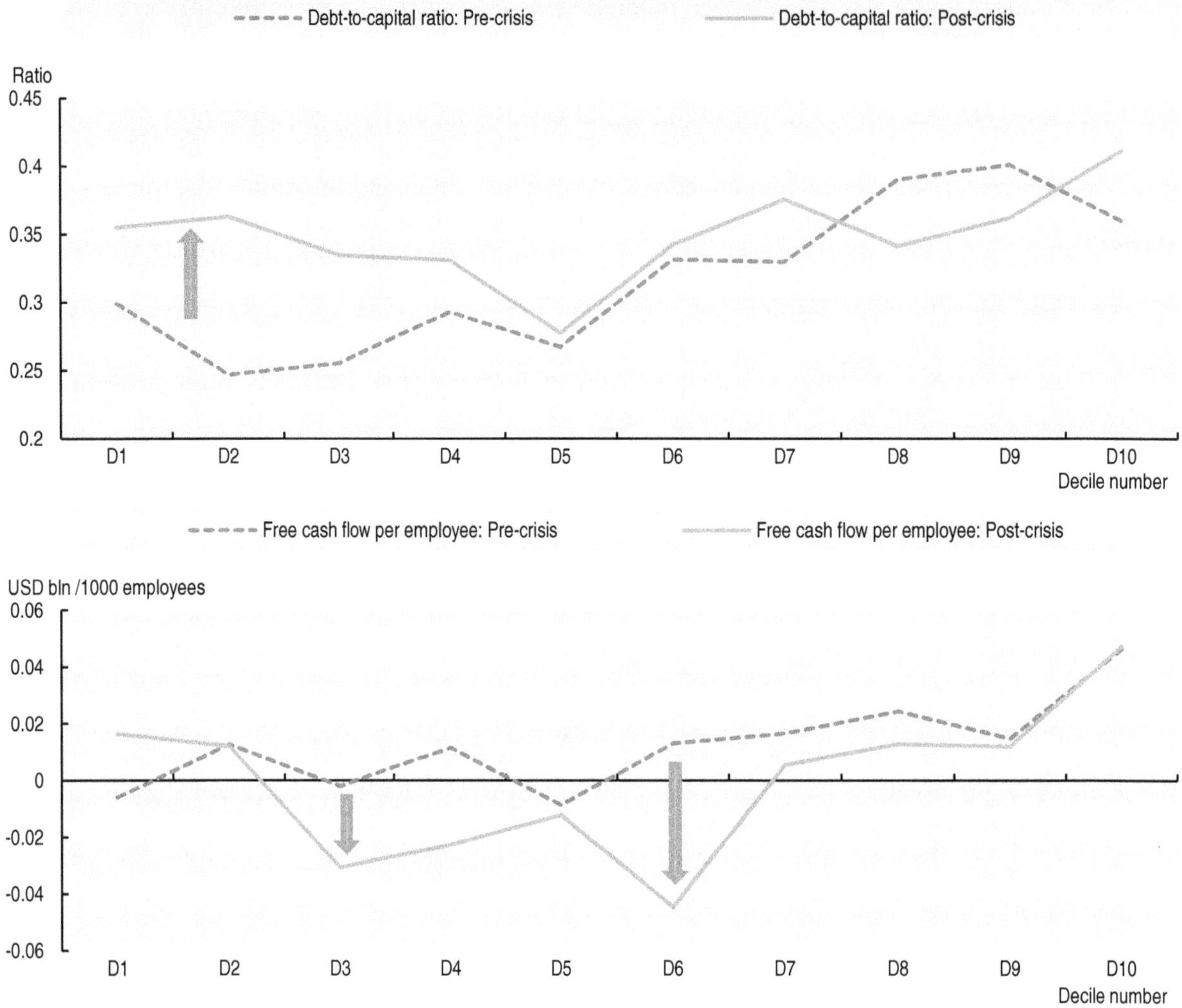

Note: The figures shown are the weighted average debt-to-capital ratio and free cashflow per 1000 employee using the geometric Törnqvist weighting procedure for the periods 2002-07 (pre-crisis) and 2008-15 (post-crisis) within each sector.
Source: OECD calculations, Bloomberg.

StatLink http://dx.doi.org/10.1787/888933362393

Mergers and acquisitions and improved productivity levels

The M&A data used in the above causality tests is based on Dealogic data and this was matched to the 11 000 companies used in this study for the period 2002-15. The level of M&A per employee was also found to be an unambiguous "causal" factor in explaining productivity growth (Box 2.2).

It is not clear whether all M&A deals should enhance productivity growth. If a large company takes over a "frontier firm" that is innovative (and would have had strong productivity growth on its own without the merger) then the impact of the deal on productivity growth in the sector will depend on the corporate strategy of the acquirer. The acquirer might buy an innovating target company because its strategy is to divest underperforming segments and replace them with segments that are a "better fit". For example, there might be important synergies: benefits to the target firm because it will

Figure 2.10. **Debt-to-capital ratios and free cash flow per employee in emerging economy companies by decile, pre-crisis versus post-crisis**

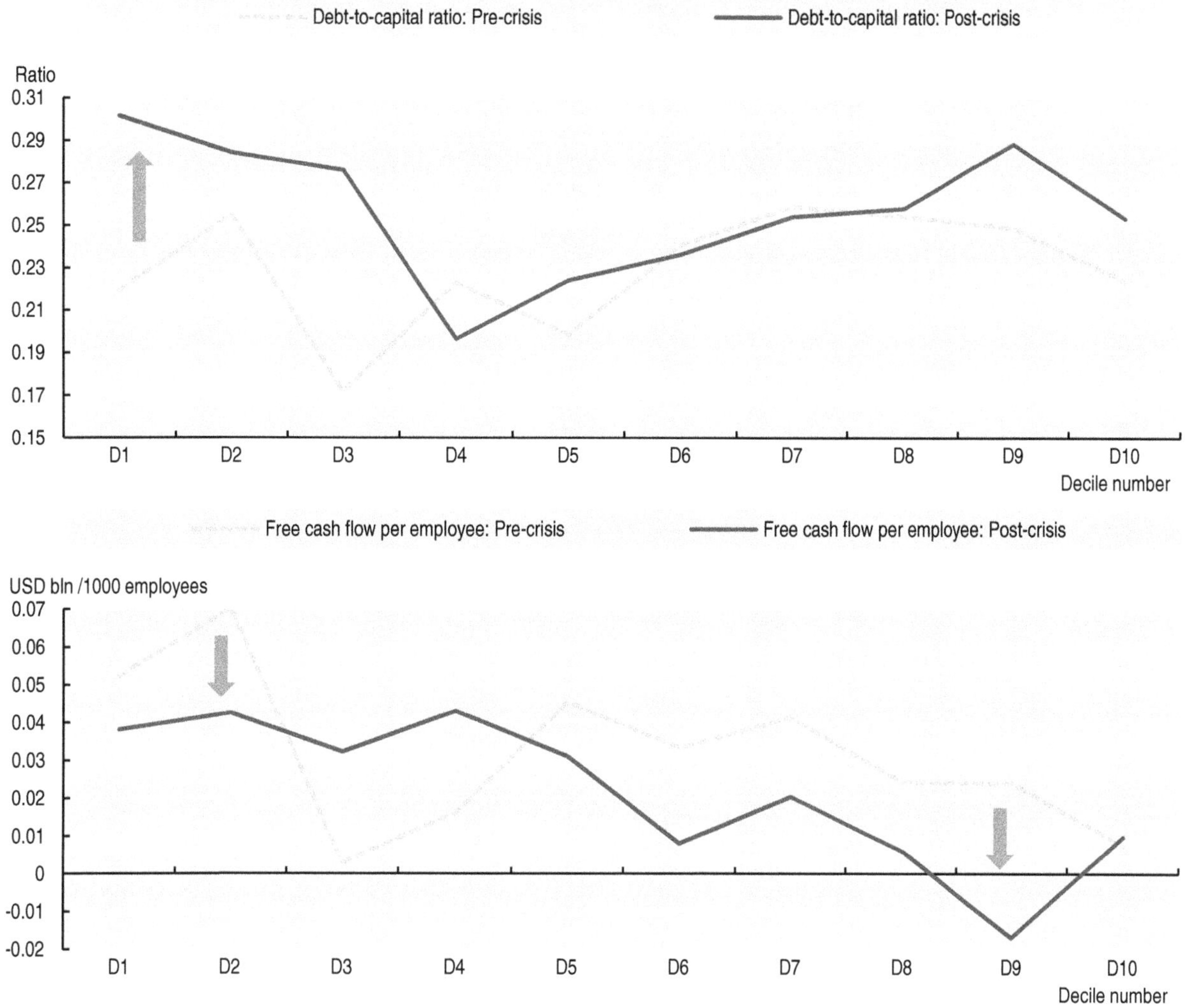

Note: The figures shown are the weighted average debt-to-capital ratio and free cashflow per 1 000 employee using the geometric Törnqvist weighting procedure for the periods 2002-07 (pre-crisis) and 2008-15 (post-crisis) within each sector.
Source: OECD calculations, Bloomberg.

StatLink http://dx.doi.org/10.1787/888933362402

have better access to markets deriving from the brand name, logistics, and complementary skills and technologies. By divesting underperforming assets and adding the target company a stronger more productive company emerges. Quite often the object of such takeovers is to acquire a unique research team rather than an existing sales business. The acquirer and the target company reinforce each other's weaknesses. This type of M&A helped propel some companies from the incumbent to the high-growth group. On the other hand, the acquirer may be a rent-seeking conglomerate which is looking to avoid another company taking advantage of its weaknesses and providing future competition. Such a company may even act to shut down the targeted innovating firm: "creative destruction" productivity growth would be harmed.[11] While this type of M&A may improve expected future profits, it may not engender better productivity.

Deal making of the companies in this sample is both continuous and extensive. During the period 2002-15, the average number of M&A deals per annum (advanced and emerging) was 1 650 in a sample of around 11 000 – that is around 15% of the companies in the sample per annum (see Figure 2.11).

Figure 2.11. **Number of M&A deals: Advanced versus emerging economy companies, by decile 2002-15**

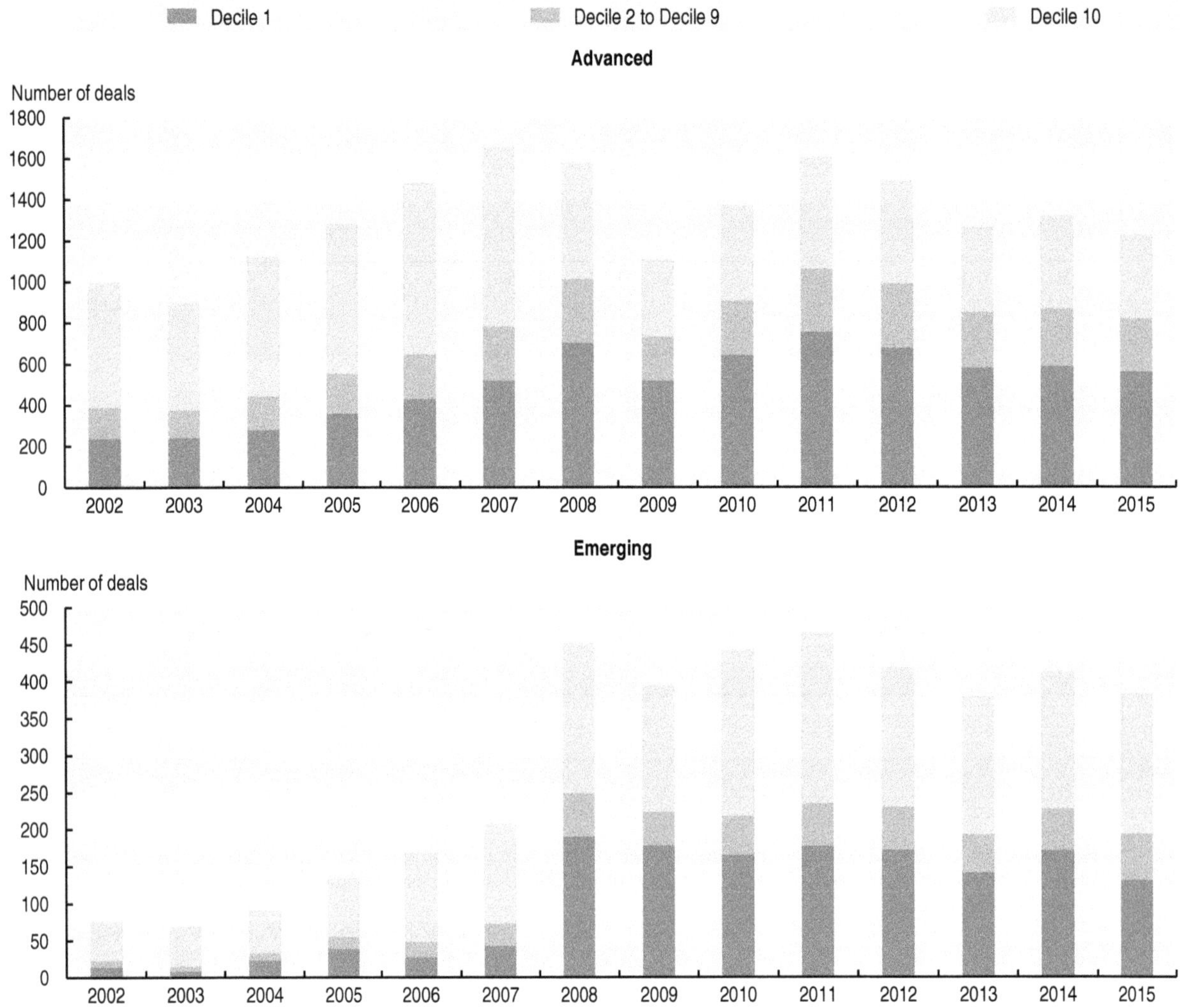

Source: OECD calculations, Bloomberg, Dealogic.

StatLink http://dx.doi.org/10.1787/888933362410

The deal making is heavily concentrated in the incumbent and high-productivity growth groups. M&A deals in the majority of companies in the middle deciles are much less pronounced.

- Deal flow has always been strong in the high-growth group of companies, both before and after the crisis. In the post-crisis period it has picked up quite strongly in the incumbent group as a way to rationalise and to get greater efficiencies.
- In emerging economies both D1 and especially D10 high-growth companies have much stronger M&A activity in the post-crisis period, presumably trying to rationalise an environment characterised by excess capacity.

Matching company names in the sample with the Dealogic M&A data leads to a similar "smile" pattern as that found for productivity levels (Figure 2.1) in the top panel of Figure 2.12.

Figure 2.12. **M&A activity associated with company decile rankings by sector, pre-crisis versus post-crisis**

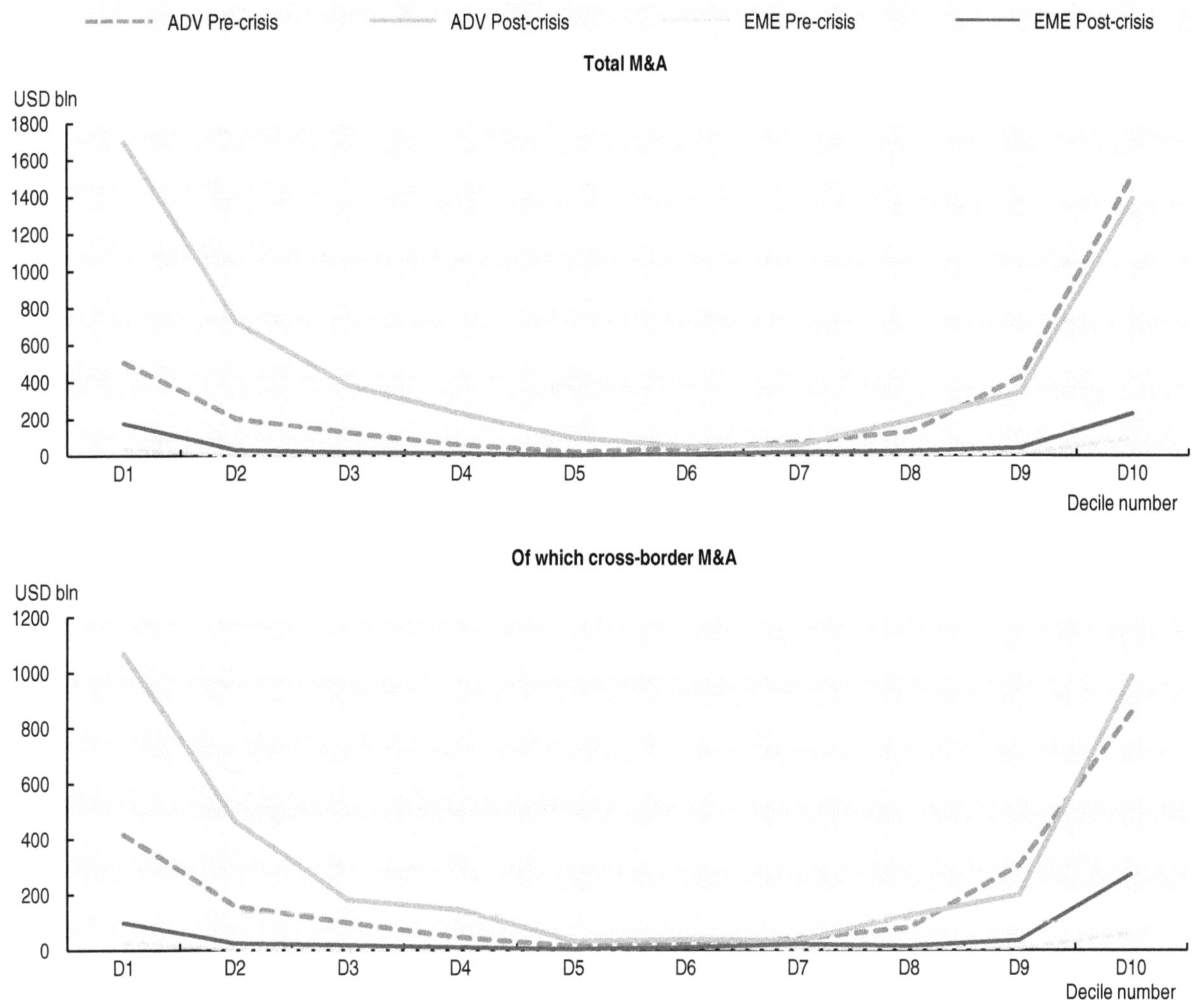

Note: Outstanding amounts in advanced (ADV) and emerging economies (EME).
Pre-crisis: 2002-07; post-crisis: 2008-15.
Source: OECD calculations, Bloomberg, Dealogic M&A Analytics database.

StatLink http://dx.doi.org/10.1787/888933362425

The cross-border-only M&A component is shown in the bottom panel of Figure 2.12 and once again the same familiar "smile" pattern is found to be present. If the analogy of a corral of horses could be used, it is as if the D1 and D10 companies try to choose the best horses in the pen and put them into their own stables to maintain some form of market and technological dominance.

M&A for the D1 and D10 companies broken out across sectors to which they belong is shown in Figure 2.13, for both advanced (top panel) and emerging (bottom panel) economies.

Figure 2.13. **M&A activity: Advanced versus emerging economy companies, post-crisis**

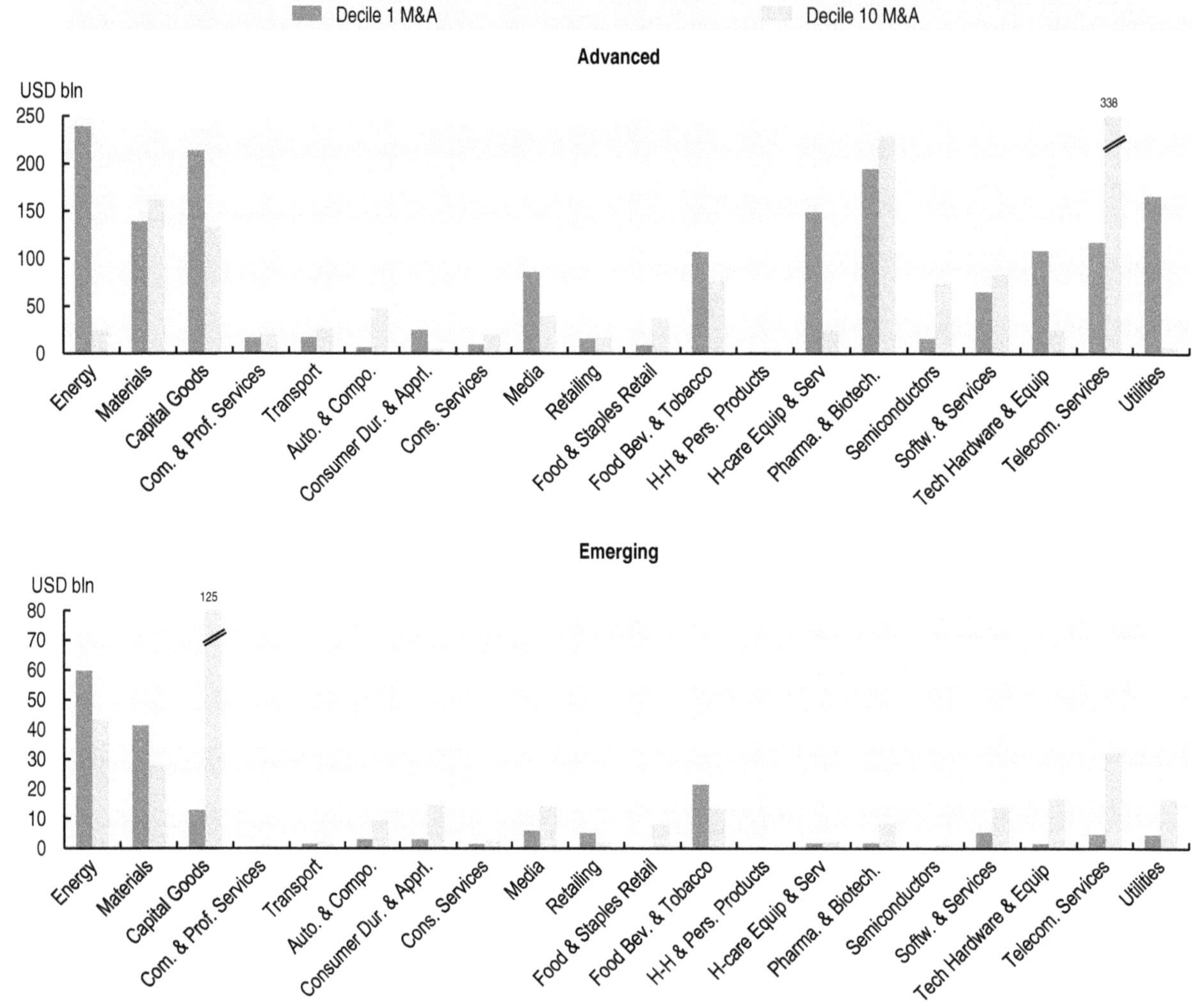

Note: Post-crisis: 2008-15.
Source: OECD calculations, Bloomberg, Dealogic M&A Analytics database.

StatLink http://dx.doi.org/10.1787/888933362431

The main features of the advanced economy companies are:

- The more dynamic D10 companies are most M&A active in: materials; capital goods; food beverages and tobacco; pharmaceuticals and biotechnology; semiconductors; software and services; and telecommunications services.
- Negative growth D1 firms are also active in most of the same sectors (though not in semiconductors) but in addition have a strong presence in: energy; healthcare equipment and services; technology hardware and equipment; and utilities. These energy companies in the negative growth group are also known to have borrowed a lot and may be facing a very tough time ahead (especially if interest rates were to rise).

With respect to emerging market economies, the M&A intensive sectors are energy, materials, and capital goods. Some of the sectors to the right also have moderate M&A. It is striking that pharmaceuticals and biotechnology are relatively small in emerging market economies in contrast to advanced economies.

What strategic decisions matter the most: R&D, debt-to-equity ratio, FCF or M&A?

This is a very difficult question to answer. The approach taken in this chapter is to use the evidence based on the preference of equity market investors over sustained periods. Equity markets discount the long-term future expected cash flow of companies based on investor perceptions of the strategy of management that ultimately drives the future of returns of the company. This should also to an extent reflect future productivity growth that managers are striving for (as well as any monopoly advantages that might arise).[12] The four strategies identified in the earlier causality analysis are examined from the perspective of equity market performance in Table 2.2.

Table 2.2. **Portfolio performance of high versus low productivity companies, pre-crisis versus post-crisis**

Companies with high productivity compound growth (Decile 10)			
Equally-weighted portfolios	Positive return strategies		*(Post crisis)-(Pre-crisis)*
	Pre-crisis	*Post-crisis*	
	High R&D		
Advanced 50 companies	12.37	4.50	-7.87
Emerging 50 companies	30.44	9.84	-20.60
	Low Debt		
Advanced 50 companies	10.15	7.53	-2.62
Emerging 50 companies	34.92	6.00	-28.93
	High FCF		
Advanced 50 companies	12.45	4.08	-8.37
Emerging 50 companies	29.65	12.47	-17.18
	High M&A		
Advanced 50 companies	16.00	5.29	-10.71
Emerging 50 companies	34.01	1.70	-32.31
Companies with low productivity compound growth (Decile 1)			
Equally-weighted portfolios	Positive return strategies		*(Post crisis)-(Pre-crisis)*
	Pre-crisis	Post-crisis	
	High R&D		
Advanced 50 companies	23.13	3.69	-19.44
Emerging 50 companies	39.97	-4.14	-44.10
	Low Debt		
Advanced 50 companies	18.68	-0.20	-18.88
Emerging 50 companies	36.73	-6.25	-42.97
	High FCF		
Advanced 50 companies	18.55	4.41	-14.14
Emerging 50 companies	42.23	-6.53	-48.76
	High M&A		
Advanced 50 companies	16.07	-0.31	-16.39
Emerging 50 companies	39.66	-6.72	-46.38
MSCI World performance	8.09	0.08	-8.01

Note: Annual average performance is shown. The companies are selected for the full period. Performance is compared between the periods 2002-07 (pre-crisis) and 2008-15 (post-crisis). Two groups of 50 companies in the D1 and D10 deciles, in both advanced and emerging countries, are considered.
Source: OECD calculations, Bloomberg, Dealogic M&A Analytics database.

StatLink http://dx.doi.org/10.1787/888933362828

All companies from the energy and materials sectors are excluded from the portfolios due to the excessive influence of the commodity price cycle. The average annual performance over the 2002-07 period and the post-crisis period 2008-15 years is shown for the D10 (high-productivity growth) and D1 (incumbent) companies. A first observation is that all portfolios in the tough post-crisis environment do less well than during the pre-crisis boom years (the far right column).

- *In the pre-crisis period:* All strategies outperformed the MSCI regardless of which productivity grouping companies were in. It is of some interest that the share price impact in the small sub-sample portfolios was mostly higher in the incumbent D1 group (in both advanced and emerging economies). Most of these 50 companies are precisely amongst those that transitioned to the post-crisis high-growth group, leaving behind those that did not adjust. All four strategies were share-price enhancing, suggesting better performance later on (in the post-crisis period).
- *In advanced economies in the post-crisis period*: all four strategies work well within the D10 high-growth group (especially equity versus debt). This is not the case for incumbent declining productivity companies, though higher R&D and better FCF always seem to work in the advanced economy portfolios of 50 companies.
- *In emerging market economies in the post-crisis period*: FCF appears to be by far the strongest influence on the high-growth frontier group (D10) and R&D is also important. For the low-productivity company portfolios (D1, containing many state-owned enterprises) none of the four financial strategies work. Even for the small subsample of the 50 best D1 company examples they do not add value. It seems that fundamental structural problems – and perhaps the over-capacity referred to in the *OECD Business and Finance Outlook 2015* – might be located to a greater extent in this group.

Conclusions

The above analysis suggests that fragmentation is a major feature of the productivity growth of companies. Companies were ranked into deciles according to their weighted productivity growth. In the pre-crisis period there was a group of high productivity companies but with negative productivity growth (referred to throughout as "incumbent"). But the crisis brought with it severe financial conditions and poor demand, requiring companies to adjust. Some incumbents did this well and moved to the high-growth rising productivity level group in the post-crisis period, while other incumbents continued to decline. Some previously high-growth companies also joined the incumbent group, often by taking poor business or financial decisions. The vast majority of middle-group companies that have low productivity levels and moderate growth appear to be "stuck" – they find it very difficult to transition to either of the high-level or high-growth groups.[13] The study suggests that the explanation of the Great Productivity Puzzle – that there is little aggregate productivity growth despite easy monetary policy since the crisis – is due to fragmentation, with very different abilities of boards to steer companies to the financial structures conducive to growth in value added per employee. The dynamic group is not large enough and the middle groups are not growing fast enough to offset the high-level declining productivity group. The possible business and financial strategy contributions to this problem were then examined.

Recognizing that decisions about innovation are taken in the board room, this chapter looked at the financial decisions that the dynamic creative destruction companies took to succeed in the post-crisis environment – focusing only on those where true one-way causality could be established. These companies had four key interrelated corporate finance characteristics:

- They expensed much more on R&D than other companies, which in turn requires risk taking and a long-term focus critical to the innovation process.
- The high productivity group did not increase borrowing compared to equity in the post-crisis period (while those that did were in the low productivity groups). Equity is for the long term and success or failure is reflected in its price, whereas debt must be serviced and the inability to do so in the short-run will lead to bankruptcy. An equity focus enabled the successful firms to focus on longer-term goals instead of altering their business model to try to generate more short-term cash to meet debt obligations.
- These same high-productivity companies had a buffer of free cash flow (FCF): i.e. their operating cash flow was in excess of that needed for capital expenditure. Such companies can maintain a focus on long-term goals in the face of short-term disruptions. Companies with high FCF typically have strong corporate governance, have penetrated new markets and use technology and flexible labour market contracts to contain costs.
- Importantly, those that succeeded used mergers and acquisitions (buying and selling business segments) to rationalise what they were doing in the tougher more competitive post-crisis environment.

Stock prices reflect expected future earnings and which benefit from productivity growth, and hence may shed light on the efficacy of these four corporate strategies. Fifty stock portfolios based on the strategies outperformed the global benchmark in most cases (except the low-productivity growth companies in emerging markets).

Some of the possible policy implications of these findings are:

- *With respect to R&D*: the consideration of improved R&D fiscal incentives and funding for basic research, including support for collaboration between firms and universities; and technology policies with respect to intellectual property rights and patents that strike a balance between encouraging innovation and facilitating reasonable spill-overs to other firms. Tax incentives for R&D are taken up in detail in the next chapter.
- *With respect to equity finance instead of debt:* Policies that would encourage equity over debt include: a) the removal of tax incentives that favour debt over equity; b) the simplification of equity listing rules that increase costs relative to private equity; c) equity market reforms that encourage IPOs including *inter alia* an examination of stock exchange fragmentation into lit exchanges and dark pools (where the latter reduce transparency and impede price discovery discussed in Chapter 5); d) financial regulations for long-term institutional investors that do not unduly penalise equity portfolios (e.g. Solvency II); and e) improvements to regulations and trading rules that create volatility and reduce investor trust in the equity market (e.g. high frequency trading arrangements and the functioning of some exchange traded funds).
- *With respect to free cash flow:* the best way to enhance this key requirement in a broader range of companies is to make it easier for them to access new markets for their core products and to adopt policies that minimise their costs (flexible labour contracts, more open cross-border and internal trade and investment regimes, access to cheaper external funding and fiscal incentives): a) Open trade and investment regimes between countries are particularly important, not only for market access, but also to ensure

policies directed at supporting specific sectors do not inadvertently fracture global value chains which add to costs for other downstream companies hurting their cash flow (see Chapter 5); b) breaking down competitive barriers to entry often granted by government rules and regulations (e.g. maritime and air transport, telecommunications network access, planning permission in retail, monopoly rules in the professions, the pharmaceutical industry, etc.) are essential for the contestability of internal markets; c) more flexible labour market rules allow companies to manage their cash flow when setbacks occur; d) recapitalising banks and dealing with their non-performing loans (NPL) problems will reduce funding costs for companies through the banking system; e) financial reforms and their interaction with monetary policy also need to be cognisant of their impact on the availability and cost of external financing (both debt and equity), and regulations and tax rules should not inhibit cheaper non-traditional sources of funds (angel investors, crowdfunding, peer-to-peer lending and distributed ledger innovations in payments technology); and f) fiscal support has a direct impact on company cash flow but needs to be well targeted: e.g. where R&D is concerned firms need a lot of up-front cash given the asymmetric information that exists between young firms and their potential investors (see Chapter 3).

- *With respect to M&A activity:* breaking down cultural and regulatory barriers to cross-border M&A consistent with allowing entry and facilitating a genuine open market for corporate control is needed. Efficiency enhancing measures include: a) cooperation between competition agencies when considering cross-border deals to speed up the M&A process, to minimise costs and to reduce inconsistent criteria; and b) eliminating the culture of "national champions" whereby governments support incumbent firms when they face challenges from new (particularly foreign) entrants. Policy makers always need to be wary of approving deals that simply increase market share and profits, which may not generate productivity-enhancing investment. However, given the post-crisis evidence that the net effect of M&A is positive for productivity growth via synergies and rationalisation channels, it might be helpful if competition authorities took note of this when assessing mergers.

Better diffusion of technology that would remove the fragmentation in productivity performance at the company level would do much to improve aggregate productivity growth. But technical progress and innovation to enhance productivity do not happen in a vacuum. Decisions affecting these things in large multinational enterprises are taken in the boardroom. Large companies set the tone for global economic growth. At present the world is characterised by excess capacity in a number of key sectors while better prospects go unexploited in others. Low interest rates (which attribute a zero time value to money) do not address this problem of fragmentation between companies holding back sustainable productivity growth and may even delay the necessary adjustments. Looking through the company lens, it is policies that foster more research and development spending, greater equity financing instead of a debt, improved company cash flows, and rationalisations by merger and acquisition that are essential for improving productivity growth.

Taking full advantage of better productivity growth will also require adjustment to take place across the global economy as a whole. If this is not done widespread improved productivity performance by companies in advanced economies only will tend to exacerbate over-supply problems that persist in emerging market economies and associated financial fragility problems throughout the world. At a minimum this requires corporate restructuring in emerging markets and continued progress in addressing remaining weaknesses in financial sectors globally. These need to be supported by broader framework conditions, notably as regards trade, cross-border investment, labour markets, social policies and tax design, which facilitate the necessary reallocation of human and physical resources smoothly.

Notes

1. Productivity went into a new phase of downward momentum after 2000, and even more so after the crisis. Furman (2015) quotes the OECD study on The Future of Productivity that recognises frontier firms and Mr Furman ponders why the spill-overs from these firms are not happening. See also Furman and Orszag (2015).
2. OECD (2015a) on the "Future of Productivity" uses firms in the 2-digit sector in the ORBIS database.
3. The GICS consists of 24 different industry sectors. This study considers 20 industry sectors by excluding financial companies and real estate.
4. The geometric Tornquist weighting procedure is used for the 2002-07 period, the 2008-15 period and, where required, the full period. The size of one sector versus another does not affect the weighting – only the size within the sector. If a company disappears, usually because it merges with another, it is excluded from the sample to avoid double counting.
5. There is a need to not weight very small companies with high productivity growth (but which have little impact on the economy) equally with larger high-productivity-growth firms.
6. Otherwise they would be advanced economies.
7. The present authors consider it erroneous to calculate year-by-year probability transition matrices in an actuarial sense, as the effect of multiplying probabilities on the assumption that movements are random biases the answer towards zero persistence. Here the performance of companies over two relatively long periods of time is calculated and the actual names of companies are traced between the two periods. The persistence in the D1 and D10 groups is very strong – it is not random. As the sample of data is "unbalanced", firms which disappear from the first period to the second period and the firms which exist only over the second period are also considered in the calculations.
8. Or alternatively, it is assets minus liabilities. Treasury stock is the amount of shares bought back by the company, often for tax purposes or to offset the dilution of employee stock ownership plans. In jurisdictions where capital gains taxes are more favourably treated, buybacks are a tax-efficient method of putting money back into the hands of shareholders. Of course buybacks can also be used by management to manipulate share prices when their own remuneration is affected.
9. However, Levine and Warusawitharana (2014) find that, for firms in large European countries, debt finance supports productivity growth at the firm-level.
10. This is done to show better earnings growth than is in fact the case by manipulating accruals items (inventory, accounts receivable, accounts payable, and "other current assets and liabilities").
11. When dealing with companies in global industries in the GICS sectors used in this study, it is not possible to consider this issue in terms of concentration ratios and market power. A multinational company may have a large share of the GICS sector, but a low concentration in a number of well-defined local markets. There is a big difference between having a large share of a global market such as oil, for which there is something close to a global price and, for example, concentration in the electricity market in Washington versus that in Paris.
12. An error-correction model relating productivity growth to the lagged levels of the stock price and productivity shows the long-run effect of stock prices indeed to be significantly positive for the 11000 companies included in the sample.
13. A process that would raise the overall level of productivity.

References

Aghion, P., R. Blundell, R Griffith, P. Howitt and S. Prantl (2004), "Entry and Productivity Growth: Evidence from Micro level Panel Data, *Journal of the European Economics Association*, MIT Press.

Baily, M., C. Hulten and D. Campbell (1992), "Productivity Dynamics in Manufacturing Plant's", *Brookings Papers on Economic Activity: Microeconomics*, Vol 4, The Brookings Institute.

Blundell-Wignall, A. and Caroline Roulet (2014), "Problems in the international financial system", *OECD Journal: Financial Market Trends*, Vol. 2014/1, *http://dx.doi.org/10.1787/fmt-2014-5jxzmkg91s0t*.

Foster, L., J.C. Haltiwanger and C.J. Krizan (2001), "Aggregate Productivity Growth: Lessons for Microeconomic Evidence", *New Developments in Productivity Analysis*, University of Chicago Press.

Furman, J. (2015), "Productivity Growth in the Advanced Economies: The Past, the Present, and Lessons for the Future", Remarks by the Chairman of the Council of Economic Advisers.

Furman, J. and P. Orszag (2015), "A Firm-Level Perspective on the Role of Rents in the Rise in Inequality", Presentation at "A *Just Society*" Centennial Event in Honour of Joseph Stiglitz, Columbia University.

Griliches, Z. and H. Regev (1995),"Firm Productivity in Israeli Industry: 1979-1988", *Journal of Econometrics*.

Melitz, J.A. and S. Polanec (2012), "Dynamic Olley-Pakes Productivity Decomposition with Entry and Exit", *NBER Working Paper* 18182, NBER.

Levine, O. and M. Warusawitharana (2014), "Finance and productivity growth: firm-level evidence", *FEDS Working Paper* #2014-17.

Melitz, J.A. and S Polanec (2012), "Dynamic Olley-Pakes Productivity Decomposition with Entry and Exit", *NBER Working Paper* 1818, NBER.

OECD (2015a), *The Future of Productivity*, Paris, *http://dx.doi.org/10.1787/9789264248533-en*.

OECD (2015b), *OECD Business and Finance Outlook 2015*, Paris, *http://dx.doi.org/10.1787/9789264234291-en*.

Olley, G.S. and A. Pakes (1996), "The Dynamics of Productivity in the Telecommunications Equipment Industry", *Econometrica*, Vol. 64, No. 6.

ANNEX 2.A1

Company data and sample description

Company data are based on the Bloomberg World Equity Index (BWEI). The sample includes all companies which have been listed in the BWEI over the period 2002-15. 10 098 listed companies in 76 countries were selected (i.e. 6 460 in advanced economies and 4 638 in emerging economies) operating in 20 GICS industry sectors.[1] Annual consolidated financial statements were extracted from Bloomberg. All unbalanced panel data are denominated in current US dollars.[2] Potential outliers were removed from the sample. Table 2.A1.1 presents the number of companies by country and sector.

Companies are ranked by their decile of Törnqvist weighted productivity growth rate within sector.[3] Productivity is measured as the total value added per employee of individual companies. The compound growth rate of productivity for each company is calculated for the period under consideration and this number is multiplied by the average share in sector value added (between the start and the last dates of the considered time period) to define the decile within which it sits. When deciles are aggregated across sectors average sector weights are used. Table 2.A1.2 shows weighted average company productivity growth by sector and decile.

To examine the financial characteristics of firms that succeed, the several following financial variables are considered and are defined as follows:

- **Value added:** Sum of personnel expenses and EBITDA, i.e. income before interest, taxes, depreciation and amortisation. Personnel expenses include wages and salaries, social security, pension, profit-sharing expenses and other benefits related to personnel.
- **Number of employees:** Number of people employed by the company, based on the number of full time equivalents. If unavailable, then the number of full time employees is used, excluding part time employees.
- **Net sales:** Total operating revenues less various adjustments (i.e. returns, discounts, allowances, excise taxes, insurance charges, sales taxes, and value added taxes) to gross sales. It includes revenues from financial subsidiaries in industrial companies if the consolidation includes those subsidiaries throughout the report. It also includes subsidies from federal or local government in certain industries (i.e. transportation or utilities). However, it excludes intra-company revenue and revenues from discontinued operations.
- **Capital expenditure:** Amount the company spent on purchases of tangible fixed assets. It may include intangible assets when not disclosed separately.

- **Free cash flow:** Operating cash flow minus capital expenditures. It represents the cash that a company is able to generate after laying out the money required to maintain or expand its asset base.
- **Dividends and buybacks:** Sum of dividend paid and buybacks of common shares. Dividend paid corresponds to all dividends actually paid out as cash disbursements for both common shareholders and preferred shareholders. It may include dividends paid to minority interests and dividends paid by subsidiaries if they are not disclosed separately. Common share buybacks correspond to the monetary amount that a company spent to repurchase common shares during the period. It includes all share buybacks, including, but not limited, to the share buyback program or plan.
- **R&D expenditure:** Operating expense related to the research and development of a company's products or services.
- **Debt-to-enterprise value ratio:** Total long-term borrowings divided by the sum of long-term borrowing and equity capital. Long-term borrowing includes all interest-bearing financial obligations that are not due within a year (i.e. convertible, redeemable, retractable debentures, bonds, loans, mortgage debts, sinking funds, and long-term bank overdrafts, subordinated capital notes, long-term hire purchase, finance lease obligations, long-term bills of exchange, bankers acceptances and other debt which is interest bearing). It may also include shares issued by subsidiaries if the group has an obligation to transfer economic benefits in connection with these shares. Long term borrowings are net with unamortised premium or discount on debt. Equity capital is share capital, plus retained earnings and minus treasury stock.
- **Return on equity (ROE):** Ratio of net income to common equity. Net income is the profit after all expenses have been deducted. It includes the effects of all one-time, non-recurring, and extraordinary gains, losses, or charges. Common equity is the amount that all common shareholders have invested in a company.
- **Value of completed M&A deals:** Declared amount effectively paid by the acquirer for the target. "Acquisitions" include all deals with a 100% takeover of another entity (such as, acquisitions of business units, divisions, product lines or other operations of another entity, acquisitions of stakes, acquisition of pharmaceutical rights and brands). In "Mergers", the target is deemed to be the company for which the offer is being made, the owner of the smaller equity stake in the combined entity, or the one with smaller market capitalisation. If the merger is a 50/50 split of equals, and there is no clear indication of the larger firm, Dealogic will use its discretion in the selection of target. Joint ventures are eligible if two or more companies combine their existing assets or equity to form a new entity. Spin-offs and split-offs are eligible. Privatisations (but not government carve outs), government-awarded PCS/wireless licenses, real estate property transactions (excluding purchases consisting solely of land which fall outside the oil and gas and mining industries) and buy-back transactions structured as public tender offers are tracked and also eligible.

Table 2.A1.1. Distribution of companies by country and sector

Advanced economies	Number of companies	Emerging economies	Number of companies	Sector	Industry group	Advanced economies	Emerging economies
Australia	457	**Argentina**	17	**Energy**	Energy	607	220
Austria	25	**Bahrain**	2	**Materials**	Materials	838	870
Belgium	38	**Bosnia-Herzegovina**	14	**Industrials**	Capital goods	869	849
Canada	808	**Brazil**	144		Commercial and professional services	247	51
Cyprus[1]	22	**Bulgaria**	25		Transportation	250	191
Czech Republic	6	**Chile**	43	**Consumer discretionary**	Automobiles and components	146	187
Denmark	43	**China**	1 407		Consumer durables and apparel	287	315
Estonia	4	**Colombia**	14		Consumer services	293	148
Finland	48	**Croatia**	51		Media	208	119
France	205	**Egypt**	35		Retailing	334	149
Germany	208	**Gabon**	1	**Consumer staples**	Food and staples retailing	105	64
Greece	79	**Hungary**	9		Food beverage and tobacco	245	340
Hong Kong, China	129	**India**	971		Household and personal products	52	43
Ireland	30	**Indonesia**	114	**Healthcare**	Health care equipment and services	280	86
Italy	91	**Israel**[2]	46		Pharmaceuticals and biotechnology	373	222
Japan	1 099	**Jordan**	9	**Information technology**	Semiconductors	151	60
Latvia	7	**Kenya**	3		Software and services	448	213
Lithuania	9	**Korea**	515		Technology hardware and equipment	389	195
Luxembourg	6	**Kuwait**	20	**Telecommunication services**	Telecommunication services	110	93
Malta	5	**Macedonia**	4	**Utilities**	Utilities	228	223
Netherlands	58	**Malaysia**	226				
New Zealand	18	**Mexico**	55				
Norway	37	**Montenegro**	1				
Portugal	19	**Morocco**	8				
Singapore	57	**Oman**	5				
Slovakia	8	**Pakistan**	21				

Table 2.A1.1. **Distribution of companies by country and sector** *(cont.)*

Advanced economies	Number of companies	Emerging economies	Number of companies	Sector	Industry group	Advanced economies	Emerging economies
Slovenia	13	**Peru**	17				
Spain	65	**Philippines**	29				
Sweden	149	**Poland**	190				
Switzerland	81	**Qatar**	9				
Chinese Taipei	192	**Romania**	138				
United Kingdom	365	**Russia**	120				
United States	2 079	**Saudi Arabia**	53				
		Senegal	1				
		Serbia	39				
		South Africa	81				
		Sudan	1				
		Thailand	50				
		Turkey	98				
		Ukraine	21				
		United Arab Emirates	15				
		Venezuela	2				
		Vietnam	14				
TOTAL	6 460		4 638				

Notes:

1. Note by Turkey. The information in this document with reference to "Cyprus" relates to the southern part of the Island. There is no single authority representing both Turkish and Greek Cypriot people on the Island. Turkey recognises the Turkish Republic of Northern Cyprus (TRNC). Until a lasting and equitable solution is found within the context of the United Nations, Turkey shall preserve its position concerning the "Cyprus issue".

   Note by all the European Union Member States of the OECD and the European Union. The Republic of Cyprus is recognised by all members of the United Nations with the exception of Turkey. The information in this document relates to the area under the effective control of the Government of the Republic of Cyprus.

Source: OECD compilation.

StatLink http://dx.doi.org/10.1787/888933362834

Table 2.A1.2. Productivity growth by sector and decile, post-crisis

	D1		D2		D3		D4		D5		D6		D7		D8		D9		D10	
	ADV	EME	ADV	EME	ADV	EME	ADV	EME	ADV	EME	ADV	EME	ADV	EME	ADV	EME	ADV	EME	ADV	EME
Energy	-15.22	-6.20	-11.27	-10.42	-8.04	-5.65	-6.63	-1.25	-2.91	-1.50	-0.94	0.27	0.92	5.79	3.09	4.72	5.28	9.26	11.92	6.69
Materials	-11.64	-18.55	-3.31	-8.33	-2.99	-4.63	-1.45	-2.52	-1.00	-0.21	0.59	2.33	1.34	2.75	1.66	6.12	3.87	5.95	5.96	14.55
Capital goods	-7.25	-15.88	-2.46	-4.39	-1.42	-7.12	-1.52	-2.37	-1.15	1.05	0.41	3.86	1.44	5.12	2.40	6.76	2.44	6.46	7.28	16.38
Commercial and professional services	-18.37	-3.72	-4.83	-2.36	-2.66	-1.48	-2.10	-1.08	-2.47	1.76	-0.33	1.65	0.49	4.82	2.79	7.63	2.70	6.29	10.87	29.69
Transportation	-10.74	-13.07	-3.71	-7.42	-3.86	-2.69	-1.49	-1.57	-0.69	0.61	0.45	2.88	0.94	6.96	2.70	8.83	3.50	7.74	12.09	27.47
Automobiles and components	-6.24	-10.95	-3.06	-3.27	-1.64	-0.56	-0.94	0.46	0.44	2.37	1.45	3.00	2.78	5.41	2.81	5.82	3.58	9.50	4.67	8.24
Consumer durables and apparel	-15.45	-11.57	-3.02	-7.07	-1.06	-3.24	-0.89	-0.30	0.13	2.21	1.23	3.93	2.79	7.58	1.92	7.04	3.06	9.55	8.80	8.45
Consumer services	-14.60	-8.13	-5.40	-2.59	-2.95	-8.14	-1.56	-0.70	-1.53	1.81	0.12	2.16	1.18	4.21	1.44	3.80	3.63	3.90	13.76	12.48
Media	-9.17	-23.67	-4.63	-20.27	-3.30	-4.55	-3.19	0.70	-0.70	3.24	0.08	17.65	1.79	7.18	1.85	8.54	2.61	14.84	13.47	13.37
Retailing	-12.77	-14.87	-3.91	-6.64	-3.17	-4.16	-3.36	-1.15	-0.97	0.42	0.11	4.52	1.67	4.49	1.25	4.14	3.42	6.57	8.23	10.38
Food and staples retailing	-6.59	-9.52	-2.58	-2.48	-8.18	-2.23	-6.97	-1.54	-1.54	1.10	-2.79	7.85	-0.73	7.81	0.56	5.12	2.33	4.62	7.08	9.67
Food beverage and tobacco	-28.18	-7.68	-3.53	-3.90	-1.62	-2.79	-1.03	-0.80	-0.63	0.62	0.05	4.85	0.96	5.16	1.87	6.63	2.55	7.88	5.90	8.79
Household and personal products	-12.46	-1.93	-1.81	-0.08	-0.57	2.04	-3.26	2.65	-3.18	6.24	-0.38	2.36	0.16	10.14	1.80	8.22	0.85	14.36	7.03	18.04
Health care equipment and services	-14.91	-5.73	-10.60	-4.82	-5.60	-2.97	-2.64	0.54	-1.49	2.37	-0.61	5.26	0.30	10.25	1.46	6.32	1.13	5.96	11.01	11.44
Pharmaceuticals and biotechnology	-13.61	-12.57	-6.91	-2.49	-7.55	-0.28	-2.89	3.69	-1.88	8.55	-0.54	4.15	1.20	6.55	0.70	7.67	1.25	8.57	8.05	12.26
Semiconductors	-12.25	-22.53	-4.79	-10.42	-1.59	-3.81	-6.02	4.09	1.13	11.86	1.84	7.49	2.91	9.18	2.81	7.64	6.24	23.88	8.33	16.24
Software and services	-20.24	-2.87	-8.92	-3.66	-7.19	-2.95	-2.50	-0.06	-2.38	3.57	-1.67	7.01	0.54	9.12	0.94	3.22	1.94	7.42	8.68	8.30
Technology hardware and equipment	-11.27	-11.76	-3.83	-7.44	-2.02	-5.34	-1.91	-0.91	-0.74	1.72	0.75	2.25	3.73	9.06	3.51	8.01	2.78	6.71	12.14	3.68
Telecommunication services	-6.68	-21.42	-5.62	-9.98	-4.46	-2.79	-3.54	-2.86	-1.23	-0.82	-0.47	0.27	1.24	3.99	1.56	3.55	3.10	6.25	4.38	6.75
Utilities	-6.02	-11.89	-3.48	-5.48	-2.47	-2.15	-0.63	-2.34	-0.10	1.70	1.43	3.33	1.40	4.90	3.04	6.95	5.02	7.18	5.42	14.46

Note: The figures shown are the weighted average productivity compound growth rate using the geometric Törnqvist weighting procedure for the period 2008-15 within each sector.
ADV: advanced economies; EME: emerging economies.
Source: OECD calculations, Bloomberg.

StatLink http://dx.doi.org/10.1787/888933362843

Notes

1. See Annex 2.A2 for further details about the composition of each sector and industry group.
2. Balance sheets are reported at an exchange rate set on the date of publishing. Income statements and statements of cash flow are averaged over the period. The pricing source is the Bloomberg composite rate (CMP). It is a composite based on contributing banks prices. The time the exchange rate is taken is at 6:00pm in London time. Neither the pricing source (Bloomberg composite) nor the closing time can be modified;these are fixed for everyone.
3. A Törnqvist index is a discrete approximation to a continuous Divisia index. A Divisia index is a theoretical construct, a continuous-time weighted sum of the growth rates of the various components, where the weights are the component's shares in total value. The growth rates are defined to be the difference in natural logarithms of successive observations of the components (i.e. their log-change) and the weights are equal to the mean of the value added shares at the start and end of the period under consideration.

ANNEX 2.A2

The structure of the Global Industry Classification Standard

In 1999, MSCI and Standard & Poor's developed the Global Industry Classification Standard (GICS), seeking to offer an efficient investment tool to capture the breadth, depth and evolution of industry sectors. GICS is a four-tiered, hierarchical industry classification system. Companies are classified quantitatively and qualitatively. Each company is assigned a single GICS classification at the sub-industry level according to its principal business activity. MSCI and Standard & Poor's use revenues as a key factor in determining a firm's principal business activity. Earnings and market perception, however, are also recognised as important and relevant information for classification purposes, and are taken into account during the annual review process. Excluding financial companies, GICS classification consists of nine sectors, 20 industry groups, 60 industries and 130 sub-industries. GICS structure is detailed in Table 2.A2.1.

Table 2.A2.1. **The Global Industry Classification Standard (GICS)**

Sector	Industry sector	Industry group	Sub-industry
Energy	**Energy**	**Energy equipment and services**	Oil and gas drilling
			Oil and gas equipment and services
		Oil, gas and consumable fuels	Integrated oil and gas
			Oil and gas exploration and production
			Oil and gas refining and marketing
			Oil and gas storage and transportation
			Coal and consumable fuels
Materials	**Materials**	**Chemicals**	Commodity chemicals
			Diversified chemicals
			Fertilisers and agricultural chemicals
			Industrial gases
			Specialty chemicals
		Construction materials	Construction materials
		Containers and packaging	Metal and glass containers
			Paper packaging
		Metals and mining	Aluminium
			Diversified metals and mining
			Gold
			Precious metals and minerals
			Steel
		Paper and forest products	Forest products
			Paper products

Table 2.A2.1. **The Global Industry Classification Standard (GICS)** *(cont.)*

Sector	Industry sector	Industry group	Sub-industry
Industrials	**Capital goods**	**Aerospace and defence**	Aerospace and defence
		Building products	Building products
		Construction and engineering	Construction and engineering
		Electrical equipment	Electrical components and equipment
			Heavy electrical equipment
		Industrial conglomerates	Industrial conglomerates
		Machinery	Construction and farm machinery and heavy trucks
			Industrial machinery
		Trading companies and distributors	Trading companies and distributors
	Commercial and professional services	**Commercial services and supplies**	Commercial printing
			Data processing services
			Diversified commercial and professional services
			Human resource and employment services
			Environmental and facilities services
			Office services and supplies
			Diversified support services
			Security and alarm services
		Professional services	Human resource and employment services
			Research and consulting services
	Transportation	**Air freight and logistics**	Air freight and logistics
		Airlines	Airlines
		Marine	Marine
		Road and rail	Railroads
			Trucking
		Transportation infrastructure	Airport services
			Highways and rail tracks
			Marine ports and services
Consumer discretionary	**Automobiles and components**	**Automobile components**	Auto parts and equipment
			Tires and rubber
		Automobiles	Automobile manufacturers
			Motorcycle manufacturers
	Consumer durables and apparel	**Household durables**	Consumer electronics
			Home furnishings
			Homebuilding
			Household appliances
			Housewares and specialties
		Leisure equipment and products	Leisure products
			Photographic products
		Textiles, apparel and luxury goods	Apparel, accessories and luxury goods
			Footwear
			Textiles
	Consumer services	**Hotels, restaurants and leisure**	Casinos and gaming
			Hotels, resorts and cruise lines
			Leisure facilities
			Restaurants
		Diversified consumer services	Education services
			Specialised consumer services
	Media	**Media**	Advertising
			Broadcasting
			Cable and satellite
			Movies and entertainment
			Publishing
	Retailing	**Distributors**	Distributors
		Internet and catalogue retail	Catalogue retail

Table 2.A2.1. **The Global Industry Classification Standard (GICS)** *(cont.)*

Sector	Industry sector	Industry group	Sub-industry
			Internet retail
		Multiline retail	Department stores
			General merchandise stores
		Specialty retail	Apparel retail
			Computer and electronics retail
			Home improvement retail
			Specialty stores
			Automotive retail
			Home furnishing retail
Consumer staples	**Food and staples retailing**	**Food and staples retailing**	Drug retail
			Food distributors
			Food retail
			Hypermarkets and super centres
	Food, beverage and tobacco	**Beverages**	Brewers
			Distillers and vintners
			Soft drinks
		Food products	Agricultural products
			Meat, poultry and fish
			Packaged foods and meats
		Tobacco	Tobacco
	Household and personal products	**Household products**	Household products
		Personal products	Personal products
Healthcare	**Healthcare equipment and services**	**Healthcare equipment and supplies**	Healthcare equipment
			Healthcare supplies
		Healthcare providers and services	Healthcare distributors
			Healthcare services
			Healthcare facilities
			Managed Healthcare
		Healthcare technology	Healthcare technology
	Pharmaceuticals and biotechnology	**Biotechnology**	Biotechnology
		Pharmaceuticals	Pharmaceuticals
		Life sciences tools and services	Life sciences tools and services
Information technology	**Software and services**	**Internet software and services**	Internet software and services
		IT services	IT consulting and other services
			Data processing and outsourced services
		Software	Application software
			Systems software
			Home entertainment software
	Technology hardware and equipment	**Communications equipment**	Communications equipment
			Networking equipment
			Telecommunications equipment
		Computers and peripherals	Computer hardware
			Computer storage and peripherals
		Electronic equipment and components	Electronic equipment and instruments
			Electronic components
			Electronic manufacturing services
			Technology distributors
		Office electronics	Office electronics
	Semiconductors and equipment	**Semiconductors and equipment**	Semiconductor equipment
			Semiconductors

Table 2.A2.1. **The Global Industry Classification Standard (GICS)** *(cont.)*

Sector	Industry sector	Industry group	Sub-industry
Telecommunication services	**Telecommunication services**	**Diversified telecommunication services**	Alternative carriers
			Integrated telecommunication services
		Wireless telecommunication services	Wireless telecommunication services
Utilities	**Utilities**	**Electric utilities**	Electric utilities
		Gas utilities	Gas utilities
		Multi-utilities	Multi-utilities
		Water utilities	Water utilities
		Independent power producers and energy traders	Independent power producers and energy traders

Source: OECD compilation, MSCI.

Chapter 3

Fiscal incentives for R&D and innovation in a diverse world

Public policy has an important role to play in promoting research and development (R&D) and the development, diffusion, and use of new knowledge and innovations. Fiscal incentives, including tax policies, should be directed at specific barriers, impediments or synergies to facilitate the desired level of investment in R&D and innovations. Without careful design, policies can have unintended consequences such as favouring incumbent firms, encouraging small firms to undertake less efficient activities, or creating arbitrage and rent-seeking activity. R&D tax policy needs to be considered in the context of the country's general tax policies, its broader innovation policy mix and its other R&D support policies. More R&D activity in one country does not necessarily result in an overall increase in global innovation if it is simply shifted from another country. More research is needed to determine the extent to which R&D fiscal incentives in one country increase overall R&D, the quality of that R&D, and its positive spillovers to other sectors of the economy and other countries.

The statistical data for Israel are supplied by and under the responsibility of the relevant Israeli authorities. The use of such data by the OECD is without prejudice to the status of the Golan Heights, East Jerusalem and Israeli settlements in the West Bank under the terms of international law.

Main findings

- Government support for business research and development (R&D) seeks to encourage firms to invest in knowledge that can result in innovations that transform markets and industries and result in benefits to society. Most often, support is provided to firms with the intention of correcting market failure such as difficulties in appropriating the returns to investment in R&D and difficulties in finding external finance, in particular for small or young firms.
- Fiscal incentives should be directed at specific barriers, impediments or synergies to promote research and development (R&D) among other innovation activities and facilitate innovation within each country and region. Public policy must recognise the heterogeneity of the markets and individual actors involved in developing and using innovations, as well as the heterogeneity of alternative fiscal incentives and their design.
- Tax policy is an increasingly important element of these incentives. The most widely used types of tax incentive include tax credits or favourable tax deductions for R&D expenditures, but other types are focused on income from certain R&D activities, on certain types of R&D financing, and are, in some cases, provided directly to researchers.
- Most countries providing R&D tax incentives focus the incentives on reducing the cost and encouraging increased expenditures on R&D. This can take the form of credits against income and/or payroll taxes for expenditures on wages and/or capital investments for R&D. It can also take the form of accelerated depreciation, allowing recovery of the investment faster than the underlying economic depreciation of the long-lived asset; or enhanced depreciation, where taxpayers can recover more than 100% of the cost of the R&D expenditures.
- An increasing number of countries have adopted, or are considering adopting, income-based tax incentives, often in addition to their expenditure-based incentives. These provide for lower tax rates on the future income from investments in R&D and increase the after-tax rate of return to those investments. The assets are highly mobile, however, allowing both the assets and future income from them to be located away from the activity that generated the assets and income. This is often in low-tax jurisdictions to reduce their corporate tax liabilities, which erodes tax revenues in the other countries where the R&D investments were actually made.
- To avoid harmful tax practices preferential tax regimes for research and development should be consistent with a "nexus" approach. This uses expenditure as a proxy for real activity and allows a taxpayer to benefit from the preferential regime only to the extent that the taxpayer itself incurred the qualifying expenditures that gave rise to the income generated by the research and development investment.

Introduction

Innovation is key to economic growth and productivity increases and will also play a role in helping to find solutions to many global challenges from climate change to ageing populations. Although not all firms that innovate carry out R&D, investment in R&D plays a major role in facilitating technology-based innovations that bring new and significantly improved products and processes to the market. The slowdown of productivity growth is currently a focus of many countries, however, this slowdown has not been uniform across countries, industries or firms. Chapter 2 in this Outlook highlights the importance of R&D for productivity growth in listed companies. The research finds that while innovation is high among global frontier firms, productivity growth is highly concentrated among some firms and industries, because innovation is not being sufficiently diffused or taken up by many other firms and industries (OECD, 2015d). There is significant heterogeneity across and within sectors with respect to the development and take-up of innovation.

Public policy must recognise the heterogeneity of the markets and individual actors involved in developing and using innovations. It must also recognise the heterogeneity of alternative fiscal incentives and their design.

This chapter discusses the rationales for government R&D incentives, alternative innovation fiscal policies, different innovation-focused tax incentives and general tax issues, and policy design considerations for R&D in a heterogeneous and fragmented world.

Rationales for government incentives for business R&D

Government support for business R&D seeks to encourage firms to invest in knowledge that can result in innovations that transform markets and industries and result in benefits to society. All industries rely extensively on fundamental science and ideas largely originating from or developed within the government sector itself or publicly-funded institutions, but additional support of a financial nature is also provided to private sector firms for a number of reasons. Most often, support is provided to firms with the intention of correcting market failure (OECD, 2015e), including:

- **Difficulties by firms to fully appropriate the returns to their investment.** Returns on investments in R&D are difficult to appropriate by firms as some of the resulting knowledge – non-rival and partially non-excludable in nature – will leak out or "spill over" to other firms, to the benefit of society. This leads firms to underinvest in innovation relative to what would be the socially optimal level.
- **Difficulties in finding external finance, in particular for small or young firms.** Innovation is a highly uncertain activity with large differences between the information available to inventors and that available to investors. This may imply that external capital for innovation will only be available at too high a cost or will not be available at all. This is especially the case for small start-up firms without collateral

Public support for business R&D is typically justified as a means of overcoming these market failures. In addition, countries may use support measures to attract the R&D activities, investments and jobs of multinational enterprises (MNEs) which typically account for a substantial share of R&D expenditure. For example, in some small open economies, such as Ireland, Belgium and Israel, more than 60% of business R&D is accounted for by affiliates of foreign companies (OECD, 2015e).

Alternative R&D and innovation policies

Where human capital is relatively abundant and infrastructure relatively well supplied, the focus often first shifts to resolving market and institutional failures, as noted above. However, for R&D and innovation policies to have the intended impact, attention also needs to be paid to some of the disadvantages that new firms and technologies may have relative to incumbents and existing technologies and policies that help overcome these. While there are many barriers and obstacles to innovation, and there are many reasons governments may wish to take action to encourage R&D and innovation, policy makers will always need to consider carefully whether they have a sufficient understanding of innovation in their economy and an understanding of the appropriate policy tools to take effective and efficient government action.This involves consideration of alternative policy actions where governments can best add value, and consideration of how governments can engage with other actors and encourage them to take action.

OECD analysis suggests that innovation thrives in an environment characterised by the following features (OECD, 2015e):

- A skilled workforce that has the knowledge and skills to generate new ideas and technologies, to bring them to the market, and to adapt to technological changes across society;
- A sound business environment that encourages investment in technology and in knowledge based capital (KBC) including R&D, that also enables innovative firms to experiment with new ideas, technologies and business models, and that helps them to grow, increase their market share and reach scale;
- A strong and efficient system for knowledge creation and diffusion that engages in the systematic pursuit of fundamental knowledge, and that diffuses that knowledge through society; and
- Policies that encourage firms to engage in innovation and entrepreneurial activity.

The latter may include targeted innovation policies to tackle a range of barriers to innovation. The appropriate policy mix might include tax incentives for investments in R&D; direct public support through grants, subsidies and innovation competitions; and policies to facilitate co-operation and networking, but also indirect incentives through public procurement and other so-called demand-side policies. As noted above, fiscal incentives must be part of a broader innovation-friendly environment and policies that are shaped by intellectual property protection, sound bankruptcy rules, STEM (science, technology, engineering and mathematics) training, etc. There are many non-tax policy tools available to governments, including public R&D by government, not-for profit and research sectors as well as support for public sector R&D through government grants, loans, guarantees and legal protection of intellectual property (IP) rights.

As Table 3.1 highlights, the market for innovation and R&D within which fiscal incentives operate is very complex and comprises a range of heterogeneous players and activities. R&D is one innovation activity and firms can engage in many non-R&D activities that can be part of innovation.[1] R&D comprises three types of activity (OECD, 2015b): basic research, applied research and experimental development. Companies may carry out R&D in-house and/or procure R&D services from other parties. They may also acquire from third parties the rights to use intellectual property (IP) arising from R&D (R&D assets) or other innovation activities carried out in the past by third parties on their own account. Some

Table 3.1. **Heterogeneity in fiscal incentives for innovation activities**

Sources of heterogeneity in the market (potential eligibility for incentives):

- Types of innovation: R&D (basic research, applied research, experimental development), non R&D activities (e.g. acquisition of other external knowledge, acquisition of machinery, equipment and other capital goods, training in support of the introduction of new products and processes).
- Types of R&D expenses: in-house R&D; procurement of R&D services; acquisition of rights to use IP (R&D assets).
- Types of R&D business models: internally developed combined with commercialisation; develop and sell; acquire R&D and commercialise.
- Types of firms: start-ups, incumbents, small and medium-sized enterprises; multinational enterprises.
- Types of financing: equity, debt, founder, angel investor, venture capital, private vs. public.
- Other economic and policy conditions in a country: bankruptcy laws, patent protection, STEM education, immigration laws.

Sources of heterogeneity in fiscal incentives:

- Types of fiscal incentives: grants, public procurement, loans, guarantees, tax.
- Types of tax incentives: general/targeted; input/output; volume-based/incremental, temporary/permanent.
- Targeted (complex, more subject to gaming) vs general (more likely to create windfalls).
- Type of tax: corporate income, personal income (including stock options), payroll, value added, property taxes.

Source: (OECD, 2015b).

firms will have business models that internally engage in R&D and also produce and distribute the resulting goods and services with the embedded KBC. Other firms will specialise in R&D, but then sell the resulting KBC to acquiring firms that will commercialise the products. The financing of innovation can also occur in a number of different ways. Equity and debt both play a role, with capital being provided by founders, angel investors and venture capitalists, as well as being raised with initial public offerings.

Large enterprises are disproportionately represented in some areas, notably patents, as a large share of patents is held by a small number of large MNEs. In 2012, the 250 leading R&D global corporations and their affiliates accounted for 70% of patents filed by the 2000 largest R&D performers at the largest five intellectual property offices worldwide. They also accounted for almost 80% of information and communications technology (ICT) related patents (OECD, 2015e).

There is also considerable heterogeneity within types of fiscal incentives. Fiscal incentives can include grants, public procurement, loans, guarantees as well as tax incentives (OECD, 2015e, Table 6.1). Tax incentives are provisions of the tax system that favour a particular type of activity relative to the general tax treatment of business activity. Within tax, multiple types of incentives are possible including up-front input incentives, such as tax credits and enhanced and accelerated tax depreciation allowances, as well as back-loaded output incentives, such as income-based IP or knowledge boxes and favourable capital gain tax rates. Incentives can be provided through relief to corporate income, personal income, payroll, consumption and property taxes. They can be targeted or general, temporary or permanent, volume-based or incremental. Various hybrids and combinations are possible.

As of 2013, approximately 6.9% of business R&D was directly funded (e.g. through R&D procurement and grants) by governments. R&D tax incentives accounted for the equivalent of an additional 5.2% of public funding of business R&D.[2] So tax incentives are at least 43% of fiscal support for business R&D. The level of tax incentives for business R&D increased in many countries between 2006 and 2013, although Mexico and New Zealand ended their tax incentives during that period (Figure 3.1). A number of countries such as Germany and Mexico do not provide dedicated R&D tax incentives. All OECD countries provide some form of direct financial support for R&D through grants or subsidised loans. For example, in Mexico, although there are no tax incentives for R&D, the National Council of Science and Technology (CONACYT) provides firms with grants and funding for these activities.

Figure 3.1. **Direct government funding and tax incentives for business R&D, 2013**

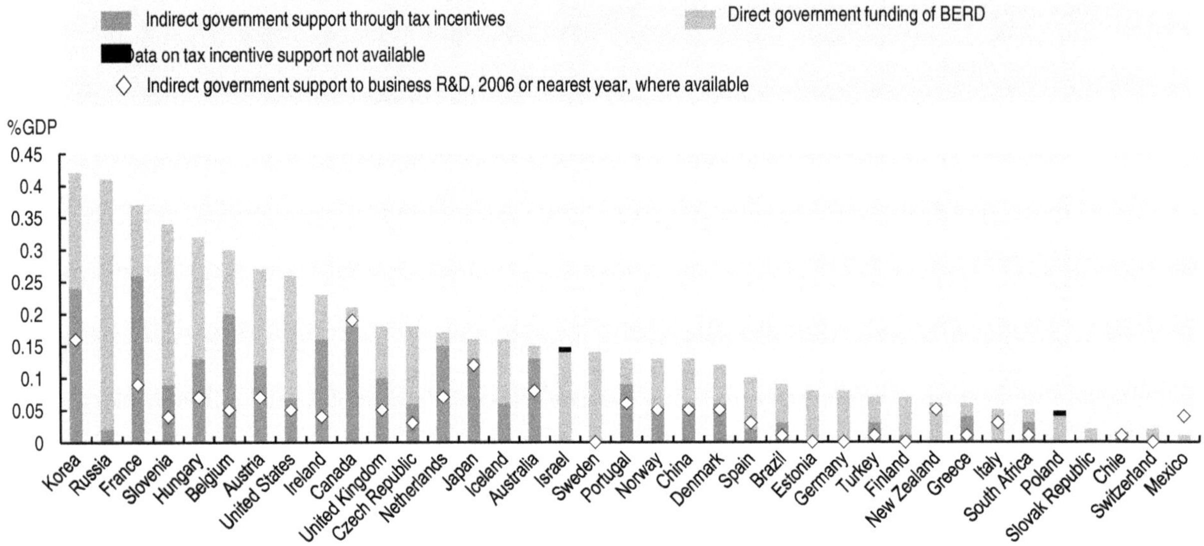

Note: All data are expressed in percent of GDP.
Source: OECD (2015d).

StatLink http://dx.doi.org/10.1787/888933362440

Overall, and leaving aside differences in design and implementation that can blur the dividing line between tax support and grants, there appears to be broad consensus that tax incentives are more suited in principle to encouraging R&D activities oriented towards the development of applications that have the potential to be brought to the market within a reasonable timeframe. In contrast, direct grant support is more suitable for supporting longer-term, high-risk research and for targeting specific areas that generate public goods (defence, environment, medical research, etc.) or that have particularly high potential for spillovers. Direct grant support may be designed to allow for an assessment of the quality of the underlying R&D activity being funded, whereas most tax incentives provide a general incentive for any activities falling within a defined category of eligible R&D activity.

How should R&D tax incentives be designed?

Fiscal incentives for business R&D are close substitutes for each other. Any direct government support or loan programme could be designed in principle as a tax incentive, or vice versa. Tax incentives are often chosen for particular design features which are characteristics of tax incentives but which generally are not characteristics of direct spending programmes. Two design features particularly favour tax incentives in many countries. First, tax incentives are often open-ended entitlements which do not typically require annual spending authorisation and are often unlimited in the amount of qualifying activity undertaken by the private company. Second, tax incentives reduce the scope for discretionary selection of individual firms or projects as they often do not have the pre-approval process or extensive reporting and audit requirements of most government funding programmes.[3] Qualified activity is defined in the statutory language and voluntary self-compliance with low levels of audit by tax authorities is generally the amount of oversight.

The term "tax expenditures" is used for government intervention programmes that are run through the tax system, but which could be administered through direct subsidies or loan programmes. Tax expenditures often include some disadvantages, in particular, limitations on the amount of the subsidies to the amount of pre-credit or pre-deduction tax liability of the company. Such tax liability limitations are generally designed to prevent fraudulent claims for the subsidy, given the typical low level of programmatic audits, and to reduce the fiscal cost of the generally open-ended entitlement programmes. Limitations to income tax liability can significantly reduce or eliminate the value of a R&D incentive for start-up companies, and thus favours larger incumbent companies that may have other sources of taxable income which can be offset by the R&D tax subsidy.

Countries can make tax subsidies more like direct subsidies. In some countries, tax credits are immediately refundable or can offset non-income taxes. In some countries, audits of R&D tax credits claimed are extensive and done by specialised teams. An increasing number of countries have put caps on the amount of the R&D tax credit that can be claimed, so it is not an open-ended entitlement programme, but which then eliminates the incentive at the margin for additional R&D activity.

General vs. targeted tax incentives

As noted above, OECD analysis suggests that innovation thrives in a sound business environment that fosters investment, risk-taking and experimentation, a skilled labour force, and protection of property rights. A country's tax system is an important part of a sound business environment. Predictable low tax rates with broad tax bases to minimise inefficiencies across types of activities provide all companies with higher after-tax rates of return on their investments. OECD analysis suggests that in countries that have experienced a large number of R&D tax policy reversals, the impact of R&D tax credits on private R&D expenditures is greatly diminished (Westmore, 2013).

A country's general tax rules can be an important attraction or deterrent to risk-taking innovators and their companies. One study found that tax rates matter to the location of inventors and their patent registrations. The tax rates that mattered were personal income tax rates of the inventors, and those who were employed by MNEs were more likely to take advantage of personal income tax differentials (Akcigit and Stantcheva, 2015). Favourable tax treatment of employee stock options can make them more attractive to employers than paying cash salaries, as they help to reduce cash out-flows (OECD, 2006). Labour taxes, particularly employer payroll taxes, can significantly increase the cost of doing business in a particular country. Tax loss limitation rules and choice of business entity (e.g. corporation vs. partnership) can affect the general business tax climate as well as the value of particular targeted R&D tax incentives.

As noted in Table 3.1, considerable heterogeneity exists in the design of R&D tax incentive provisions. Table 3.2 shows the main features of current R&D tax incentives across OECD and selected other countries. Thirty of the 34 OECD countries offer some type of R&D tax incentive. Only four OECD countries did not offer R&D tax incentives (expenditure or income-based) in 2015: Estonia, Finland, Germany and Mexico. Most countries have increased the total value of tax incentives relative to GDP between 2006 and 2013, as shown in Figure 3.1.

Twelve OECD countries offered more generous R&D tax incentives for SMEs. In the direct subsidy area, a notable trend among practitioners is a gradual move away from using firm size as a segmentation criterion, towards other differentiators, such as firm age or growth rate (OECD, 2015e, p. 147-148). Using firm age to determine subsidy eligibility could raise difficult issues to prevent aggressive tax planning, while using growth rates for subsidy eligibility would have similarities to incremental tax subsidies.

Table 3.2. **Main features of R&D tax incentives in selected OECD and other countries, 2015**

Design of the R&D tax incentive scheme	
Expenditure-based R&D tax incentives	
• Volume-based R&D tax credit	Australia, Austria, Belgium, Canada, Chile, Denmark, France, Hungary, Iceland, Ireland, New Zealand, Norway, United Kingdom
• Incremental R&D tax credit	United States (credit on fixed, indexed base and incremental for simplified credit)
• Hybrid system of volume and incremental credits	Italy, Japan, Korea, Portugal, Spain
• R&D tax deduction beyond 100% recovery	Belgium, Brazil, People's Republic of China, Czech Republic, Greece, Hungary, Netherlands, Poland, Russian Federation, Slovenia, Slovak Republic, South Africa, Turkey, United Kingdom
Tax relief on wage taxes or related contributions	Belgium, France, Netherlands, Hungary, Russian Federation, Spain, Sweden, Turkey
More generous R&D tax incentives for SMEs, young firms or start-ups	Australia, Belgium, Canada, France, Italy, Japan, Korea, Netherlands, Norway, Portugal, Spain, United Kingdom
Ceilings on amounts that can be claimed for specific incentives	Australia, Canada, Chile, Denmark, France, Hungary, Iceland, Italy, Japan, Korea, New Zealand, Norway, Portugal, Slovak Republic, Spain, Sweden, Turkey, United Kingdom, United States
Income-based R&D tax incentives[1]	Belgium, People's Republic of China, Colombia, France, Hungary, Ireland, Israel, Italy, Luxembourg, Netherlands, Portugal, Spain, Switzerland (Canton of Nidwalden), Turkey, United Kingdom
No R&D tax incentives	Estonia, Finland, Germany, Mexico

1. OECD (2015c).
Source: OECD Directorate for Science, Technology and Innovation.

Several key features are whether the incentive is linked to the current expenditure on R&D or on the future income of the R&D; whether the incentive is volume-based or incremental; whether the incentive is capped on the amount claimed or more generous for SMEs; and whether the incentive is corporate income tax-based or provided through other taxes, such as personal income or payroll taxes.[4]

Expenditure (input) vs. income (output) incentives

Most countries providing R&D tax incentives focus the incentives on reducing the cost and encouraging increased expenditures on R&D. This can take the form of credits against income and/or payroll taxes for expenditures on wages and/or capital investments for R&D. An increasing number of countries have adopted or are considering adopting income-based R&D tax incentives, often in addition to their expenditure-based R&D tax incentives.

Expenditure-based incentives can also take the form of accelerated or enhanced tax depreciation. Accelerated depreciation is when the recovery of the R&D investment is faster than the underlying economic depreciation of the long-lived asset for tax purposes. Most countries allow companies immediate deductions of employee compensation and capital purchases for R&D, even though the underlying R&D investment is expected to generate income over a number of future years. Accelerated tax depreciation is equivalent to an interest-free loan from the government to the taxpayer, which reduces the cost of the investment and the effective tax rate on the income generated from the investment. Ten OECD countries and several BRIICS countries provide enhanced depreciation, where taxpayers can recover more than 100% of the cost of the R&D expenditures. Enhanced tax depreciation is similar to an R&D tax credit. Enhanced depreciation of 200% of R&D investment (100% more than the actual cost) deducted immediately at a 25% tax rate is equivalent to a 25% expenditure-based tax credit.

The benefit of accelerated or enhanced depreciation can also vary by the heterogeneity of the economic depreciation of R&D investments. A recent study finds the pharmaceutical industry has the lowest R&D economic depreciation rate and longest useful life, which may reflect the fact that R&D resources in pharmaceuticals are more appropriable than in other industries due to effective patent protection and other entry barriers (Li, 2012). A similar accelerated tax depreciation rate provides greater benefit to longer-lived investments than shorter-lived investments.[5]

Income-based incentives via lower tax rates on the future income from R&D investments increases the after-tax rate of return to those investments, which can attempt to address the market failure from firms not fully appropriating the returns to their investment (spillovers). Just as tax and non-tax fiscal incentives are close substitutes, income-based and expenditure-based tax incentives can be designed to provide approximately the same level of tax incentive in present value terms. A 15% lower tax rate on future income for a firm earning a 30% pre-tax return on its R&D investment is the equivalent of a 31% expenditure-based tax credit (Modica and Neubig, 2016).

Income-based incentives, often referred to as patent, IP or knowledge boxes, have raised a number of questions about their effectiveness. Due to the highly mobile nature of IP assets, such as patents, copyrights, trademarks, and brands, the assets and future income from them can be located away from the activity that generated the assets and income. MNEs often locate their intangible assets in jurisdictions which offer relatively lower tax rates for the relevant income to reduce their corporate tax liabilities. The OECD study *Supporting Investment in Knowledge Capital, Growth and Innovation* (2013) shows that a 15% reduction in the corporate tax rate on R&D-created intangible assets transferred to an off-shoring holding company can result in -32% R&D tax wedge, compared to a +16% tax wedge if the R&D is used with a domestic license and production (OECD, 2013). A recent European Commission study found that a lower tax rate on patent income encouraged shifting of patent registrations and taxable income without a significant change in real economic activity (European Commission, 2015). However, patent box regimes that required a connection with local innovative activity found some positive impacts on real activity (number of resident inventors) within the country providing such qualified incentives.

An income-based incentive by its design gives an *ex post* reward only to successful innovators who already hold a monopoly right on their inventions. Experimentation is a risky activity, which naturally entails high rates of failure, so an income-based incentive may not benefit many firms undertaking R&D activity, and are more likely to benefit incumbent firms that have a diversified set of R&D activities to benefit from higher returns on their successful investments.

On the other hand, it is possible that an income-based incentive could increase the availability and terms of financing by investors given the higher after-tax returns of potentially successful R&D investments. The extent to which income-based incentives provide better financing of R&D that has not yet generated any income has not been analysed. Credit-constrained, innovative firms need funds to conduct their research as early as possible. Policies that provide funds with a lag, relative to research effort, might not be suitable for this group of firms and might make the playing field uneven (Andrews and Criscuolo, 2013). Income-based incentives are likely to have similar tax design issues as tax credits that are not immediately refundable.

An income-based incentive tied to a patent registration may push firms to focus on innovations that lead to outcomes susceptible to protection by patents, and may lead them to focus too much on applied research (Akcigit, Hanley and Serrano-Velarde, 2014) or products that are closer to market. In the long run this may have costs in terms of productivity enhancement. It also may push firms to seek patent protection for innovations for which they would not have sought patent protection in the absence of the tax incentive. Many innovation surveys report that several innovative firms choose not to seek any IP protection, but might if required to obtain a tax benefit.

Future empirical studies might find IP boxes have a positive effect on patent registrations, yet some of this increase could be due only to a re-labelling or reporting change, not a real increase in total R&D activity or the quality of the resulting R&D. Similarly, calculating the income eligible for R&D tax incentives is difficult, because identifying the stream of income generated by a single patent when multiple patents – often granted at different points in time – are used to produce a complex product (such as semiconductors). Measuring the income from a patent is already difficult because the income flows between related parties has to be imputed in the absence of an explicit price for the use of the IP with an unrelated third party. Measuring particular activity is also a problem with expenditure-based R&D incentive studies which may find higher R&D expenditures due to relabelling of activity or resulting from higher wages paid to R&D staff, not from an actual increase in the amount of R&D and innovation.

Volume-based vs. incremental incentives, ceilings and other limits

As countries have moved to strengthen their budget positions, they have aimed to improve the cost-effectiveness of their tax incentives. This has led to targeting tax incentives at firms and activities with the highest productivity-enhancing potential.

Countries vary in their use of volume-based R&D tax credits versus incremental-based tax credits. R&D tax incentives may apply to all qualified R&D expenditures (volume-based credits) or only to the additional amount of R&D expenditures above a certain base amount (incremental credits). The base amount usually takes the form of a rolling average of several prior year expenditures or a fixed base during a reference period which may be indexed to sales or inflation to stay relevant.

Using a volume-based approach has the advantage of being simple and predictable. Firms know they will get the credit on all eligible investments. From the government perspective, however, the volume-based approach is more costly as some of the support subsidises R&D that would have been performed without the incentive, and is likely to benefit mostly large firms in the absence of any ceilings.

An incremental R&D incentive seeks to minimise the amount of "subsidised" R&D that would have been undertaken even in the absence of support. However, the incremental approach also presents some undesirable features. Incremental incentives are more complex to design and use, as it increases transaction costs for firms and governments as well as uncertainty about the availability of future subsidies. Incremental incentives are possibly less effective in slow or no-growth economic environments when incremental incentives might be zero or negative. Heterogeneity across firms in their R&D investments year-over-year could exclude some firms from eligibility for an incremental incentive even though they would respond with more expenditure if the incentive were available. Finally, incremental incentives can elicit strategic behaviours to time R&D investment to maximise the tax benefits, thus distorting the temporal profile of the R&D investment.

Increasingly, countries are adopting hybrid systems that combine a volume and incremental tax credit. In order to manage the overall cost of R&D incentives and target the incentives to smaller firms, some countries apply upper ceilings or thresholds to eligible R&D expenditures or tax benefits. While they reduce the overall cost of the incentive, caps can eliminate the incentive effect of the incentive at the intensive margin (e.g. an additional dollar of R&D expenditure) among firms with particularly high levels of R&D. Aggregation rules can play an important role in minimising tax arbitrage in the case of ceilings and targeting, as some groups may be able to break down their R&D tax credit claims across separate enterprises to meet size, growth, or "young firm" eligibility rules.

Cash refunds, carry back/forward, claw backs, transferability

The value of tax incentives can be significantly reduced if the benefits are delayed or potentially lost due to lack of taxable income or tax liability. Due to concerns about open-ended tax entitlements and low levels of tax audits, most countries limit tax benefits to firms with positive taxable income or income (or other) tax liability. Some countries give immediate refunds of R&D tax credits, while others allow taxpayers to either carry tax credits or losses back against prior tax liability (and thus provide immediate refunds) or carry them forward against future tax liability.

Table 3.3 shows the effect of the immediate refundability of tax losses compared to loss carry forwards without an interest adjustment for two types of KBC investments, which can include R&D: one where the KBC is developed and then sold to a third-party producer and another where the KBC is internally developed and used in the production of goods. In both cases, the lack of immediate refundability increases both the marginal effective tax rate (for investment levels at the intensive margin) and the average effective tax rate (for location decisions). Table 3.3 also shows that expensing of investment favours companies that can both develop KBC and produce goods resulting from the KBC themselves, compared to companies that specialise in developing KBC but then sell to other companies that may be more efficient at producing goods embedded with the purchased KBC.

Table 3.3. **Average effective tax rates for different loss refundability treatment and different types of knowledge-based capital development**

Development of knowledge-based capital (KBC) scenarios	Marginal effective tax rate %	Average effective tax rate %
Internal development followed by sale of rights to other users		
Expensing with immediate refundability	0.0	25.0
Non-refundable with loss carry forward	21.8	29.1
Internal development followed by internal use for production and sale of the output		
Expensing with immediate refundability	0.0	22.5
Non-refundable with loss carry forward	11.9	23.4

Source: Modica and Neubig (2016). Statutory corporate tax rate in example is 25%.

Given the importance of cash-flow for new firms undertaking R&D investments, the delay of tax benefits until they become profitable and tax paying reduces the effectiveness of the incentive.[6] Many R&D investments made by firms that are not successful will not receive any direct tax benefit. The ability to carry forward tax credits and tax losses is important, but delayed receipt of the credits or losses reduces their value compared to an immediate refund.

Some countries are evaluating whether tax incentives achieve the stated objectives of the programme. In the case of some discretionary tax incentives, including R&D incentives, if the company does not achieve the projected number of jobs or investment, the government may "claw back" or reclaim the tax incentives. There is an issue of the potential transferability of tax incentives to other companies if the R&D investing company is not able to benefit from the credit or deduction. In many incumbent firms, tax benefits can be transferred to related companies within a consolidated group who can benefit from the incentive. Tax policy design could allow companies to sell the tax incentive, typically at less than full value, to an unrelated company that can immediately use the benefit. This is not an efficient means of providing a government incentive, but has been one approach used to get around the tax incentive design limitation of lack of immediate refundability due to the open-ended low-enforcement entitlement approach of many tax incentives.

Types of research activity or knowledge-based capital

OECD research finds that direct subsidies are more targeted towards long-term research, while R&D tax schemes are more likely to encourage short-term applied research and boost incremental innovation rather than contribute to radical breakthroughs (OECD, 2015e). Recent OECD analysis suggests that direct support measures – e.g. contracts, grants, awards for mission-oriented R&D or support for networks – may be more effective in stimulating R&D than previously thought for young firms that lack the upfront funds to start an innovation project (Westmore, 2013). Income-based tax incentives may push firms to focus on development to the detriment of research, since the incentive is only earned if the inventions earn immediate and attributable income, rather than reducing the cost of the investment (Akcigit, Hanley, and Serrano-Velarde, 2014).

The type of income and IP currently qualifying for tax relief through income-based incentives varies greatly. Royalties represent the most common category of income to qualify for tax relief, followed by capital gains and production income. Different categories of IP qualify. Patents feature as the most prominent, but a majority of countries allow for additional categories of IP, such as trademarks, designs and software copyrights. Countries also vary in the extent to which they allow for a preferential tax treatment of IP which is self-developed, existing or acquired.

Recent research finds that while innovation is high among frontier firms, productivity growth is highly concentrated among some firms and industries, because innovation is not being diffused or taken up by many other firms and industries (OECD, 2015d). There is significant heterogeneity across and within sectors with respect to both the development of innovation and the take-up of innovation, as described in Chapter 2 in this Outlook. General tax policies encouraging economic growth and labour mobility should be considered in addition to R&D incentives to ensure that innovations are diffused and taken up by non-innovative companies.

Other tax incentives for R&D

The tax incentives discussed above generally apply to business entities and income taxation. A number of countries have R&D tax incentives that provide tax benefits to other stakeholders and using other taxes (OECD, 2015c). Some examples include an exemption on payroll withholding taxes for qualified R&D workers; personal wage tax reduction for foreign researchers and key staff; wealth tax exemption for business angels; lower tax rates on capital gains for qualified R&D investments; and favourable tax treatment of employee stock options for R&D researchers and managers. Tax relief from consumption taxes, land and property taxes are also provided. Some of these incentives are a large part of the total

R&D incentives in some countries, e.g. Belgium and the Netherlands. An advantage of these other tax incentives is they support R&D independent of whether the firm is profitable or loss-making.

Base erosion and profit shifting concerns (spillovers)

Fiscal incentives for R&D investments are intended to create positive spillovers which will diffuse the benefits widely, enhancing consumer welfare and productivity. However, by attracting jobs and investments of MNEs to the country offering incentives, these incentives may prove harmful to trading partners who face the loss of associated fiscal revenues. It is important that the design of these incentives avoids harmful tax practices.

Activities, such as financial and other service activities, including the provision of intangibles generated by R&D, are geographically lmobile and very easy to shift from one country to another. Globalisation and technological innovation have further enhanced that mobility. The OECD has worked since 1998 in this area to secure the integrity of tax systems by addressing the issues raised by regimes that apply to mobile activities and that unfairly erode the tax bases of other countries, and potentially distort the location of capital and services. The work on harmful tax practices is not intended to promote harmonisation of tax structures or to dictate an appropriate level of tax rates. The work is about reducing the distortionary influence of taxation on the location of mobile activities, thereby encouraging an environment in which free and fair tax competition can tax place. This is essential in moving towards a "level playing field" and a continued expansion of global economic growth (OECD, 2015a).

The OECD/G20 Base Erosion and Profit Shifting (BEPS) Project addressed the issue of the separation of taxable profits with the substantial activities that generate them in the context of the Forum on Harmful Tax Practices. Countries in the Project agreed that a substantial activity requirement used to assess preferential tax regimes should be strengthened and a consensus was reached on a "nexus approach." This approach was developed in the context of IP regimes, and it allows a taxpayer to benefit from an IP regime only to the extent that the taxpayer itself incurred qualifying R&D expenditures that gave rise to the IP income (OECD, 2015a).

The nexus approach uses expenditure as a proxy for activity and builds on the principle that, because IP regimes are designed to encourage R&D activities and to foster growth and employment, a substantial activity requirement should ensure that taxpayers benefiting from these regimes did in fact engage in such activities and did incur actual expenditures on these activities. Future IP and Knowledge Boxes will be less susceptible to taxable income shifting and eroding the tax bases of other countries, but there are still many other important design features that countries need to consider before embracing them as the policy instrument of first choice.

In addition, the BEPS Project recognises that transparency is important and that tax rulings that could give rise to BEPS concerns should have compulsory spontaneous exchange of information.

Sixteen IP regimes were identified in 2015 as potentially harmful tax practices, in that all were considered inconsistent either in whole or in part, with the OECD/G20 BEPS Action 5 nexus approach. They and future such IP regimes will be subject to an ongoing monitoring and review mechanism. New entrants will not be permitted in any existing IP regime that is inconsistent with the nexus approach after 30 June 2016. If a new regime consistent with the nexus approach takes effect before 30 June 2016, no new entrants will be permitted in the existing IP regime after the new IP regime has taken effect. For purposes of the grandfathering, "new entrants" include both new taxpayers not previously benefiting from the regime and new IP assets owned by taxpayers already benefiting from the regime. Taxpayers benefiting from an existing regime may keep such entitlement until an abolition date, which can be no later than 30 June 2021. After that date, no more benefits stemming from old regimes not meeting the nexus requirement may be given to taxpayers.

Special IP regimes with nexus requirement can provide significantly reduced tax rates on income from R&D investments, but whether such income-based incentives are efficient and effective compared to alternative fiscal incentives requires further investigation. As noted above, income-based incentives only directly reward successful innovators, and thus are more likely to benefit incumbent firms rather than start-ups that need funds to conduct their research. Income-based incentives may push firms to focus on more applied research closer to commercialisation, and encourage firms to seek patent or other legal protection for their innovations. Income-based incentives are also more susceptible to tax avoidance than expenditure-based incentives, since measuring income attributable to a specific patent when the company has multiple patents and royalty payments with related parties is complex and requires significant tax administration enforcement.

Conclusions

Policy makers are increasingly recognising that, for efficient and effective incentives, the heterogeneity and fragmentation of not only different types of businesses, but different types of economic activity and alternative policies, need to be considered. What works for one country may be inappropriate for another country. What is a strong inducement for one type of business is detrimental for another. What achieves one objective may have unintended consequences or be difficult to administer.

Tax policy research is increasingly being done with firm-level data to reflect differences in types of firms and types of businesses. Tax rate reductions or tax credits that would appear to be a strong incentive for more R&D investment may not be beneficial to start-up companies that are credit-constrained. Accelerated tax depreciation may help profitable private companies with their cash-flow, but often are not viewed favourably by public companies since accelerated tax depreciation does not change public companies' reported profits or effective tax rates (Neubig, 2006, Edgerton (2010) and Zwick (2016). Tax incentives focused on businesses may be more beneficial to incumbents and multinational companies focused on R&D commercialisation, while grants and loans to individual inventors and small businesses may result in more innovative R&D breakthroughs.

Certainty and predictability of tax incentives may be more important than the reduction in tax liability for companies that are already taking significant risks in their R&D development and business. Thus, R&D fiscal incentives need to be considered as part of a country's total tax system, total innovation strategy, and overall economic and investment environment. More research is needed on the different fiscal incentives to identify the fiscal and economic conditions that will provide the biggest improvement in productivity and well-being from governments' significant investments in R&D given the significant heterogeneity of businesses and different type of R&D investments.

Given the heterogeneity of innovation across markets and firms, combined with the heterogeneity of countries' innovation policies, including innovation-specific tax incentives and general tax rules, further analysis at the firm level, across countries and across time can provide new and valuable insights. In order to address questions, such as which support design features contribute to higher levels of R&D performance and innovation-driven economic growth, the OECD has launched a new project that explores the variation in public support and business performance within and across countries, taking account of the wide heterogeneity in eligibility for support. The project is based on the analysis of micro-data through which the OECD collaborates with national experts with access to R&D and public support micro-data.[7] This entails undertaking a co-ordinated statistical analysis of the utilisation and impact of policy design features and their interaction with direct forms of public R&D funding.

Notes

1. The Oslo Manual distinguishes product, process, marketing and organisational innovations.
2. The amount of tax incentives only includes R&D tax credits and enhanced depreciation allowances. Other forms of tax incentives, such as accelerated depreciation, reduced tax rates on income derived from R&D activities, and personal income tax incentives for R&D investment, such as angel financing tax preferences, are not included in the total.
3. South Africa moved from a retrospective submission process to a pre-approval procedure for investments to qualify for enhanced (150%) depreciation. The Department of Science and Technology (DST) administers the programme, and companies must now apply to the DST for approval of qualifying R&D activities. Republic of South Africa DST (2014).
4. Some countries' tax incentives provide additional support to recipients that collaborate with universities or other publicly-funded research bodies.
5. Modica and Neubig (2016). It should be noted that the OECD B-Index does not measure the value of accelerated depreciation.
6. Caps on loss offsets could be restricted above a monetary threshold, thereby not limiting smaller firms.
7. For example, the measurement of R&D tax incentives: *www.oecd.org/sti/rd-tax-stats.htm*.

References

Akcigit, U., S. Baslandze and S. Stantcheva (2015), "Taxation and the International Mobility of Inventors", *National Bureau of Economic Research Working* Paper 21024.

Akcigit, Hanley and Serrano-Velarde, (2014), "Back to basics: Basic research spillovers, innovation and growth", *NBER Working Paper Series*, No. 19473.

Andrews, D. and C. Criscuolo (2013), "Knowledge-Based Capital, Innovation and Resource Allocation: A Going for Growth Report", *OECD Economic Policy Papers*, No. 4, OECD Publishing, Paris, *http://dx.doi.org/10.1787/5k46bh92lr35-en*.

Andrews, D., C. Criscuolo and P.N. Gal (2015), "Frontier Firms, Technology Diffusion and Public Policy: Micro Evidence from OECD Countries", *OECD Productivity Working Papers*, No. 2, OECD Publishing, Paris, *http://dx.doi.org/10.1787/5jrql2q2jj7b-en*.

Edgerton, J., "Investment incentives and corporate tax asymmetries", *Journal of Public Economics* 94.11 (2010): 936-952.

European Commission (2015), "Patent boxes design, patents location and local R&D", *IPTS Working Papers on Corporate R&D and Innovation*, No. 6/2015.

Li, W. (2012), "Depreciation of Business R&D Capital", Bureau of Economic Analysis/National Science Foundation R&D Satellite Account Paper, October, *www.bea.gov/national/pdf/WendyLiDepreciation BusinessR&DCapital20130314BEAwebversion.pdf*.

Modica, A. and T. Neubig (2016), "Taxation of Knowledge-Based Capital: Non-R&D Investments, Average Effective Tax Rates, Internal Vs. External KBC Development and Tax Limitations", *OECD Taxation Working Papers*, No. 24, OECD Publishing, Paris, *http://dx.doi.org/10.1787/5jm2f6sfz244-en*.

Neubig, T. 2006, "Where's the applause? Why most corporations prefer a lower tax rate", *Tax Notes*, April 24: 483-486.

OECD (2006), *The Taxation of Employee Stock Options*, OECD Tax Policy Studies, No. 11, OECD Publishing, Paris, *http://dx.doi.org/10.1787/9789264012493-en*.

OECD (2013), *Supporting Investment in Knowledge Capital, Growth and Innovation*, OECD Publishing, Paris, *http://dx.doi.org/10.1787/9789264193307-en*.

OECD (2015a), *Countering Harmful Tax Practices More Effectively, Taking into Account Transparency and Substance, Action 5 – 2015 Final Report*, OECD/G20 Base Erosion and Profit Shifting Project, OECD Publishing, Paris, *http://dx.doi.org/10.1787/978926241190-en*.

OECD (2015b), *Frascati Manual 2015 – Guidelines for Collecting and Reporting Data on Research and Experimental Development*, OECD Publishing, Paris, *http://dx.doi.org/10.1787/9789264239012-en*.

OECD (2015c), *OECD Science, Technology and Industry Scoreboard 2015: Innovation for growth and society*, OECD Publishing, Paris, *http://dx.doi.org/10.1787/sti_scoreboard-2015-en*.

OECD (2015d), *The Future of Productivity*, OECD Publishing, Paris, *http://dx.doi.org/10.1787/9789264248533-en*.

OECD (2015e), *The Innovation Imperative: Contributing to Productivity, Growth and Well-Being*, OECD Publishing, Paris, *http://dx.doi.org/10.1787/9789264239814-en*.

Republic of South Africa, Department of Science and Technology (2014), Performance of the Research and Development Tax incentive Programme Report to Parliament 2013/14, *www.dst.gov.za/index.php/services/41-rad-tax-incentives-programme/1288-reports-to-parliament-20132014*.

Westmore, B. (2013), "R&D, Patenting and Growth: The Role of Public Policy", *OECD Economics Department Working Papers*, No. 1047, OECD Publishing, Paris, *http://dx.doi.org/10.1787/5k46h2rfb4f3-en*.

Zwick, E. and J. Mahon, *Tax Policy and Heterogeneous Investment Behavior*, No. w21876, National Bureau of Economic Research, 2016.

OECD Business and Finance Outlook 2016

Chapter 4

Changing business models of stock exchanges and stock market fragmentation

This chapter provides an overview of structural changes in the stock exchange industry. It provides data on mergers and acquisitions as well as the changes in the aggregate revenue structure of major stock exchanges. It describes the fragmentation of the stock market resulting from an increase in stock exchange-like trading venues, such as alternative trading systems (ATSs) and multilateral trading facilities (MTFs), and a split between dark (non-displayed) and lit (displayed) trading. Based on firm-level data, statistics are provided for the relative distribution of stock trading across different trading venues as well as for different trading characteristics, such as order size, company focus and the total volumes of dark and lit trading. The chapter ends with an overview of recent regulatory initiatives aimed at maintaining market fairness and a level playing field among investors.

Main findings

- Regulatory reforms and developments in information and communication technology have increased competition between different types of stock trading venues. The result is fragmentation in two dimensions. First, we find extensive fragmentation of trading between stock exchanges and off-exchange venues, such as alternative trading systems (ATSs) and multilateral trading facilities (MTFs). Second, we also find an increased fragmentation between dark (non-displayed) trading and lit (displayed) trading.
- In 2015, two thirds of all stock trading in the United States took place on 11 different exchanges and the remaining 33% on numerous off-exchange venues. Of all trading, 42% was in the form of dark trading, of which about one-fifth was carried out on exchanges. In the European countries, around 50% of all trading takes place on exchanges and the rest on off-exchange venues. The amount of dark trading in Europe varies across countries from 35% to 48% of all trading.
- Off-exchange trading and dark trading have often been seen as a way for investors to reduce the market impact that could occur if they place large orders on a stock exchange. However, our analysis of trading data for the United States indicates that average order sizes do not differ significantly between off-exchange venues and traditional exchanges.
- Fragmentation does not seem to have affected the distribution of trading in large and small company stocks. Moreover, the distribution of trading in large and small company stocks is fairly similar in countries with fragmented trading venues and countries where trading is concentrated. Since 2000, trading in the 10% largest companies has accounted for 70-90% of all trading, both in the United States and Japan.
- The main concerns with respect to increased off-exchange and dark trading are the quality of the price discovery process, the fairness of markets, and the level playing field among investors. Together with recent enforcement actions against some dark pools, this has opened up a discussion about the rationale for existing differences in regulatory regimes between trading venues that seem to serve similar functions.
- Looking ahead, it is likely that regulatory initiatives in both Europe and the United States will come to focus on regulatory convergence between exchanges and off-exchange venues. It remains to be seen what the effects will be in terms of stock market fragmentation.

Introduction

From a company's perspective, there are two characteristics that make equity capital different from other forms of capital that the company can use. First, providers of equity capital (the shareholders) are not guaranteed any fixed interest rate or any given rate of return on the money that they invest. Second, once the equity capital is provided to the company, shareholders cannot withdraw their individual stakes. These characteristics mean that equity capital is crucial to, and particularly well suited for, long-term corporate investments that have an uncertain outcome, such as research, innovation and the development of new technologies.

Based on firm-level data, Chapter 2 also demonstrated that greater equity financing in relation to debt is essential to promote the long-term focus that is needed for productivity growth. It showed that a higher debt-to-capital ratio was negatively correlated with productivity growth. A recent OECD report (Cournède et al., 2015) addressed the use of equity at an aggregate level, highlighting the role of equity for overall economic growth. The report noted that while an increase in outstanding bank credit was associated with a reduction in long-term growth across OECD countries, further expansion of equity financing was likely to promote economic growth.

There are a number of different sources of equity capital, including the founder's initial equity capital and the retained earnings that are re-invested in the company rather than taken out in the form of dividends. Importantly, a company may also raise equity in the capital market. And since 2000, companies around the world have used public stock markets to raise a total of USD 11 trillion in equity.

During this period the stock exchange industry has experienced profound structural changes. Most traditional stock exchanges have either been acquired by another entity or become subsidiaries of an upstream parent company. The ultimate parent company of an exchange may in turn be a public company with its shares listed and traded on one or more of its own stock exchanges. As part of this transformation many of the national stock exchanges today form part of an international group structure.

At the same time, public equity markets have also been characterised by fragmentation along two lines. First, there has been a fragmentation of trading between stock exchanges (on-exchange trading) and other trading venues (off-exchange trading). Second, there has been a fragmentation between lit (displayed) and dark (non-displayed) trading. Among the driving forces behind these fragmentation trends are advancements in information and communication technology, supported by regulatory reforms aiming to promote competition between different trading venues.

This chapter describes the features and functioning of this new stock market ecosystem. It also discusses how developments may have influenced access to equity capital for smaller growth companies and concerns that have been raised with respect to market fairness and a level playing field among equity investors.

The changing landscape of the stock exchange industry

In advanced economies, stock exchanges were traditionally established as member-owned organisations or government institutions. Since the mid-1990s, however, most stock exchanges have been transformed into privately owned for-profit corporations. Today, all major stock exchange operators in advanced economies have their shares listed and traded on their exchanges, while the mutual form based on brokers' membership has almost disappeared.

In emerging markets, stock exchanges were often established in the form of state-owned corporations and their transformation into listed corporations has been more gradual. While the stock exchanges in Brazil and Mexico are now listed companies, those in Turkey and Saudi Arabia are still run as state-owned enterprises. Furthermore, the largest emerging market stock exchanges, which are in the People's Republic of China, operate as semi-public institutions and are membership institutions directly governed by the China Securities Regulatory Commission (CSRC).

During this transformation, there have been a large number of mergers and acquisitions (M&A) in the stock exchange industry, involving companies from sectors such as electronic trading platforms, financial information providers, financial index providers, data management and asset management. Figure 4.1 shows the number of M&A transactions in the stock exchange industry between 2000 and 2014. The figure covers a total of 169 buy-side deals and mergers involving publicly listed stock exchange operators. In 26 of these transactions, a stock exchange acquired an equity stake in another stock exchange or stock exchange group. In 18 cases, the stock exchange acquired a 100% or majority stake and in eight cases, a minority stake. There were an additional 19 transactions where stock exchanges acquired an exchange that was trading securities and derivatives other than stocks. After 2005, a significant number of buy-side deals, with respect to related businesses such as information technology and post trade services, can be observed.

Figure 4.1. **Mergers and acquisitions in the stock exchange industry**

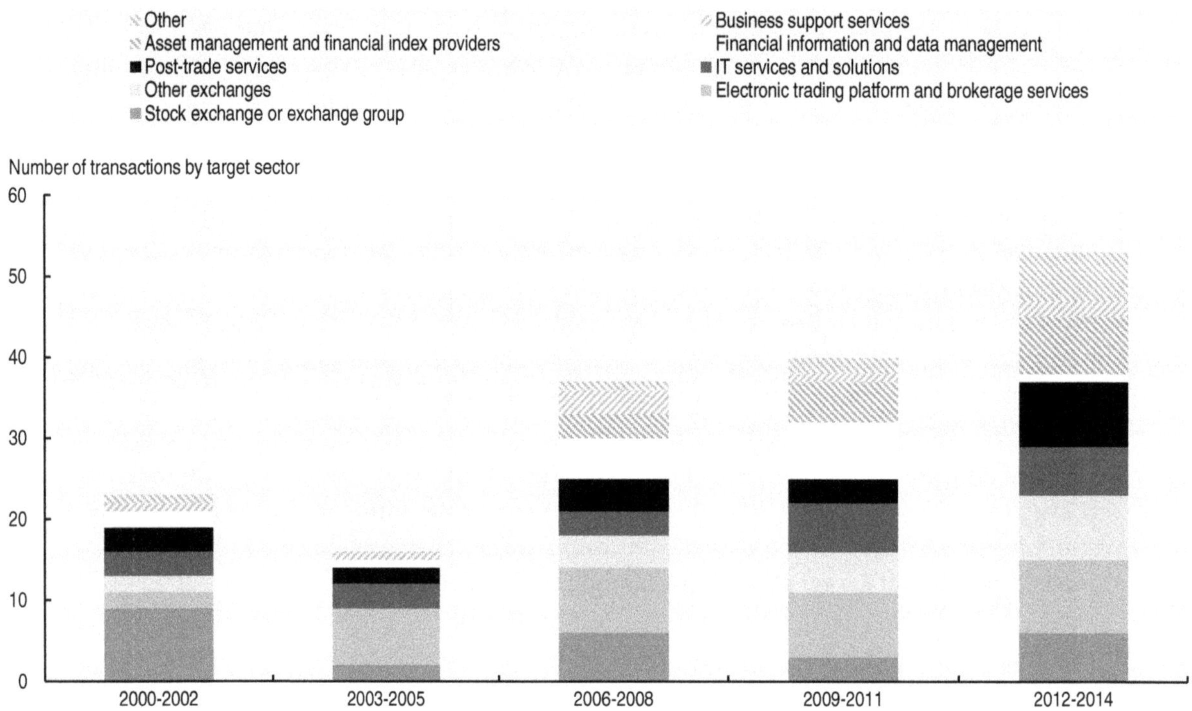

Note: Based on data from 16 stock exchanges.
Source: Factset, OECD calculations.

StatLink http://dx.doi.org/10.1787/888933362454

The changes in the ownership structure of stock exchanges, as well as the structural changes that followed from M&A activities have been accompanied by a shift in the revenue structure of stock exchanges. Figure 4.2 compares in some detail the revenue structure of listed stock exchanges in 2004 and 2014. The share of revenues from listing new companies and issuer services, which consists of new listing fees – including from exchange-traded funds (ETFs) – and fees paid by existing listed companies dropped from 14% in 2004 to 8% in 2014. During the same period the share of revenues from derivatives trading and over-the-counter (OTC) markets increased by almost half and represented 22% of total revenues in 2014. This makes income from trading (cash, capital markets, derivatives and OTC) the largest source of revenue with a total share of 48% in 2014.

Figure 4.2. **Revenue structure of stock exchanges**

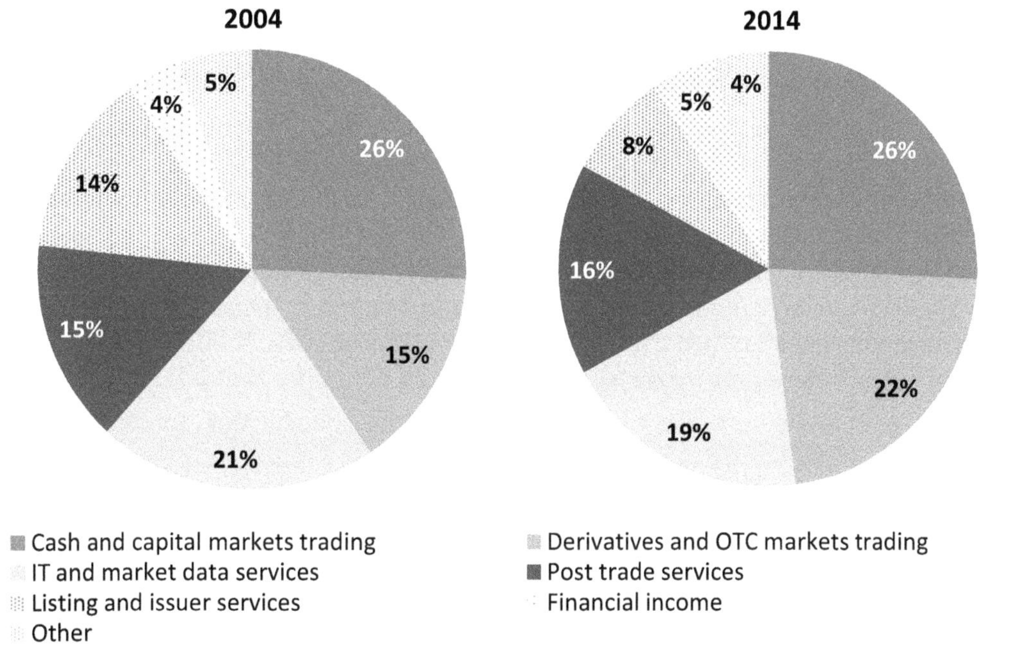

Note: Aggregated revenue data from 18 stock exchanges.

Source: Thomson Reuters, stock exchanges' websites and annual reports.

StatLink http://dx.doi.org/10.1787/888933362462

Fragmentation of public equity markets

Traditionally, trading a specific stock in a single venue generated economies of scale and network externalities that made stock exchanges considered as natural monopolies sustained by regulatory advantages (Kay, 2006). However, technological advances have come to challenge that; notably, communication technology that makes the geographical location of a trading venue less important and information technologies that have drastically decreased costs and time required for processing and disseminating large amounts of information, such as orders and quotes.

Today, trading is fragmented in two dimensions: 1) between stock exchanges (on-exchange) and a large number of other trading venues (off-exchange); and, 2) between transactions where investors have access to pre-trade information about buying and selling interests (lit or displayed trading) and transactions where pre-trade information is not made available (non-displayed trading, often referred to as dark trading).

In most advanced economies, trading in a company's shares now takes place in many different venues in addition to the stock exchange where the company's shares are actually listed. Most important among these "off-exchange" venues are alternative trading systems (ATSs) in the United States and multilateral trading facilities (MTFs) in Europe, which match buyers and sellers for a transaction. ATSs are not regulated like national securities exchanges. They must register as broker-dealers and comply with Regulation ATS. Unlike national securities exchanges, ATSs are not required to publicly disclose their trading services, operations or fees. MTFs are regulated as investment services under the EU regulatory framework.

In addition to exchanges and off-exchange trading venues such as ATSs and MTFs, trading can also be executed in a firm's internal trading system (e.g. broker, dealer or investment bank). When a firm "internalises" a client's order in this way, it generally matches the order with its own inventory of securities. This means that the client's order is not routed to an exchange or an off-exchange trading venue. Instead, it is executed on a bilateral basis within the internal trading system of the firm and against its own portfolio.

Taking advantage of advancements in information and communication technology has been facilitated by regulatory changes. For example, the EU's Markets in Financial Instruments Directive (MiFID 1), which was adopted in 2007, abolished the "concentration rule" that allowed EU member countries to require investment firms to route equity orders only to stock exchanges, in particular to the company's listing exchange. Together with the recognition of the MTFs and systematic internalisers as trading venues, the abolition of the concentration rule amplified competition between exchanges and off-exchange trading venues in European equity markets.

Initiatives to the same effect have been taken in the United States. The US Regulation National Market System (Regulation NMS) adopted in 2005 is a collection of existing and new rules issued by the US Securities and Exchange Commission (US SEC). A new key rule was the "Order Protection Rule" which requires trading centres to enforce policies and procedures that prevent the execution of trades at prices inferior to protected quotations displayed by other trading centres. The objective is to ensure that investors receive an execution price equivalent to the best price available in all trading venues. A second change was the "Access Rule" which was aimed at ensuring a level playing field among trading venues by improving access to quotes in different trading venues. The third major change was to amend the market data rules to further promote market data availability and to allocate market data revenues to those Self-Regulatory Organisations[1] that produce the most useful data for investors.

One of the key objectives of the US SEC's new rules in Regulation NMS was to promote competition among trading venues. First, Regulation NMS assured new or smaller trading venues that if they displayed the best prices, they would attract order flows since larger, dominant venues, according to the Order Protection Rule are not allowed to ignore their quotations.[2] Second, Regulation NMS provided new or smaller trading venues with access to displayed quotations of dominant venues as required in the Access Rule (US SEC, 2005).

As mentioned above, the fragmentation of trading into multiple venues has been accompanied by an increase in dark trading in the last decade. The difference between dark and lit trading lies in the transparency of trade information. The information can be transparent either pre-trade, which gives investors access to information about buying and selling interest before trading, or post-trade, which means that trade information is disseminated to the public after the execution of the trade. In both the United States and Europe, post-trade disclosure is required for all trades, including trades that are executed on off-exchange platforms and internal trading systems of firms. Therefore, the distinctive character of dark trading is that there is no pre-trade transparency with respect to buyer and seller interests.

While dark trading is often associated with off-exchange trading, the picture is not that clear-cut. In fact, there are off-exchange venues that can carry out lit trading and there are regulated exchanges that execute a significant amount of dark trading based on so-called hidden orders. For example, one type of ATS, an Electronic Communication Network (ECN) in the United States, is organised as a publicly displayed limit order book that is fully electronic. An ECN automatically and anonymously matches and executes orders, avoiding the need for a third party to be involved in the transaction.

Equity market structure in the United States

Stock trading in the United States is fragmented into a number of different venues that fall into three main categories: 1) 12 national securities exchanges; 2) 44 ATSs,[3] including off-exchange visible trading venues (ECNs) and dark pools; and 3) various OTC systems, including internal trading systems of firms. It is worth noting that trading in off-exchange venues is not a new phenomenon. Already in 1990, 17% of the volume traded in shares that were listed on the New York Stock Exchange (NYSE) took place in venues other than NYSE itself.[4] This share remained stable until 2005 when it started to successively increase. Figure 4.3, shows that in 2015 only 33% of the trade in NYSE-listed shares actually took place on the three NYSE Group exchanges. The remaining two thirds of all trades were carried out in other venues. Similarly, the three NASDAQ exchanges' share of the total trading in NASDAQ Stock Market listed firms was just 31% in 2015.

Out of the 18 national securities exchanges registered with the US SEC at the end of 2015, 12 exchanges traded equity securities in the United States. However, 10 of these 12 exchanges belong to one of three exchange groups (Intercontinental Exchange/New York Stock Exchange [ICE/NYSE], NASDAQ and Bats Global Markets [BATS]).[5] Figure 4.3 shows how the trading volume in companies that are listed on NYSE and NASDAQ is distributed among these three exchange groups and the only independent securities exchange, the Chicago Stock Exchange (CHX). CHX share of trading volume was less than 1% in both NYSE and NASDAQ-listed shares.

Figure 4.3. **Market shares in the trading of NYSE and NASDAQ-listed shares among trading venues in the United States, 2015**

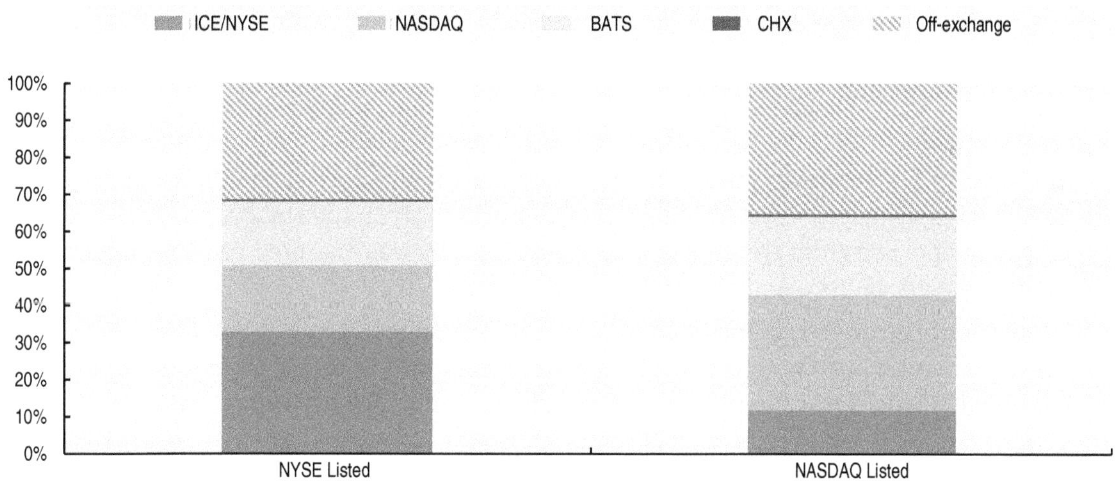

Note: Off-exchange volume includes ATS, internal trading systems of firms and other OTC trading that are reported to the FINRA. This is primarily done through the two Trade Reporting Facilities (TRFs) operated by the two exchanges or through the Alternative Display Facility (ADF) directly operated by FINRA.
Source: BATS Global Markets.

StatLink http://dx.doi.org/10.1787/888933362472

Figure 4.3 also shows the off-exchange trading in shares listed on NYSE and NASDAQ. In 2015, 31% of all trading in NYSE-listed and 35% of all trading in NASDAQ-listed shares took place in off-exchange venues.

In January 2014, the US SEC approved a rule that requires all broker-dealers that operate an ATS to report the aggregate weekly trading information for each security to the Financial Industry Regulatory Authority (FINRA). FINRA has made this information available since July 2014.

As of 1 December 2015, there were 85 trading venues operating as ATSs.[6] Of these, 44 venues traded NMS stocks.[7] Figure 4.4 displays the distribution of traded volume among the different ATS venues based on data retrieved from FINRA. As seen in Figure 4.4, ATS trading is quite concentrated to the five largest venues that trade NMS stocks, which account for about half of the total ATS trading volume for both NASDAQ-listed and NYSE-listed stocks. The two largest ATSs by trade share, Credit Suisse's CrossFinder and UBS, account for about 25% of the total.

Figure 4.4. **Market shares in total alternative trading system volume in NYSE and NASDAQ-listed shares, 2015**

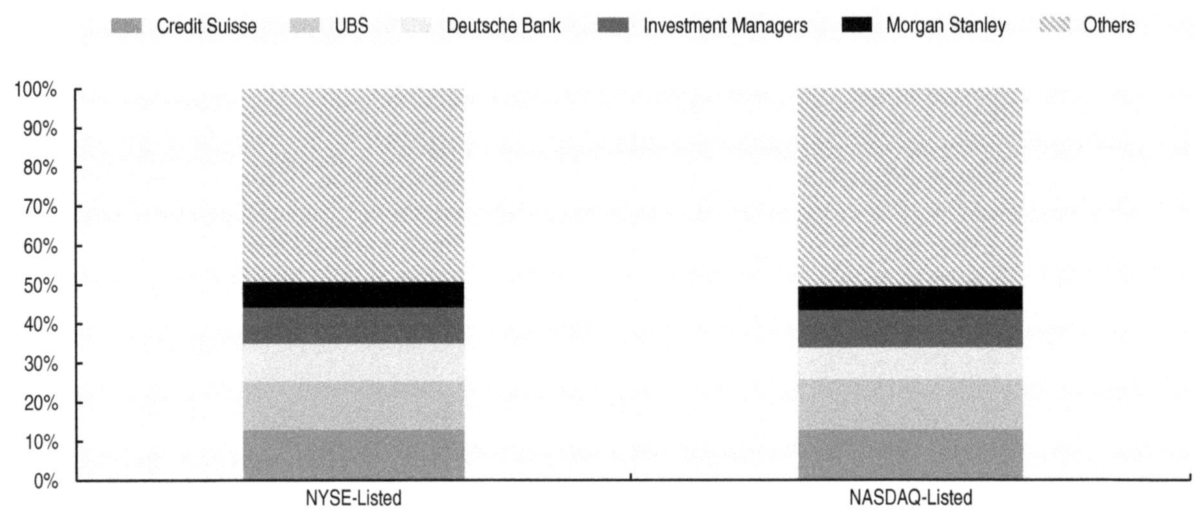

Note: The category "Others" includes 39 ATSs.
Source: FINRA, OECD calculations.

StatLink http://dx.doi.org/10.1787/888933362480

Figure 4.5 summarises the secondary equity market structure in the United States in 2015 and shows that 67% of all trading in shares listed on NYSE and NASDAQ was executed on 11 national securities exchanges. The remaining 33% was executed on ATSs, internal trading systems of firms and other OTC trading centres.

With respect to the second dimension of fragmentation, Figure 4.5 clearly shows that the demarcation line for fragmentation between dark and lit trading is not necessarily between exchange and off-exchange trading. The reason is that ATS venues can indeed be lit, for example, in the form of an ECN venue while part of the exchange trading is actually dark.[8] However, ATSs in the form of lit ECNs play an insignificant role in terms of total trading today. On the other hand, there is a significant portion of dark trading on regulated exchanges, which is estimated to be 9% of total trading volume. This overlap between dark trading volume across off-exchange trading venues and exchange trading is identified in Figure 4.5. Adding the volume of dark trading in exchanges to the dark trading in off-exchange trading venues (including ATS and non-ATS OTC volume) shows that about 42% of the total trading volume in US equity markets in 2015 was in the form of dark trading.

Equity market structure in Europe

Fragmentation in European equity markets accelerated after MiFID 1 came into effect in November 2007. The Directive allowed equity trading to be executed on MTFs, as well as on

Figure 4.5. **The two dimensions of fragmentation in United States equity markets, 2015**

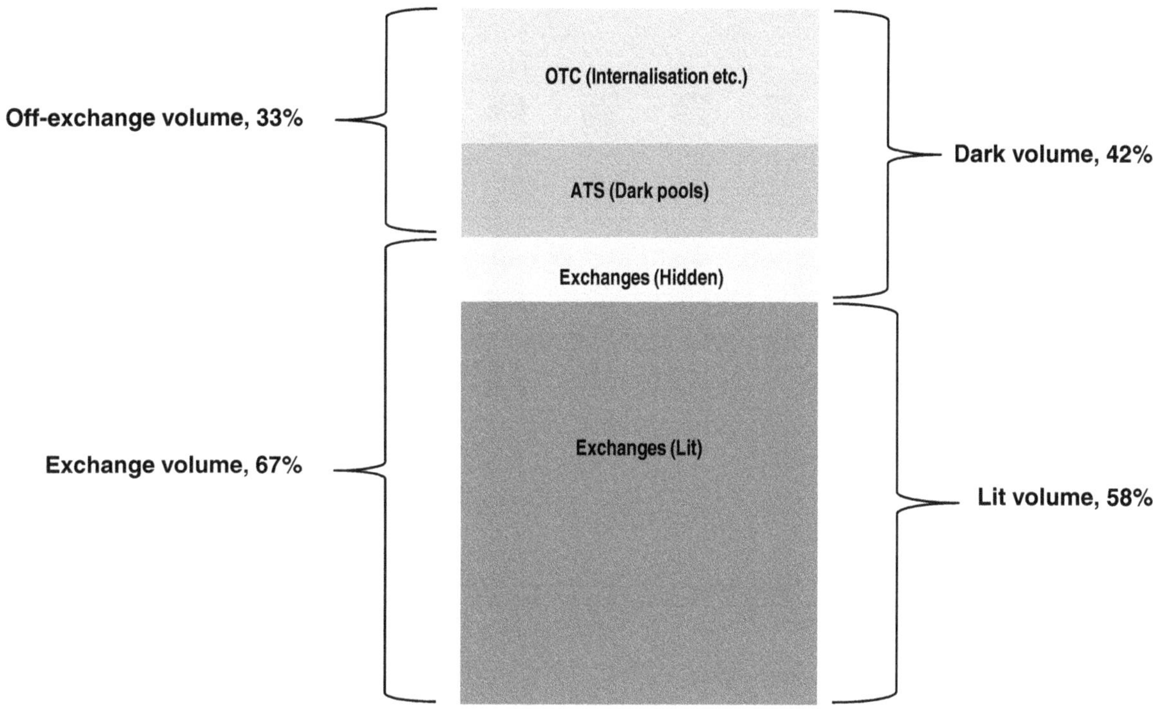

Note: Data include NYSE and NASDAQ-listed securities. Lit volume in ATSs in 2015 was insignificant and is not included in the figure.
Source: BATS Global Markets, US SEC, FINRA, Thomson Reuters.

traditional stock exchanges, and to be matched internally by investment firms (systematic internalisers). The impact of MiFID 1 on market fragmentation in Europe has been significant. Starting with the launch of the first MTF in 2007, in January 2016 there were 103 regulated exchanges, 151 MTFs and 11 systematic internalisers in Europe according to the European Securities and Markets Authority's (ESMA) database on MiFID.

Comparing the fragmentation between exchange and off-exchange trading in the United States and Europe is not straightforward. The main reason is that in Europe, there is no publicly available standardised and consolidated trading information for all trading venues, including OTC and internalised trading. Using trading information available from BATS for stocks listed on 12 major European exchanges in 2015 gives the distribution between exchange and off-exchange trading illustrated in Figure 4.6. For the London Stock Exchange (LSE), for example, the use of BATS data shows that 57% of the trading in stocks listed at LSE is actually traded on the LSE. Another third is traded on BATS and Turquoise;[9] less than 1% in other lit venues and about 11% is in the form of dark volume. However, unlike Figure 4.3 for the United States, the numbers for London and other European exchanges in Figure 4.6 do not take into account trading on off-exchanges venues other than MTFs and off-order book trading on exchanges.[10] This poses particular challenges when it comes to estimating the extent of dark trading in equities listed on European exchanges.

Moreover, since the trading data in Europe is not standardised across trading venues, concerns have been raised about the quality and consistency of the data provided by different venues or data providers. For example, a study by the Association of Financial Markets in Europe (AFME, 2011) which analysed data from a number of brokers in Europe, found that approximately 60% of all reported MiFID OTC trading between Q1 2008 and

Figure 4.6. **Market shares among trading venues in Europe, 2015**

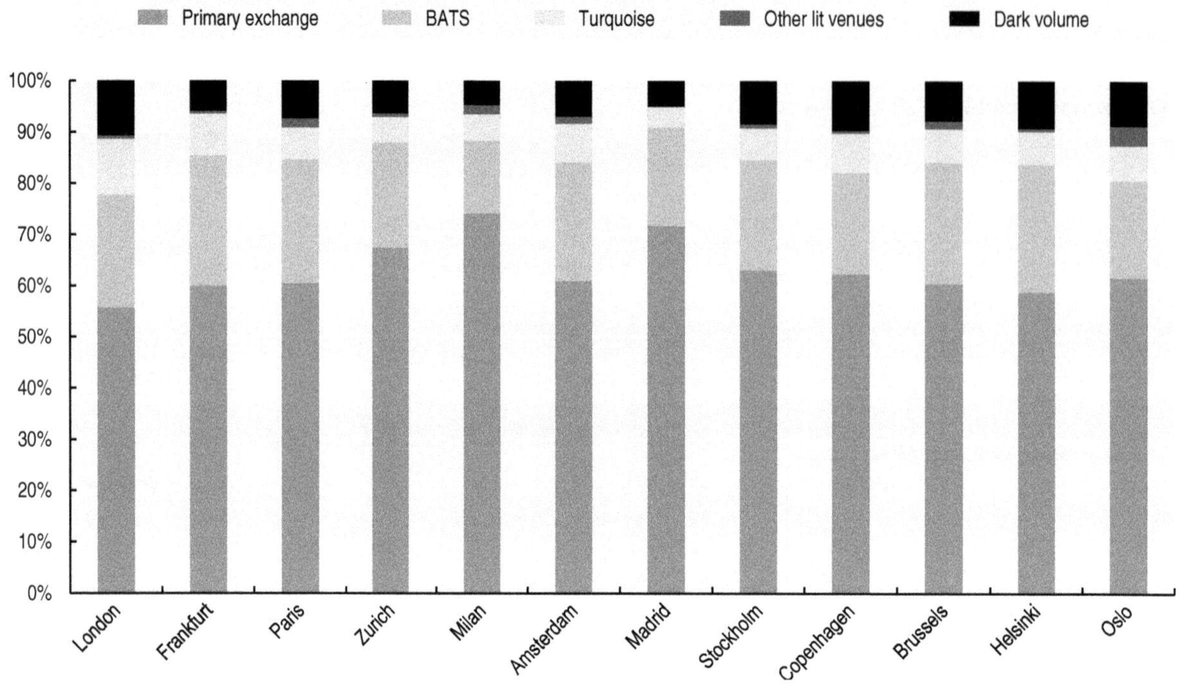

Source: BATS Global Markets.

StatLink http://dx.doi.org/10.1787/888933362490

Q3 2010 was duplicate trades already reported elsewhere. A major source of double counting in trading data is that "give up/give in" trades, which transfer ownership of stocks from one broker to another to execute an order on behalf of the broker, are reported by both of the two brokers involved.

In an attempt to provide a more comparable picture between trading in US and European equity markets, we have collected firm-level data on the trading volume of individual stocks that are included in three major European stock indices (i.e. FTSE 100 in the United Kingdom, CAC 40 in France and DAX 30 in Germany) for the period from 1 December 2015 to 31 March 2016. Based on this data, we have calculated how the trading is distributed among all the individual trading venues, including exchanges, MTFs and other OTC trading.

Given the difficulties with analysing the trading data in Europe, potentially double-counted trades have been excluded, based on the explanations provided for each trading category in the dataset, including give up/give in trades. Each trading category has also been categorised as on/off exchange and lit/dark volume using the same explanations. The aggregated results are summarised in Figure 4.7.

Using this method, the figure shows that the share of on-exchange volume is similar across the three markets, between 48%-52% of all trading volume, but considerably lower than in Figure 4.6. This also includes on exchange off-order book trading and hidden orders on exchanges, which are both classified as dark volume. With respect to off-exchange venues, the market share of MTFs is around 12% in the United Kingdom, 10% in France and 8% in Germany, while the lion's share of the off-exchange volume was executed on non-MTF OTC centres.

Figure 4.7. **An illustration of the distribution of trading among trading venues and between lit and dark volume in France, Germany and the United Kingdom, December 2015 – March 2016**

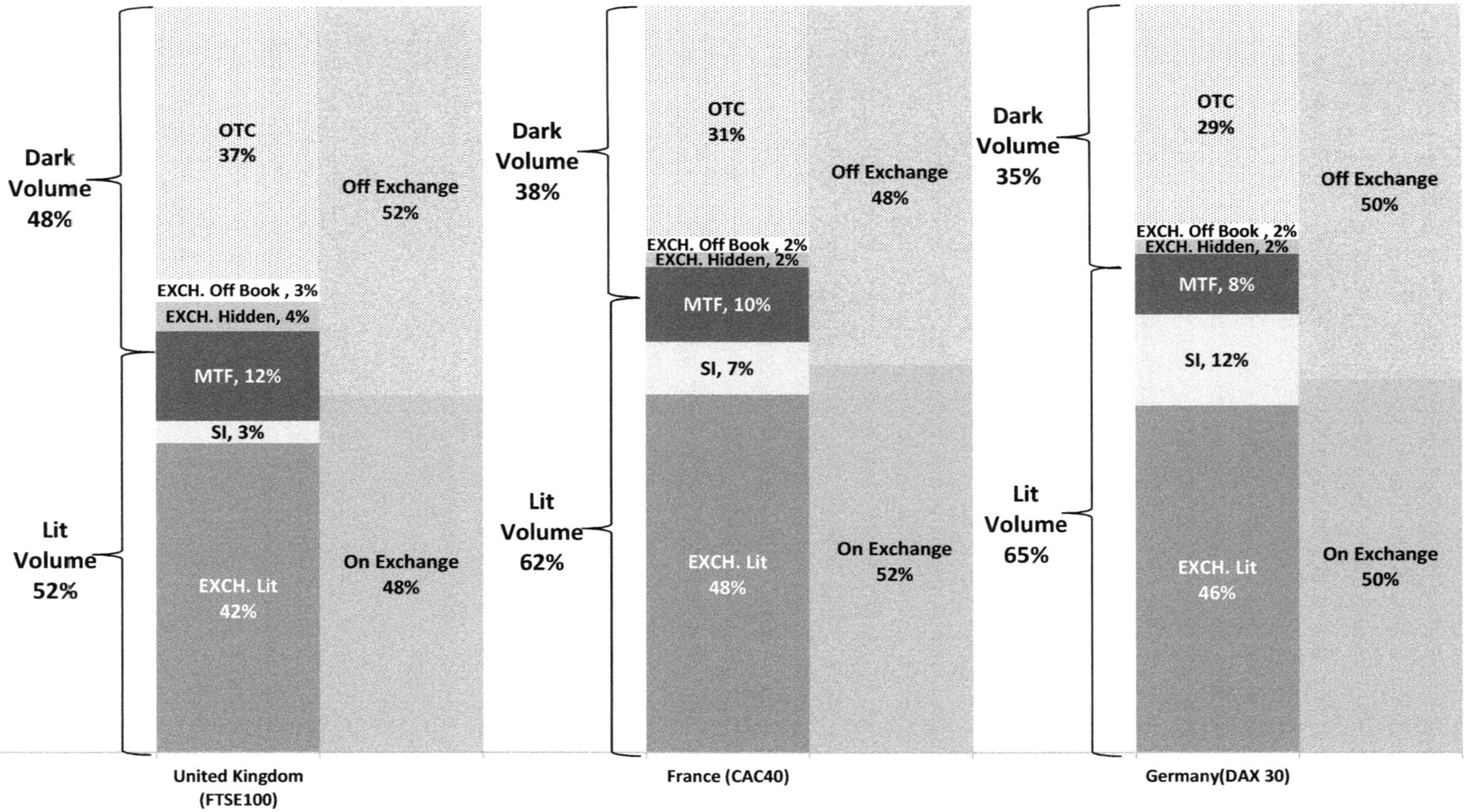

Note: For each index constituent company, the trading volume across all European venues between 1 December 2015 and 31 March 2016 is included. The figure covers only EUR volume for France and Germany, and GBP volume for UK companies. All firm-orders are classified according to their visibility, on/off exchange trading and the type of the venue. For example, transactions reported by exchanges on behalf of Systematic Internalisers (SI) or over-the-counter (OTC) are reclassified as SI and OTC transactions respectively. Transactions that are recorded as give up/give in trades are excluded.

Transactions reported on behalf of SIs are classified as visible, off-exchange transactions and SI. Transactions reported as OTC of any type are classified as non-visible, off-exchange transactions and OTC. Hidden transactions executed in the order books of regulated markets are classified as non-visible, on-exchange and exchange hidden. Transactions executed in the dark order books of regulated markets are classified as non-visible, on-exchange and exchange hidden. Off-book transactions reported and executed in exchanges are classified as non-visible, on-exchange and exchange off-order book. Transactions executed in an MTF's order book are classified as visible, off-exchange and MTF. Transactions executed in an MTF's dark order book are classified as non-visible, off-exchange and MTF.

Source: Thomson Reuters, Factset, OECD calculations.

StatLink http://dx.doi.org/10.1787/888933362502

Since the data used for Figure 4.7 includes all OTC trading, any on exchange off-order book trading, hidden orders on exchanges and dark order book volume of MTFs, it is possible to arrive at a more accurate picture of the amount of dark trading in Europe. As a result of using more complete trading data, the total amount of dark trading in European listed stocks is estimated to be 48% in the United Kingdom, 38% in France and 35% in Germany, which is significantly higher than the 10% indicated in Figure 4.6.

Since there are certain pre-trade transparency requirements for Systematic Internalisers in Europe, unlike the US data, they were classified as part of the lit volume. In addition, the market share of dark pools (dark MTFs) in Figure 4.7 is lower than their share in Figure 4.6 because of the fact that the latter figures are calculated by including OTC and on-exchange off-order book trading to the total trading volume. For example, the market share of dark MTFs in the United Kingdom drops from around 7% to 4% when all trading volume is taken into account. It should be noted that the dataset used in Figure 4.7 covers a shorter time period (four months instead of one year) and a somewhat different period, which may limit the comparability of the two figures.

The increase in dark trading

Dark trading has existed for a long time in many stock markets. As noted above, it can take place in many different forms including undisclosed orders on regulated exchanges, trading on alternative trading platforms, off-order book trading on exchanges and other OTC centres. Trading by using orders that do not appear in the visible order book has traditionally been associated with the needs of institutional investors that want to reduce the market impact of large orders. This need has become increasingly relevant as algorithmic trading and high frequency trading (HFT) have increased in importance.

With respect to the argument that dark pools meet the needs to place large orders, Table 4.1 shows the average trade sizes in ATSs in the United States in 2015. As seen in the table, some ATSs execute large trade sizes of up to 500 000 shares. However, the top five ATSs in terms of average trade size account for less than 3% of the total share volume executed in ATSs. The top five ATSs in terms of volume traded, which account for 49% of total share volume traded, had an average trade size between 153 and 233 shares. The average trade size in all ATSs was 207 shares, which is very close to the average trade size in stock exchanges for the same period (209 shares). These findings suggest that ATSs, with respect to the execution of large orders, do not distinguish themselves from the regulated exchanges whose listed shares they are trading.

The increase in dark volume, particularly in the form of dark pools, has raised concerns about the efficiency of the price discovery process, the fairness of markets and the level playing field among investors. For example, the US SEC in a recent release (US SEC, 2015a) on proposed rules with respect to Regulation of NMS Stock ATSs, expressed concerns that;

- In terms of trading, ATSs operate in a similar manner to securities exchanges with whom they compete for business. However, unlike securities exchanges, there is limited public information available to market participants about their operations. These differences may create a competitive imbalance between two functionally similar[11] trading venues that may trade the same security but are subject to different regulatory requirements.
- This difference in operational transparency is to the disadvantage of market participants, since it limits their ability to adequately assess the relative merits of many trading

Table 4.1. **Average trade sizes in ATSs in the United States, 2015**

Top 5 ATS sorted by Volume Traded			Top 5 ATS sorted by Average Trade Size		
ATS	Average trade size (shares)	% of total ATS share volume	ATS	Average trade size (shares)	% of total ATS share volume
Credit Suisse	177	12.62	Dealerweb	494 877	1.49
UBS	153	12.31	Barclays	75 430	0.02
IEX Services	225	8.52	LEHM Barclays	70 464	0.00
Deutsche Bank	184	8.29	Liquidnet	39 116	1.24
Morgan Stanley	233	6.79	Luminex	30 544	0.02
Cumulated volume		**48.54**[1]	**Cumulated volume**		**2.78**[2]
ATS average trade size:		**207**			
Exchange average trade size[3]**:**		**209**			

1. Top 5 ATSs in terms of share volume traded account for 47.26% of total ATS USD volume.
2. Top 5 ATSs in terms of average trade size account for 7.22% of total ATS USD volume.
3. Exchange average trade size is calculated based on information reported by BATS Global Markets and includes the three US exchange groups: NYSE, NASDAQ and BATS.

Source: FINRA, OECD calculations.

venues and to adequately discern how their orders interact, match, and execute on ATSs and to find the optimal venue or venues for their orders.

- There is a lack of transparency around potential conflicts of interest that arise from the activities of the broker-dealer operator of the ATS and its affiliates in connection with the ATS.

Recent US SEC enforcement actions highlighting the difference in regulatory frameworks between national securities exchanges and ATSs have attracted public attention in the United States. In 2011, for example, the US SEC settled an enforcement action against a dark pool operator who advertised that no proprietary trading took place in its dark pool while, on the contrary, the overwhelming majority of the shares traded on its ATS were bought or sold by an operator's wholly owned subsidiary. In addition, the operator provided its subsidiary with certain access and information that improved the subsidiaries ability to trade advantageously and were not known to other customers (US SEC, 2011). In a more recent case, the US SEC has settled another enforcement action against a dark pool operator who had also not disclosed that it was engaged in proprietary trading within its ATS and gave its proprietary trading desk access to live feeds of highly confidential order and execution information that were used to inform the desk's trading decisions (US SEC, 2015b).

Changes in market structure and the decline in smaller growth company IPOs

Markets where companies raise external equity financing are referred to as the primary public equity markets. In the last two decades, advanced economies have experienced a significant decline in both the average number of non-financial companies who use primary markets to make an initial public offering (IPO) and in the average annual amount of equity they raise. Between 1994-2000, there were on average 1 152 IPOs per year. That number fell to 853 in the period 2001-07 and again to just 453 per year in the period 2008-15. This decrease in number of companies has been accompanied by a significant decline also in the amount of capital raised over the three periods; from USD 147 billion in the period 1994-2000, to USD 88 billion in the period 2001-07 to USD 67 billion in the period 2008-15.[12]

An important aspect of this trend is the steep decline in smaller, growth company IPOs, particularly in the United States and Europe. Figure 4.8 shows the trends in IPOs by non-financial growth companies in advanced economies, both the absolute amount of equity raised by growth companies as well as the decline in the relative share of all equity raised that goes to growth companies. In the period from 1994-2000, IPOs smaller than USD 100 million represented 19% of all funds raised. Since 2004 however, this proportion has declined almost monotonically and in 2015 it amounted to just 13%. As a result, in advanced economies there are fewer but larger IPOs. Considering the importance of access to equity funding for innovation, productivity and overall economic growth, discussed earlier in this chapter, this development has given rise to discussions about the causes behind these trends.

Figure 4.8. **The decline in small company IPOs in advanced economies**

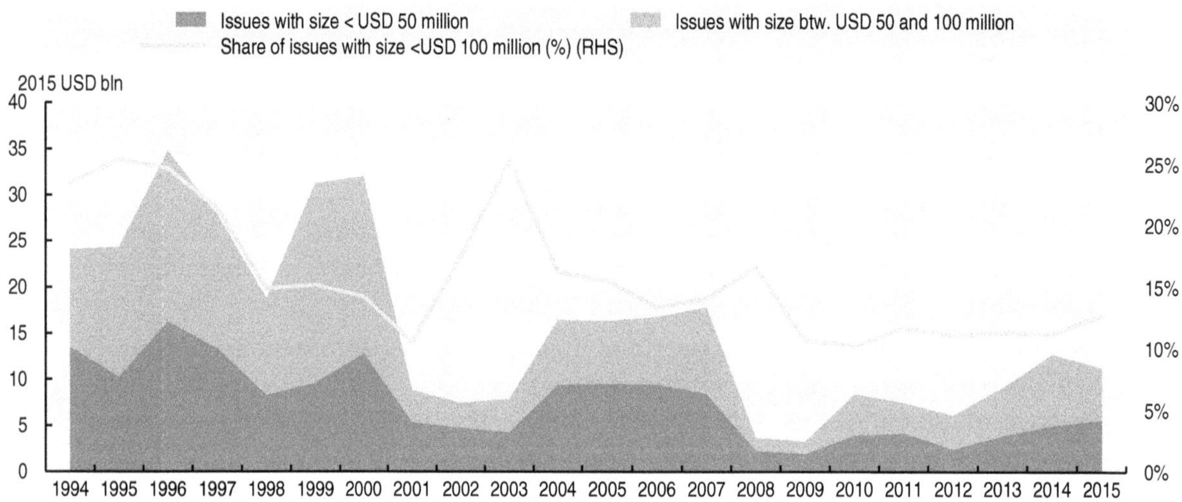

Source: Thomson Reuters, OECD calculations.

StatLink http://dx.doi.org/10.1787/888933362512

Many different explanations have been proposed for the decline in non-financial company IPOs in advanced economies (Isaksson and Çelik, 2013). One of them focuses on the impact of structural changes in stock markets, including the effects of fragmentation and new investment techniques and instruments, such as ETF and high-frequency trading (HFT), on the lower liquidity of small company stocks. It has been claimed that the new market structure encourages a focus on large liquid company stocks and less appetite to hold and trade in small company stocks. As a result, the attention of investors has been diverted away from potential growth companies that in turn have been discouraged from going public (Economist, 2009; Bradley and Litan, 2010; Haslag and Ringgenberg, 2015).

One way to illustrate the relative level of attention that secondary markets give to companies of different sizes is to look at the distribution of trading in companies of different sizes. To start with, Figure 4.9 shows the share of total market capitalisation represented by the 1, 5, and 10% largest companies measured by market capitalisation and the share of total trading that is attributed to these largest companies as of December 2015. In Japan, for example, 80% of total market capitalisation is attributable to the 10% largest companies measured by market capitalisation. Similarly, slightly more than 30% of market capitalisation is attributable to the 1% largest companies.

Again, for Japan, about 75% of the total trading volume is attributed to the trading of shares in the 10% largest companies. Similarly, about 25% of all trading in Japan is in the shares of the 1% largest companies measured by market capitalisation. Overall, in all the markets featured in Figure 4.9, the share of total trading volume attributed to the largest 10% of companies in terms of market capitalisation was over 70%, with the exception of Indonesia (68%). Moreover, in most markets 20% of all trading was attributed to the largest 1% of companies. Figure 4.9 does not only show that trading volume is highly concentrated to large companies. It also shows that the share of trading in large companies typically is proportional to their share of total market capitalisation.

Figure 4.9. **Concentration of market capitalisation and trading volume in public equity markets, December 2015**

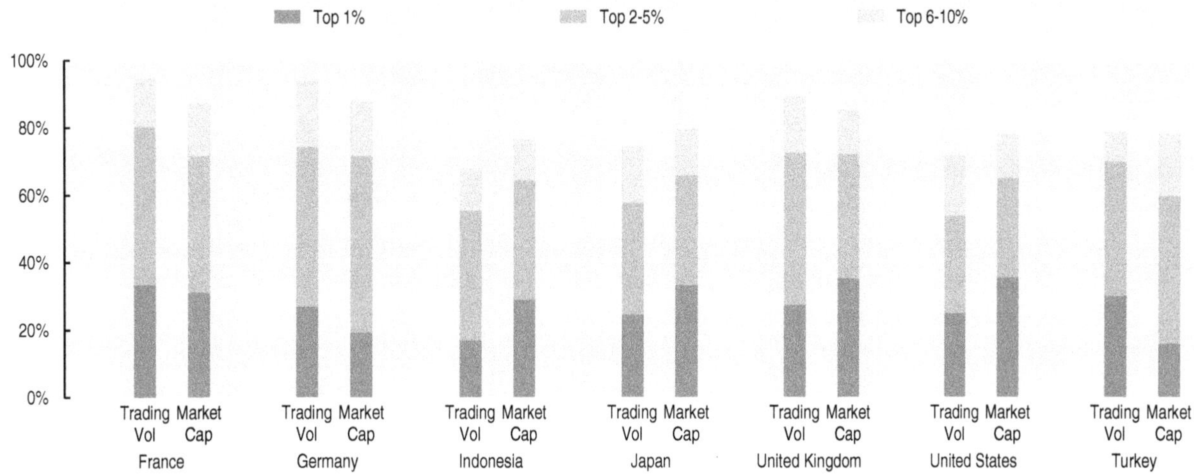

Source: Thomson Reuters, OECD calculations.

StatLink http://dx.doi.org/10.1787/888933362523

In order to analyse the long-term trends in the distribution of trading among companies of different size and the possible link to changes in stock market structure, Figure 4.10 shows the 10% largest companies' share of total trading volume in Japan and the United States since 2000. The data is computed based on firm-level monthly consolidated trading volume for all listed companies, their respective mid-month prices and end-month market capitalisation. Despite the fact that throughout the period almost all trading in listed companies in Japan was executed on exchanges, whereas United States trading developed in an increasingly fragmented trading environment following the adoption of Regulation NMS, the two markets follow each other closely both in terms of level and trends. Throughout the 15 year period, between 70% and 90% of all trading was attributed to shares in the 10% largest companies, indicating rather limited variations over time.

In order to track overall variations in trading concentration over time, Figure 4.11 shows developments in the form of the Herfindahl concentration index. The index has been calculated based on the same firm-level data used for Figure 4.10 and includes five more countries: France, Germany, Indonesia, Turkey and the United Kingdom. Although there has been some difference in terms of the volatility of the index in different periods in some countries, the figures do not indicate an overall trend towards higher concentration in large company trading. This is particularly marked for the last two-year period. The exception is Turkey with a relatively small public equity market. Interestingly, despite the

Figure 4.10. **Share in total trading volume of 10% largest companies in Japan and the United States, 2000-15**

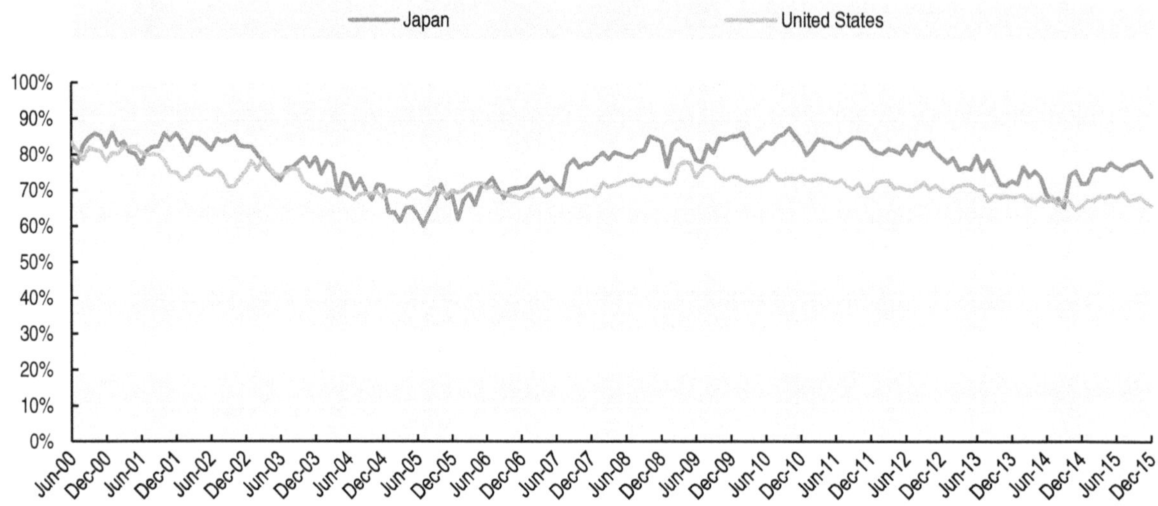

Source: Thomson Reuters, OECD calculations.

StatLink http://dx.doi.org/10.1787/888933362530

fact that the market structures have undergone significant changes in Europe since 2007, with the implementation of MiFID 1, the distribution of total trading between companies of different size has remained fairly stable.

The results presented above do not indicate an overall increase in the equity market trading concentration for the period from 2000-15. However, since the share of trading in small company stocks of the total volume of trading has been very low throughout the period, relatively small changes may also merit attention.

While the analysis above describes the overall distribution of trading between large and small companies, it may also be of interest to look at any potential differences between exchange and off-exchange venues. Having concluded above that in general, there were no significant differences in order size between exchange and off-exchange venues, the next question is if there are any major systemic differences in off-exchange trading with respect to the distribution of trading in the stocks of small and large companies.

To identify any such differences in the United States, we have used firm-level data from Thomson Reuters on consolidated traded volume and company characteristics, which has been analysed together with the data, obtained from FINRA on ATS trading volume. In a population of almost 4 200 United States listed companies in our dataset, almost all of them had shares traded in an ATS at least once during 2015.

Figure 4.12 compares the distribution of stock trading among companies of different size on ATSs with the overall market pattern (including stock exchanges, ATSs and non-ATS OTC trading). Firms are sorted according to their market capitalisation as of December 2014. Across company sizes, our data reveals very small differences between the trading patterns in ATSs and the overall market. Trading in ATSs is also highly concentrated with the largest 1% of the companies accounting for 23.8% of the trading, which is actually at par with the overall concentration in United States trading volume. The share of the top 5% and top 10% largest companies in total trading on ATSs was somewhat higher than their share in total United States trading volume. The results do not change significantly when company size is measured by the total value of assets instead of market capitalisation.

Figure 4.11. **Equity market trading concentration index, 2004 = 100**

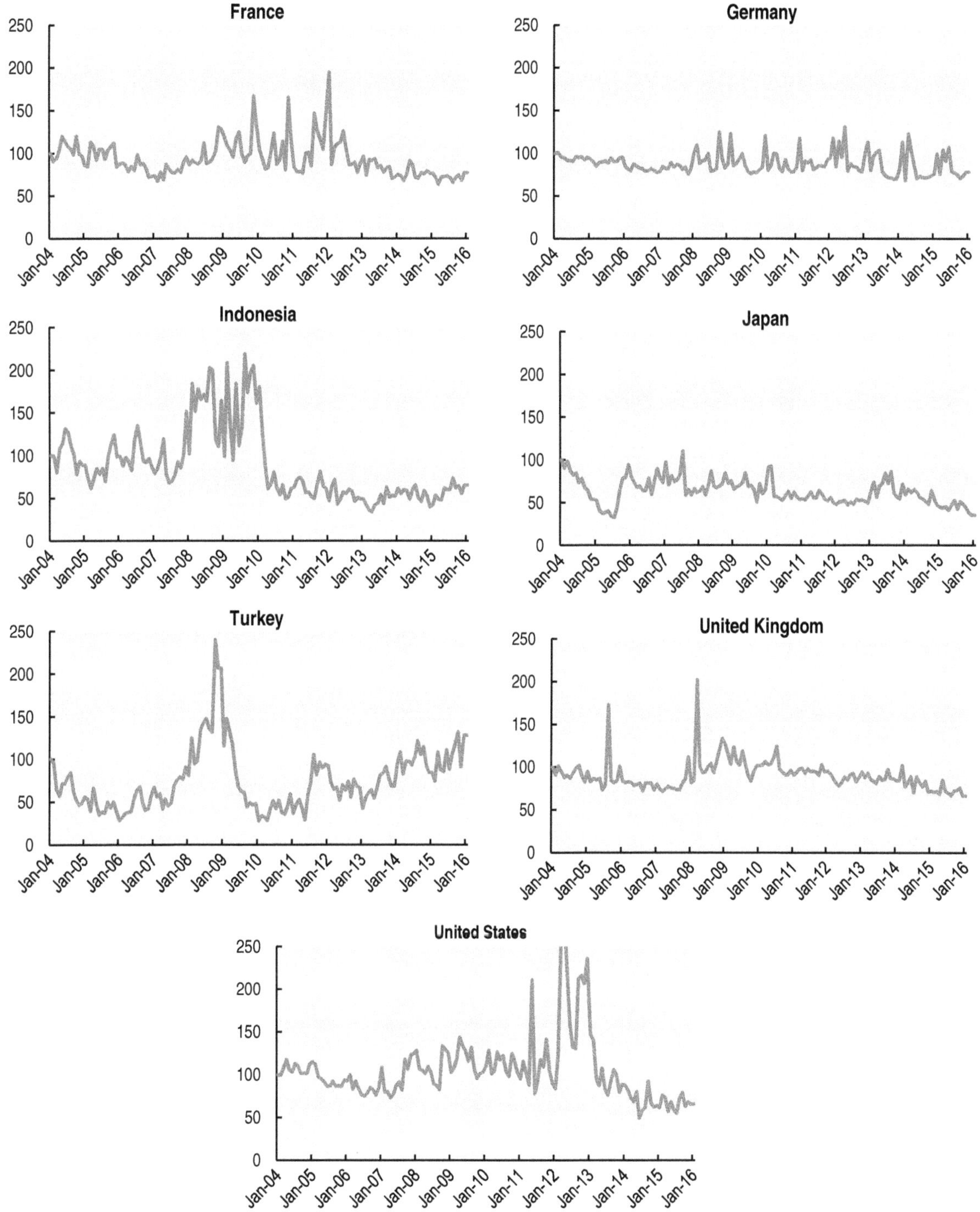

Source: Thomson Reuters, OECD calculations.

StatLink http://dx.doi.org/10.1787/888933362543

In addition to order size and company size, it has also been suggested that ATS trading may serve the purpose of specialising in specific industries. In order to investigate this, Table 4.2 compares the distribution of ATS and total trading among different industry groups as defined by Thomson Reuters. Columns 2 and 3 show how the total volume traded

Figure 4.12. **The share of large companies in trading in the United States, 2015**

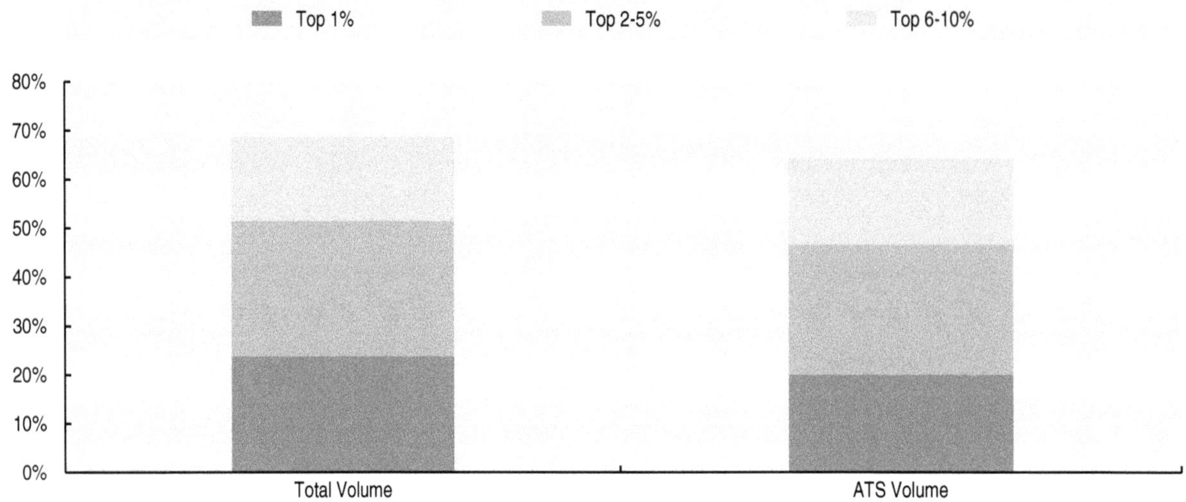

Source: FINRA, Thomson Reuters, OECD calculations.

StatLink http://dx.doi.org/10.1787/888933362555

Table 4.2. **Top 10 industry sectors traded in ATSs (volume), 2015**

	(2)	(3)	(4)	(5)	(6)	(7)
Industry Sector	Consolidated Ex. ATS	Alternative systems Vol. (ATS Vol.)	Ranking Consolidated Ex. ATS. Vol.	Ranking ATS Vol.	As a % of Total ATS Vol.	As a % of Total Consolidated Vol ex ATS. Vol.
Software and Computer Services	81.8	18.2	3	1	9.6	8.6
Pharmaceuticals and Biotechnology	83.5	16.5	2	2	8.6	8.7
Technology Hardware and Equipment	85.7	14.3	1	3	8.5	10.2
General Retailers	84.7	15.3	4	4	6.6	7.4
Oil and Gas Producers	84.3	15.7	5	5	5.5	5.9
Travel and Leisure	83.3	16.7	6	6	5.0	5.0
Media	76.7	23.3	12	7	4.7	3.1
Health Care Equipment and Services	81.9	18.1	9	8	4.5	4.1
Financial Services	83.0	17.0	8	9	4.3	4.2
Banks	85.1	14.9	7	10	3.8	4.4

Note: Column (2) shows for each industry sector, the share of non-ATS USD volume over the total consolidated USD volume; column (3) shows for each industry sector, the share of USD volume traded in alternative systems over the total consolidated USD volume; column (4) shows the industry sector ranking in terms of non-ATS USD volume; column (5) shows the industry sector ranking in terms of ATS USD volume; column (6) shows the industry sector volume traded in ATS over the total volume traded in ATSs across all industry sectors; and column (7) shows the industry sector volume traded in non-ATSs over the total volume traded in non-ATSs across all industry sectors.

Source: FINRA, Thomson Reuters, OECD calculations.

is split between non-ATS venues and ATS venues. The analysis concludes that on average, each industry group trades around 14% on ATSs and 86% on other venues, mostly stock exchanges. Columns 6 and 7 compare the distribution of trading in different industry groups for ATS and non-ATS venues. The comparison shows that the distribution of trading in different industry groups on ATS venues generally mirrors the distribution for overall stock market trading.

Policy responses

The increase in market fragmentation and dark trading has been associated with a growing debate about the consequences for essential market qualities, such as the efficiency of price formation, fairness between investors, level playing field between venues and conflicts of interest between service providers and clients. In several countries, this has already led to regulatory responses. Australia and Canada for instance, have both introduced so-called "trade-at" rules which allow a trade to be executed on an off-exchange trading venue only if it provides a price or size improvement over exchanges (Shorter and Miller, 2014). In other jurisdictions, recently launched initiatives may lead to substantial changes. The two most important regulatory initiatives currently undertaken by advanced economies includes the US SEC's recent proposal to change the regulatory framework for ATSs in the United States and the announcement by the European Commission that MiFID 2 will enter into application in January 2018.

The proposed reforms in the United States

In November 2015, the US SEC submitted an extensive proposal to amend the regulatory framework for ATSs that trade NMS stocks in the United States. The main focus is on differences in operational transparency between ATSs and national securities exchanges and the lack of transparency around potential conflicts of interest between the broker-dealer operator of the ATS and the ATS's subscribers. An important reason for these differences is that national securities exchanges and ATSs today operate under different regulations. National securities exchanges must, for example, be registered with the US SEC. They must fully disclose their operations and procedures, establish publicly disclosed rules for trading, and submit any changes in their rules to US SEC's for approval. In contrast, ATSs must register as broker-dealers, which includes becoming a member of a Self-Regulatory Organisation (SRO), and comply with Regulation ATS, which includes noticing its operations to the US SEC on Form ATS. Form ATS is not approved by the US SEC and it is deemed confidential upon filing. ATSs are not required to publicly disclose the character of their trading services, operations, and fees and are not required to file proposed rule changes that national securities exchanges are required to file.

The US SEC's reform proposal from November 2015 would require that ATSs that trade NMS stocks and that want to be exempted from registering as a national securities exchange, comply with additional conditions and increase the transparency of their operations. The proposal would increase the filing requirements regarding the activities of the ATS operator (broker-dealer) and its affiliates in connection with the ATS that trades NMS stocks. The ATS broker-dealer operator would be required to disclose certain information through Form ATS-N and the US SEC would make it available to the public. The US SEC would also determine whether ATSs that trade NMS stocks would qualify for the exemption from registration as an exchange and would review the Form ATS-N for compliance with the form's requirements. The proposal would also allow the US SEC to suspend, limit or revoke the exemption provided. Under the proposed regulation, ATSs would also be required to have the ATS's safeguards and procedures in writing to protect their subscribers' confidential trading operations.

Overall, the US SEC proposal aims to level the regulatory environment between ATSs that trade NMS stocks and national securities exchanges by means of increasing the requirements for ATSs that trade NMS stocks and increasing the information available to market participants.

The European Union and MiFID 2

MiFID 1 was adopted in 2007 and covers a broad range of market rules related to market structure, transparency, supervision and investor protection. It also includes rules related to trading and clearing of financial instruments, such as shares, bonds and derivatives and the venues on which they are listed or admitted to trading. MiFID 2, which replaces MiFID 1, was approved by the European Council in May 2014. The European Commission has extended the original application date for MiFID 2 which was January 2017 to January 2018 in order "to take account of the exceptional technical implementation challenges faced by regulators and market participants" (European Commission, 2016).

An important rationale for MiFID 1 was to promote competition between different trading venues and decrease the costs for investors. MiFID 1 explicitly allows equity trading to be executed on stock exchanges, MTFs and internal trading systems of firms (systematic internalisers). However, and outside the scope of MiFID 1, it is also possible to execute trading on an OTC basis outside of all these three venue types. Broker crossing networks, for example, without being classified as any of these three categories and without being subject to related regulatory requirements, are frequently used to execute trades in listed equities. MiFID 2 aims to ensure that all multilateral trading is executed either on exchanges or MTFs; and that bilateral transactions are carried out on the internal trading systems of firms. Under certain conditions, it will still be possible to carry out trading on a traditional OTC basis.

MiFID 1 also allows trading to be executed without orders being subject to pre-trade transparency. There are four types of waivers from pre-trade transparency of orders: 1) large in scale transactions, 2) transactions based on a reference price generated by another system, 3) negotiated transactions; and 4) orders held in an order management facility of the trading venue. MiFID 2 will maintain these waivers but introduce certain restrictions. Of particular interest regarding fragmentation between lit and dark trading is the so-called "double volume cap mechanism". This mechanism stipulates that the dark volume of trading on any trading venue for a particular share should not exceed 4% of the total trading volume on all trading venues in the European Union, and 8% across all trading venues based on a 12-month rolling calculation. The caps will only be applied to dark trading that is making use of the reference price waiver and some types of negotiated transactions. Importantly, the caps will not target dark trades under the waivers for large in scale transactions and trades executed on an OTC basis. This means that the total volume of dark trading under MiFID 2 may amount to 8% of the total trading volume that uses the reference price waiver and some types of negotiated transactions plus all trading that makes use of the large in scale and order management facility waivers plus all trading that is executed outside of the three venues defined by MiFID 2.

A main difference between the United Stated and European equity markets is access to reliable and consistent aggregate trading data. In the United States, the Consolidated Tape Association, which is a membership organisation of exchanges, oversees the dissemination of real-time trade and quote information in listed securities. For the time being, there is no similar pan-European facility. While recognising the need to improve the situation in Europe, MiFID 2 takes a somewhat different approach to the organisation of consolidated data dissemination. The Directive envisages that a consolidated tape will be established by data providers that collect trade reports from the exchanges, MTFs and other reporting mechanism used by investment firms and consolidate this information into a continuous electronic live data stream providing price and volume data for each financial instrument.

Conclusions

In addition to changes in market structure and the business models of stock exchanges, secondary stock markets are today fragmented along two lines. First, trading is fragmented between stock exchanges and a large number of off-exchange venues, such as stock exchange-like alternative electronic trading platforms and OTC centres, including internal trading systems of firms. In the United States, about 30% of all trading takes place in off-exchange venues and in Europe about 50% of the total trade volume is executed outside of the traditional exchanges.

Second, there is fragmentation between lit volume where investors have access to pre-trade information about buying and selling interests, and dark volume where pre-trade information is not available to the public. Lit and dark trading both occur on exchanges and off-exchange venues. In 2015, the total volume of dark trading in the United States – including dark trading in both exchanges and off-exchange venues – was 42%. In Europe the share of dark volume with respect to total trading volume varies between countries from 35% to 48%.

Commitment to maintain market fairness and a level playing field among investors have given rise to regulatory initiatives in both Europe and the United States. As part of this, it is expected that the rationale for existing differences in regulatory regimes between different types of trading venues will be scrutinised. It remains to be seen what the effects will be in terms of stock market fragmentation.

Notes

1. For example, the National Association of Securities Dealers (NASD) in the United States was established as a national securities association and is a Self-Regulatory Organisation (SRO). In July 2007, the Securities and Exchange Commission (US SEC) approved the merger of NASD and the regulatory operations of the NYSE to form the Financial Industry Regulatory Authority (FINRA). It is important to note that national securities exchanges in the United States are also SROs with regulatory obligations, such as enforcing their rules and the federal securities laws with respect to their members. These obligations do not apply to ATSs (US SEC, 2015a).
2. Since the adoption of Regulation ATS in 1998, ATSs have become more prevalent in equity trading in the United States. It is important to note, however, that dark ATSs are not covered by the Order Protection Rule of Regulation NMS, which means that exchanges and ECNs are not required to route orders to dark venues.
3. Out of 85 trading venues operating as ATSs as of 1 December 2015, we have identified 44 venues that in 2015 traded NMS stocks based on data retrieved from FINRA.
4. NYSE, Market Share of consolidated tape volume by year (1976-2003), *www.nyxdata.com*.
5. The National Stock Exchange (NSX) ceased trading operations in May 2014, but continued to be registered as a national securities exchange during 2015. Since trading did not resume on NSX until the end of 2015, market share data for NSX is not included in Figure 4.3.
6. US SEC, Alternative Trading Systems with Form ATS on File with the SEC as of 1 December 2015, *www.sec.gov/foia/ats/atslist1215.pdf*.
7. Rule 600 of Regulation NMS defines an "NMS stock" as "any NMS security other than an option" and defines an "NMS security" as "any security or class of securities for which transaction reports are collected, processed, and made available pursuant to an effective transaction reporting plan, or an effective national market system plan for reporting transactions in listed options." In general, the term "NMS Stock" refers to exchange-listed equity securities.
8. On US stock exchanges, however, displayed orders are given execution priority over non-displayed orders at the same price.
9. Turquoise is an MTF which is majority owned by the London Stock Exchange, in partnership with 12 investment banks.

10. A trade that is executed bilaterally off the order book of an exchange, but executed subject to the exchange's rules and reported to the exchange, is classified as an off-order book on exchange trade.
11. The European Union has also stated that the definitions of regulated markets and MTFs "should be clarified and remain closely aligned with each other to reflect the fact that they represent effectively the same organised trading functionality." (Source: Regulation No. 600/2014 in markets in financial instruments and amending Regulation No 648/2012).
12. OECD calculations based on data from Thomson Reuters New Issues Database.

References

AFME (2011), "The Nature and Scale of OTC Equity Trading in Europe", April.

Aguilar, L.A. (2015), "Shedding Light on Dark Pools", *Public Statement by SEC Commissioner*, 18 November, *www.sec.gov/news/statement/shedding-light-on-dark-pools.html#_edn5*.

Bradley, H. and R.E. Litan (2010), *Choking The Recovery: Why New Growth Companies Aren't Going Public and Unrecognised Risks of Future Market Disruptions*, Ewing Marion Kauffman.

Cournède, B., O. Denk and P. Hoeller (2015), "Finance and Inclusive Growth", *OECD Economic Policy Papers*, No. 14, OECD Publishing, Paris.

Economist (2009), "High-speed slide: What is good for cutting-edge traders may be bad for the market as a whole", 12 November.

European Commission (2016), Press release: Commission extends by one year the application date for the MiFID II package, 10 February.

Haslag, P. and M.C. Ringgenberg (2015), "The Causal Impact of Market Fragmentation on Liquidity", WFA – *Center for Finance and Accounting Research Working Paper*, No. 15/001.

Isaksson, M. and S. Çelik (2013), "Who Cares? Corporate Governance in Today's Equity Markets", *OECD Corporate Governance Working Papers*, No. 8, OECD Publishing, Paris, *http://dx.doi.org/10.1787/5k47zw5kdnmp-en*.

Kay, J. (2006), "A giant's strength is valuable – if not used like a giant", *Financial Times*, 27 November.

Shorter, G. and R.S. Miller (2014), "Dark Pools in Equity Trading: Policy Concerns and Recent Developments", *Congressional Research Service Report*.

The European Parliament (2014), "Directive 2014/65/EU of the European Parliament and of the Council of 15 May 2014 on markets in financial instruments and amending Directive 2002/92/EC and Directive 2011/61/EU", *Official Journal of the European Union*.

The European Parliament (2014), "Regulation (EU) No 600/2014 of the European Parliament and of the Council of 15 May 2014 on markets in financial instruments and amending Regulation (EU) No. 648/2012", *Official Journal of the European Union*.

Tuttle, L. (2013), "Alternative Trading Systems: Description of ATS Trading in National Market System Stocks", *SEC Working Paper*.

US Securities and Exchange Commission (2005), *Regulation NMS*, Release No. 34-51808.

US Securities and Exchange Commission (2011), Securities Exchange Act of 1934 Release No. 65609, 24 October, *www.sec.gov/litigation/admin/2011/33-9271.pdf*.

US Securities and Exchange Commission (2015a), *Regulation of NMS Stock Alternative Trading Systems*, Release No. 34-76474.

US Securities and Exchange Commission (2015b), Securities Exchange Act of 1934 Release No. 75672, 12 August , *www.sec.gov/litigation/admin/2015/33-9887.pdf*.

Chapter 5

Fragmentation in clean energy investment and financing

This chapter reviews how policy and market fragmentation is constraining financing of, and investment in, renewable electricity projects. Scaling-up investment in renewable electricity is critical for reducing greenhouse gas emissions from the power sector, and is therefore important for implementing the 2015 Paris Agreement on climate change. Despite increasing cost-competitiveness of renewable electricity technologies, overall investment in renewables projects remains constrained by policy and market obstacles. These hinder development of a sufficient pipeline of bankable projects and affect the risk-return profile of renewable electricity projects. This chapter reviews recent trends in renewable electricity investment and financing and identifies policy misalignments and market barriers constraining investment in renewable electricity, with a focus on fragmentation issues.

Main findings

- An increase in the scale and pace of climate change mitigation efforts, including mobilising investment and financing for renewable electricity generation, is necessary to successfully implement the 2015 Paris Agreement concluded by the 21st Conference of the Parties (COP21) of the United Nations Framework Convention on Climate Change (UNFCCC).
- Global new investment in renewable energy has rebounded since its decline in 2012-13 to an all-time record of USD 286 billion in 2015, with a shift in geographic focus towards Asia. The growth in investment flows has been sustained by an evolution in financing models and financial stakeholders for renewable electricity projects, coupled with significant policy support to renewable energy.
- The struggling finances of many utilities have contributed to new ownership and financing models in certain renewable electricity technologies such as wind energy. Traditionally, utilities and project developers have provided the majority of equity in large renewable projects through their balance sheet. In the past five years, other types of investors have increased their commitments to renewable electricity. A large number of institutional investors have notably recognised infrastructure investments through debt and equity finance as a source of inflation-linked, long-term and stable cash flows.
- Partnerships between financial actors are increasingly used to recycle capital from the balance sheets of utilities through the sales of project stakes or refinancing. Institutional investors have an important role in freeing up debt and equity capital in operating-stage renewable electricity projects. Banks, private equity funds, project developers and utilities can then redeploy the proceeds into the development and construction of new projects. Innovative financing structures are now being used during construction and operational stages of renewable electricity projects. Since 2013, some utilities and other corporate entities have notably launched "yieldcos",[1] publicly traded companies whose growth is one of the main trends affecting renewables investment.
- Even though technology costs are falling fast, policy and market obstacles still constrain overall growth in investment in renewable electricity, limiting the pipeline of bankable projects and affecting the risk-return profile of renewable electricity investments. As well as insufficiently ambitious climate mitigation policies, the misalignment of other policies and regulations with respect to climate goals can act to hinder investment in renewable electricity. Misalignments can occur across the general investment environment, such as in the areas of investment policy, competition policy and electricity market design, trade and financial markets policy.
- Trade and investment policies that are inconsistent with climate change goals can create barriers to cross-border trade and investment in renewable electricity generation. The increasing use of local-content requirements in solar photovoltaic (PV) and wind energy since 2008 threatens to fragment rather than optimise global renewable electricity value

chains. Other outstanding trade and investment barriers in solar PV and wind energy include trade remedies and divergent national technical standards.

- Fragmentation in electricity markets, including in the development of transmission and distribution infrastructure, can favour fossil-fuel incumbency in the power sector and increase the cost of further integration of renewables. Factors include insufficient cross-border interconnection of transmission networks, which limits the flexibility of electricity systems and hinders integration of renewables, and heterogeneous design of capacity mechanisms with insufficient regional planning.[2]
- In order to unlock investment in renewable electricity, policy makers need to consider options to address existing obstacles to investment, especially concerning existing fragmentation in electricity markets and policy misalignments with climate change goals. Additional research is needed to help G20 and OECD policy makers address key policy priorities to overcome barriers to renewable energy investment and financing.

Introduction

Implementing the 2015 Paris Agreement concluded by the 21st Conference of the Parties (COP21) of the United Nations Framework Convention on Climate Change (UNFCCC) will require increasing the scale and pace of climate change mitigation efforts. At COP21, parties agreed to transition to "aggregate emission pathways consistent with holding the increase in the global average temperature to well below 2°C above preindustrial levels", going further than the previous agreement at Cancun in 2010.[3]

Yet a large gap remains between the action pledged by countries and the emission pathways consistent with the "well-below-2°C" target. As the OECD Secretary-General has emphasised, meeting the climate challenge requires achieving zero net greenhouse gas (GHG) emissions globally by the end of this century. The power sector will be crucial for these efforts (accounting for around 40% of global primary energy use and carbon dioxide (CO_2) emissions in 2012). Fortunately, though, it offers high potential for "decarbonisation" (IEA, 2015b).

Mobilising investment and financing in low-carbon energy technologies, and especially in renewable electricity, is therefore central to implementing the Paris Agreement. Although investment in renewable electricity generation has increased significantly over the past decade, achieving the energy transition will require considerable new private investment in both mature and early-stage clean energy technologies in the power sector. In addition to renewable electricity generation, this will include carbon capture and storage, electricity storage and demand-side management technologies such as smart grids.

The costs of many renewable electricity technologies are falling fast and some are becoming increasingly cost-competitive against fossil-fuel-based alternatives in a number of countries. So why is renewable electricity investment not growing faster? There is no shortage of available capital globally. The problem is the absence of a sufficient pipeline of bankable projects in renewable electricity. This is because renewable electricity investment and finance remain constrained by serious barriers linked to market and policy failures, along with country-specific impediments, market conditions (including fossil fuel prices)[4] and technical challenges. Such barriers can inhibit the development of renewable electricity-generating projects vis-à-vis fossil fuel-based infrastructure projects.

A key cause of the problem of insufficient investment opportunities in renewable electricity is a misalignment between climate goals, investment policies and the underlying economic conditions. The complexity of policy packages used around the world both to address climate change and to stimulate investment in renewable electricity has led to a web of different policies, resulting in a fragmented business environment. Furthermore, the layer of broader business regulations on which climate and renewables policies are overlaid can create conflicting incentives, increasing overall risk and constraining investment. Policy makers therefore have a role in setting coherent and predictable policies to send consistent signals to investors and financiers in renewable electricity. Future regulatory uncertainty makes it difficult for investors to formulate risk and return expectations, causing hesitation and preventing capital inflows.

This chapter reviews recent trends in renewable electricity investment and financing. It then focuses on key trends and policy misalignments that contribute to the fragmentation problem hindering renewable electricity development. These include:

- lack of coherent and sufficiently ambitious climate mitigation policies, such as insufficient carbon prices, inefficient fossil-fuel subsidies and policy uncertainty about renewable-energy incentives;
- misalignment of broader policies with climate change goals, e.g. within the general investment environment;
- inconsistent trade and investment policies that create barriers to cross-border trade and investment in renewable electricity and threaten to fragment rather than optimise global clean-energy value chains, especially in solar PV and wind energy;
- fragmentation in electricity markets and the development of electricity infrastructure, favouring fossil-fuel incumbency in the power sector and restricting further integration of renewable electricity.

Annex 5.A1 provides more information on the dataset used in the equity investment section. A glossary of technical terms used in this chapter can also be found in the annex.

The challenges ahead

The scale of greenhouse gas emissions reductions needed is large

The intended nationally determined contributions (INDCs) submitted prior to COP21, outlining countries' mitigation targets and actions starting in 2020, remain insufficient to achieve the agreed global climate change goals. By some estimates full implementation of all the INDCs would lead to a global temperature rise of around 3°C by 2100 (UNEP, 2015). In particular, energy-sector investment implied by the INDCs would remain insufficient to get the world on a path to achieve the 2°C target.

Given the scale of the climate challenge, recent emissions trends and developments relating to climate change mitigation policies in OECD countries and partner economies[5] suggest that enhanced action and co-ordination are required between all actors, including businesses, investors and governments. As highlighted by the recent OECD report *Climate Change Mitigation: Policies and Progress*, aggregate GHG emissions from OECD countries and partner economies have been increasing since the 1990s. In addition, although the use of renewable electricity is increasing, most countries still rely on fossil fuels and support the production and consumption of fossil fuels through subsidies and other budgetary measures. In particular, coal (the most carbon-intensive fuel) still accounted for 45% of electricity generation in OECD countries and partner economies in 2012 (OECD, 2015k). The share of total emissions covered by energy and carbon taxes also remains too low to spur technological change and shift investment decisions away from fossil fuels and towards renewable electricity.

The scale of the investment gap is also large but technology costs are falling

Despite recent growth, private sector investment in renewable electricity needs to be scaled up significantly to meet climate change goals. According to the International Energy Agency (IEA), to limit the temperature increase to 2°C, investment in "low-carbon power generation"[6] would need to triple between 2013 and 2035, and investment for energy efficiency across energy sectors would have to rise by a factor of eight (Figure 5.1).

Figure 5.1. **Growth in investment needs in low-carbon power generation and energy efficiency**

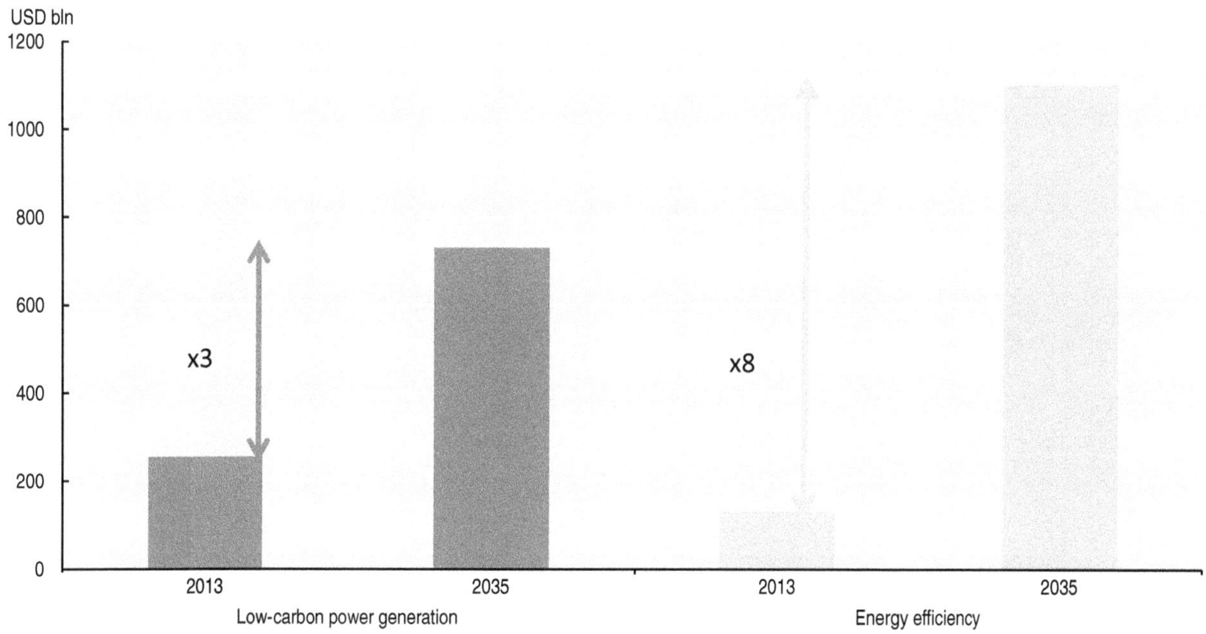

Note: All figures are expressed in USD billion.
Source: IEA (2014a).

StatLink http://dx.doi.org/10.1787/888933362568

The good news is that, on aggregate, scaling-up renewable electricity investments should not cost much more than the investment that would be required in energy infrastructure under business-as-usual assumptions. The IEA estimates that cumulative investment in energy supply and energy efficiency will need to reach USD 53 trillion by 2035. This is only 10% more than investment needs in the energy sector that are likely under current policies (IEA, 2014a).

These projections of modest incremental costs are driven in part by rapidly falling technology costs. From 2010-15, average costs for new onshore wind plants fell by 30% and average costs for new utility-scale solar PV installations declined by two-thirds (IEA, 2015c). The cost of solar components has halved since 2010, making current solar PV module costs just 1% of the price prevailing 35 years ago, while wind turbines can now generate 100 times more power than 30 years ago (Global Commission on the Economy and Climate, 2014). Utility-scale solar PV projects are now competitive against peaking gas generation in several countries in terms of costs to generate electricity.[7] Figure 5.2 presents recent IEA estimates of levelised costs of electricity for various renewable electricity technologies in the power sector, and shows that several of these technologies can now be competitive against fossil-fuel-based alternatives under certain conditions.

Figure 5.2. **Levelised cost of electricity using various technologies, 2015**

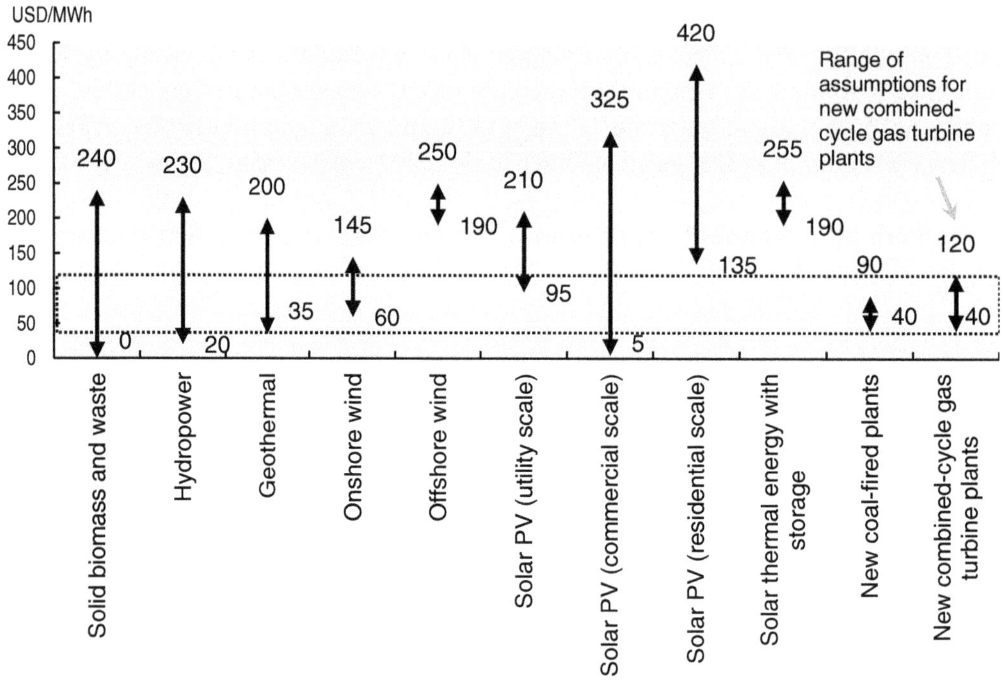

Note: The grey band represents the range of IEA assumptions for new combined cycle gas turbine (CCGT) plants.
Source: OECD calculations based on IEA (2015c).

StatLink http://dx.doi.org/10.1787/888933362571

Increased deployment of renewable electricity projects will also yield major economic and climate benefits, such as better health and reduced local air pollution, improved energy security and reduced traffic congestion, in addition to substantial fuel savings (OECD, 2015c; IEA, 2015d). The economic cost of damage to health from poor air quality, for instance, amounts to about 4% of GDP on average in the 15 countries with the highest GHG emissions; in the People's Republic of China, this value exceeds 10% of GDP (Global Commission on the Economy and Climate, 2014).

Key trends in renewable electricity investment and financing

This section provides a brief background overview of renewable electricity investment financing. It then describes the main trends and innovations occurring financing of renewable electricity projects. Subsequent sections of the chapter then turn to policy and market barriers related to fragmentation constraining overall investment and financing.

Overview: the shifting base of investment financing for renewable electricity

The United Nations Environment Programme (UNEP), based on Bloomberg New Energy Finance (BNEF) data, reports global new investment in renewable electricity and biofuels has reached a new record of USD 286 billion in 2015, an increase of 5% on 2014.[8] A major contributor was the installation of 118 Gigawatts (GW) of solar PV and wind capacity. Growth was largely driven by the Asian region where more than half of the total investment took place, with over one third of total investment in China alone. For the first time, developing countries accounted for more than half of global new investment in renewable electricity and biofuels (54.5%) (McCrone et al., 2016).

Figure 5.3 shows the full range of investment activity in renewable electricity and biofuels by asset class. It runs from the early stages of financing for companies and investment in research and development (R&D) at the left and moves to the roll-out phase on financing of new build assets (projects) in the middle. The right-hand side covers secondary market activities not associated with new activity, including investment projects that do not contribute directly to new assets or company financing, such as corporate mergers and acquisitions (M&As), private equity buyouts, investor exits and asset refinancing and acquisitions.

Figure 5.3. **Renewable electricity and biofuels investment financing, 2015**

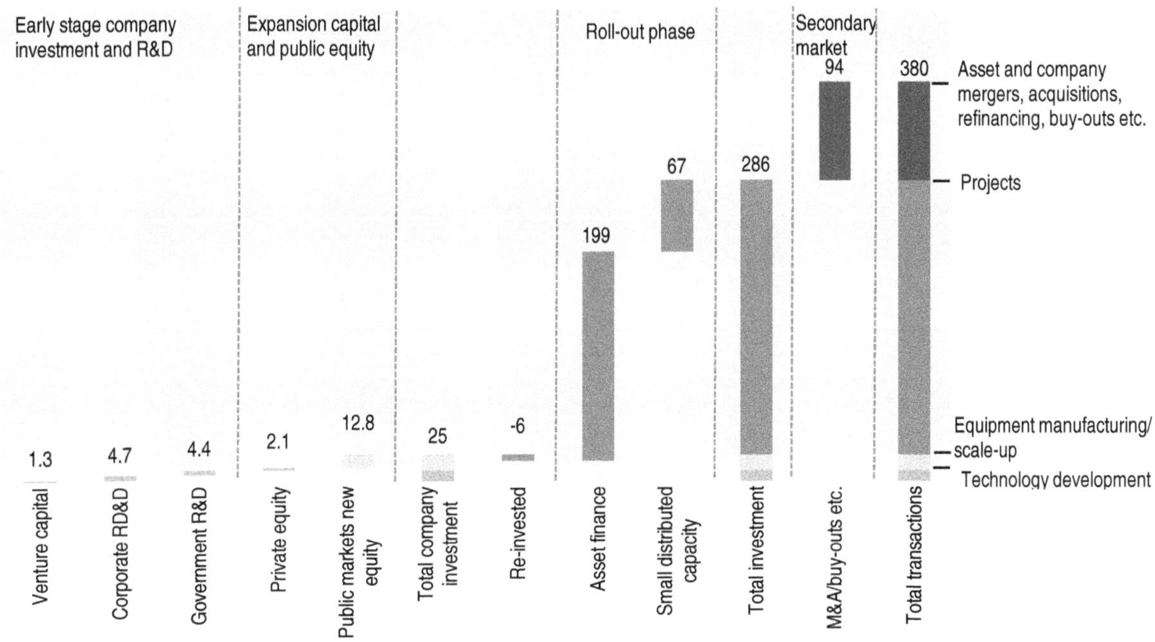

Note: All figures are expressed in USD billion. RD&D: research, development and demonstration. Total values include estimates for undisclosed deals. Figures may not add up exactly to totals, due to rounding.
Source: OECD calculations based on McCrone et al. (2016) and BNEF data.

StatLink http://dx.doi.org/10.1787/888933362587

Asset finance[9] of utility-scale[10] renewable electricity projects accounts for the largest share of new (or "greenfield") investment in renewable electricity and biofuels (i.e. in primary markets), accounting for USD 199 billion in 2015 (Figure 5.4). This is up from USD 188 billion in 2014.

In 2015, wind energy was the largest sector in terms of new utility-scale asset finance, rising 9% to USD 107 billion. Driven by growth in Europe and China, offshore wind energy rose 40% in 2015, accounting for USD 23.2 billion. The next largest sector, solar power, grew faster and advanced by 13% to USD 80.9 billion. Other sectors were much smaller, the next largest being biomass and waste-to-power, with USD 5.2 billion (down 46% from the previous year).

Financial markets support the renewable electricity sector through a variety of investors (e.g. utilities, banks or institutional investors) and financial structures (such as debt, equity or mezzanine). Figure 5.4 shows the split in global asset financing by type of

Figure 5.4. **Asset financing of new investment in renewable energy by type of financing, 2004-15**

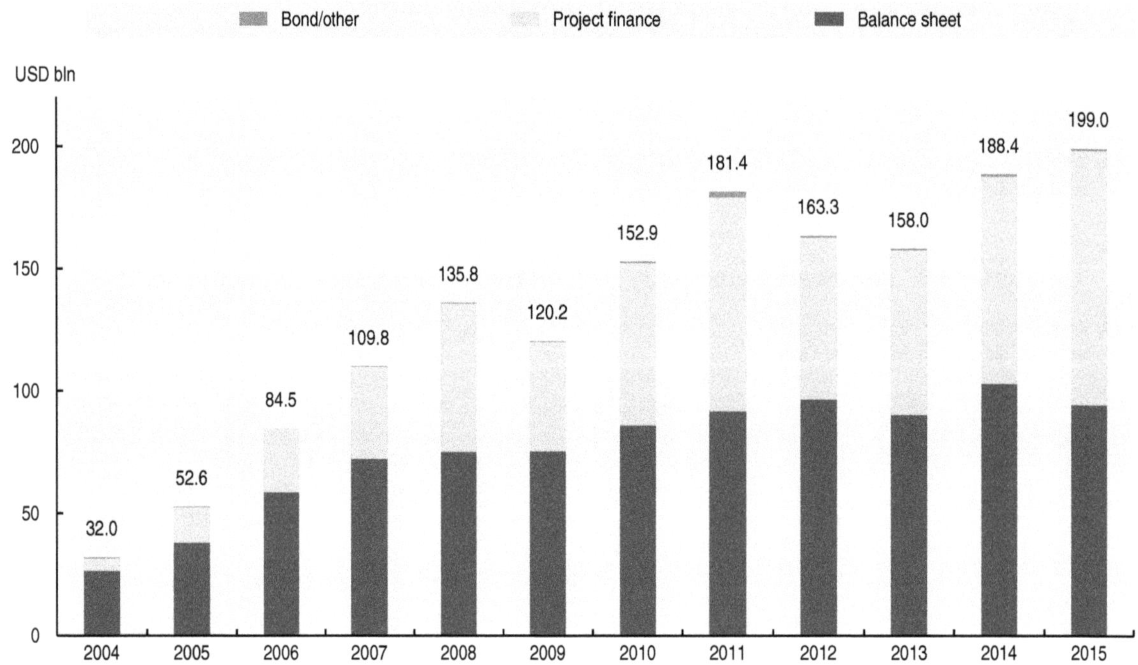

Note: All figures are expressed in USD billion. Total values include estimates for undisclosed deals. "Bond" refers to project bonds, and does not include corporate bonds and public bonds. In this graph, "renewable energy" refers to renewable electricity generation and biofuels.
Source: McCrone et al. (2016), based on BNEF data.

StatLink http://dx.doi.org/10.1787/888933362596

arrangement.[11] Renewable electricity projects can be financed in three ways (OECD 2015b, j, 2016c forthcoming):

- **Project finance,** involving a mixture of debt (mainly banks) and equity capital. Based on available equity and debt data from BNEF, 2015 marked the first year in which project finance represented more than half of total asset finance in renewable electricity and biofuels McCrone et al., 2016). Project financing of renewable projects has been growing strongly in the last few years, reflecting preference for term loans structures in developing countries such as China and South Africa. In 2015, non-recourse project finance[12] made up 52% of total asset financing, at USD 104 billion, up from 45% in 2014.
- **On-balance-sheet corporate financing,** by utilities, independent power producers, project developers and other corporates. In 2015, on-balance-sheet financing of projects by utilities, corporate actors (non-energy corporations and manufacturers), independent power producers and developers made up approximately USD 94 billion, representing about 47% of total asset finance in renewable electricity and biofuels.
- **Project bonds and other types of transactions** accounted for a small residual of asset finance flows.

Additional sources of finance and new financial structures are emerging. Utilities and power producers continue to be substantial providers of equity capital in the renewable sector. However, due to the large scale investment and stable income returns, there is greater interest from the financial services industry. As renewable electricity becomes increasingly cost-competitive, and the low-risk and stable-return profile of assets becomes more apparent, the largest institutional infrastructure investors are accessing renewable

Box 5.1. **Drivers of funding and financing models for renewable electricity projects**

What are possible factors influencing the funding and financing models such as corporate, project finance or bond structures? Possible drivers and parameters may include:

- *The financing profile of the investment*: a large initial investment followed by significant operating and maintenance costs could for instance indicate advantages from bundling the construction, operation and maintenance of the assets in a single contract. In the wind- and solar-power sectors, most of the costs are incurred upfront, so concessions are often used by governments to procure projects. Project finance structures matching the long term nature of the concessions and relying on the cash flows during the operation period then become the preferred route for financing renewable projects.
- *The potential for cost recovery from users*: for investments in sectors that have a non-excludable nature for example, user fees will not be practicable and the project will need to be funded via government spending.
- *The extent to which quality is contractible*: When quality is difficult to specify and monitor for instance, contracts are likely to be costly and time consuming to develop, and will be highly vulnerable to renegotiation.
- *The level of uncertainty, especially within broader enabling conditions, and attractiveness of domestic policy frameworks*: projects may face significant speculative risks that are difficult for the private sector to quantify and mitigate, linked notably to unstable and unpredictable legal and regulatory frameworks, high political risk and construction risk. In the offshore wind-power sector for example, as projects scale up and move into deeper water, newer technologies also add to construction risk, which may discourage some investors from participating. The political and regulatory regime, and the risk that support will erode over time, are key considerations for investors when investing in renewable electricity projects.
- *Financial market conditions*, such as difficulties in securing project finance debt, development of capital markets and corporate constraints (i.e. deleveraging, impact of oil prices), high costs of capital.
- *Optimal allocation of risks*: the ability to identify, assess and allocate risk appropriately is an important consideration driving the decision about funding and financing structures.

Source: OECD (2016c, forthcoming), *Infrastructure Financing: Partnering with the Private Sector*, OECD Publishing, Paris; and the OECD Public Investment Framework.

projects through direct investment (OECD, 2015b, j, 2016c, forthcoming). In some cases, project bonds are another emerging way to raise debt financing compared to more established sources of corporate debt or project finance (OECD, 2016b). As recently surveyed by the OECD (2015j), investment is also channelled through public-market vehicles such as "yieldcos", real estate investment trusts (REITs) and other publicly listed vehicles (see Annex 5.A2). Finally, investment growth and recent trends, such as divesting of assets from utilities, are contributing to the development of a secondary market for renewable electricity.

The equity mix in wind energy is changing

This section analyses the evolution of the equity mix in ownership and financing models for both onshore and offshore wind energy in Europe.[13] The equity mix for renewable electricity projects has changed vastly in the last five years. Recent developments in the wind energy sector in Europe between 2010 and 2015 are illustrative.

The first offshore wind-power farms were typically financed on the balance sheets of the utilities that conceived, built, and operated them. Now banks, private equity funds, pension funds, state-backed "green" banks and insurance companies have all invested in these projects. Figure 5.5 highlights changes to the equity mix of wind energy deals, comparing deals which reached financial closure in Europe in 2010 and 2015.[14]

Figure 5.5. **Change in equity mix in wind energy projects in Europe, 2010 and 2015**

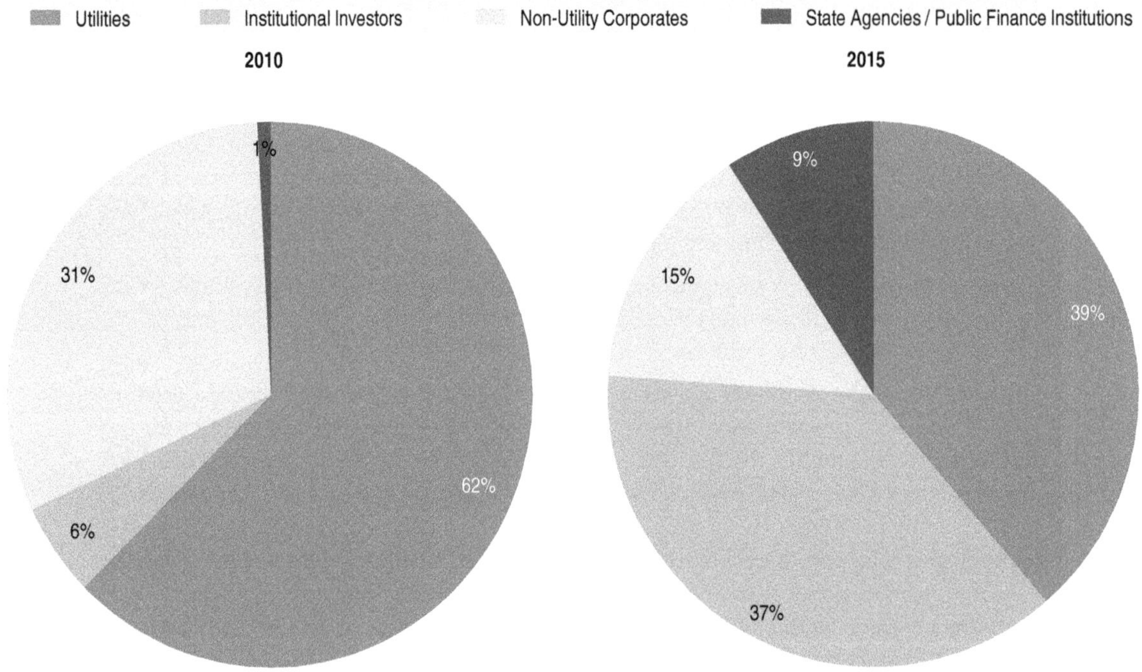

Note: Figures correspond to shares of total equity in sample.
Source: BNEF (2016), OECD calculations.

StatLink http://dx.doi.org/10.1787/888933362600

The share of total equity provided by utilities (state-owned and private) decreased from 62% in 2010 to 39% in 2015, that of non-utility corporates from 31% to 15%. In other words, the combined share of the two traditional equity investors in the wind energy sector decreased substantially, from 93% in 2010 to 54% in 2015. Accordingly, other investors have stepped up their activities. Further research is needed to understand the decreased role of utilities beyond deleveraging as a consequence of the crisis.

Institutional investors[15] drive this development, at least for brownfield projects; pension funds, insurance companies, private equity and infrastructure funds have become major equity investors in the European wind sector. Their share in total equity provision increased from 6% in 2010 to 37% in 2015, making them the second most important equity providers in the 2015 sample, just 1% behind utilities. The increase of equity provision by institutional investors in the sample can be traced mainly to the acquisition of brownfield assets or portfolios for onshore wind deals. Pension funds and insurers were not involved in any greenfield onshore wind-power transactions included in the 2015 sample. This suggests that institutional investors look to the onshore wind sector mainly for the acquisition of existing projects.

Equity investment in wind energy assets by state agencies and public finance institutions grew significantly from a marginal share in 2010 to 9% of total equity invested in 2015.

In the sample, this increase can be attributed mostly to the activities of the UK Green Investment Bank. This institution was created by the UK government in 2012 to attract private sector financing for green infrastructure projects. The creation or expansion of similar institutions is a trend observable at the global level, and is important for risk sharing with newer technologies. In the offshore wind sector, for example, as projects scale up and move into deeper water, newer technologies also add to construction risk. This may discourage some investors from participating. In Europe, commercial banks have invested in partnership with government supported banks (e.g. United Kingdom's Green Investment Bank, Germany's KfW Development Bank), export credit agencies (e.g. Denmark's EKF and Belgium's Delcredere – Ducroire), and multilateral banks (e.g. the European Investment Bank; see OECD, 2016a forthcoming).

On the project level, large offshore wind deals illustrate the diversifying equity mix. The largest wind energy deal in Europe to reach financial closure in 2015, the Galloper Offshore Wind Farm, provides an example of a project in which equity investors include a utility (the German company RWE), a public finance institution (the UK Green Investment Bank) and institutional investors (Macquarie Capital). The equity part of the second largest deal, the Veja Mate Offshore Wind Farm, was provided by two institutional investors, while mezzanine finance was provided by another. Finally, the UK Green investment Bank and the utility E.ON collaborated for the financing of the Rampion Offshore Wind Farm. All three deals were greenfield projects (albeit offshore) with a transaction value of over USD 2 billion each.

Renewable electricity infrastructure can offer an attractive return profile for long-term investors

Many institutional investors, notably pension funds, have long-dated liabilities and may not necessarily face short-term liquidity needs. These investors are increasingly seeking to invest in lower beta assets where risk-return trade-offs may be better than in public equity markets. Indeed, the recent OECD Survey of Large Pension Funds (LPFs) and Public Pension Reserve Funds (PPRFs) (OECD, 2016d) indicates that allocations to listed equities declined from 2010-14, confirming that large pension funds are shifting return-seeking assets to alternative investments.

As part of the overall trends in alternative investments and demand for higher-yielding assets, pension fund demand for investment in illiquid unlisted infrastructure equity markets has increased over the past five years. Despite this strong demand, the funds that reported their unlisted infrastructure equity allocation have only increased this allocation slowly over the past five years, occupying around 3.5% of portfolios, on average, in 2014 (Figure 5.6). At the same time, many funds reported that they were below their investment targets for infrastructure. This suggests that funds have some capacity to increase their investment in unlisted infrastructure equity. By investing directly in renewable electricity projects or through funds that invest in renewable electricity assets, some pension funds have included renewable electricity as part of their illiquid infrastructure allocation. These findings confirm the above analysis on the changing sources of finance in renewable electricity sectors, particularly in pension fund investment in onshore wind.

Additionally, renewable electricity has potential to contribute to meeting institutions' liability-driven investment objectives. A 25-year power purchase agreement on a solar project, for example, creates a predictable stream of future cash flows, providing a bond-like return profile. Renewable electricity projects with a strong yield component and

Figure 5.6. **Historical unlisted infrastructure equity allocation of selected pension funds, 2010-14**

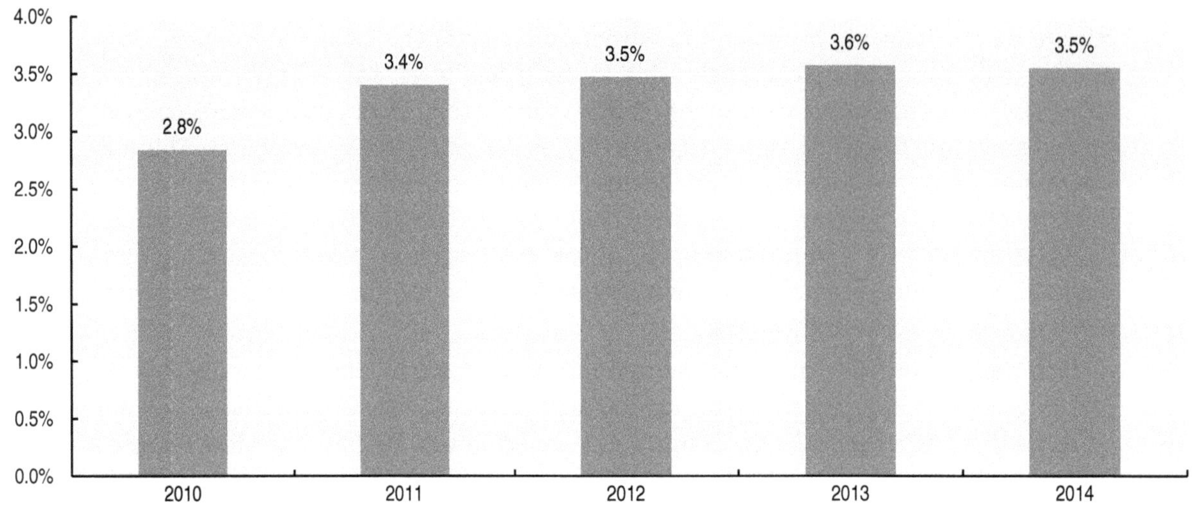

Note: Pension funds refer to large pension funds (LPFs) and public pension reserve funds (PPRFs). Values are a simple average invested in unlisted infrastructure equity for those LPFs and PPRFs that reported unlisted infrastructure equity exposure in Part B of the 2015 survey, independently of their size in terms of assets. The data track a total of 24 LPFs and PPRFs over the period 2010-14.
Source: OECD (2016d).

StatLink http://dx.doi.org/10.1787/888933362617

suitable risk profiles may diversify liability-driven investment portfolios and benchmarks of pension funds, which tend to be dominated by fixed income.

Despite the increasing interest, renewable electricity is still a small component of the total infrastructure allocation by pension funds. This reflects the overall investment environment for renewables: market barriers and policy risks (described later in this chapter) mean that opportunities are fewer than in more traditional infrastructure sectors such as transport or conventional energy.[16] Of the 26 pensions and reserve funds that reported sector allocations in their infrastructure portfolios, only nine reported exposure to renewable electricity. The largest allocation of an infrastructure portfolio to renewables was 19% (PFA Pension, Denmark), while the smallest was less than 1% of total infrastructure investment (OMERS, Canada). It is noteworthy that OMERS, the fund with the largest allocation to infrastructure in absolute terms in the survey population, had a very small weight in renewable electricity, given the long history of the fund's investment in infrastructure and expertise in due diligence and deal sourcing. Most funds reported exposure to renewables in unlisted infrastructure equity, either through private equity-style funds or through direct investment and co-investment in renewable electricity projects.

Public equity markets have provided innovative finance for renewable electricity

While pension funds and other institutional investors have been active in financing renewable electricity projects in illiquid private markets, some new equity instruments have become available through public equity markets. This trend has increased competition for renewable electricity assets in some regions, especially in the United Kingdom and the United States. Different investor bases can have differing costs of equity. Competition amongst equity sources of capital that minimise the cost of equity has been a driving source of these financing trends and has spurred innovations to create new vehicles to access renewable electricity investment.

Over the past few years, a handful of exchange-listed closed-end funds have emerged in the United Kingdom. These funds raise capital by issuing shares and debt to acquire wind and solar assets. The funds are designed to pay a significant amount of earnings as dividends to shareholders. Closed-end funds have been used for a number of years in infrastructure finance, particularly in Australia where some funds have lengthy track records.

In the United States, yieldcos have emerged as a new form of public equity market finance for renewable electricity. Yieldcos differ from closed-end funds in that they are essentially publicly listed companies that hold renewable electricity assets. Most often these assets are acquired directly from a sponsoring parent such as a utility. But yieldcos are similar to closed-end funds in that they are designed to pay out a significant amount of earnings in the form of dividends.

Recent developments in the United States yieldco market have tested their structures and raised questions about their future. Since yieldcos were established to hold cash-flow generating assets and are committed to distribute all, or substantially all, of available cash to investors as dividends,[17] this would imply that much of the expected return to investors would be in the form of income instead of capital growth. Yet many yieldcos included aggressive dividend growth policies as part of their earnings guidance. This strong growth had been fuelled through direct acquisitions of assets and drop-downs from the sponsoring entity. Such growth through investment required a strong pipeline of projects and near continuous access to capital markets – both in debt markets, and the ability to tap equity markets through new share issues.

A steep drop in yieldco equity prices in 2015, prompted by flaws in the business model and also contagion from falling fossil fuel prices, closed off access to capital markets and brought the yieldco machine to a halt. While falling stock prices lead to rising dividend yields, they made growth through new acquisitions unfeasible due to depressed stock prices. As a result, investors are re-evaluating the yieldco model.

Investors may also be hesitant with the yieldco model due to lacklustre performance. Comparing yieldco performance to that of master limited partnerships (MLPs),[18] the return on equity for the five largest yieldcos was consistently below that of the five largest MLPs (Figure 5.7). An unproven yieldco business model combined with a relatively short operational history and weak performance leaves many investors on the side-lines.

In order to build confidence in the yieldco model, greater transparency of asset transactions (drop-downs from sponsor) is necessary, along with stronger and more responsible corporate governance. Additionally, reforms such as higher carbon prices and stronger climate mitigation policies (described in detail in further sections) could make investment in renewable energy, through public equity markets, more attractive by making returns more competitive with conventional energy.

Further innovation is afoot in public equity markets for the finance of renewable electricity. Proposed legislation in the United States seeks to include projects in wind and solar as qualifying assets under securities laws that govern MLPs, potentially expanding the field of listed equity finance for renewable electricity. The growth of closed-end funds, such as in the United Kingdom, shows signs of attracting higher levels of investment. Public equity markets have the potential to meet the growing financing needs of renewable energy, yet the market is still in a state of development where new business models seek greater acceptance from investors, combined with the need for mitigating policies, that make renewable energy assets more attractive for investment.

Figure 5.7. **Average ROE of largest yieldcos and master limited partnerships in the United States, 2013-15**

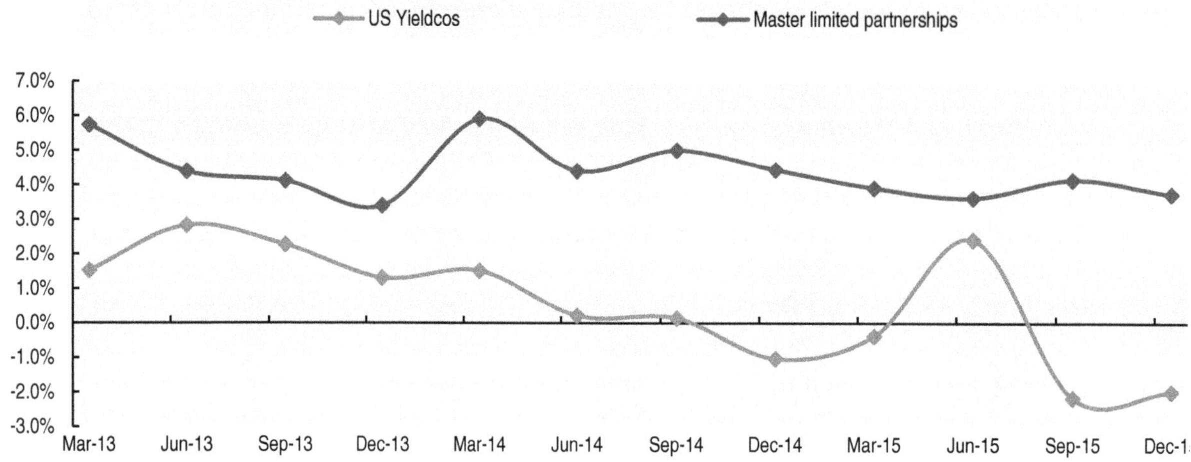

Note: ROE: return on equity.
Source: Reuters, OECD calculations.

StatLink http://dx.doi.org/10.1787/888933362625

A secondary market for renewable electricity projects has developed

Corporate asset disposals from utilities and refinancing of projects in operation, coupled with a strong appetite from investors, are contributing to the increase in global secondary market acquisition transactions in the renewable sector. Figure 5.8 shows corporate M&A, private equity buy-outs and public market investor exits, as well as the refinancing and acquisition of renewable assets.

Figure 5.8. **Acquisition transactions in renewable energy by type, 2004-15**

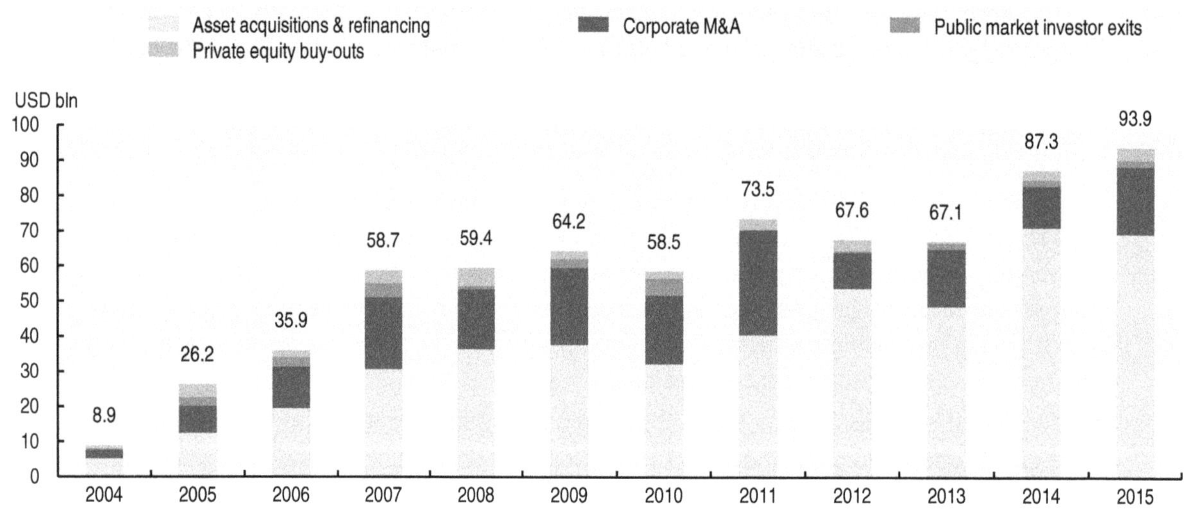

Note: All figures are expressed in USD billion. Total values include estimates for undisclosed deals.
Source: McCrone et al. (2016), based on BNEF data.

StatLink http://dx.doi.org/10.1787/888933362632

In the United States and the European Union, competition from renewable electricity and lower demand for energy are putting pressure on utilities and developers. In order to preserve the balance sheet or undertake new projects, many utilities are now seeking to recycle capital through sales of equity stakes. In December 2015, for example, the yieldco TerraForm Power acquired more than 90% of the North American wind energy portfolio from the developer Invenergy, for USD 2 billion. Almost USD 300 million was financed via commercial debt, while TerraForm financed the remaining amount through its balance sheet. Three of the seven wind farms included were under construction at the time, and the acquisition will be completed upon operation, providing an example of secondary market transaction at the construction stage.

A range of financial institutions has provided capital for the refinancing of operating offshore wind projects on a project finance basis, including banks, export credit agencies, multilateral development banks, pension funds and sovereign wealth funds. In December 2015, the investor Blackstone issued USD 1.067 billion in bonds to refinance Phase I of the MeerWind Sud und Ost Offshore Wind Farm (OECD 2015a, 2016b). Table 5.1 summarises other recent prominent examples in the secondary market.

Table 5.1. **Top transactions in secondary markets in Q4 2015**

Organisation	Country	Sector	Type of transaction	Acquirer	Value (USD mln)
Invenergy North American Wind Portfolio TerraForm Acquisition	Canada	Wind	Term loan	Terraform Power	2 000
Meerwind Sud und Ost Offshore Wind Farm Phase I Refinancing	Germany	Wind	Bond	Blackstone Group	1 067
Benedict First State Investment Portugal Wind Farm Portfolio Acquisition	Portugal	Wind	Bond	First State Wind Energy	1 012
Finerge-Gestao de Projectos Energeticos	Portugal	Wind	Equity (company)	First State Wind Energy	956
GDF Suez Mitsui Axium Infrastructure Canadian Wind/Solar Portfolio Refinancing	Canada	Wind	Term loan	Fiera Axium, IPR-GDF, Mitsui & Co	464

Source: BNEF (2016).

Given these trends in the renewable electricity market, it is not surprising to see increased co-operation between utilities and other market participants. This can be observed at the project level, as highlighted in Table 5.1, but also at the institutional level, where formal partnerships have been emerging. In particular, utilities have recently established joint ventures with financial companies to invest in renewable electricity. The aim is to combine the operational expertise of energy companies with the financing know-how and long-term capital fundraising of established investment companies. For example:

- The French utility EDF and Amundi partnered in 2014 to create a joint asset management company that will finance energy-related projects. This partnership initially plans to raise EUR 1.5 billion for the financing of renewable electricity generation and energy efficiency projects.
- In Italy, EDF and Edison, two utilities, and the infrastructure fund F2i established the third-largest operator in the Italian renewable energy sector in 2014. EDF is responsible for the operation of the facilities while Edison is in charge of the marketing.
- In Germany, the utility RWE, along with 29 municipal utilities, established Green GECCO in 2010, a joint-venture company for renewable projects which operates five wind farms to date.

Policy misalignment and fragmentation: implications for renewable electricity investment

The evolution and innovation in financing models described above have led to a return to growth in total investment in renewable electricity. Nevertheless, investment remains constrained by policy and market obstacles that either hinder the development of a sufficient pipeline of bankable clean-energy projects or affect the risk-return profile of renewable projects. These barriers include policy stability and alignment, market design issues, technology risk and prevailing fossil-fuel energy prices. Taken together they can lead to weaker returns for renewables investments, as reflected, for example, in the returns on equity for clean energy companies (Box 5.1).

Box 5.1. **Returns on renewables investments: The case of equity for large listed companies**

As noted in the *OECD Business and Finance Outlook, 2015*, returns on equity have tended to be insufficient to cover costs of capital for large listed companies specialised in clean energy, at least since 2008. (Figure 5.9 considers a group of large publicly-listed clean-energy companies cited within the Bloomberg "Clean Energy" index.) The discrepancy between falling technology costs and poor returns on equity can be explained by a number of market and policy factors.

Figure 5.9. **ROE on clean energy investments minus COE, public companies 2002-15**

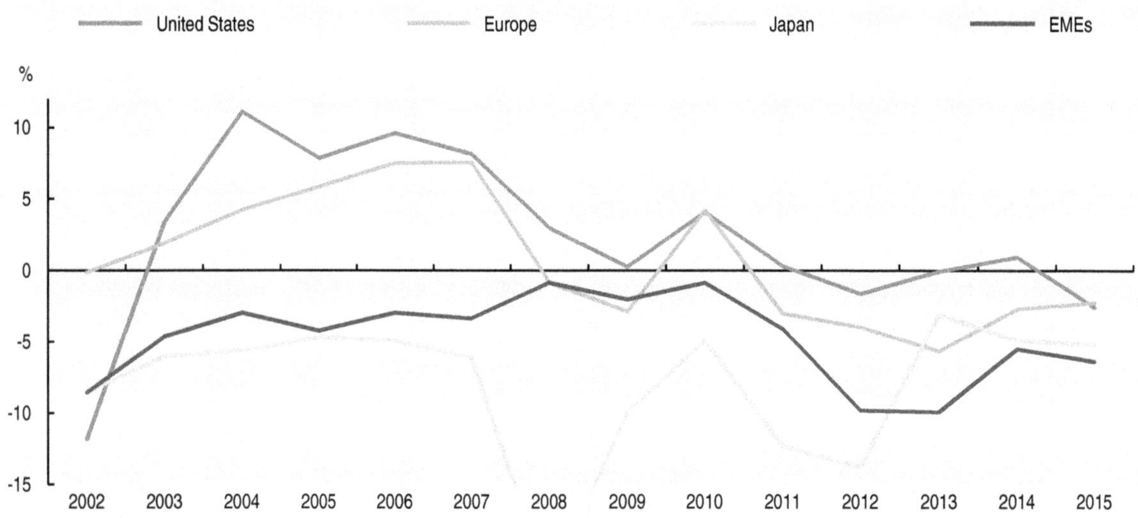

Note: ROE: return on equity. COE: cost of equity. Europe refers to the European Union and Switzerland.
Source: Bloomberg, *OECD Business and Finance Outlook 2015*.

StatLink http://dx.doi.org/10.1787/888933362646

This section discusses the key role policy makers can play to remove outstanding investment barriers and scale up attractive investment opportunities in renewable electricity. A broad approach is necessary, combining strong climate change policies with efforts to ensure that policies affecting the broader investment environment for renewable electricity (such as investment policy or the design of electricity markets) are coherent and aligned with climate goals. A more aligned policy landscape can strengthen the confidence of private financiers in renewable electricity investments.

Set stronger climate mitigation policies

As highlighted by the report *Aligning Policies for a Low-carbon Economy* (OECD/IEA/NEA/ITF, 2015), economy-wide shifts in investment away from fossil-fuel-based options remain constrained by the absence of coherent and strong climate mitigation policies. These policies are needed to internalise climate change costs and to create incentives for the private sector to shift investment away from fossil-fuel-based technologies towards "low-carbon" technologies, including renewable electricity. When developing climate change policies aimed at the electricity sector, priorities for policy makers include:

- Setting a robust, credible long-term price on GHG emissions. Putting a price on carbon is critical to send long-term signals to investors. OECD analysis shows that explicit carbon-pricing tools, such as carbon taxes and emissions-trading schemes, are more effective than other policy instruments (such as mandates) in abating GHG emissions (OECD, 2013c). In the electricity sector, carbon pricing acts to increase wholesale prices due to the extra cost levied on carbon-intensive generation. Currently however, carbon prices generally remain too low to encourage investment in renewable electricity technologies. Supporting climate policies are thus needed to achieve GHG emissions reductions in the electricity sector without compromising other policy goals such as energy security and energy access.
- Developing targeted investment incentives, designed to complement carbon pricing policies and help deploy renewable electricity projects. In addition to carbon pricing, policy makers have provided significant support in the past decade to help deploy renewable electricity technologies at commercial-scale through targeted incentives. For renewable electricity, some of these measures offer a fixed tariff to generators and so operate largely independently of the electricity market (e.g. feed-in tariffs). Others, such as feed-in premiums, offer a premium to wholesale electricity prices. Globally, government support for renewable energy amounted to USD 121 billion in 2013 – of which 80% went to renewable electricity generation and 20% to biofuels. As of early 2015, 145 countries had implemented renewable-energy incentives, including feed-in tariffs, renewable electricity certificates, public auctions and tax incentives (REN21, 2015).
- Eliminating inefficient subsidies and other forms of support to fossil fuels, which create disincentives to renewable investment, including in the electricity sector. Such support undermines global efforts to achieve zero net emissions in the second half of this century. Although government support for fossil fuels seems to have peaked in 2011-12, such support in OECD countries and the BRIICS[19] still amounted to USD 160-200 billion annually (OECD, 2015m).
- Providing targeted technology support to innovation, e.g. through targeted, technology-neutral public support for research, development and demonstration.

Aligning the broader investment environment

Adopting a portfolio of climate policies is critical to address the gap between current and desired GHG emissions trends, but is not in itself sufficient. The overall investment environment still collectively favours investment in fossil-fuel-based options. Achieving the desired emissions reductions – including scaling up investment in renewable electricity – also requires that broader policies affecting investment are not misaligned with climate goals (OECD/IEA/ITF/NEA, 2015). Such misalignment of policies increases the public cost of climate-specific policies and can even lead to retroactive policy changes, for example retrospective changes to solar PV feed-in tariff contracts in several countries. These changes can increase investors' risk and increase market fragmentation. Policy misalignment can also unnecessarily add to the cost of renewable electricity investments.

In accordance with the OECD *Policy Framework for Investment*, the investment environment or business climate can be defined as the range of policy fields that form a country's enabling environment for all types of investment (OECD, 2015e). Potential misalignments with climate goals can be identified in many different policy areas, including trade and investment policies affecting manufacturing, electricity market design features and financial and banking regulations. Some of these are considered in the following sections.

However, more empirical evidence is needed to help policy makers improve the effectiveness of policy support to investment in renewable electricity, including through aligning the broader investment environment and addressing fragmented business conditions. Ongoing OECD work is undertaking new econometric analysis to estimate the impact of climate mitigation policies and investment conditions – and their interactions – on investment flows in renewable electricity generation in OECD and G20 countries (OECD, 2017a forthcoming). The report seeks to build on qualitative conclusions in the *Aligning Policies for a Low-Carbon Economy* report and assess empirically how the investment environment influences the "effectiveness"[20] of climate mitigation policies in mobilising investment flows in renewable electricity generation in OECD and G20 countries. Based on this analysis, the report will seek to identify which climate mitigation policies are more effective in driving investment flows and encouraging patent activity in renewable electricity generation in OECD and G20 countries. It will also consider the hypothesis that the effectiveness of such policies depends on the broader investment environment.

Avoid fragmenting global renewable electricity value chains

Over the past decade, governments have provided substantial support to the deployment of renewable electricity, and both international and domestic investors have benefited. Applied import tariffs on solar PV and wind energy equipment are relatively low across OECD and emerging economies, and *de jure* restrictions to foreign direct investment (such as limits on foreign ownership) in clean electricity generation remain limited, especially in OECD countries.

Since the 2008 financial crisis, however, the perceived potential of renewable electricity to promote growth and employment has led several governments to implement trade and investment measures protecting domestic solar panel and wind turbine manufacturers, with a view to creating local jobs and promoting exports (OECD, 2015a; Bahar et al., 2013). In particular, the OECD report *Overcoming Barriers to International Investment in Clean Energy* (OECD, 2015a) highlights that:

- Policy makers have increasingly used local-content requirements in solar PV and wind energy since 2009. Local-content requirements typically require project developers or investors to source a specific share of manufactured components or equipment locally to be eligible for policy support or public tenders. Such requirements have been planned or implemented in solar and wind energy sectors in at least 21 countries, including 16 OECD countries and emerging economies, mostly since 2009.[21]
- The alleged use of dumping or actionable subsidies has resulted in an escalation in the use of trade remedies in solar PV energy, and to a lesser extent, in wind energy. Between

January 2010 and September 2014, OECD countries and emerging economies have imposed nine anti-dumping duties and seven countervailing duties on products and components associated with solar PV and wind energy, and launched 24 WTO investigations for anti-dumping or countervailing duties.

- There are outstanding non-tariff barriers to trade and investment in solar and wind energy, such as divergent domestic technical standards in wind energy.

Such measures can seriously disrupt global value chains. They are misaligned with climate goals. In particular, according to recent OECD work (OECD, 2015a):

- The increasing use of local-content requirements in solar PV and wind energy in OECD and emerging economies since 2008 has had a detrimental effect on global international investment flows in solar and wind energy. Midstream manufacturing and downstream activities (such as power plant project development) in solar PV and wind energy sectors are increasingly global, i.e. solar and wind-power generation relies on an increasing share of imported intermediate products. This means that by raising the cost of inputs for downstream businesses, local-content requirements can hinder the profitability of downstream investors and lead to increased overall costs, weakened price competitiveness, reduced international investment flows and higher electricity prices. The rise of green industrial policies, especially through local-content requirements, threatens to fragment solar PV and wind energy value chains into regional and domestic markets. This may prevent supply chain optimisation and cost reductions.
- Analysis of the solar PV and wind energy value chains suggests that local content requirements may have limited or even negative impacts on value added and job creation. This is because downstream activities represent the largest share of job creation and value added potential in solar PV and wind energy. In the solar PV sector in particular, manufacturing activities represent only 18%-24 % of total jobs, according to recent estimates. At least 50% of solar PV jobs and value-added are located in downstream activities. This means that policies targeting manufacturing activities may not be effective in creating domestic jobs and value across the entire value chains.
- In addition, the increasing use of trade remedies against imports of solar PV and wind turbine components has led to large reductions in global trade, especially for solar PV, amounting to around USD 14 billion annually (Cimino and Hufbauer, 2014).

Reduce the fragmentation of electricity networks and markets

The characteristics of electricity markets and systems may themselves be constraining investment in renewables. Liberalised electricity markets, as they are designed today, can be considered misaligned with climate change objectives. Indeed, "current designs of wholesale electricity markets in many OECD countries are not strategically aligned with the low-carbon transition. They do not deliver the long-term price signal that investment in high capital cost, low-carbon technologies […] would require" (OECD/IEA/ITF/NEA, 2015). Given that renewables have often been supported by "out-of-market" incentives in parallel with wholesale markets, the integration of renewables into existing market designs has contributed to downward pressure on electricity prices (along with reduced overall demand in many OECD countries and reduced running hours for conventional power plants; see Box 5.2). Wholesale electricity prices are now at their lowest level since 2002, squeezing profit margins of conventional electricity utilities. As a result, in 2015 more than one-quarter of Standard & Poors' rated universe of Europe, Middle-East and Africa (EMEA) utilities has been subject to negative rating actions (downgrade or negative outlook revision). Combined with the policy uncertainties described above, the result is that many utilities may limit investments – including in renewables – for cash flow preservation and balance sheet protection.

Box 5.2. **Electricity market design and renewable electricity**

Several analyses have noted that the current designs of wholesale liberalised electricity markets are often not strategically aligned with the low-carbon transition (OECD/IEA/NEA/ITF, 2015; IEA, 2014c). "Energy-only" wholesale electricity markets would not attract investment in low-carbon technologies unless there was a high CO_2 price, periods of very high electricity prices and even risks of rolling brown-outs (because electricity demand remains fairly inflexible in most countries). Even if these conditions were to occur, the high risks involved would lead to higher cost of capital which would in itself hinder low-carbon investment, given that most low-carbon generation options have high upfront capital costs and low (or near-zero) variable running costs.

To stimulate investment in renewable electricity, many governments have turned to "out of market" measures that offer a fixed tariff to generators, such as feed-in tariffs. While feed-in tariffs can be effective at providing revenue certainty for investors, the challenge of setting appropriate tariff levels is important. Also, as the proportion of low-marginal-cost renewables rises due to these out-of-market agreements, the result is downward pressure on wholesale prices, especially when overall electricity demand is also falling, as has been the case in some OECD countries. This exacerbates the well-known "missing money" problem in electricity markets, whereby short-run marginal cost pricing does not guarantee full recovery of capital costs for all plants, including renewables (OECD/IEA/NEA/ITF, 2015; IEA, 2014c).

New market arrangements are needed to ensure competitive investment in low-carbon capacity, and to ensure that renewable electricity is generated when it is of most value to the overall system. Mechanisms involving price discovery are a promising step forward. Auctions for procurement of specific new capacity at new locations appear to provide a strong incentive for investment while delivering low electricity prices even for renewables, provided that the purchase agreements are for a sufficiently long duration (IEA, 2016). Some countries have also required renewable generators to sell their electricity on the wholesale market, while guaranteeing a supplementary premium payment (feed-in premiums). Further, market design issues will also be different in fast-growing regulated markets that do not rely on spot markets, such as in China.

The investment profile of renewable electricity projects can also be affected by elements of fragmentation in the development of transmission and distribution infrastructure for electricity and in some elements of electricity market design. These include:

- a lack of investment in transmission networks, including cross-border interconnections, reducing the flexibility of electricity systems;
- the design of capacity mechanisms used to ensure that sufficient generating capacity will always be available in systems based on wholesale electricity markets.

Investing in the flexibility of electricity systems

The variability of renewable electricity generation means that, to integrate high proportions of renewables into existing electricity networks at lowest cost, significant investment will be required to improve the overall flexibility of electricity systems. While technical solutions do exist, the flexibility of the whole system needs to be considered – including the demand side, transmission and distribution management, storage availability and generating patterns of both conventional generators and the renewables themselves (IEA 2014c; IEA, 2016). This includes, notably, investment in network infrastructure in two ways:

- investments and improvements in transmission and distribution networks locally;
- broadening the geographic spread of electricity systems by increasing levels of interconnection between neighbouring electricity grids (including policy harmonisation to optimise the cross-border flow of electricity).

Variable renewable electricity technologies are essential to address climate change but their integration into existing grid systems can be challenging. Weather-dependent technologies such as wind and solar PV do not generate electricity constantly, and although energy storage technologies are developing fast, cost-effective storage options do not yet exist. Recent improvements in weather forecasting have dramatically improved the predictability of wind and solar generation on a day-ahead timeframe (IEA, 2014c). However, wind and solar plants are still not fully dispatchable, meaning that the system operator cannot rely on being able to call upon them at times of high demand. Other dispatchable capacity needs to be available to allow for system balancing. The location of renewable generating sites can also pose an integration challenge as the renewable resources (such as wind and water) are often far from demand centres. This adds to pressures on the electricity transmission grid, requiring new lines extending to generating sites and increasing congestion on pre-existing trunk lines.

Significant investments in transmission and distribution infrastructure are needed, both to address local problems and to increase the geographic spread of the grid systems that renewable sources serve. It is notable that the IEA expects considerable investment in transmission and distribution infrastructure in its "New Policies Scenario" (Figure 5.10), of a similar magnitude to investment in renewable generation itself (and even more in non-OECD countries).

To date, private investment in electricity transmission and distribution infrastructure has been limited. The sector is not open to private investment in many countries, and even where it is open, attracting merchant investment has not always been easy. Nevertheless, some experience is now building up globally. In Brazil, all transmission expansion projects are put to tender and, since 1999, 50 000 km of new lines have been financed by USD 28 billion of private investment (IEA, 2016). In Europe, private investment in transmission infrastructure has been limited, partly because system operators are also owners of the infrastructure in many cases. However, the United Kingdom has begun to open up the transmission sector for investment in the particular case of offshore transmission lines connecting offshore wind farms.

The integration of renewables can also be facilitated by increasing the geographic spread of the electricity grid and encouraging trading of electricity across a broader area. National transmission grids (and in larger countries, sub-national grids) are often interconnected to neighbouring grids. Interconnectors allow for cross-border trading and, overall, a better matching of renewable electricity supply with demand centres. Nevertheless, the capacity of interconnections is still limited in many countries. For example, in Western Europe, most countries have grid interconnection of less than 10% of their total capacity, with only a few countries exceeding 15% (IEA, 2015). Low levels of

Figure 5.10. **Investment in transmission and distribution relative to power generation based on IEA New Policy Scenario 2015-40**

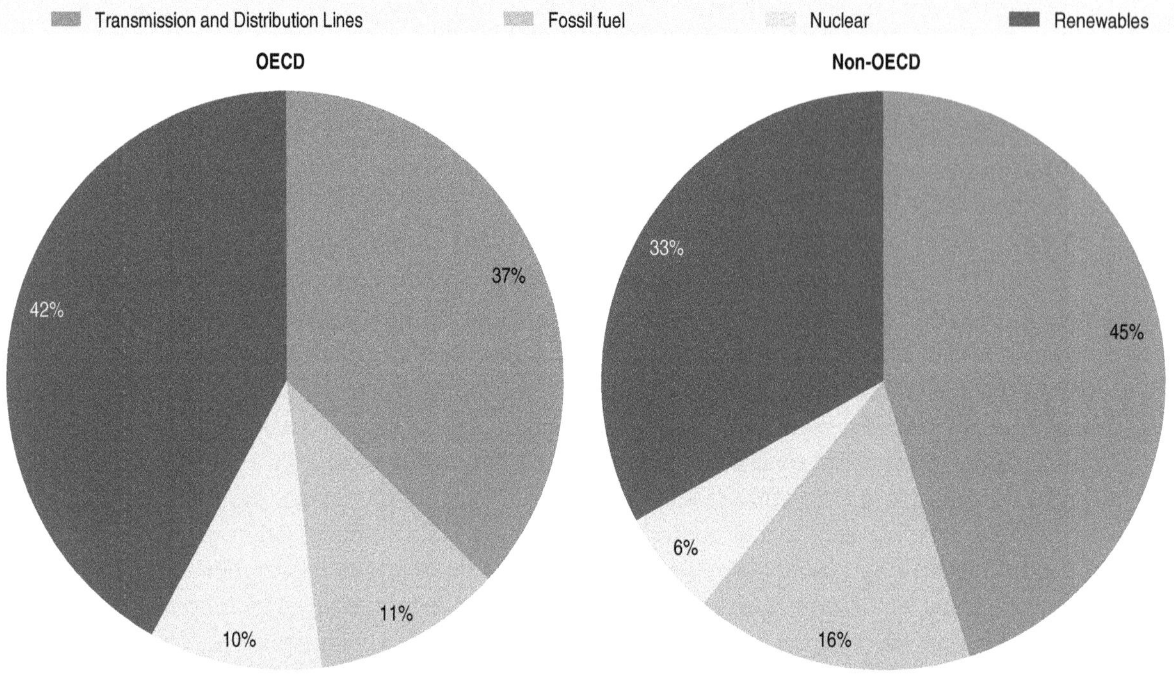

Note: Figures are expressed in percentage of total.

Source: OECD calculations based on IEA (2014d), World Energy Outlook, OECD/IEA Publishing, Paris.

StatLink http://dx.doi.org/10.1787/888933362659

interconnection make variable renewables harder to integrate and can affect the risk-return profile for potential wind and solar investors.

According to IEA analysis, interconnectors are the most cost-efficient way to integrate a high share of variable renewable electricity while maintaining a secure supply of electricity (cheaper, for example, than current options for large-scale storage or investments in extra baseload capacity). In the European Union, a better interconnected European energy grid would bring notable market benefits, with some estimates foreseeing consumer savings of between EUR 12 billion and EUR 40 billion annually by 2030 (IEA, 2016). Interconnection is particularly important for renewables because the generation patterns of weather-related technologies will be different across larger geographic areas. If the wind drops in western France, it may still be blowing in eastern Poland. Similarly, demand patterns are likely to be less synchronised across broader geographic areas. While peak demand in northern Europe may occur in the winter due to electric heating, in southern Europe it may be in summer when the demand for air-conditioning increases. Models suggest that with more than 3% penetration of wind, there are significant benefits to increasing cross-border trade through interconnection (Benatia et al., 2013).

Interconnectors, as with all transmission infrastructure, require substantial investment. Such investment is only economically justifiable when the benefits of increased power flows exceed the costs of new lines, yet elucidating the real benefits and costs can be challenging (IEA, 2016). Interconnectors pose particular opportunities and risks for investors. In theory, long-term price differences in neighbouring (but insufficiently connected) power grids can provide attractive revenue possibilities. However, the cross-border nature of interconnectors can complicate the planning and approval process, worsening the investment case. Cost-benefit analyses can be difficult due to benefits being heterogeneous across jurisdictions (e.g. interconnection can actually increase wholesale prices in isolated grids that enjoy abundant low-cost power, such as cheap hydro). Some regulators have sought to overcome these barriers by offering higher returns on capital for interconnectors (e.g. in Italy and by the Federal Energy Regulatory Commission in the United States, IEA, 2016).

Physical interconnection is not enough to guarantee cross-border trading. A range of market integration issues and administrative barriers can prevent trading even where sufficient physical interconnection capacity exists. These include different gate closure times, auction procedures and tax situations as well as conventional barriers such as language differences (Bahar and Sauvage, 2014; IEA, 2014b, 2016). Increased international co-ordination on network planning and market design could therefore facilitate increased interconnection and increased cross-border trading of electricity.

Design and use of capacity mechanisms

A further challenge for liberalised electricity markets is the need to maintain electricity generation capacity margins for security purposes at times of scarcity. While electricity markets based on wholesale marginal cost pricing can deliver reliable electricity supply over the short-term, they may not provide sufficient incentives to deliver investment in the capacity margins necessary to guarantee supply over the medium and longer term. Countries have introduced different mechanisms to tackle this problem, and the resulting policy fragmentation in regional markets, including within Europe, can distort electricity markets regionally, affecting the investment attractiveness of renewable electricity projects. Different mechanisms include:

- Market-wide capacity markets, providing payments for generating capacity or reduced demand that is guaranteed to be available at times of stress, with the price set through auctions. These provide additional revenue to generators, on top of year-round sales via the wholesale market.
- Targeted volume-specific strategic reserves, which are used to maintain strategic reserves and tend to provide payments for existing baseload capacity.

While capacity markets are important complements to wholesale markets, they should not be seen as a means to prop up revenues of otherwise unprofitable generators; in other words, capacity mechanisms should not replace good market design in the first place (IEA, 2016). Further, the design and role of capacity markets should be carefully considered in the context of a transition to low-carbon power generation. Capacity markets can provide incentives to maintain existing generation units open for longer than they would be economic in an energy-only market. While such incentives are good for security of supply, they may be misaligned with climate change objectives. This is especially likely in the absence of a robust carbon price.

Differences in the design and operation of capacity markets can, therefore, hinder cross-border trade of electricity, creating further barriers to integration of renewable electricity. The IEA identifies principles for efficient co-ordination of capacity markets to support private sector investment in renewable electricity projects (IEA, 2016). These include:

- addressing capacity adequacy requirements on a regional level (aiding both capacity market design and interconnector planning);

- aligning capacity product definitions to facilitate cross-border trade;
- ensuring that capacity markets do not interfere with forward pricing of electricity.

Conclusions

Helping policy makers mobilise private investment in renewable electricity requires addressing outstanding policy and market obstacles to such investment. The OECD has an important role to play in providing policy analysis to help countries strengthen the enabling conditions for renewable electricity investment and financing. Policy priorities for addressing fragmentation issues in renewable electricity markets and suggested ways for the OECD to continue to provide support include:

- overcoming financing challenges and mobilising private finance for renewable electricity;
- setting coherent and strong climate mitigation policies and aligning the investment environment;
- supporting electricity market integration and regional co-ordination;
- improving data collection.

Overcoming financing challenges and mobilising private finance for renewable electricity

Given the considerable need for long-term infrastructure investment, including for renewable electricity and power transmission and distribution, countries need to improve the efficiency of public investment while mobilising private investment at scale and at pace. Diversifying the types of financial stakeholders and sources of finance for such investment through new financing and funding structures, and innovative financial tools, can help align public and private sector interest in infrastructure provision and management, while optimising the capital structure and reducing the cost of capital for the public sector.

This chapter has emphasised the rising appetite from both equity and debt investors for renewable electricity projects, in various activities associated with project development, and using different financial structures employed across the spectrum of investment opportunities. Increasing numbers of institutional investors are recognising the potential for infrastructure investment to deliver inflation-linked, long-term and stable cash flows. Despite these encouraging trends, total amounts of institutional investment in renewable electricity remain relatively limited, considering the large pool of available capital from long-term investors. Various financing instruments can allow investors to tailor cash-flows to their needs. In addition, governments currently have a key role in fostering institutional investment not only by the direct use of funds, but also by playing an important catalytic role with respect to the mobilisation of private financing in renewable electricity, and other clean-energy technologies, beyond working on enhancing the macroeconomic and legal environments.

Further research and policy dialogue with regulators and investors (such as the B20) are also needed to better understand issues such as: factors driving the changing nature of banks and declining share of utilities and banks in financing renewable projects; the risk appetite of different types of investors, given the risk profile of renewable electricity projects; and new models and instruments for private sector financing of renewable projects, including through financial instruments offered by governments and multilateral development banks (MDBs). As different types of private investors are willing to take on different types of risks, risk allocation is a crucial factor in determining the pool of willing investors (i.e. the "right-siting" of capital). Attracting institutional investment may require new financial instruments and forms of collaboration beyond traditional instruments, such as direct equity stakes and bank loans. This can make infrastructure as an asset class more accessible to a broader group of investors and help diversify the large risks of infrastructure projects – currently shouldered to a large extent by the banking sector and the public sector through guarantees – across many groups of investors through capital markets.

Setting coherent and strong climate mitigation policies and aligning the investment environment

Stronger and coherent climate mitigation policies are needed to align incentives for the private sector to shift investment away from fossil-fuel-based technologies towards renewable electricity technologies and other "low-carbon" investments (in the power sector and other emissions-intensive sectors). Such policies can include a policy package of explicit carbon pricing (e.g. carbon taxes and emission rights trading), targeted investment incentives (e.g. feed-in tariffs and public tenders), reform of fossil-fuel subsidies; and targeted support to innovation, e.g. through public R&D expenditures.

Beyond the need to set strong and coherent climate policies, investment and financing in renewable electricity remains constrained when other policies and regulations are misaligned with climate goals (OECD/IEA/ITF/NEA, 2015). Such misalignments can create an unsupportive investment environment for low-carbon investment such as renewable electricity.

Further research is needed to help policy makers improve the effectiveness of policy support to investment in renewable electricity, including through aligning the investment environment. Ongoing OECD work is empirically assessing the impact of climate policies and broader investment conditions on investment in renewable electricity, as mentioned previously (OECD, 2017a forthcoming). Related work is also underway on investigating the effects of competition policy and the role of state-owned enterprises in influencing investment in renewable electricity (OECD, 2017b forthcoming). Subsequent research steps could usefully develop country-specific indicators on countries' attractiveness for renewable electricity investment, depending on domestic policies and investment conditions.

In addition, continued research is needed to further assess implications of the possible fragmentation of solar PV and wind energy value chains into regional markets, as a result of policy misalignments such as local-content requirements and trade remedies. This would build on recent OECD work (OECD, 2015a; Bahar et al., 2013).

Supporting electricity market integration and regional co-ordination

Integrating renewable electricity technologies at least cost requires flexible electricity systems and electricity markets covering large geographic areas. However, many countries are not sufficiently interconnected with their neighbours and some regions face internal congestion in domestic transmission grids, meaning that electricity cannot flow freely to where it is of most value. In addition, market arrangements are often not integrated between neighbouring systems, preventing international electricity trades and leading to inefficient use of interconnectors where they exist. These fragmented arrangements can hinder investment in renewable electricity.

To create a market design and regulatory framework fit for the low carbon transformation of the electricity system, additional research and policy efforts are needed to foster regional co-ordination for the planning and use of interconnections. While some countries have encouraged private investment in transmission capacity, including interconnectors, cross-border issues can complicate the planning and approval process. Governments and regulators need to take more regional and holistic approaches to network planning, both within countries and across borders. Finally, public financial institutions such as MDBs can play an active role in addressing obstacles encountered by projects, ranging from overseeing compliance with permit granting procedures to facilitating access to finance.

Another element of fragmentation in electricity markets is the development of diverse mechanisms for ensuring sufficient availability of capacity at times of scarcity. Again a more regional approach is desirable, such as addressing capacity adequacy requirements on a regional level (aiding both capacity market design and interconnector planning) and aligning capacity product definitions to facilitate cross-border trade.

In co-operation with the IEA, further research could focus on the investment implications of the design of electricity markets and systems, both to increase investment in renewable electricity and to stimulate private sector participation in other electricity infrastructure such as transmission and distribution (including interconnectors).

Improving data collection

To better assess the impact of fragmented climate policies and misaligned business conditions on investment and financing in renewable electricity, improved data collection and tracking is needed. The OECD is undertaking new data gathering on renewable electricity investment (OECD, 2017a forthcoming, 2017b forthcoming). It is also administering the *2016 Survey on Improving the Investment Environment for Renewable Energy*. This new survey will supplement empirical work by gaining insight into what key stakeholders consider to be the key policy barriers and drivers to private decisions to invest and innovate in renewable electricity technologies in OECD and G20 countries. The survey also includes a section on financing practices, including expected returns and risk perception.[22]

Other recent research has focused on infrastructure investment, looking at the "productivity" of capital and the determinants of investment and its financing, whether public or private (IMF, 2014; OECD, 2015). More evidence is needed about the impact and benefits of infrastructure investment on policy goals such as: economic development and wealth creation; and the investment characteristics of infrastructure.

In addition, future work could usefully gather data on the costs as well as new capacity of low-carbon technologies, and especially renewable electricity, in order to better assess the "quality" of investment flows, as well as the cost-effectiveness of policy support to the deployment of such technologies. It could also help assess how policies, such as feed-in tariffs and tenders, have contributed to driving technology cost-reductions through "learning-by-doing".

More clarity is also needed on future investment needs for infrastructure and the estimated contribution of private sector capital, by sector, region and type of financing, building on existing work (Global Commission on the Economy and Climate, 2014; Kennedy and Corfee-Morlot, 2012).

Notes

1. A publicly-traded company that is formed to hold renewable energy assets such as wind and solar power generation facilities. Most yieldcos are formed through a sponsoring entity, such as a utility, where operational assets may be sold from the sponsor to the yieldco entity. Yieldcos are designed to pay earnings as dividends to shareholders; OECD, 2015j; Annex 5.A2.

2. Capacity mechanisms are used to ensure that sufficient generating capacity will always be available in systems based on wholesale electricity markets.
3. "[...] and pursuing efforts to limit the temperature increase to 1.5°C above preindustrial levels"; UNFCCC (2015a).
4. In particular, the drop in oil prices globally since 2014 – and to a lesser extent, gas and coal prices – may create challenges for clean-energy technologies such as biofuels in the transport sector and renewable heating. At the same time, the decline of oil prices creates opportunities to reform fossil-fuel subsidies; IEA (2015b).
5. Brazil, the People's Republic of China, Colombia, Costa Rica, Indonesia, India, Latvia, Lithuania, the Russian Federation and South Africa.
6. Including in renewable electricity generation, nuclear power and carbon capture and storage (CCS).
7. Using levelised costs of electricity (LCOE) to estimate the cost of generating electricity; the LCOE calculations are based on a levelised average lifetime cost approach, using the discounted cash flow method; costs are calculated at the plant level, excluding transmission and distribution costs; IEA (2015c).
8. This is remarkable given also the shifting exchange rate and the sharp fall in oil prices.
9. As defined by the BNEF database, asset finance for renewable energy investment includes electricity generation and biofuels production assets that meet the following size criteria: one megawatt (MW) or larger for biomass and waste, geothermal, solar and wind energy generation; 1-50 MW for hydroelectric power projects; any size for marine-energy projects; and one million litres per year or greater for biofuel projects. The financing of carbon capture and storage and energy-smart technologies, along with mergers and acquisitions and refinancing deals are excluded.
10. As defined by the BNEF database, utility-scale projects refer to projects greater than 1 MW.
11. Figure 5.4 also reflects the quality of data available, which can be affected by incomplete financial disclosures for many transactions. There are major issues with data. Measuring investment flows or understanding the risk/return trade-offs in the renewables sector is challenging – the industry is young, track records are short, and a significant amount of investment has occurred in private markets. For example, the BNEF methodology regarding the accounting of Chinese asset finance deals with no disclosed financing type is an important caveat. A recent change in methodology has significantly reduced the share of balance-sheet finance for 2015 and previous years in BNEF statistics.
12. Where recovery in case of default is limited only to the collateral.
13. Based on the BNEF database (2016), including onshore wind generation as well as offshore wind-power generation and offshore wind-power transmission.
14. The data on investment, including new build and acquisition transactions, is compiled from the BNEFdatabase. The sample for 2010 includes 70 projects (57 new builds; 13 acquisitions), and the sample for 2015 includes 44 projects (29 new builds; 15 acquisitions). The total disclosed transaction value of the deals included in the sample was USD11.7billion in 2010 and USD14.9billion in 2015. The aggregated transaction value of greenfield projects stood at USD10.8billion in 2010 and USD11billion in 2015. The volume of total equity invested has decreased from USD6.6billion in 2010 to USD6.1billion in 2015. The institutional investor category includes pension funds, insurance companies, private equity and infrastructure funds; for more information on the data sample, please see Annexes 5.A1 and Table 5.A1.1.
15. Institutional investors are defined in this section as pension funds, insurance companies, asset managers, private equity funds, infrastructure funds, yieldcos, other listed vehicles and investment funds.
16. For a detailed description of infrastructure investment channels see OECD (2015b). As surveyed in detail by the OECD (2015j), institutional investors can invest in renewable electricity through a number of available channels. These include debt investments made in companies or projects, on a listed or private basis, and intermediated approaches such as fund structures.
17. NRG Yield Inc., Prospectus, Form S-1 Registration Statement Under the Securities Act of 1933.
18. Master Limited Partnerships are a type of limited partnership that is publicly traded, and is representative of the midstream conventional energy sector. Since securities law in the United States does not currently include wind and solar projects as qualifying assets, yieldcos were launched starting in 2012 as an attempt to mimic the MLP model for renewable electricity assets.

19. BRIICS stands for Brazil, Russia, India, Indonesia, China and South Africa.

20. For the purpose of this forthcoming report, the "effectiveness" of a given climate policy is determined by the fact that this policy variable has a statistically significant effect on investment flows in renewable electricity generation (or on patenting activity in renewable electricity sources); OECD (2017a, forthcoming). The analysis covers the period 2000-13.

21. Updated as of September 2014; OECD (2015b).

22. The results of the Survey will feed into the work of the OECD project on "Improving the Investment Climate to Achieve the Clean-Energy Transition" (OECD, 2017a forthcoming; 2017b forthcoming), as well as the OECD Long-Term Investment project, which aims to facilitate long-term investment by institutional investors such as pension funds, insurance companies, and sovereign wealth funds.

References

Bahar, H., J. Egeland and R. Steenblik (2013), "Domestic Incentive Measures for Renewable Energy with Possible Trade Implications", *OECD Trade and Environment Working Papers*, No. 2013/01, OECD Publishing, Paris, *http://dx.doi.org/10.1787/5k44srlksr6f-en*.

Bahar, H. and J. Sauvage (2013), "Cross-border trade in electricity and the development of renewables-based electric power: Lessons from Europe", *OECD Trade and Environment Working Papers*, No. 2013/02, OECD Publishing, Paris, *http://dx.doi.org/10.1787/5k4869cdwnzr-en*.

Benatia, D. et al. (2013), "Effectiveness of policies and strategies to increase the capacity utilisation of intermittent renewable power plants", *OECD Environment Working Papers*, No. 57, OECD Publishing, Paris, *http://dx.doi.org/10.1787/5k46j0trlrnn-en*.

Bloomberg New Energy Finance (BNEF) (2016), "BNEF database of clean energy projects", BNEF.

Cimino and Hufbauer (2014), "Trade remedies targeting the renewable energy sector," *Green Economy and Trade. Ad hoc Expert Group 2: Trade Remedies in Green Sectors: the Case of Renewables*, UNCTAD, Geneva, *http://unctad.org/meetings/en/SessionalDocuments/ditc_ted_03042014Petersen_Institute.pdf*.

Global Commission on the Economy and Climate, The (2014), *Better Growth, Better Climate – The new Climate Economy Report*, *http://newclimateeconomy.report/*.

Haščič, I. et al. (2015), "Public Interventions and Private Climate Finance Flows: Empirical Evidence from Renewable electricity Financing", *OECD Environment Working Papers*, No. 80, Editions OCDE, Paris, *http://dx.doi.org/10.1787/5js6b1r9lfd4-en*.

IEA (2016), *Re-powering Markets: Market design and regulation during the transition to low-carbon power systems*, OECD/IEA Publishing, Paris, *http://dx.doi.org/10.1787/9789264209596-en*.

IEA (2015a), *World Energy Outlook Special Report: Energy and Climate Change*, OECD/IEA Publishing, Paris, *www.iea.org/publications/freepublications/publication/WEO2015SpecialReportonEnergyandClimateChange.pdf*.

IEA (2015b), *Energy Technology Perspectives 2015*, OECD/IEA Publishing, Paris, *http://dx.doi.org/10.1787/energy_tech-2015-en*.

IEA (2015c), *Renewable electricity Medium-Term Market Report 2015*, OECD/IEA Publishing, Paris, *http://dx.doi.org/10.1787/renewmar-2015-en*.

IEA (2015d), *World Energy Outlook 2015*, OECD/IEA Publishing, Paris, *http://dx.doi.org/10.1787/weo-2015-en*.

IEA (2014a), *World Energy Investment Outlook*, OECD/IEA Publishing, Paris, *http://dx.doi.org/10.1787/weo-2014-en*.

IEA (2014b), *Seamless Power Markets: Regional Integration of Electricity Markets in IEA Member Countries*, OECD/IEA Publishing, Paris, *www.iea.org/publications/freepublications/publication/SEAMLESSPOWERMARKETS.pdf*.

IEA (2014c), *The Power of Transformation, Wind, Sun and the Economics of Flexible Power Systems*. OECD/IEA Publishing, Paris, *www.iea.org/publications/freepublications/publication/The_power_of_Transformation.pdf*.

IEA (2014d), *World Energy Outlook*, OECD/IEA Publishing, Paris, *http://dx.doi.org/10.1787/weo-2013-en*.

Kennedy, C. and J. Corfee-Morlot (2012), "Mobilising Investment in Low Carbon, Climate Resilient Infrastructure", *OECD Environment Working Papers*, No. 46, OECD Publishing. *http://dx.doi.org/10.1787/5k8zm3gxxmnq-en*.

McCrone, A. et al. (2016), *Global Trends in Renewable Energy Investment 2016*, Frankfurt School of Finance & Management – UNEP Collaborating Centre and Bloomberg New Energy Finance.

OECD/IEA/NEA/ITF (2015), *Aligning Policies for the Transition to a Low-Carbon Economy*, OECD Publishing, Paris, *http://dx.doi.org/10.1787/9789264233294-en*.

OECD (2017a, forthcoming), *Enabling Investment and Innovation in Renewable Energy*, OECD Publishing, Paris.

OECD (2017b, forthcoming), *Competition, State-Owned Enterprises and investment in the Low-Carbon Transition*, OECD Publishing, Paris.

OECD (2016a), *Green Investment Banks: Scaling up Private Investment in Low-carbon, Climate-resilient Infrastructure, Green Finance Investment*, OECD Publishing, Paris, *http://dx.doi.org/10.1787/9789264245129-en*.

OECD (2016b, forthcoming), *Green Bonds: Mobilising the debt capital markets for clean energy investment*, OECD Publishing, Paris.

OECD (2016c, forthcoming), *Infrastructure Financing: Partnering with the Private Sector*, OECD Publishing, Paris.

OECD (2016d), *Annual Survey of Large Pension Funds and Public Pension Reserve Funds: Report on Pension Fund's Long-term Investments*, OECD Publishing, Paris, *www.oecd.org/daf/fin/private-pensions/2015-Large-Pension-Funds-Survey.pdf*.

OECD (2015a), *Overcoming Barriers to International Investment in Clean Energy*, Green Finance and Investment, OECD Publishing, Paris, *http://dx.doi.org/10.1787/9789264227064-en*.

OECD (2015b), *Infrastructure Financing Instruments and Incentives*, OECD Report to G20 Finance Ministers and Central Bank Governors (September 2015), *www.oecd.org/daf/fin/private-pensions/Infrastructure-Financing-Instruments-and-Incentives.pdf*.

OECD (2015c), *Policy Guidance for Investment in Clean Energy Infrastructure: Expanding access to clean energy for green growth and development*, OECD Publishing, Paris, *http://dx.doi.org/10.1787/9789264212664-en*.

OECD (2015d), "Climate: What's changed, what hasn't and what we can do about it – Six months to COP21", Lecture by the OECD Secretary-General, Mr. Angel Gurría, London, 3 July 2015, *www.oecd.org/about/secretary-general/climate-what-has-changed-what-has-not-and-what-we-can-do-about-it.htm*.

OECD (2015e), *Policy Framework for Investment*, 2015 Edition, OECD Publishing, Paris, *http://dx.doi.org/10.1787/9789264208667-en*.

OECD (2015f), *OECD Business and Finance Outlook*, OECD Publishing, Paris, *http://dx.doi.org/10.1787/9789264234291-en*.

OECD (2015g), *OECD Companion to the Inventory of Support Measures for Fossil Fuels 2015*, OECD Publishing, Paris, *http://dx.doi.org/10.1787/9789264239616-en*.

OECD (2015h), *Taxing Energy Use 2015*, OECD Publishing, Paris, *http://dx.doi.org/10.1787/9789264232334-en*.

OECD (2015i), "Climate Change Mitigation Policies", OECD Compare Your Country online tool *www.compareyourcountry.org/cop21*, last accessed 30 March 2016.

OECD (2015j), *Mapping Channels to Mobilise Institutional Investment in Sustainable Energy*, Green Finance and Investment Series, OECD Publishing, Paris, *http://dx.doi.org/10.1787/9789264224582-en*.

OECD (2015k), *Climate Change Mitigation: Policies and Progress*, OECD Publishing, Paris, *http://dx.doi.org/10.1787/9789264238787-en*.

OECD (2014a), "2014 OECD Ministerial Statement on Climate Change", Meeting of the OECD Council at Ministerial Level Paris, 6-7 May 2014, *www.oecd.org/mcm/MCM-2014-Statement-Climate-Change.pdf*.

OECD (2013a), "The Climate Challenge: Achieving zero emissions", lecture by the OECD Secretary-General, Mr. Angel Gurría, London, 9 October 2013, *www.oecd.org/env/the-climate-challenge-achieving-zero-emissions.htm*.

OECD (2013b), *Climate and Carbon – Aligning prices and policies*, OECD Publishing, Paris, *http://dx.doi.org/10.1787/5k3z11hjg6r7-en*.

OECD (2013c), *Effective Carbon Prices*, OECD Publishing, Paris, *http://dx.doi.org/10.1787/9789264196964-en*.

OECD (2013d), *Taxing Energy Use: A Graphical Analysis*, OECD Publishing, Paris, *http://dx.doi.org/10.1787/9789264183933-en*.

REN21 (2015), *Renewables 2015: Global Status Report*, Renewable Energy Policy Network for the 21st Century (REN21), *www.ren21.net/wp-content/uploads/2015/06/REN12-GSR2015_Onlinebook_low1.pdf*.

UNEP (2015a), *The Emissions Gap Report 2015*, United Nations Environment Programme (UNEP), Nairobi, *http://uneplive.unep.org/media/docs/theme/13/EGR_2015_Technical_Report_final_version.pdf*.

UNEP (2015b), *The Financial System We Need: Aligning the Financial System with Sustainable Development*, UNEP, *http://apps.unep.org/publications/index.php?option=com_pub&task=download&file=011830_en.*

UNDP (2013), *Derisking Renewable Electricity Investment – A Framework to Support Policymakers in Selecting Public Instruments to Promote Renewable electricity Investment in Developing Countries*, UNDP.

UNFCCC (2015a), Adoption of the Paris Agreement, Conference of the Parties, Twenty-first session, Paris, 30 November to 11 December 2015, UNFCCC, UNFCCC/CP/2015/L.9/Rev.1, *http://unfccc.int/resource/docs/2015/cop21/eng/l09r01.pdf.*

UNFCCC (2015b), "GHG inventory data detailed by Party", *http://unfccc.int/di/DetailedByParty.do* (accessed 19 August 2015).

Weber, B. and H.W. Alfen (2010), *Infrastructure as an Asset Class: Investment Strategies, Project Finance and PPP*, Wiley, Chichester.

ANNEX 5.A1

Complementary information on the dataset of Figure 5.5

To study the development of the equity mix of wind energy deals, we analysed the structure of deals having reached financial closure in Europe in 2010 and 2015. The data on investment is compiled from the Bloomberg New Energy Finance asset finance database (BNEF, 2016). The database distinguishes between three types of transactions: new build, acquisition and refinancing. For the purpose of this analysis, refinancing transactions has been disregarded. New build and acquisition transactions have been included. Furthermore, only transactions in the wind sector (onshore generation, offshore generation and transmission) in Europe have been included. The BNEF database is limited to wind projects of over 1 MW capacity. Additional criteria of selection are the availability of a disclosed total transaction value and availability of sufficiently granular data to ensure consistent classification of equity investors. This could introduce a bias towards projects in countries with stronger disclosure guidelines or better coverage of BNEF data.

Some important assumptions have been made: short term debt and mezzanine debt have been included in the debt total; investment reported as balance sheet financing has been assumed to be equity financing from the sponsors; if the disclosed total transaction values differed from the sum of reported debt and equity, the discrepancy has been assumed to be balance sheet financing (sponsor equity); in the case of multiple equity sponsors, where no ownership split was available the assumption of equal ownership stakes has been made. For the classification of equity investors, the BNEF databases of organisations as well as outside sources have been used. Please refer to Table 5.A1.1 for the complete list of investors included.

The investor categories are defined as follows:

- Utilities: companies that sell and distribute electricity, gas or water to customers. It may also be the producer/energy generator and can be private or state-owned.
- Institutional Investors: investors in energy assets. The distinction between sole investors and managers/operators of the assets in the portfolio is sometimes difficult to make. Includes pension funds, insurance companies asset managers, private equity firms, yieldcos and other listed vehicles, and investment funds.
- Non-Utility Corporates: All companies involved in the energy sector which are neither financial companies nor utilities. The majority are power plant operators, electricity generators, project developers, construction companies or manufacturers of technical components. Bloomberg defines them as the sponsors of the project, the company that

has the idea for the project and carries it out. They might sell the energy they produce to utilities and can be private or state-owned.

- State Agencies/Public Finance Institutions: government institutions, such as ministries, and public finance institutions, such as the Green Investment Bank in the United Kingdom or the European Investment Bank.
- Banks.

Table 5.A1.1. **Equity investors included in the deal sample**

Category used	Included in 2010	Included in 2015
Utilities	Alpiq Holding AG	E.ON SE
	DONG Energy A/S	E.ON Thueringer Energie AG
	EDF Energy Renewables Ltd	EDP Renovaveis SA
	Fortum OYJ	Enel Green Power SpA
	GDF SUEZ Energia Polska SA	Energie AG Oberoesterreich
	Good Energy Group PLC	RWE Innogy GmbH
	Iberdrola Renovables SA	RWE NPower Renewables Ltd
	Skellefteaa Kraft AB	ScottishPower Renewables Ltd
	SSE PLC	SSE Renewables Ireland Ltd
	SSE Renewables Holdings UK Ltd	Statkraft AS
	Transpower Stromuebertragungs GmbH	Vattenfall AB
	Trianel Goup	
Non-Utility Corporates	ABO Wind AG	Balfour Beatty
	Agaoglu Group	Coillte Teoranta
	C-Power NV	Coillte Teoranta
	Elektrani na Makedonija AD	Energix-Renewable Energies Ltd
	Element Power US LLC	Enlight Renewable electricity Ltd
	Energia y Recursos Ambientales SA	Iberwind Desenvolvimento e Projectos SA
	Energiekontor AG	ImWind Elements GmbH
	Eolica Bulgaria EAD	Invenergy LLC
	Eolicas de Portugal	Momentum Renewables GmbH
	Eunice Energy Group SA	Raedthuys Groep BV
	Eurowatt SCA	Raedthuys Groep BV
	Faik Celic Holding	Raedthuys Groep BV
	Falck Renewables Wind Ltd	Statoil ASA
	Fersa Energias Renovables SA	Sumitomo Corp
	Fornax Sp zoo	Windkraft Simonsfeld AG
	Gamesa Energia SAU	Yard Energy Group BV
	Gamesa Eolica SL	
	Gecal SA	
	Gemba UAB	
	Gestamp Eolica SL	
	Gestamp Wind	
	Greentech Energy Systems AS	
	Inversiones Empresariales Tersina SL	
	Inversiones Empresariales Tersina SL	
	Jaeren Energi AS	
	Krzemien i Wspolnicy Spzoo	
	Ostwind Group	
	Petrom SA	
	PROKON Entrepreneurial Group	
	REG Windpower Ltd	
	Renewable Development Co Ltd	
	Renewable electricity Systems Ltd	
	Renovalia Energy SA	
	Umweltgerechte Kraftanlagen GmbH	
	Ventinveste SA	
	Windvision Belgium SA	
	Windway SGPS SA	
	Wpd AG	

Table 5.A1.1. **Equity investors included in the deal sample** *(cont.)*

Category used	Included in 2010	Included in 2015
Institutional Investors	Allianz Renewable electricity Management GmbH Energia UK Ltd Eolia Renovables de Inversion SCR SA HgCapital LLP Infinis PLC Inveravante Inversiones Universales SL Island Of Hoy Development Trust/The Kallista France Novera Energy Services UK Ltd PensionDanmark A/S PGGM NV Platina Partners LLP Viridian Group Ltd Wind Works Power Corp	4P Envest GmbH Allianz Global Investors Fund Management LLC AMF Fonder AB Brookfield Asset Management Inc Brookfield Renewable electricity Partners LP/CA ; Capital Stage AG Equitix Equitix Ltd First State Wind Energy Investments SA Greencoat UK Wind PLC John Laing Environmental Assets Group Ltd Laidlaw Capital Group Macquarie Capital Ltd MEAG MUNICH ERGO KAG mbH Meewind NV Parkwind NV Siemens Financial Services Inc Siemens Project Ventures GmbH
State Agencies, Public Finance Institutions	EU (European Energy Programme for Recovery (EEPR)) Polish Ministry of Economy Polish Ministry of Energy	Green Investment Bank Ltd

ANNEX 5.A2

Glossary of clean energy investment and financing terminology

Asset finance	The new-build financing of renewable electricity generating projects. As defined by Bloomberg New Energy Finance (BNEF) database, asset finance for renewable energy investment includes electricity generation and biofuels production assets that meet the following size criteria: one megawatt (MW) or larger for biomass and waste, geothermal, solar and wind energy generation; 1-50 MW for hydroelectric power projects; any size for marine-energy projects; and one million litres per year or greater for biofuel projects. The financing of carbon capture and storage and energy-smart technologies, along with mergers and acquisitions and refinancing deals are excluded. Projects may be financed via the balance sheets of the project owners, or through financing mechanisms such as syndicated equity from institutional investors, or project debt from banks. *Source:* BNEF.
Brownfield projects	Brownfield or secondary projects are already operational and/or have a predecessor of some form at the same location. These projects may involve the reconstruction, renovation or expansion of existing assets. *Source:* Weber and Alfen, 2010.
Clean energy	According to BNEF definition and classification, "clean energy" includes the following sectors: renewable electricity generation (solar, wind, small and large hydroelectric, geothermal, marine, biomass and waste-to-energy power plants); carbon capture and storage (CCS) technologies; energy-efficient technologies (digital energy and smart grids, power storage, hydrogen and fuel cells, advanced transportation and energy efficiency on both the demand and supply side); low-carbon service providers (consultants, government agencies, policy makers, NGOs, financial service providers, investors and clean energy information providers); *Source:* BNEF.
Greenfield projects	Greenfield or primary projects are assets generally constructed for the first time at a specific site. They may be in the planning, development, financing or construction stage. *Source:* Weber and Alfen, 2010.
Institutional investor	Entities which mainly provide financing for clean energy projects. Includes pension funds, insurance companies, asset managers, private equity firms, yieldcos and other listed vehicles, and investment funds. The distinction between sole investors and managers/operators of the assets in the portfolio is sometimes difficult to make.
Liability Driven Investment (LDI) and Asset Liability Management (ALM)	The task of managing the funds of a financial institution to accomplish two goals: i) to earn an adequate return on funds invested and ii) to maintain a comfortable surplus of assets beyond liabilities. *Source*: OECD 2015j.
Non-utility corporates	All companies involved in the energy sector which are neither financial companies nor utilities. The majority are power plant operators, electricity generators, project developers, construction companies or manufacturers of technical components.
On-balance-sheet financing	Where a renewable electricity project is financed entirely by a utility or developer, using money from their internal resources. *Source*: McCrone et al., 2016.
Project bond	Project bonds are standardised securities that finance individual stand-alone infrastructure projects. They can be issued in public markets, or placed privately. Projects bonds are issued by a project company (distinct legal entity). *Source*: OECD 2015b.
Project finance	Project finance is the financing of long-term infrastructure, industrial, extractive, environmental and other projects / public services (including social, sports and entertainment PPPs) based upon a limited recourse financial structure where project debt and equity used to finance the project are paid back from the cash flow generated by the project (typically, a special purpose entity (SPE) or vehicle (SPV)). *Source*: OECD 2015b.

Renewable electricity	Assets generating energy from renewable sources. Includes: Wind, solar, small hydro, marine, geothermal, biomass & waste, offshore wind transmission. *Source*: BNEF.
State agencies and public finance institutions	Government institutions, such as ministries, and public finance institutions, such as the UK Green Investment Bank or the EIB.
Utility	A company that sells and distributes electricity, gas or water to customers. It may also be the producer/generator of energy.
Yieldco	A publicly-traded company that is formed to hold renewable energy assets such as wind and solar power generation facilities. Most yieldcos are formed through a sponsoring entity, such as a utility, where operational assets may be sold from the sponsor to the yieldco entity. Yieldcos are designed to pay earnings as dividends to shareholders. *Source*: OECD 2015j.

Chapter 6

Fragmentation of retirement markets due to differences in life expectancy

This chapter provides evidence of the differences in life expectancy around retirement age across different socio-economic groups in selected OECD countries based on measures of education, income and occupation. Evidence shows that higher socio-economic groups live longer than those in lower socio-economic groups and these differences may be increasing over time. Fragmentation of mortality rates has implications for pensions, annuity markets and public policy. It makes it more challenging for pension funds and insurance companies to manage longevity risk. However, it also presents an opportunity to better tailor retirement solutions to the needs of different segments of society. Policy makers need to be aware of these differences to ensure that rules governing access to pensions and retirement savings do not put those in lower socio-economic groups at a disadvantage.

The statistical data for Israel are supplied by and under the responsibility of the relevant Israeli authorities. The use of such data by the OECD is without prejudice to the status of the Golan Heights, East Jerusalem and Israeli settlements in the West Bank under the terms of international law.

Main findings

- There are significant differences in life expectancy across socio-economic groups, as measured by education, income and occupation, and there are also differences in the gradient of improvements over time in mortality and life expectancy across socio-economic groups.
- Differences in life expectancy present a challenge for pension funds and annuity providers in managing longevity risk; both in terms of establishing appropriate mortality assumptions and of effectively mitigating exposure to the risk.
- These differences also present an opportunity for pensions and insurers to expand their markets and diversify their longevity risk exposure by adapting product offerings to different segments of society.
- Policy makers should help to facilitate the measurement and management of the longevity risk exposure of pension funds and annuity providers by making accurate and timely mortality data available by socio-economic group.
- Policy makers should encourage and facilitate product innovation to meet the various needs of different market segments, though they should also ensure that the risks arising from these products are managed appropriately.
- Policy makers should be aware of these differences in mortality rates to ensure that the rules governing overall access to funds earmarked for retirement do not put lower socio-economic groups at a disadvantage, as policies defined "on average" may be regressive.

Introduction

The growing fragmentation in mortality rates across socio-economic groups has exacerbated the problem of increases in life expectancy. These increases have been putting pressure on pension systems to provide adequate and sustainable incomes in retirement as people are not necessarily working longer but are spending more years in retirement. As long as life expectancy differs significantly across the various socio-economic groups of the population, the challenge of ensuring sufficient income in retirement cannot be only assessed "on average".

This chapter provides evidence on the differences in life expectancy around retirement age across different socio-economic groups in selected OECD countries. The chapter also assesses the implications of this fragmentation for pensions and annuity markets and for public policy. Not only are there differences in current levels of mortality and life expectancy, but growing evidence shows that there are also differences in the gradient of improvements in mortality and life expectancy over time across socio-economic groups. In many countries, those in higher socio-economic groups have benefited from larger improvements in mortality and life expectancy over the last few decades than those in the lower socio-economic groups.

As a result of these differences, two individuals of different socio-economic groups retiring at the same age can expect very different lengths of retirement. Policies encouraging people to work longer following the average increases in life expectancy may therefore disproportionately penalise individuals in lower socio-economic groups who would be working longer but not necessarily living longer. Additionally, pension pay-out rules may have unintended consequences for total pension payments that individuals in lower socio-economic groups can expect to receive.

These differences also present challenges for pension funds and insurance companies in measuring and managing longevity risk. The actual longevity improvements experienced by pensioners and insured populations will be heavily dependent on the demographic mix of these populations. Unpredictable changes in demographics lead to higher uncertainty about the future life expectancy of these populations. Furthermore, anti-selection in annuity markets implies a higher cost of mitigating the longevity risk of annuity beneficiaries. While lower cost index-based hedges could present a solution to this problem (OECD, 2014) the uncertainty around the efficacy of these instruments due to the differences in mortality trends across socio-economic groups presents a barrier for their widespread use.

Nevertheless, these differences also present opportunities to better serve society's financial needs for retirement through increased market segmentation. Different segments of the population have different needs with respect to financing their retirement. Product innovation should better adapt to meet these diverse needs. Enhanced annuities, for example, have emerged as a solution to provide higher annuity incomes to more disadvantaged groups with lower life expectancies. Other types of products could be structured to provide unique solutions for different segments of society.

The chapter is structured as follows. The first section presents evidence of differences in mortality rates and improvements in life expectancy according to three socio-economic indicators: education, income and occupation. These differences are quite significant across all countries assessed here. The second section discusses implications of these differences for pensions and insurance. It highlights the types of challenges that pension systems and annuity providers may encounter in managing the longevity risk as a result of these differences. It also highlights that this heterogeneity presents an opportunity to innovate and provide services to better meet the varied needs of the populations according to the diverse longevity risk they face. The third section discusses issues that policy makers may need to consider. The final section concludes.

Life expectancy according to socio-economic indicators

Countries vary with respect to the socio-economic indicators used to report mortality data. The three main types of socio-economic variables used are: education, income and occupation measures.[1] Life expectancies based on each of these measures are presented for selected countries. Evidence by education is presented for Australia, Canada, Czech Republic, Denmark, Estonia, Finland, France, Greece, Hungary, Ireland, Italy, Norway, Poland, Portugal, Slovak Republic, Slovenia, Sweden, Turkey and the United States. Evidence by income is presented for Australia, Canada, Chile and New Zealand. Finally, evidence by occupation is presented for England and Wales, France and Ireland. Nevertheless, as definitions of the referenced categories can vary from one country to the next, comparison of the magnitude of differences across countries remains limited.[2]

Education

Education is the most common socio-economic indicator used to assess differences in mortality across population segments. As a measure of socio-economic status, education has the advantage that it is generally established early in life and therefore should not be affected by health outcomes later in life which correlate with mortality. It also can be clearly measured at an individual level. However, given the general increase in the average level of education of the population over time, assessing a trend in mortality based on absolute levels of education could be misleading, as those not completing high school, for example, would be relatively more disadvantaged today compared to a generation ago. It may therefore be preferable to establish socio-economic categories by relative levels of education for any given period in time if comparing the change in the life expectancy by educational attainment over time.

Figure 6.1. **Difference in life expectancy at age 65, by level of education, relative to the population average**

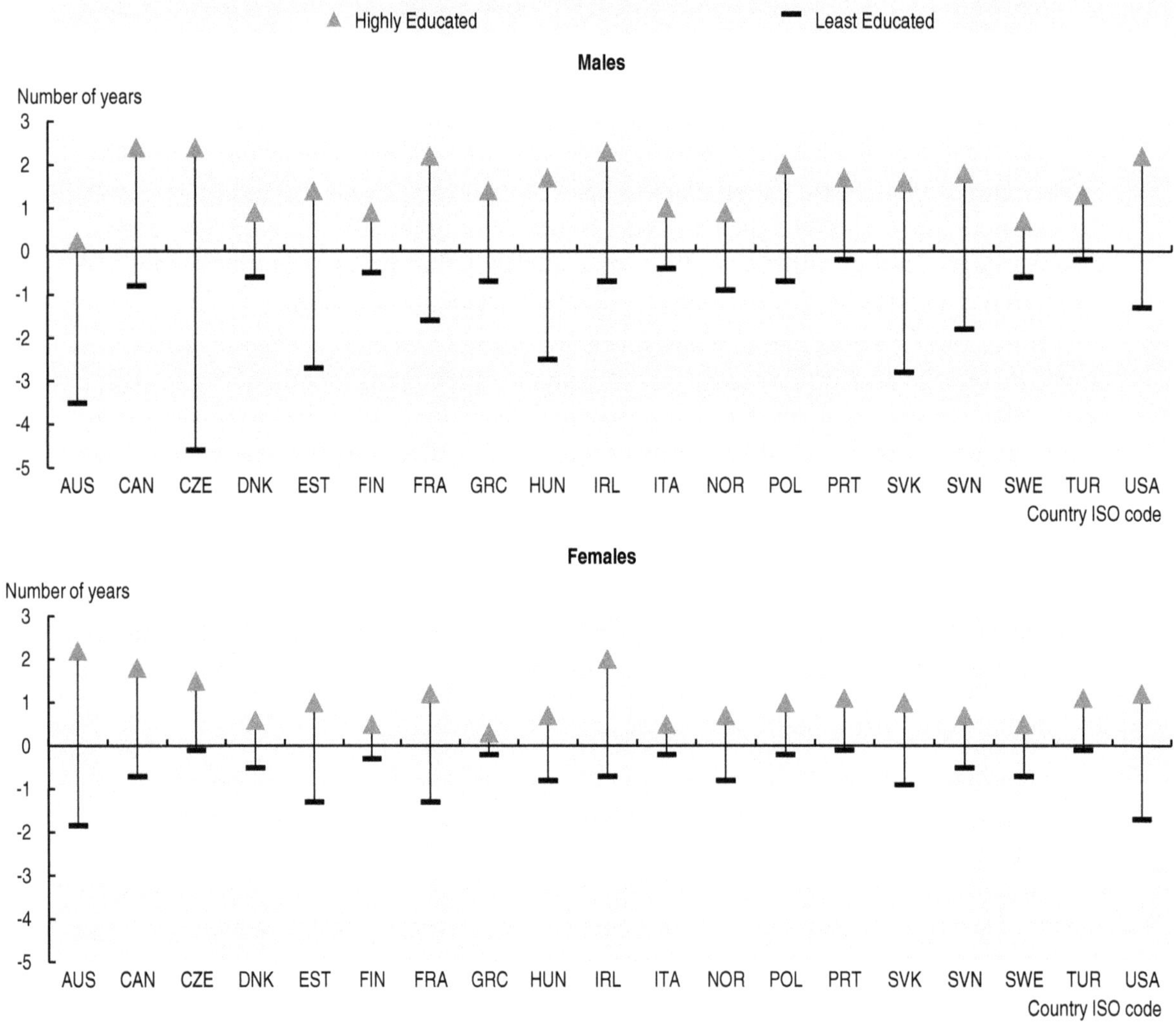

Note: Australia figures shown for age 60. Reference years and categories differ across countries and are for the lastest year available, see Annex 6.A1.

Source: OECD calculations based on sources given in Annex 6.A1.

StatLink http://dx.doi.org/10.1787/888933362667

There are significant differences in life expectancy by educational attainment. Figure 6.1 shows the difference in life expectancy at age 65 between the lowest and highest categories of educational attainment for males and females compared to the population average for the OECD countries for the last year of available data.[3] While definitions of the highest and lowest categories of educational attainment vary by country, the most common measure is based on the International Standard Classification of Education (ISCED). For this classification, the lowest category includes education through the lower secondary level and the highest category includes tertiary education. However as a result of different category definitions, reference years and average educational attainment in each country, cross-country comparisons will not necessarily be representative of the true differences across countries. Nevertheless the differences between the highest and lowest categories indicate the magnitude of differences in life expectancy in each country across the population segments observed.[4]

Differences for males are generally significantly higher than for females. The only exception is Australia, where females with more than 12 years of education can expect to live four years longer than those with less than 12 years, only 0.3 more years than the difference for males. Czech males have a significant gap in life expectancy between the most and least educated. Males with a tertiary education have a life expectancy at age 65 of seven years longer than those with only lower secondary education.[5]

Differences in life expectancy for the least educated groups, compared to the total population, provide an indication of how disadvantaged the lowest socio-economic groups are compared to the average. For males, the largest disadvantage is observed in the Czech Republic, though Australia, Estonia, Hungary and the Slovak Republic also present rather large differences from the population average, with the lowest educated males having over two years lower life expectancy than the total population. For females, Australia and the United States present the largest differences at just less than two years lower. Highly educated males live over two years longer than the population average in Canada, the Czech Republic, Ireland, Poland and the United States. Highly educated females in Australia and Ireland enjoy the biggest advantage over the population average.

In most countries, higher educated groups have higher gains in life expectancy than the lower educated groups, indicating that not only do these groups have a higher life expectancy but also higher mortality improvements. Figure 6.2 shows how differences in life expectancy across socio-economic groups have changed over time, although the period over which data is available for most countries is relatively short (less than 10 years). Highly educated males in the Czech Republic, Hungary and Portugal have increased their life expectancy by over two months more per year than the lowest educated males. In the United States, which has the longest period of observation available, the highest quartile of educated males has gained over two years more in life expectancy than the lowest quartile over the last three decades, which equates to just over three quarters of a month per year.[6] However, there are some countries where inequalities in life expectancy have improved, namely in Estonia, France and Italy, with France showing an improvement of 6 months per year over a relatively longer period of 16 years.

Figure 6.2. **Additional months of life expectancy at age 65 gained per year by those in the highest category of educational attainment compared to the lowest category**

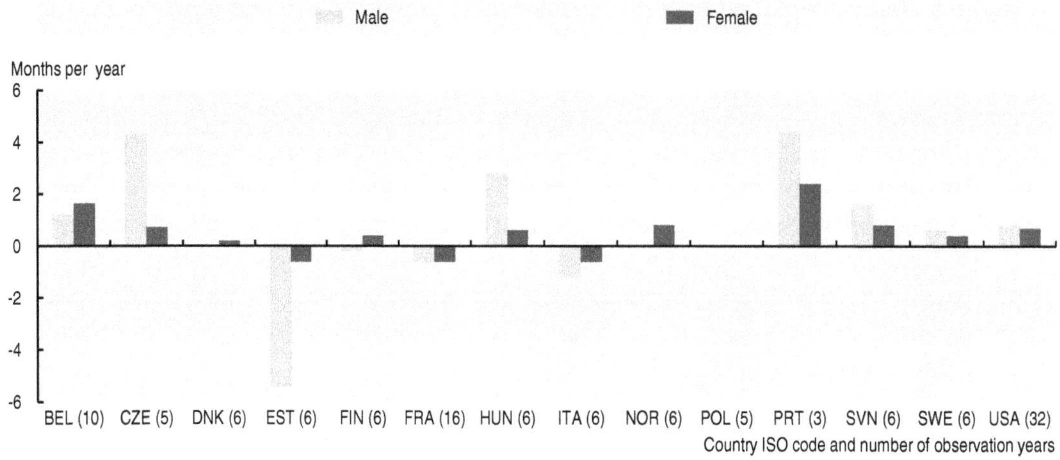

Note: The number in parenthesis refers to the number of years used to measure the difference. Reference years and categories differ across countries, see Annex 6.A1.

Source: OECD calculations based on sources given in Annex 6.A1.

StatLink http://dx.doi.org/10.1787/888933362678

Income

Income is a more direct measure of socio-economic status, although data is not as widely available as for education. Career average income is a better measure than income at a given point in time which could be subject to temporary shocks, for example from a decline in health, part-time work or unemployment, which could create a bias in the measurement of mortality. Wealth is also a relatively good indicator of social status and may be more stable than income; however this variable is not widely available as a measure.

The most commonly used measure for income in this context is a relative measure by average income quintiles. This is the measure used for comparison for all countries in Figure 6.3, apart from New Zealand where categories are based on tertiles of household income. For Chile, income quintiles are based on final salary rather than an average salary measure, which could potentially result in an overestimation of the difference in life expectancy across socio-economic groups. Those with the highest final salaries would also be those most likely to still be working and in good health, and therefore also be those who can expect to live longer. Lower final salaries could be due to reasons such as health problems, increasing the mortality risk for those with the lowest salary.

Differences in life expectancy across income groups are larger than across education groups for the two countries where both categorisations are available – Australia and Canada.[7] Shown in Figure 6.3 for the latest year of available data, Australia presents the largest gap in life expectancies between the highest and lowest income quintile of 5 years for males and 5.4 years for females. Canada and New Zealand present similar differences of around 4 years for males and 2.75 years for females. However the less dispersed categories for New Zealand likely result in an understatement of the differences across socio-economic groups compared to the differences across quintiles. Differences in Chile are approximately the same for both males and females, at just over 2 years.

Gains in life expectancy may also be higher for those with higher incomes. The only country for which life expectancy by income level is available over a given time period is New Zealand, where life expectancies are available for five periods starting in 1981-84 through 2001-04. Figure 6.4 shows that over this twenty year period, males in the highest

Figure 6.3. **Difference in life expectancy at age 65 by income group, relative to the population average**

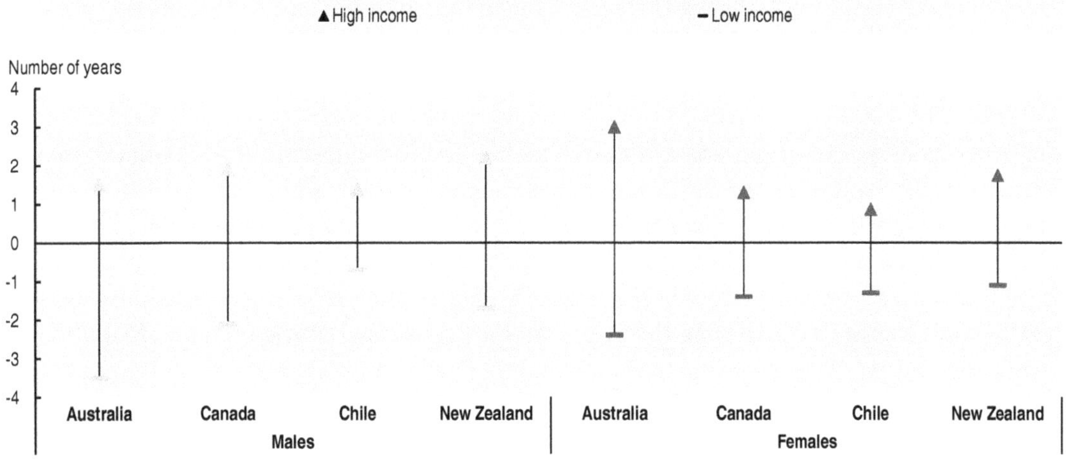

Note: Australia figures shown for age 60. The reference years and categories differ across countries and are for the latest year available, see Annex 6.A1.

Source: OECD calculations based on sources given in Annex 6.A1.

StatLink http://dx.doi.org/10.1787/888933362683

Figure 6.4. **Life expectancy and its evolution at age 65 in New Zealand, by income tertile**

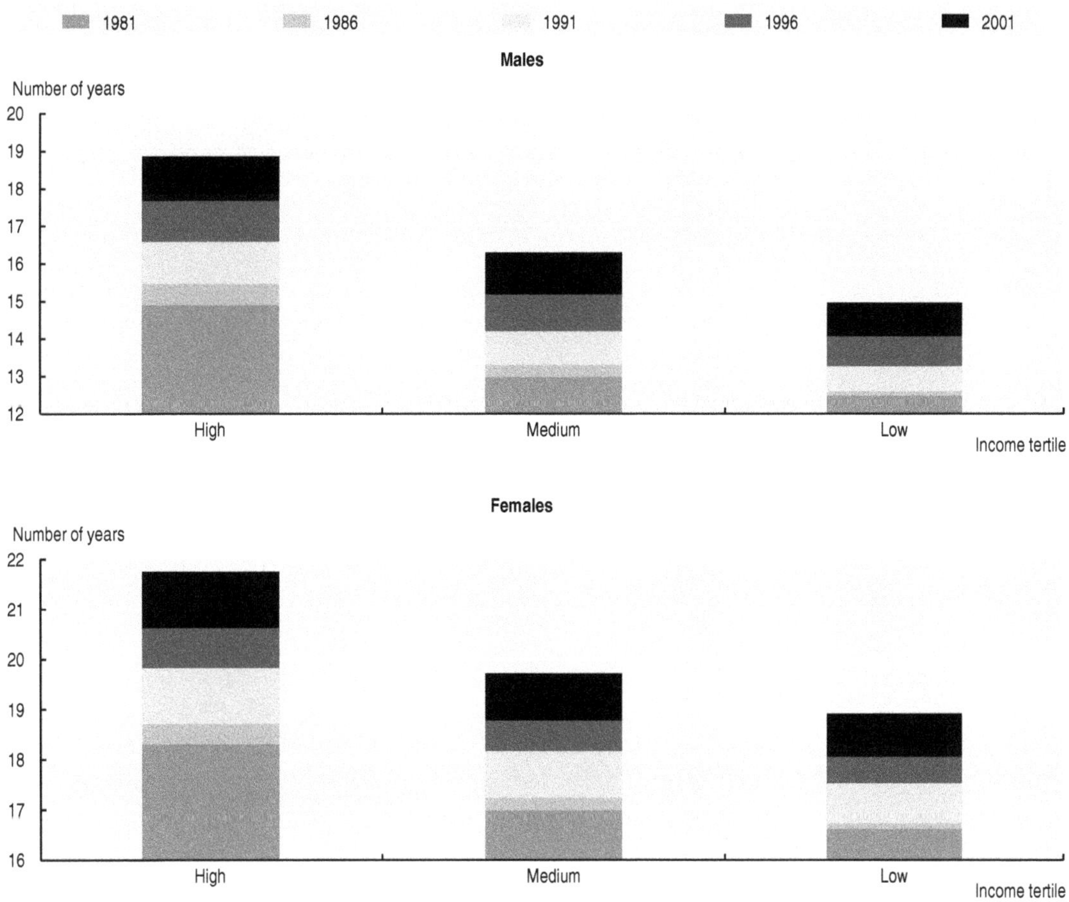

Source: OECD calculations based on the New Zealand Census Mortality Study, Carter et al. (2010).

StatLink http://dx.doi.org/10.1787/888933362698

income tertile gained 1.5 years more in life expectancy than those in the lowest tertile, and high income females gained 1.1 years more than those with low incomes. These results are therefore consistent with the measures by education in that they indicate that inequalities in life expectancy are increasing over time.

Occupation

Occupation as a socio-economic indicator has the advantage that it relates more directly to mortality outcomes, since the physical environment and social and behavioural factors which influence mortality tend also to be influenced by one's occupation. Occupation is also measured at the individual level, though categorisation of every occupation can be challenging, and occupations may change over time for a given individual. Furthermore, despite the International Standard Classification of Occupations, 2012 (ISCO 2012) which defines standardised occupational categories to be used for statistical purposes, there are variations in classifications across countries, which can make comparisons on this basis more difficult.

Despite the differences in categorisations, the differences in life expectancies between the highest and lowest categories are relatively consistent for males in the three countries where figures by occupation are available, with gaps falling between 3.6 and 3.9 years, as shown in Figure 6.5 for the latest year of available data (see Annex 6.A1 for the occupational categories used). This difference is significantly lower for females in France, at just over two years, yet slightly higher for females in Ireland at 3.9 years. The magnitude of these differences compared to the measure based on educational attainment is greater in Ireland where both of these categorisations are available.

Figure 6.5. **Difference in life expectancy at age 65, by level of occupation, relative to the population average**

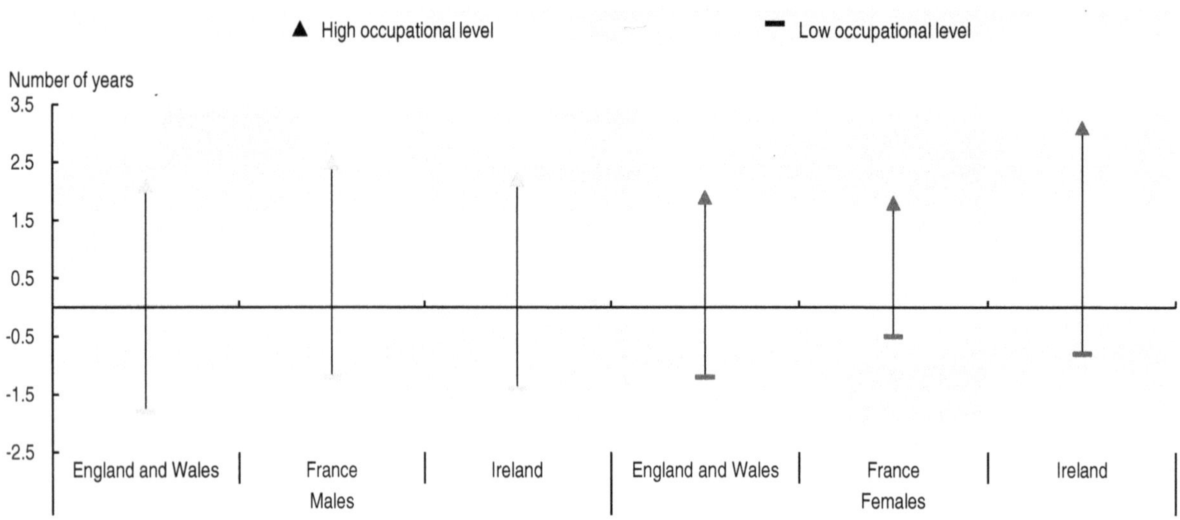

Note: The reference years and categories differ across countries and are for the latest year available, see Annex 6.A1.
Source: OECD calculations based on sources given in Annex 6.A1.

StatLink http://dx.doi.org/10.1787/888933362708

The limited evidence available indicates that people at higher managerial and professional occupational levels have also experienced higher gains in life expectancy. Life expectancy figures by occupational level are available since the 1980s for both England and

Wales, and France, allowing for a comparison of the change in these inequalities over time. In both regions, those in the highest occupational levels have enjoyed greater gains in life expectancies than those at the lowest routine and manual occupational level. In England and Wales, shown in Figure 6.6, males in the highest category have gained 1.5 years more than those in the lowest category from 1984 to 2009, though the gains for the highest group slowed down compared to other categories over the latest period observed.

Figure 6.6. **Life expectancy and its evolution at age 65 in England and Wales, by occupational category**

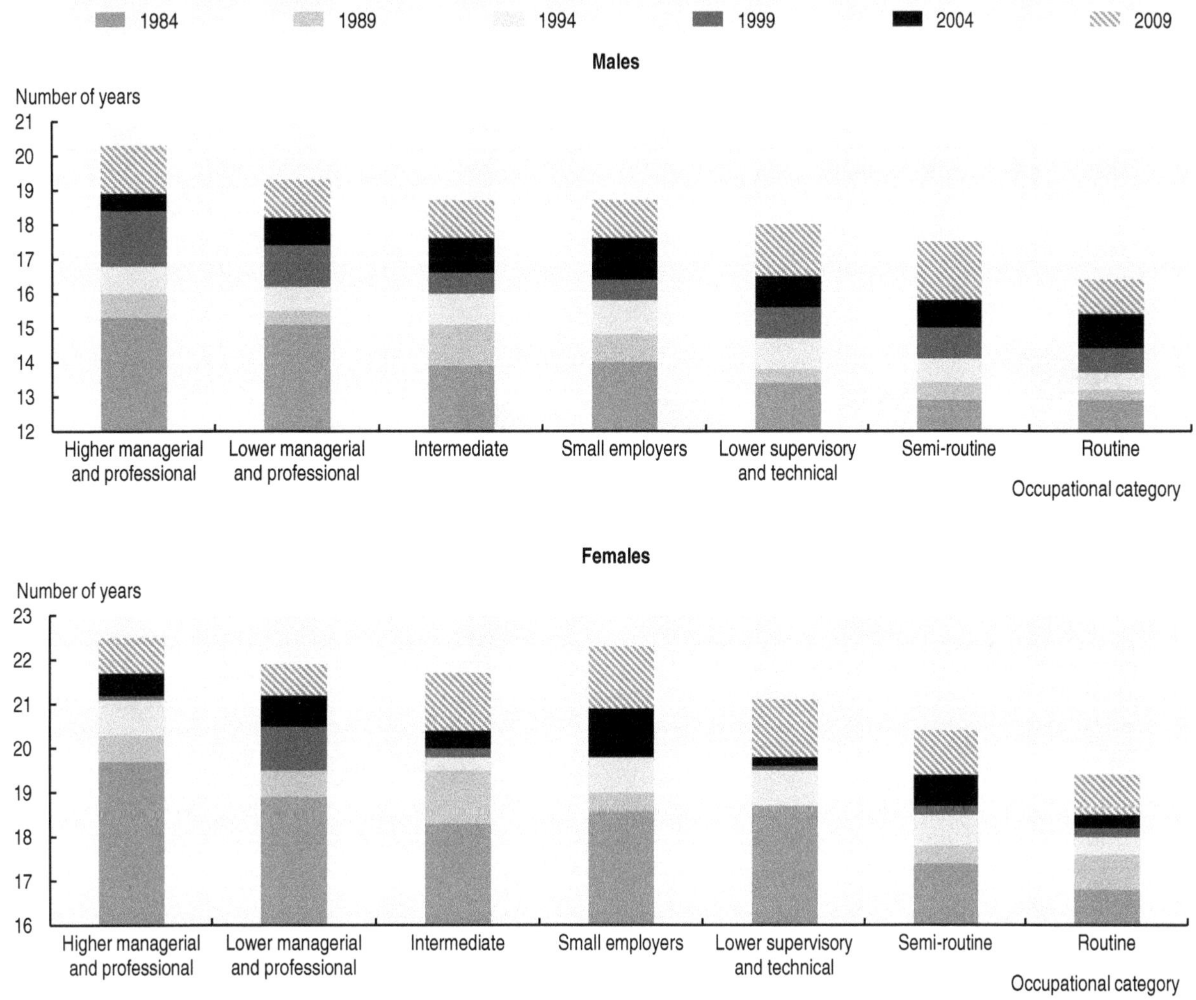

Source: UK Office of National Statistics.

StatLink http://dx.doi.org/10.1787/888933362716

Overall, gains in life expectancy have diverged less for females across categories, though over the entire period observed those in the highest category have gained slightly more years in life expectancy compared to the lowest category.

In France, gains in life expectancy for males in the highest category relative to the lowest category have been similar to those observed in England and Wales, with this inequality increasing by 1.1 years over from 1980 to 2011 (Figure 6.7). This divergence has not been as obvious for females, with manual workers actually having gained the same

Figure 6.7. **Life expectancy and its evolution in France at age 65, by occupational category**

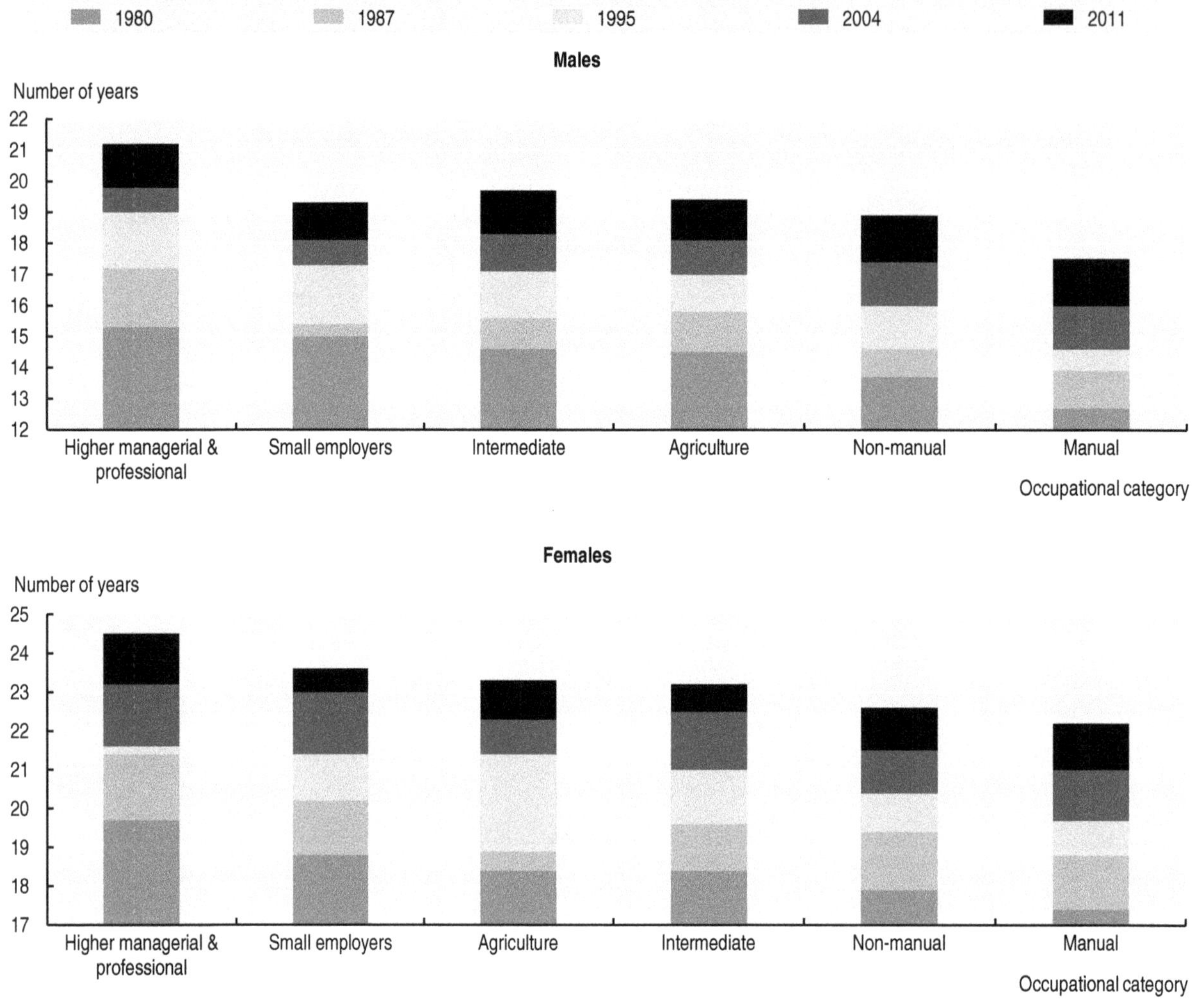

Source: *Institut national de la statistique et des études économiques* (INSEE).

StatLink http://dx.doi.org/10.1787/888933362722

number of years of life expectancy as those in higher managerial positions, though the speed of these gains has varied over time.

The significant differences in life expectancies at age 65 for different socio-economic groups are clear across all measures of socio-economic status: educational attainment, relative income and occupational level. Furthermore, these disparities have increased over time for most countries where data is available, resulting in an increased fragmentation of mortality.

These underlying differences and the increasing divergence of mortality present a challenge for measuring and managing the longevity risk by pension funds and annuity providers, given that this risk is heavily dependent on the demographic composition of the pensioner and annuitant populations. Solutions adapted to the various segments of society need to be found. Policy makers considering the design of the payout phase of pensions should keep these differences in mind when establishing limits which could impede lower socio-economic groups from optimising their consumption in retirement.

Implications for pensions and insurance

The longevity risk faced by pension funds and annuity providers depends on the population segment that they cover. External factors, such as regulatory changes which influence either the demographic make-up of these populations or improvements in mortality for certain segments can change this exposure, complicating the measurement and management of the risk. These populations tend to be skewed towards the higher socio-economic groups in most countries. To the extent that the divergence of life expectancies for these groups relative to the lowest socio-economic groups continues in the future, mitigating the longevity risk for these populations could prove to be more expensive than anticipated, and could potentially result in limited reinsurance capacity for these risks. This divergence could also hinder the development of the market for longevity risk, as standardised longevity index-based instruments, which this market would require could prove to be less effective in mitigating the longevity risk for these populations.

On the upside, this heterogeneity presents an opportunity for pension funds and annuity providers to adapt their services to better meet the varied needs of the population and diversify the longevity risks they face.

Diverse demographics pose a challenge for the measurement of mortality improvements for sub-populations

The potential differences in mortality improvements across socio-economic groups pose a challenge for pension funds and annuity providers to establish appropriate mortality improvement assumptions on which to base the valuation of their liabilities. First, available data for these populations may not be of sufficient quantity – both in terms of length of historical period and volume across age groups – to establish robust mortality improvements based on these subpopulations. Secondly, even where data for the subpopulation is sufficient, measured improvements may not be representative of the expected mortality improvements of the population if the demographics of this population have shifted over time.

Setting mortality improvement assumptions requires a reasonably long historical period and sufficient volume across different age groups. As such, the mortality improvement assumptions embedded in the standard mortality tables used in many countries are based either on the general population mortality or on the mortality of several of these subpopulations combined.

Many mortality tables used by pension funds and annuity providers rely on general population data, though certain adjustments may also be made to account for expected differences. The table used for Spanish annuitants (PERM/F P) and the tables used for pensioners in Switzerland (BVG 2010, VZ 2010) are examples of tables which rely on general population data to establish the mortality improvement assumptions used to value annuity and pension liabilities. The table used for annuitants in Germany (DAV 2004) also relies on general population data, but includes an additional buffer on these improvement assumptions in recognition of the fact that annuitants tend to be from higher socio-economic groups and therefore may also experience higher improvements than the general population. Mortality improvements published by the Continuous Mortality Investigation (CMI) in the United Kingdom rely on mortality data from England and Wales rather than the entire UK population. Large geographical differences in mortality have been observed in the United Kingdom, with England and Wales having a higher life expectancy at age 65 compared to Northern Ireland and Scotland, so this choice allows the model to reflect the specificities for the segment of the population in England and Wales, and the potentially higher mortality improvements which have been experienced by this population.

Other tables have based their assumptions on a combination of data from several pensioner or annuitant subpopulations. The Canadian Pension Mortality (CPM) study developed tables based on the population having Registered Pension Plans (RPP), covering both public and private sector plans. Recent tables developed in the United States (RP2014/MP-2015) also rely on pooled data from a number of private sector pension plans. Both of these tables therefore pool experience across different occupational sectors. As such, their accuracy for any given subsector or occupational category may be uncertain given the large differences in life expectancies observed across these categories, presenting a challenge for these plans to measure the longevity risk to which they are exposed.

The necessity of using sufficiently large data sets to develop mortality improvement assumptions presents a challenge to the ability of the resulting tables to reflect the expected mortality experience of the subpopulation. However, the underlying dataset itself may also pose problems for the measurement of accurate mortality improvement assumptions for that same population.

The demographics of annuity beneficiaries and pensioner populations may change over time as a result of external factors such as the maturing of pension systems and regulatory changes. Assessing the mortality improvements of a population whose demographics have not been stable with respect to different socio-economic groups could result in a significant mis-estimation of the expected mortality improvements going forward. Box 6.1 illustrates the potential impact of regulatory changes by providing examples in two countries, Chile and the United Kingdom.

Box 6.1. **Regulatory changes in Chile and the United Kingdom and their effect on mortality improvement calculations**

The 2008 Pension Reform in Chile provides an example of such an external regulatory shock on the demographic mix of the pensioner population. This reform effectively increased the coverage of the pension system for the lowest income segments of the population, dramatically increasing the proportion of low income pensioners. Given the evidence above regarding the differences in Chilean pensioner mortality across different income segments, it is clear that this influx of low income pensioners would have the effect of reducing the average life expectancy of the entire pensioner population.

In 2014-15, the pension and insurance regulators in Chile updated the mortality tables established in 2009 to better reflect mortality improvements experienced by the Chilean population, as the table in force at the time seemed to be significantly underestimating mortality improvements (OECD, 2014). While annual mortality improvements for the Chilean population had been between 2-3% over the last several decades, the improvements assessed on pensioner population data at an aggregate level were significantly below this.* This result was directly attributed to the increase in the proportion of low income pensioners from the 2008 reform. If the mortality improvements for the new tables had been based on the pensioner mortality data, these assumptions would have significantly

* Improvements had to be assessed at an aggregate level as there was not sufficient granularity across ages to robustly infer the differences in improvements across ages.

Box 6.1. **Regulatory changes in Chile and the United Kingdom and their effect on mortality improvement calculations** *(cont.)*

underestimated the life expectancy for pensioners and annuitants, resulting in insufficient provisions for annuity reserves and presenting pensioners with an increased longevity risk of running out of savings in retirement.

The recent pension freedoms granted in the United Kingdom provide a complementary example of a regulatory shock potentially changing the annuitant demographics going forward. Until 2014, 75% of the assets accumulated in a defined contribution pension plan were effectively required to be annuitised. This requirement was removed in 2014, resulting in a dramatic drop in annuity sales.

This exit from the annuity market is likely to be driven by individuals who have less to benefit from the longevity insurance that annuities provide and those who have lower life expectancies. These individuals are also more likely to come from lower income segments of the population. The Financial Conduct Authority found that in 2012 over a quarter of annuities sold to existing pension customers were for accumulated assets of under GBP 5 000, which would translate into a monthly income of less than GBP 20 per month. As these consumers now have the option to take a lump sum, it is quite likely that they will do so rather than take an income guarantee which is insufficient to keep them out of poverty. Indeed, the Financial Conduct Authority found that 90% of individuals who accessed their pensions in July-September 2015 and did not take the guaranteed annuity rate offered by their pension provider, had pension pots of less than GBP 10 000 (Financial Conduct Authority, 2016). This exit would affect the annuitant population going forward, in this case by removing the lowest wealth groups from the population, increasing the average socio-economic status for those who continue to buy annuities going forward. Basing mortality improvement assumptions on historical annuitant experience without accounting for this change would therefore be also likely to underestimate the life expectancy for annuitants going forward.

There is therefore a need to monitor mortality experience and changing demographics. Pension funds and annuity providers must be aware of the differences in the socio-economic compositions between their populations and the populations on which the mortality assumptions being used are based. Where assumptions are based on their own populations, they should ensure that the demographic mix of their pensioners or annuitants has been relatively stable so that the derived assumptions are appropriate for the population going forward. In either case, the need to monitor mortality experience and changing demographics of the underlying population is clear in order to ensure that the mortality assumptions used remain appropriate.

In addition to challenges for measuring the expected longevity risk of pension and annuity populations going forward, differences in mortality across socio-economic groups also presents challenges to the mitigation of this risk. The anti-selection common in annuity markets is a main driver of this challenge.

Anti-selection in annuity markets leads to increased difficulty in risk mitigation

Individuals choosing to purchase life annuities which provide protection from longevity risk also tend to be those who have higher life expectancies than the population average, and are generally from higher than average socio-economic groups. This phenomenon is referred to as anti-selection, meaning that these individuals are self-selected into the annuity market. Given that annuitants also tend to be from higher socio-economic groups, the evidence above indicates that they also present a greater risk of having higher than average mortality improvements. This greater risk can translate into a greater cost for annuity providers to mitigate their longevity risk. The potentially greater mortality improvements can also reduce the effectiveness of lower cost index-based solutions to mitigate this risk, presenting a real challenge for annuity providers to efficiently mitigate the longevity risk to which they are exposed.

Anti-selection in annuity markets is a common observation across most jurisdictions, particularly where the purchase of an annuity is voluntary. Figure 6.8 shows the differences in life expectancy at age 65 for the general population in each country and the annuitant or pension population for which the standard mortality tables are used.[8] This shows that it is

Figure 6.8. **General population life expectancy at age 65 compared to pensioners or annuitants**

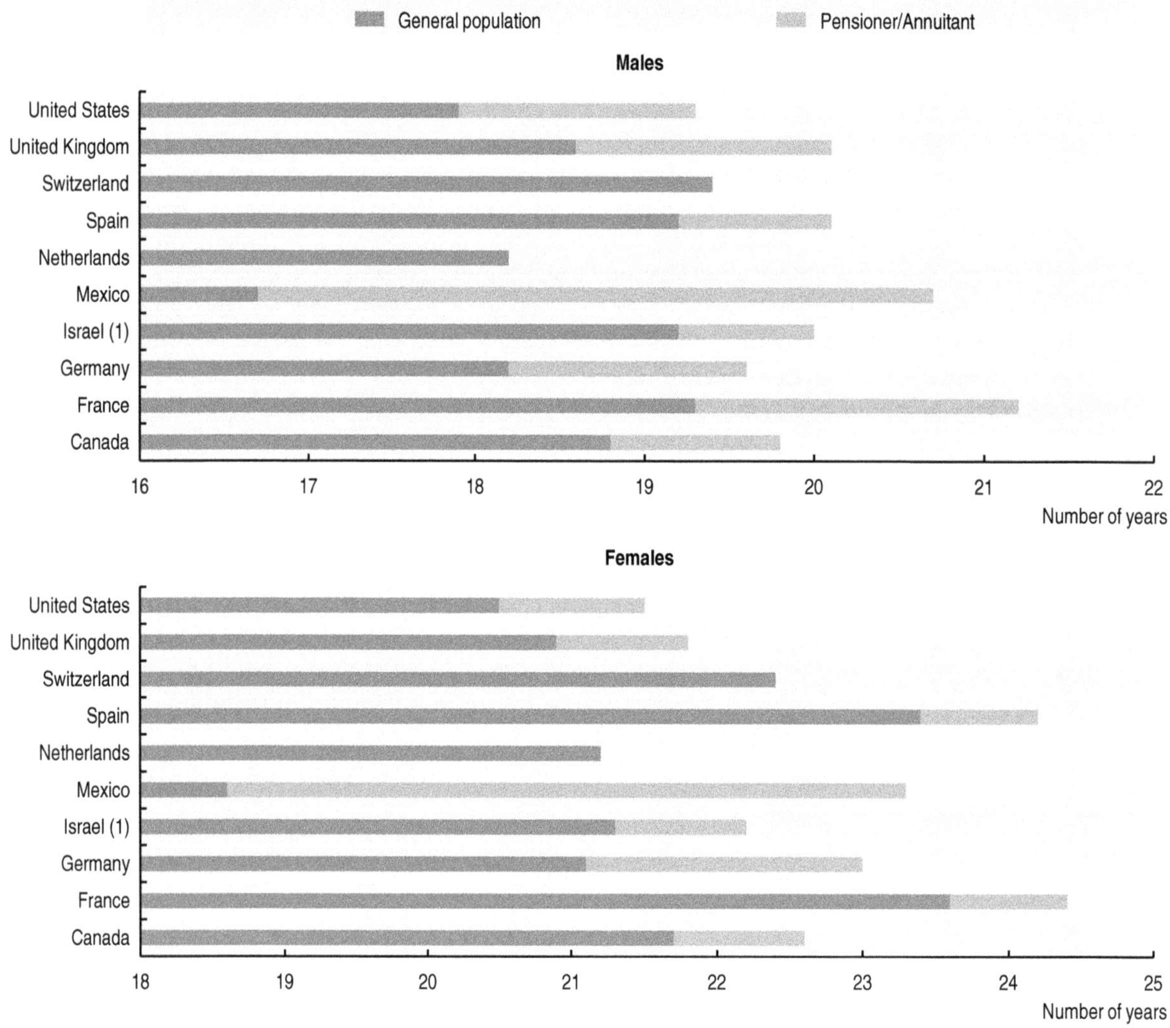

Note: Pensioner/annuitant mortality based on the following mortality tables: Canada (CPM 2014), France (TGH/F05), Germany (DAV 04, 2nd order Aggregate Target), Israel (Pension Best Estimate), Mexico (EMMSA 09), Netherlands (AG-Prognosetafel), Spain (PERM/F P), Switzerland (BVG 2010), United Kingdom (SAPS 2), United States (RP-2014).
Source: General population figures, OECD 2013 (except Canada, 2011).

StatLink http://dx.doi.org/10.1787/888933362736

not uncommon for annuitants or pensioners to have life expectancies at age 65 of over one year higher than the population average. The difference, however, depends in part on the underlying pension system and the nature of the liabilities being valued. This difference will be much smaller where the coverage of the pension system in question is high, as is the case in the Netherlands. In Mexico, where the coverage of individual annuities within the defined contribution system is currently rather low, the observed difference is much larger.

As discussed above, it is relatively challenging to establish appropriate mortality improvement assumptions for specific annuitant or pensioner populations. As a result, these assumptions are commonly based on the experience of a much larger population, either the general population or the pooled mortality experience of several populations. However, given the observation that pensioners and annuitants tend to be from higher socio-economic groups, there is also a greater risk that they may experience higher than average mortality improvements than a larger, more diverse, population.

This increased risk of higher than assumed improvements implies that reinsurers will need to charge an adequate risk premium to accept this risk from pension funds or annuity providers. This makes reinsuring the longevity risk for higher socio-economic groups relatively more expensive for the annuity provider or pension fund. If reinsurers are not able to diversify the longevity risk exposure that they are reinsuring, this could potentially lead to a capacity constraint for them to accept longevity risk from these segments of the population, further complicating the mitigation of this risk for annuity providers and pension funds.

Passing the longevity risk to the capital markets could be an alternative solution for annuity providers and pension funds to access additional capacity for longevity risk. However, this would require transacting with index-based longevity instruments in order to address the needs of capital markets investors for transparency and flexibility in the transaction (OECD, 2014).

The payments from index-based longevity swaps are based on a measure of mortality which is objective and independent from the actual pensioner or annuitant population for which the longevity risk is being hedged. This index is typically based on the mortality of the general population of a given country. In exchange for a fixed and regular payment from the pension fund or annuity provider based on the expected improvements in mortality at the onset of the contract, the counterparty will return regular payments based on the actual evolution of the index of mortality. Therefore if mortality improvements for the index population turn out to be higher than expected, the annuity provider or pension fund will receive additional payments to compensate them for the additional pension or annuity payments which they would be expected to make as a result of higher than expected survival rates.

While longevity index-based instruments are more appealing to the capital markets investor, they present some drawbacks for the annuity provider or pension fund looking to hedge their longevity risk. This is mainly because index-based instruments do not provide a full transfer of the risk, and a portion of this risk is retained by the pension or annuity provider. For a standard longevity swap, the risk retained is the difference between the evolution of the index mortality and the mortality of the pensioner or annuitant population whose longevity risk is being hedged, otherwise referred to as longevity basis risk. If the pensioners or annuitants experience mortality improvements which are higher than the population on which the index is based, the payments made by the counterparty will not be sufficient to cover the additional payments owed. Given that these populations tend to be from higher socio-economic groups, it is also likely that they will experience higher mortality improvements than the general population. A longevity swap based on an index for the general population would therefore likely to be insufficient to cover higher than expected pension or annuity payments.

Based on the evidence presented in the first section of this chapter, the magnitude of this basis risk can be significant, reducing the effectiveness of the longevity swap to hedge the longevity risk of the pensioners or annuitants. Figure 6.9 demonstrates the potential impact of this divergence in mortality improvements on the ability for the swap payments to cover hedged annuitant payments for a higher socio-economic group. The illustration is based on the actual evolution in mortality for the average French male population compared to males having a higher managerial or professional occupation since 1980. If an annuity provider had hedged its longevity exposure coming from a cohort of 65 year old males in this occupational category using a longevity swap indexed to the French population, payments owed to the annuitants would have totalled approximately 15% more than the payments received from the swap over a period of 25 years.

Figure 6.9. **Hedging shortfall from an index-based swap**

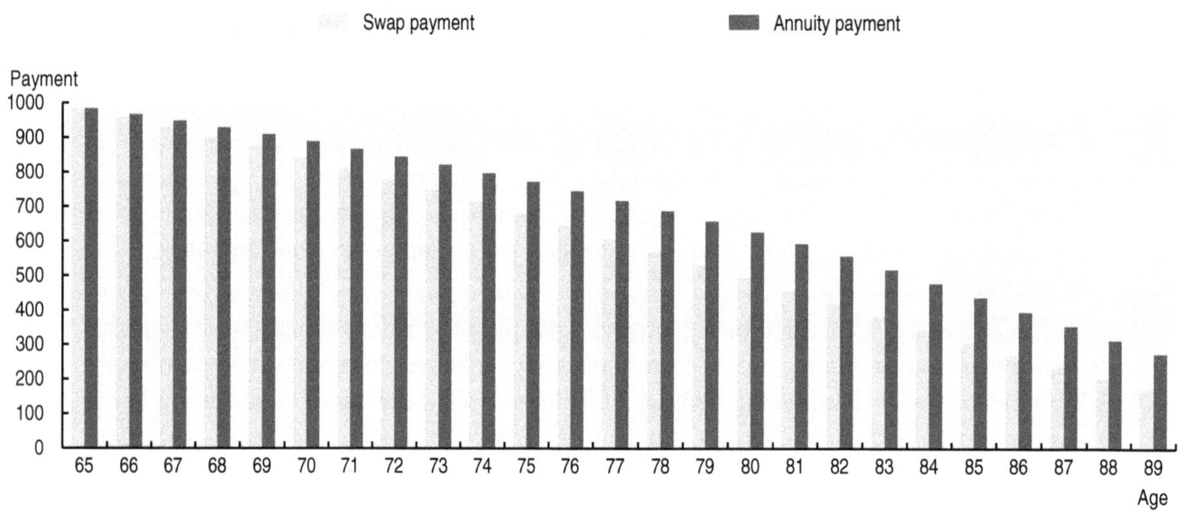

Note: Annuity payments for a cohort of 65 year old French professional males and longevity swap payments indexed to the French population.
Source: OECD calculations based on INSEE.

StatLink http://dx.doi.org/10.1787/888933362749

The uncertainty around the actual magnitude of this risk and the lack of historical data on which to measure differences in mortality improvements may lead annuity providers and pension funds to be reluctant to use index-based instruments to hedge their longevity risk, presenting a barrier to the development of a market for longevity risk. Indeed, very few index-based longevity hedges have been executed. The four largest public index-based transactions have all been indexed to Dutch population mortality. Anti-selection in the Dutch market is more limited than many other jurisdictions due to the very high coverage of the quasi-mandatory private pension system. This is also evidenced in the lack of difference between the life expectancy of the general population and the insured population in Figure 6.8. Due to this high coverage, the annuitant mortality is more likely to closely follow the trends of the general population, minimising basis risk and resulting in higher hedge effectiveness. Reduced anti-selection in the Dutch market may therefore be a driver in higher volume of index-based transactions to hedge longevity risk compared to other jurisdictions.

The differences in mortality improvements across socio-economic groups increase the cost of mitigating longevity risk for annuity providers and pension funds, and present a barrier to the increased use of index-based instruments to hedge longevity risk and therefore to the development of a market for this risk. Diversifying longevity risk exposure across socio-economic groups with adapted product offerings could provide one solution to reducing the cost of mitigating longevity risk for pension funds and annuity providers.

Heterogeneity presents an opportunity for market segmentation to diversify risk and better serve financial needs of consumers in retirement

In light of the large heterogeneity in mortality across socio-economic groups, pension funds and annuity providers may have an opportunity to diversify their concentrated exposure to the longevity risk of higher socio-economic groups by offering benefits or products which better serve the retirement needs of the various market segments.

Paradoxically, despite the observed anti-selection in annuity markets, the stated preference for traditional annuity products has been shown to be negatively correlated with education and income, two key indicators of socio-economic status (e.g. Agnew et al., 2008). This implies that there may exist an opportunity for traditional annuity products to adapt their pricing and risk profile to better target middle to lower socio-economic groups, and that product features have room to adapt from the traditional model to appeal more to higher socio-economic groups. Lower socio-economic groups may have a higher need for the consumption protection that standard annuities can offer, while higher socio-economic groups may have a higher desire for flexibility and/or market participation than the traditional model offers.

The enhanced annuity market in the United Kingdom seems to have successfully segmented the market to offer higher levels of income to individuals having lower life expectancies and therefore presenting lower longevity risk. These types of products are offered to individuals presenting certain health or behavioural factors which are correlated with lower life expectancies, such as smoking, obesity or cardiovascular disease. These types of risk factors have also been shown to be more prevalent for those in lower socio-economic classes. At the end of 2014, enhanced annuities made up 28% of the total market for annuities, demonstrating that these types of products can capture a significant portion of the total market (Gatzert and Klotzki, 2015). Providers offering both standard and enhanced annuities may be better able to diversify the longevity risk that they face by capturing a broader segment of the population. Nevertheless, enhanced annuities are not widely available in jurisdictions outside of the United Kingdom.

For the higher socio-economic segments, annuity products offering market participation may be more appealing. One reason put forward to explain the decreased preference for traditional annuities by higher socio-economic groups is that this segment of individuals has more familiarity with investing in markets. They may therefore prefer to retain control of their investment due to optimism and overconfidence in their abilities to generate higher returns than a traditional annuity could offer (e.g. Agnew and Szykman, 2010). Indeed, the average premiums for investment-linked annuity products in the United States in 2012 were nearly 40% higher than the average premium for a fixed payment annuity product, indicating that they were bought by wealthier people on average.[9] These types of products also tend to offer a certain level of liquidity, even during the payout phase, allowing the consumer to maintain access to their assets. The Guaranteed Minimum Withdrawal Benefit for Life allows this liquidity, and is the most popular annuity-type guarantee offered with variable annuity products in the United States, with over 40% of assets backing these products having this type of benefit in 2012 (The Geneva Association, 2013).

Opportunities such as these to adapt product designs to better meet the needs of different socio-economic segments and expand into different markets are clear given the diversity and divergence of mortality across these segments and the varying levels of longevity protection needed in retirement. Diversifying longevity risk exposure across these segments may help to facilitate the management of this risk for pension funds and annuity providers going forward.

Considerations for policy makers

Differences in mortality across socio-economic groups have implications for policy makers concerned with ensuring that the retirement financing needs are met for all segments of society. First, policy makers should consider ways to facilitate the measurement and management of longevity risk given the challenges faced by pensions and insurance providers outlined above. Second, product innovation and adaptation for the different market segments should be encouraged. However, policy makers must also make sure that providers measure and manage any new risks coming from these products and that the products remain accessible and suitable for the targeted population segment. Finally, mortality differences have more wide-reaching implications with respect to the rules governing access to pension money in retirement, and policy makers should establish these rules to ensure that lower socio-economic groups are not unnecessarily put at a disadvantage with respect to this access given their lower life expectancies.

Facilitating the measurement and management of longevity risk

To facilitate the management and mitigation of longevity risk, policy makers have an interest in ensuring that mortality data by socio-economic indicators is widely available in a timely and accessible manner. The key obstacle outlined above for pensions and insurance providers to measure and manage their longevity risk is the lack of adequate mortality data linked to the different socio-economic indicators identified. National statistics institutes or, alternatively, actuarial associations could be in charge of making such data available.

Having access to mortality data by socio-economic groups would help to overcome the difficulties pensions and insurers have in measuring expected mortality assumptions and the longevity risk they face. Despite the well-known differences in mortality across socio-economic groups, detailed mortality data is not easily accessible in many countries. This presents a challenge to establish mortality improvement assumptions reflective of the particular population in question and to measure the expected differences in these improvements compared to the population average.

Encouraging the development of sustainable products to meet the needs of different segments of society

Policy makers should also consider ways to encourage the development of sustainable products to finance retirement which are adapted to the needs of the different segments of society. To take enhanced annuities as an example, despite the potential for these products to serve the needs of lower socio-economic groups for protection against investment and longevity risk, they are not widely available outside of the United Kingdom. Barriers cited as a reason for this include inflexible reserve requirements, legal or regulatory challenges and insufficient demand to achieve the volume of sales necessary to create a sustainable business line. Policy makers could therefore ensure that the related rules and regulations accommodate such products by creating incentives for providers to compete and innovate, but they must also make sure that the risks of these products are appropriately managed.

Inflexible reserve requirements could make certain types of products unprofitable for insurance companies to offer. For example, insurers in the United States are required to hold reserves based on standard mortality assumptions unless the mortality for the insured is greater than 25% lower than the standard rates (Drinkwater et al., 2006). This requirement could make insurance companies unwilling to offer enhanced annuities for individuals having lower life expectancies because they would have to hold the same level of reserves as for standard annuities.

There may also be legal barriers to using certain risk factors for pricing annuity products, which could impede increased market segmentation for annuity products. Policy makers should ensure that increased market segmentation does not result in discrimination, but likewise should not impose legal restrictions which could prevent access to annuity products for certain segments of society. Gender, for example, has not been allowed to be used for pricing annuity products in the European Union since 2012 on the grounds that it is discriminatory. This ban would be expected to increase the price that males would pay for the equivalent annuity product. To the extent that this leads to males opting out of the market because they see annuities as too expensive relative to the length of time they expect to live, this could further increase the price to reflect the higher life expectancies of those continuing to purchase annuities. Indeed, evidence in Germany, where gender-based pricing of annuities has been forbidden since 2006, indicates that prices following the ban were much closer to the prices which had been charged to females before the reform (von Gaudecker and Webter, 2006). Bans on market segmentation may therefore not result in any benefit for society and can result in an exclusion of certain groups from the market.

Policy makers must carefully consider the costs and benefits in allowing or banning certain risk factors to be used for the pricing of annuity products. Drawing the line between acceptable segmentation and discrimination is not always easy, particularly where risk factors are strongly correlated with race or ethnicity. For example it is common practice in the United Kingdom to segment markets by postcode, which can be a proxy for socio-economic status. In the United States, on the other hand, a postcode could be viewed as a proxy for race and thereby seen as discriminatory. Factors having a more direct and causal link such as health problems or behavioural factors such as smoking may therefore be a preferable basis for market segmentation.

The lack of demand for annuity products could also present a barrier for further product innovation and market segmentation, as annuity providers need volume in order to have a sufficient pooling of risk and for products to be sustainable. In general, the demand for annuity products remains low in most jurisdictions. One main driver of the development of enhanced annuities in the United Kingdom seems to be the existence of the requirement to annuitise a portion of assets accumulated at retirement. Making the annuity offer more attractive to individuals who had lower life expectancies was a strategy for annuity providers to gain additional market share.

Nevertheless, consumers also need to be aware of the different products available and how to access the products in order to generate demand. In the United Kingdom, the lack of consumer engagement in the selection of their annuity product presented a barrier for the uptake of enhanced annuities, even for individuals who could have received a better income from them. The majority of consumers who could benefit from these products remained unaware of their existence and/or did not take advantage of the opportunity to purchase an enhanced annuity instead of a standard annuity. A third of individuals were not aware that purchasing an enhanced annuity was an option, and of the 60% of individuals taking an annuity from their existing pension provider, only 5% took an enhanced annuity (Financial Conduct Authority, 2014). The Financial Conduct Authority has taken numerous measures to try to address this problem, including requiring that pension providers inform their customers of their right to shop around (the Open Market Option) and are now considering requiring pension providers to show side-by-side comparisons of annuity quotes to encourage consumers to compare prices and select the best annuity product for them. Firms are also required to direct their consumers to the Pension Wise information service provided by the government for additional information and guidance.

The provision of information may therefore be the most important tool for policy makers to use to encourage a demand for innovative products to meet the needs of various segments of society in retirement. Individuals need to be informed of their options and the potential benefits of the various financial strategies they can employ for their retirement given their socio-economic level and situation. More importantly, however, this information needs to be easily accessible and simple to understand for consumers to be able to use it effectively to inform their decisions.

While encouraging product innovation is important, policy makers must also ensure that providers are appropriately managing any new risks presented by these products. Variable annuity products targeted to higher socio-economic groups for example, offered increased flexibility and market participation combined with the guarantees which significantly increased the risk exposure of the annuity providers offering these products. The financial crisis revealed that not all variable annuity providers were appropriately managing these risks, however, with several pulling out of the market as a result. Variable annuity providers have since de-risked these products, reducing somewhat the flexibility they offer, and in many jurisdictions providers are required to submit a clearly defined hedging strategy to the regulators to demonstrate that they are effectively managing the risks. Risk-based reserve and solvency requirements are also increasingly being imposed to ensure that sufficient capital is being held to cover the risks presented by different types of products.

Ensuring that rules governing access to pensions do not put lower socio-economic groups at a disadvantage

More broadly, given the differences in mortality across socio-economic groups, policy makers should ensure that the general rules governing the access to pensions and retirement savings do not put those in lower socio-economic groups that have lower life expectancies at a disadvantage. Age is often used as a reference to define limits around the ability to access money which has been earmarked for retirement, either for the amount received or the time at which it can be accessed. These limits are increasingly being linked to the realised increases in life expectancy which, as shown above, have not been equal across all socio-economic groups. Lower socio-economic groups may therefore be more limited in the amount of pension income they can expect to receive and the relative length of time they spend in retirement compared to higher socio-economic groups, and this disadvantage may be increasing over time.

Maximum limits imposed on the level of programmed withdrawals from retirement savings which are based on average life expectancy for the population could lead to lower socio-economic groups being allowed to withdraw less over their lifetime than those in higher socio-economic groups. These limits can be established based on life expectancy at the beginning of withdrawal or updated each year to reflect life expectancy conditional on surviving another year, and can account for future improvements in mortality (cohort life expectancy) or not (period life expectancy). Given the lower life expectancy of lower socio-economic groups, under such rules they would expect to withdraw a smaller proportion of their retirement savings over their lifetime compared to higher socio-economic groups. This difference could be worsened if limits are based on cohort life expectancies to the extent that lower socio-economic groups tend to also have lower mortality improvements.

Similarly, any mandatory annuitisation based on the actuarially fair values for the population average would provide lower total levels of lifetime income for lower socio-economic groups. Annuity factors calculated on health or behavioural factors, like the income provided by enhanced annuities is calculated, would help to resolve this problem as certain risk factors are also more prevalent in lower socio-economic groups, and calculating the annuity rate taking these factors into account would result in a higher level of income.

The age at which money earmarked for pensions can be accessed can also be linked to age or life expectancy, either through indirect incentives or explicit limits, and thereby can influence the age at which individuals are able to retire. For example, tax penalties can be imposed if retirement savings are accessed before a certain minimum age, effectively imposing a minimum retirement age on individuals. Alternatively, minimum age limits at which a full pension can be accessed can explicitly be imposed. Both of these approaches can directly impact the ratio of years spent in retirement to the years spent working and contributing.

The increasingly prevalent policy of linking these age limits to realised increases in life expectancy intends to maintain the proportion of life spent in retirement relatively constant, as the longer individuals live the longer they will need to work and contribute to finance the longer retirement. However, given the differences in life expectancy across socio-economic groups, lower groups will be allowed a lower proportion of their lifetime in retirement than higher groups as a result of such policies. Furthermore, to the extent that they also experience lower than average mortality improvements, these ratios would be expected to diverge over time, increasing the relative disadvantage for lower socio-economic groups.

This disparity and divergence is illustrated in Figure 6.10 for males in the United States and France. Figure 6.10 shows the evolution of this ratio over time with actual data keeping the years contributing constant assuming that individuals began working at age 22 and retired at age 65. For the least educated group in the United States, this ratio increased from 0.29 to 0.38 from 1979 to 2011, whereas it increased from 0.32 to 0.46 for the most educated. In France, the ratio went from 0.3 to 0.41 for manual workers between 1980 and 2011 and from 0.36 to 0.49 for higher managers and professionals.

The divergence in these ratios across socio-economic groups shows that higher socio-economic groups are spending an increasingly longer proportion of time in retirement relative to lower socio-economic groups. In order to keep this ratio constant across socio-economic groups, those in higher socio-economic classes would need to work and

Figure 6.10. **Ratio of years in retirement to contribution years, United States and France**

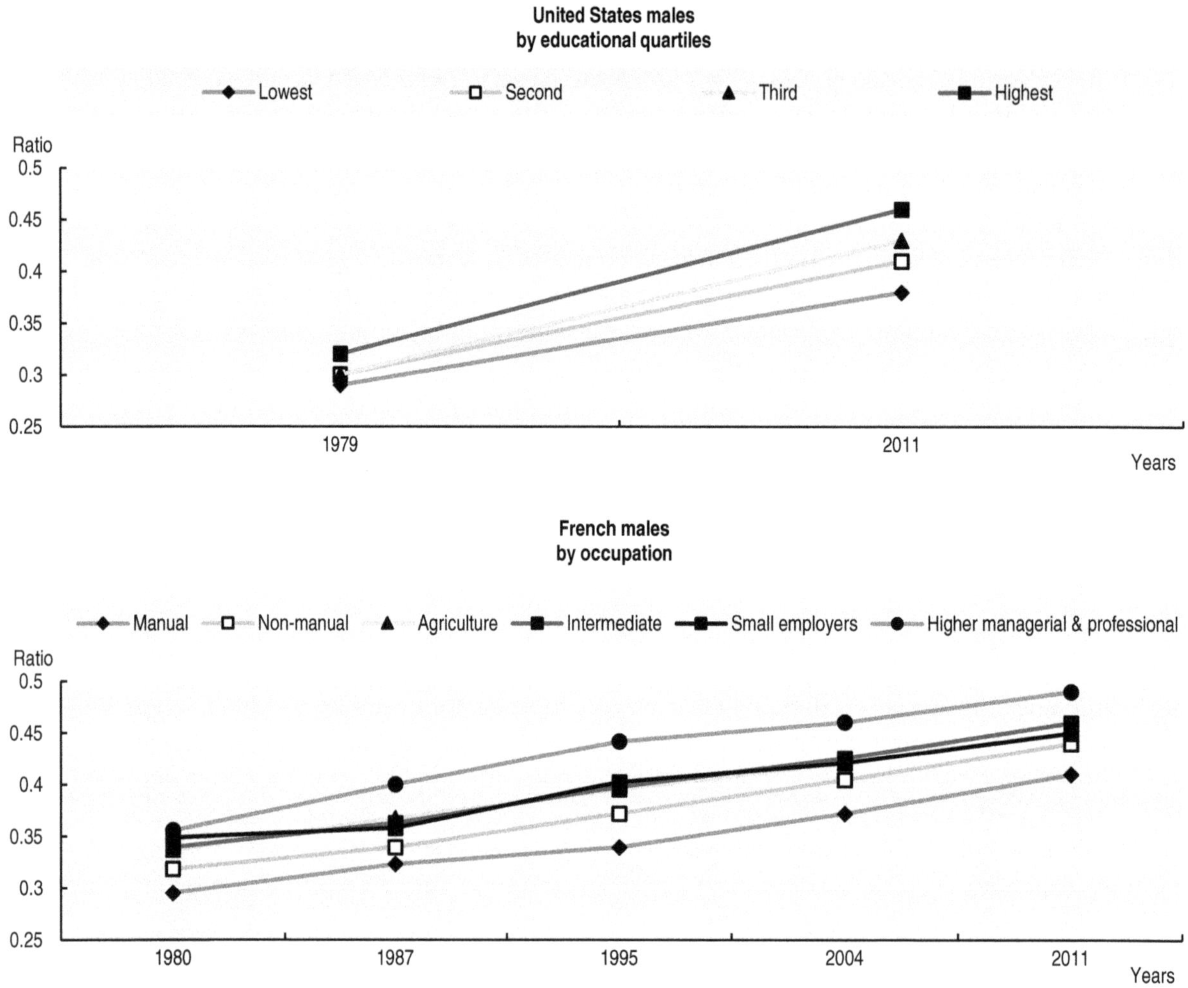

Note: Assumes age of entry into the labour force at 22, retirement at age 65, and is conditional on survival to age 65.
Source: OECD calculations based on Sanzenbacher et al. (2015) for the United States, and INSEE for France.

StatLink http://dx.doi.org/10.1787/888933362757

contribute for a longer period of time. Figure 6.11 shows the additional number of years beyond age 65 that each class would be required to work to maintain this ratio at a constant level across time, assumed to be 0.3 for the United States and 0.33 for France.[10] In the United States, those in the highest socio-economic class would have to work 5.4 additional years, whereas those in the lowest class would only have to work 2.7 additional years, since life expectancy improved for the latter group by 2.1 years less than for those with the highest education. If we further assume that those with the lowest educational attainment also began working at an earlier age of 18, this would reduce the age at which these individuals should retire by nearly one additional year. Therefore to maintain a ratio of years in retirement to years working of 0.3 in 2011, the highest educated males would need to work until age 70.4, whereas the lowest educated could retire at age 66.8, 3.6 years earlier. For the case of France, the manual workers could retire at age 67.5 in 2011 while those in higher managerial and professional roles would need to work 2.8 years longer until age 70.3. Assuming manual workers enter the labour force at the age of 18, however, they would be able to retire even earlier at age 66.5.

Figure 6.11. **Additional contribution years required to maintain a constant ratio of years in retirement to contribution years**

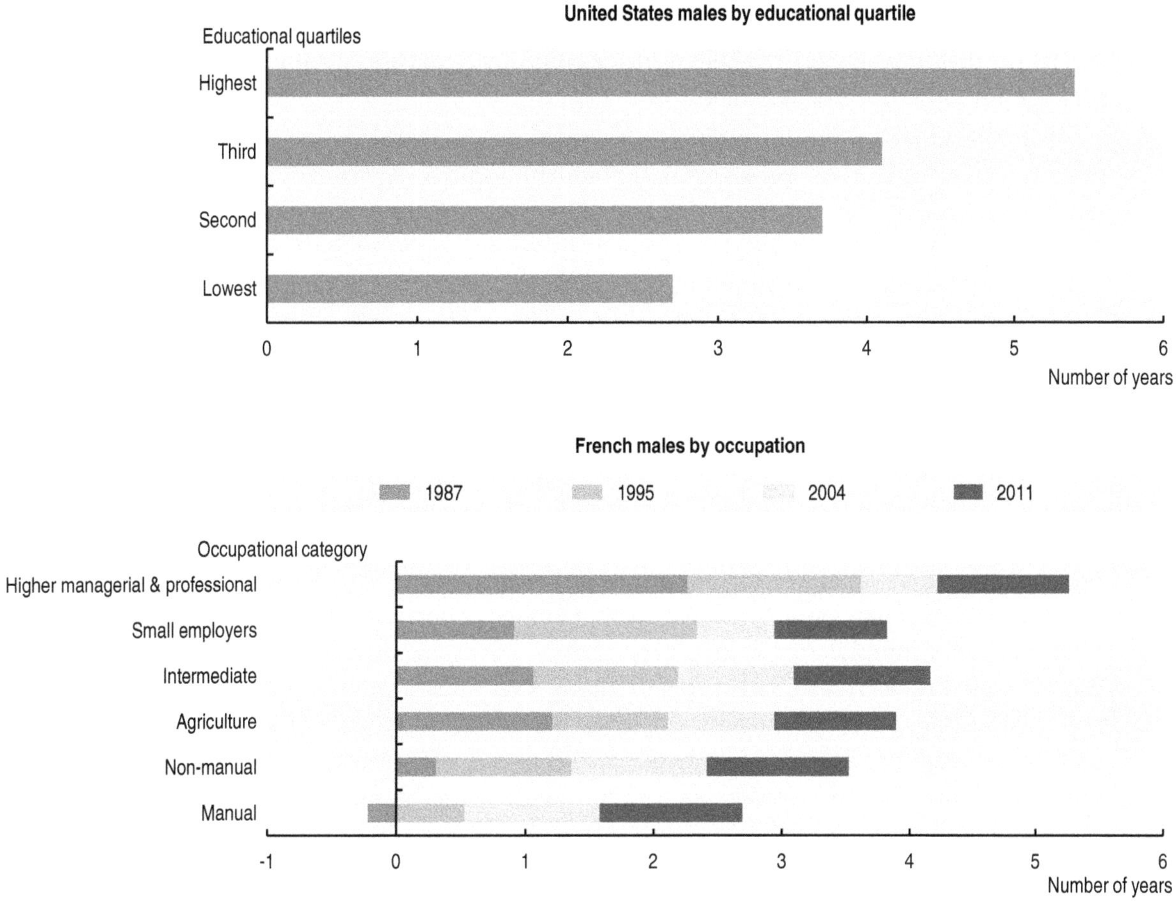

Note: Shows additional years beyond age 65, assumes age of entry into the labour force at 22 and is conditional on survival to age 65.
Source: OECD calculations based on Sanzenbacher et al. (2015) for the United States, and INSEE for France.

StatLink http://dx.doi.org/10.1787/888933362762

Policy makers should therefore consider keeping the ratio of years in retirement to years contributing equal across socio-economic groups and constant over time. Policies basing the age at which full pension can be accessed on average life expectancy will result in lower socio-economic classes spending fewer years in retirement compared to years spent working, and linking this age to increases in average life expectancy can further put these groups at a disadvantage. To the extent that lower socio-economic groups begin working earlier, for example if everyone begins working after completing their education, basing the age at which full pension can be accessed on the number of years working and contributing, as well as life expectancy, would help indirectly to reduce the discrepancy. With this policy, those beginning to work at an earlier age could also retire at an earlier age maintaining the ratio of years in retirement to years contributing equal across different socio-economic groups and constant over time. Other distributional mechanisms could also serve to offset the relative disadvantage of lower socio-economic groups, however, so policy makers need to consider these benefits as well for any solution. Attention should also be paid to any adverse incentives such policies could create, for example to retire early. However, these solutions do not necessarily address the problem with respect to the divergence of life expectancies over time, a much more challenging issue for pension policy makers to tackle.

Conclusions

The fragmentation of mortality across socio-economic groups, both with respect to the level of mortality, but also with respect to the mortality improvements experienced over time, presents significant challenges for pensions funds and insurance companies to manage the longevity risk they face.

The first challenge relates to establishing appropriate mortality assumptions for their pensioner and annuitant populations. Given the large quantity of data necessary to determine expected trends in mortality and life expectancy, these assumptions are usually based on a larger population which may not be as representative of the demographics of the population to which the assumptions are applied. Furthermore, external shocks such as regulatory changes can impact the socio-economic mix of these populations, complicating the measurement of improvements in mortality even where sufficient data exist.

The second challenge these differences present relates to the mitigation of the longevity risk exposure of pension funds and annuity providers. The exposure of these entities tends to be more concentrated towards higher socio-economic groups, meaning that there is also an increased risk that mortality improvements will be higher than those experienced by the population as a whole. This increased risk implies that a higher risk premium would be demanded by reinsurers to accept to take this risk from the pension funds and annuity providers. To the extent that longevity risk also remains concentrated in higher socio-economic groups, reinsurance capacity could potentially become limited. While using index-based instruments to pass this risk to the capital markets could potentially offer additional capacity at a lower cost, pension funds and annuity providers may be reluctant use these instruments because of the differences in expected mortality improvements across socio-economic groups and the longevity basis risk that this implies.

Policy makers could help to facilitate the measurement and management of the longevity risk exposure of pension funds and annuity providers by making accurate and timely mortality data available by socio-economic groups. These data could provide a benchmark which entities could use to establish their own assumptions, and make it easier to assess the risk that certain segments will have higher improvements in mortality.

Despite the challenges coming from the differences in life expectancies, these differences also present an opportunity for pensions and insurers to expand their markets and diversify their longevity risk by adapting product offerings to different segments of society. Enhanced annuities in particular offer a retirement financing solution for lower socio-economic groups, who are also more likely to have certain health problems or behavioural risk factors such as smoking. More flexible product offerings such as variable annuities may be more adapted to higher socio-economic groups.

Policy makers should encourage and facilitate product innovation to meet the various needs of different market segments, though they should also ensure that the risks arising from these products are managed appropriately. Attention should be paid in particular to the risk factors which are allowed to be used by annuity providers to price their products, as overly restrictive requirements could result in the exclusion of certain groups from the market. Policy makers could also help to encourage competition for the business of lower socio-economic groups in particular by helping consumers gain easy access to information regarding their options to finance their retirement, which would encourage the demand for products which best meet their needs.

The differences in mortality across socio-economic groups, however, have broader implications with respect to how the overall access to funds earmarked for retirement is governed, as policies defined "on average" may be regressive. Rules referencing average life expectancies to establish the amount of allowable income or the age at which funds can be accessed can result in lower socio-economic groups spending less time and receiving less money in retirement. To the extent that these groups also experience lower than average mortality improvements, linking these rules to the changes in average life expectancy could exacerbate the disadvantage of lower socio-economic groups over time. One approach could be to keep the ratio of years in retirement to years contributing equal across socio-economic groups and constant over time.

This dilemma is not a simple problem for pension policy makers to resolve, and any solution will undoubtedly be complex. However policymakers must be aware of this fragmentation of mortality across socio-economic groups so as to not worsen the disadvantage of lower groups with respect to the amount of pension they can expect to receive in retirement. To assist with this, the next step in the research agenda of the OECD is to estimate and quantify the potential impact of differences in mortality and life expectancy (in both levels and gradients) by socio-economic factors on the well-being of retirees. The ultimate solution will be to target the causes of these differences in order to reduce this mortality disadvantage for the future.

Notes

1. For a detailed discussion on the use of these measures as a proxy for socio-economic status see Groenwald et al., 2008.
2. See Annex 6.A1 for the definitions of the categories used for each country.
3. Except for Australia where figures are based on life expectancy at age 60.
4. The OECD is preparing more comparable estimates of inequalities in life expectancy by education based on consistent assumptions and data treatments across a large number of OECD countries. Murtin et al. 2016 explains the problems with the data and proposes consistent procedures to produce better quality figures of inequalities in life expectancy by education. The main trends and tendencies highlighted in this paper will not change.
5. Figures for the Czech Republic are based on 2012 due to observed inconsistencies in the latest available data for 2013.
6. Bosworth et al. (2016) also found that the inequalities in life expectancy at age 50 with respect to both educational attainment and income have increased for both genders when comparing the cohort born in 1920 and the cohort in 1940.
7. The educational categories used for Australia are less dispersed so likely result in a smaller difference than the comparable figures in Canada.
8. Period life expectancy is shown, which does not account for future expected improvements in mortality.
9. Based on figures provided by LIMRA in an OECD survey on annuity products.
10. These represent the average ratios observed in the United States and France in 1979 and 1980, respectively.

References

Agnew, J.R. et al. (2008), "Who Chooses Annuities? An Experimental Investigation of the Role of Gender, Framing, and Defaults", *American Economic Review* 98, No. 2, pp. 418-422.

Agnew, J. and L. Szykman (2010), "Annuities, Financial Literacy and Information Overload", *Working Paper, Pension Research Council*, Philadelphia.

Blainpain, N. (2016), "L'espérance de vie par catégorie sociale et par diplôme : Méthode et principaux résultats" *Document de travail* No. F1602, INSEE, Paris.

Bosworth, B., G. Burtless and K. Zhang (2016), "Later Retirement, Inequality in Old Age, and the Growing Gap in Longevity Between Rich and Poor", *Economic Studies at Brookings*.

CANSIM, Statistics Canada, accessed November 2015.

Carter, K.N., T. Blakely and M. Soeberg (2010), "Trends in survival and life expectancy by ethnicity, income and smoking in New Zealand: 1980s to 2000s." *The New Zealand Medical Journal* 123, No. 1320.

Central Statistics Office, Ireland (2010), "Mortality Differences in Ireland: Analysis based on the census characteristics of persons who died in the twelve month period after Census Date 23 April 2006".

Clarke, P. and A. Leigh (2011), "Death, Dollars and Degrees: Socio-economic Status and Longevity in Australia" *Economic Paper,* The Economic Society of Australia, pp. 348-355.

Deboosere, P., S. Gadeyne and H. Van Oye (2009), "The 2991-2004 Evolution in Life Expectancy by Educational level in Belgium Based on Linked Census and Population Register Data", *European Journal of Population*, pp.175-196.

Drinkwater, M. et al. (2006), "Substandard Annuities", LIMRA International Inc., Society of Actuaries, in collaboration with Ernst & Young LLP.

Eurostat Database, *Life expectancy by age and educational attainment*, accessed November 2015.

Financial Conduct Authority (2016), "Retirement Income Market Data: July-September 2015", London.

Financial Conduct Authority (2014), "Thematic Review of Annuities", London.

Gatzert, N. and U. Klotzki. "Enhanced Annuities: Drivers of and Barriers to Supply and Demand", *The Geneva Papers on Risk and Insurance – Issues and Practice*.

Groenwold, G., J. van Ginneken and C. Masseria (2008), "Towards comparable statistics on mortality by socio-economic status in EU Member States", European Commission.

Murtin, F., J. Mackenbach, D. Jasilionis and M. Mira d'Ercole (2016), "Inequalities in Mortality by Education in OECD Countries: Insights from New OECD Estimates", forthcoming *OECD Statistics Directorate Working Paper*.

OECD (2014), *Mortality Assumptions and Longevity Risk: Implications for pension funds and annuity providers*, OECD Publishing, Paris, *http://dx.doi.org/10.1787/9789264222748-en*.

Office for National Statistics (2015), "Statistical Bulletin: Trend in life expectancy at birth and at age 65 by socio-economic position based on the National Statistics Socio-economic Classification, England and Wales: 1982-1986 to 2007-2011".

Sanzenbacher, G.T. et al. (2015), "Calculating Neutral Increases in Retirement Age by Socio-economic Status", Center for Retirement Research at Boston College.

The Geneva Association (2013), "Variable Annuities – An Analysis of Financial Stability", Geneva.

von Gaudecker, H and C. Weber (2006), "Mandatory Unisex Policies and Annuity Pricing: Quasi-Experimental Evidence from Germany", Universitat Mannheim.

ANNEX 6.A1

Sources and details of life expectancy figures

	Socio-economic indicator	Categories available	Period(s)	Source
Australia	Education	12 years > 12 years	2001-09	(Clark & Leigh, 2011), derived from the Household, Income and Labour Dynamics in Australia (HILDA) survey
	Income	Low Quintile High Quintile	2001-09	
Belgium	Education	No Diploma Primary Low secondary High secondary Tertiary	Change 1991-> 2001	(Deboosere, Gadeyne, & Van Oyen, 2009)
Canada	Education	< Secondary Secondary Post-secondary University degree	1991-2006	CANSIM, Statistics Canada
	Income	1st Quintile 2nd Quintile 3rd Quintile 4th Quintile 5th Quintile		
Chile	Income	1st Quintile 2nd Quintile 3rd Quintile 4th Quintile 5th Quintile	2008-13	Superintendencia de Pensiones, Chile
Czech Republic	Education	ISCED Levels 0-2 ISCED Levels 3-4 ISCED Levels 5-8	2007; 2008; 2009; 2010; 2011; 2012	Eurostat Database, Life expectancy by age, sex and educational attainment
Denmark	Education	ISCED Levels 0-2 ISCED Levels 3-4 ISCED Levels 5-8	2007; 2008; 2009; 2010; 2011; 2012; 2013	Eurostat Database, Life expectancy by age, sex and educational attainment
England and Wales	Occupation	Routine Semi-routine Lower supervisory & technical Small employers Intermediate Lower managerial and professional Higher managerial and professional	1982-86; 1987-91; 1992-96; 1997-2001; 2002-06; 2007-11	Office of National Statistics, 2015
Estonia	Education	ISCED Levels 0-2 ISCED Levels 3-4 ISCED Levels 5-8	2007; 2008; 2009; 2010; 2011; 2012; 2013	Eurostat Database, Life expectancy by age, sex and educational attainment

	Socio-economic indicator	Categories available	Period(s)	Source
Finland	Education	ISCED Levels 0-2 ISCED Levels 3-4 ISCED Levels 5-8	2007; 2008; 2009; 2010; 2011; 2012; 2013	Eurostat Database, Life expectancy by age, sex and educational attainment
France	Occupation	Unemployed Manual Non-manual Agriculture Intermediate Small employers Higher managerial and professional	1976-84; 1983-91; 1991-999; 2000-08; 2009-13	INSEE, 2016
	Education	No diploma Lower secondary Vocational diploma High school Tertiary	1991-99; 2000-08; 2009-13	
Greece	Education	ISCED Levels 0-2 ISCED Levels 3-4 ISCED Levels 5-8	2013	Eurostat Database, Life expectancy by age, sex and educational attainment
Hungary	Education	ISCED Levels 0-2 ISCED Levels 3-4 ISCED Levels 5-8	2007; 2008; 2009; 2010; 2011; 2012; 2013	Eurostat Database, Life expectancy by age, sex and educational attainment
Ireland	Education	Primary Secondary Third	2006-07	Central Statistics Office Ireland, 2010
	Occupation	Unskilled Semi-skilled Skilled manual Non-manual Managerial and technical Professional		
Italy	Education	ISCED Levels 0-2 ISCED Levels 3-4 ISCED Levels 5-8	2007; 2008; 2009; 2010; 2011; 2012; 2013	Eurostat Database, Life expectancy by age, sex and educational attainment
New Zealand	Income	Low Medium High	1981; 1986; 1991; 1996; 2001	New Zealand Census Mortality Study, University of Otago Wellington
Norway	Education	ISCED Levels 0-2 ISCED Levels 3-4 ISCED Levels 5-8	2007; 2008; 2009; 2010; 2011; 2012; 2013	Eurostat Database, Life expectancy by age, sex and educational attainment
Poland	Education	ISCED Levels 0-2 ISCED Levels 3-4 ISCED Levels 5-8	2008; 2009; 2010; 2011; 2012; 2013	Eurostat Database, Life expectancy by age, sex and educational attainment
Portugal	Education	ISCED Levels 0-2 ISCED Levels 3-4 ISCED Levels 5-8	2010; 2011; 2012; 2013	Eurostat Database, Life expectancy by age, sex and educational attainment
Slovak Republic	Education	ISCED Levels 0-2 ISCED Levels 3-4 ISCED Levels 5-8	2011; 2012; 2013	Eurostat Database, Life expectancy by age, sex and educational attainment
Slovenia	Education	ISCED Levels 0-2 ISCED Levels 3-4 ISCED Levels 5-8	2007; 2008; 2009; 2010; 2011; 2012; 2013	Eurostat Database, Life expectancy by age, sex and educational attainment
Sweden	Education	ISCED Levels 0-2 ISCED Levels 3-4 ISCED Levels 5-8	2007; 2008; 2009; 2010; 2011; 2012; 2013	Eurostat Database, Life expectancy by age, sex and educational attainment

	Socio-economic indicator	Categories available	Period(s)	Source
Turkey	Education	ISCED Levels 0-2 ISCED Levels 3-4 ISCED Levels 5-8	2010; 2011; 2012	Eurostat Database, Life expectancy by age, sex and educational attainment
United States	Education	1st quartile 2nd quartile 3rd quartile 4th quartile	1979; 2011	(Sanzenbacher, Webb, Cosgrove, & Orlova, 2015) from the National Longitudinal Mortality Study

OECD Business and Finance Outlook 2016

Chapter 7

Is foreign bribery an attractive investment in some countries?

One of the most basic legal principles is that crime should not pay. Yet this chapter will show that, in many jurisdictions with weak sanctions, foreign bribery may be an attractive investment. In others, foreign bribery is subject to strong penalties, although some of these penalties exist only on paper because they are not backed up by effective enforcement. Only a few countries combine strong sanctions with active enforcement of anti-bribery laws. Thus, this chapter paints a picture of fragmented deterrence across the 41 Parties to the Anti-Bribery Convention. This patchwork of incentives and disincentives for foreign bribery is explored using simulations of "net present value" for "investments in foreign bribery" under assumptions of both certainty and uncertainty. The simulations draw on sanctions data produced by the OECD Working Group on Bribery for each of the 41 Parties to the Anti-Bribery Convention and on the cash flows – including both bribes and benefits – associated with a real-world bribery scenario. They show, in particular, that in many countries having low fines for paying bribery, a company would still be willing to "invest" in a foreign bribery scheme even if it knew in advance that it would be caught and fined at the end of the bribery scenario. This implies that fines for bribery are set too low in many jurisdictions.

Main findings

- Fragmentation across jurisdictions of fines and enforcement effectiveness create both strong incentives and disincentives for foreign bribery across the Parties to the Anti-Bribery Convention. This fragmentation is documented by simulations of returns on investments in foreign bribery for Parties to the Convention.
- The simulations are based on the cash flows from a real-world bribery scheme. For each Party that has a maximum sanction for foreign bribery, this maximum sanction is applied to the cash flow analysis to calculate a net present value for the investment in the bribery scheme.
- The results show that, because of low sanctions in many jurisdictions, companies would still have an interest in investing in the bribery scheme, even if they knew with certainty that they would be caught at the end of the scheme.
- Simulations under an uncertainty scenario where a firm faces at least some probability of getting caught and sanctioned for bribery in each year of the scheme also show a strong fragmentation of incentives. This implies that an appropriate balance between enforcement effort and levels of sanctions needs to be found in order to establish an effective system of deterrence.
- The simulations also show that the availability of effective systems of confiscation – that is, the deprivation of property by a competent authority, such as a court – has the potential to significantly reduce the fragmentation of incentives, but in many cases the Parties to the Convention lack the necessary expertise and legal infrastructure to establish such systems.

Introduction

Foreign bribery is subject to severe penalties in a handful of jurisdictions – and these penalties are enforced in even fewer. However, in other jurisdictions, foreign bribery can still be a good "investment" because of low sanctions and/or weak enforcement. The varying types and levels of sanctions across jurisdictions, combined with varying detection and punishment probabilities, create financial and economic fragmentation by making foreign bribery a viable option in some jurisdictions and an unattractive one in others.

This chapter explores the widely divergent incentive systems that companies face when it comes to foreign bribery. It focuses on sanctions, which are a crucial aspect of any legal regime. As legal incentives have important effects on economic activity, the extraordinary variability in sanctions for foreign bribery are an important source of fragmentation in the global economy. This is because diverging sanctions regimes around the world create an uneven playing field for companies in different jurisdictions and widen the scope for cross-border legal engineering designed to lower companies' exposure to sanctions for foreign bribery. The next section briefly describes the existing comparative data for the 41 Parties to the OECD Anti-Bribery Convention, which shows wide variability in sanctions policies.

This chapter then presents two simulation scenarios designed to facilitate comparison across sanctions regimes, including the regimes' rules for imposing corporate fines and confiscating the bribe and/or the proceeds from bribery from convicted companies. The two scenarios convert the cash flows from a bribery scheme and the maximum available sanctions for bribery in each jurisdiction into comparable values across jurisdictions by calculating the net present value of the investment in the bribe scheme. This net present value of bribery may be positive or negative. These simulations – which are based on the cash flows associated with an actual foreign bribery scheme uncovered by real world enforcement actions – document the extent to which foreign bribery remains a highly profitable activity in some jurisdictions but is potentially heavily sanctioned in others. In other words, it quantifies fragmentation in incentives and disincentives for foreign bribery. Because the chapter only considers two types of sanctions – fines and confiscation – it does not capture the full set of incentives facing companies.[1] Nevertheless, it provides a vivid illustration of the why enforcement and adequate fines and confiscation matter.

Dissuasive sanctions regimes and foreign bribery as an investment opportunity

One of the most basic objectives of law enforcement is to ensure that crime does not pay. For foreign bribery, this means that paying bribes to foreign public officials is (or should be), on average, a money-losing proposition. The Anti-Bribery Convention states that penalties for foreign bribery should be, among other things, "dissuasive" (see Box 7.1).

Box 7.1. **The OECD Anti-Bribery Convention and sanctions for foreign bribery**

The Preamble to the OECD Anti-Bribery Convention states *inter alia* that the purpose of the Convention is to prevent foreign bribery from distorting "international competitive conditions". It recognises that "achieving equivalence among the measures to be taken by the Parties is an essential object and purpose of the Convention".

Article 3 of the Convention requires each Party to ensure that legal persons (essentially, companies) are subjected to penalties – which may be criminal or non-criminal – that are "effective, proportionate and dissuasive". Under Article 3(3), each Party must ensure that they can confiscate "the bribe" plus "the proceeds of the bribery of a foreign public official" (or property whose value is equivalent to such proceeds), unless the Party would apply "monetary sanctions of comparable effect".

Significantly, however, the Convention does not require complete uniformity. In numerous places, the Convention expressly limits the Parties' obligations concerning foreign bribery to measures that are "in accordance" with their national legal principles.[1] Indeed, the *Commentaries*, which were adopted along with the Anti-Bribery Convention, clarify that the Convention merely "seeks to assure a functional equivalence among the measures taken by the Parties".[2] Article 3 is no exception, as Article 3(1) provides that the "range of penalties" for foreign bribery "shall be comparable to that applicable to the bribery of the Party's own public officials".

Fifteen years after the Convention went into force, 40 of the 41 Parties to the Convention can now impose sanctions on legal persons (for example, companies) for foreign bribery. While the WGB has not concluded that all of these regimes for legal persons satisfy the obligations under Articles 2 and 3 of the Convention, it has collected data on the Parties' types and levels of sanctions through the first three phases of monitoring.[3]

1. See, e.g. OECD Anti-Bribery Convention, art. 2 ("Each Party shall take such measures ..., in accordance with its legal principles, to establish the liability of legal persons...."); *see id.* at art. 4(2) ("Each Party which has jurisdiction to prosecute its nationals for offences committed abroad shall take such measures ... to establish its jurisdiction [over foreign bribery] according to the same principles").
2. *Commentaries on the Convention on Combating Bribery of Foreign Public Officials in International Business Transactions* (21 Nov. 1997) (hereinafter the *Commentaries*), comment 2.
3. As of December 2015, the WGB has finished the third phase of monitoring for all but two of the Parties to the Convention. The fourth phase of monitoring began in 2016.

At a minimum, the concept of "dissuasive" means that companies' expected gains from bribes, after accounting for legal sanctions, should be negative. Foreign bribery is not supposed to be an attractive investment.

Seen from the perspective of a company engaged in international business transactions, the expected gains or losses from foreign bribery (or other economic crimes) will depend on, first, the probability that a crime will be detected and successfully prosecuted and, second, the sanctions imposed as a result of a successful prosecution. Higher probabilities of being sanctioned for a crime and higher sanctions both produce lower expected net present values for crime. Thus, making sure that "crime doesn't pay" implies that effective law enforcement and sanctions regimes should, at a minimum, create conditions which make the expected net present value of the crime negative for most bribe scenarios. The simulation scenarios presented in this chapter show that this is not always the case.

Comparative data on sanctions for foreign bribery

OECD data published in the monitoring reports of the OECD Working Group on Bribery in International Business Transactions (WGB) show that sanctions on companies for foreign bribery take a variety of forms: fines; confiscation; and debarment, which is the exclusion (often temporary) from public procurement processes or obtaining public advantages.

Fines are monetary penalties. Depending on the jurisdiction, they can result from judicial or administrative proceedings or from settlement agreements with prosecutors. The WGB monitoring reports show that:

- Many countries establish maximum fines, which place an upper limit on the size of the fine that a company can be forced to pay. These limits are established in various ways:
  - Some countries impose simple maximum thresholds for monetary fines. These vary greatly in size from about USD 580 000 in the country with the lowest threshold to over USD 10 million in the highest threshold.[2]
  - Other countries have more complex rules for maximum fines. For example, fines may be set at multiples of bribe amounts (e.g. one country sets the maximum at 100 times the bribe amount for very large bribes). Other rules (of which there are many) include: setting the maximum as a multiple of the benefit (or "proceeds") received; as a function of the gravity of the bribery offence or as a combination of the considerations just listed.
- Eight countries do not set "maximum" thresholds for fines.

Confiscation is "the permanent deprivation of property by order of a court or other competent authority".[3] In practice, confiscation regimes are highly fragmented across the 41 Parties to the Anti-Bribery Convention. In addition, the WGB has found that confiscation regimes are rarely or only occasionally used in most jurisdictions. In contrast, a few jurisdictions have active confiscation regimes.[4] Other features of these regimes include:

- The rules for confiscation vary in important ways. Some allow confiscation only of assets directly involved in illegal acts, whereas others allow confiscation of indirectly related assets or of equivalent values.
- Experience with confiscation in the context of bribery cases involving companies is uneven. Some countries lack legislation and jurisprudence. In most jurisdictions, little is known about how courts would handle confiscation in complex foreign bribery cases.

This is especially true because such cases often involve assets held in several jurisdictions and multi-tiered company groups.

- The different ways that countries determine how much and what should be confiscated further reinforces the theme of fragmented jurisdictions. The Anti-Bribery Convention obliges Parties to provide that the bribe and the "proceeds" of a bribe or "property the value of which corresponds to that of such proceeds, are subject to seizure and confiscation or that monetary sanctions of comparable effect are applicable." However, countries have different rules for determining what constitutes the "proceeds" of the bribe.[5]
- In addition, some countries appear to be hampered by lack of expertise or legislation. In effect, they do not have an operative mechanism for confiscation. Such situations leave "many corporate wrongdoers unpunished, walking away with their ill-gotten proceeds".[6]
- In some countries, monetary sanctions (fines) are mutually exclusive with confiscation.

The simulations discussed below will focus only on the monetary fines and confiscation.

The net present value of foreign bribery: description of simulation scenarios

The simulation results presented in this chapter show that the large variation in sanctions regimes across the Parties to the Convention translates into analogous variations in the profitability of foreign bribery for companies operating in different jurisdictions. The overall picture painted by these simulations is one of widely diverging incentive systems for foreign bribery and myriad opportunities for escaping sanctions by judicious corporate structuring across jurisdictions.

To explore the dissuasiveness of the sanctions that Parties to the Convention can impose on legal persons for foreign bribery, this chapter applies the sanctions available in each Party to the facts arising out of an actual foreign bribery case. The bribery scenario draws on the facts of a bribery scheme involving a major multinational enterprise operating in the electrical power field. This scheme involved USD 1.9 million in improper payments (including cash and in-kind gifts) made over the period 1997-2004 in order to obtain tainted contracts with two electrical power companies in the host country. The contracts yielded a profit for the bribing company of some USD 13 million. For the criminal part of this case the company pleaded guilty to violating anti-bribery laws and was ordered to pay a USD 17.1 million criminal fine in September 2010. Thus, from the initiation of bribe payments to the settlement of the criminal enforcement action, this bribery episode covered the 1997 to 2010 period.

The simulations produce estimates of the net present value (NPV) of the "investment" in foreign bribery: i.e. the value – positive or negative – of the decision to bribe. While the amount and timing of the cash flows relating to both the bribe payments and the benefits received are held constant for each simulation of NPV, the sanctions vary by jurisdiction. Specifically, the simulated sanctions for the different jurisdictions are calculated under the assumption that the country will impose the maximum fine available given the nature of the offence. Thus the simulations are only calculated for the 33 countries that have maximum sanctions.[7] (Eight of the 41 Parties can impose sanctions on companies but do not set maximum sanctions). The simulations assume that the simulated sanction is paid on the date that it was actually paid in the bribe scheme under consideration (e.g. at the end of September 2010).

- *Perfect certainty*. This scenario presents a hypothetical company with certain knowledge of the cash flows associated with a bribery scheme – that is, with the actual sequence of bribe payments, the actual sequence of benefits and the simulated amount of sanctions to be paid at the date the case is resolved (e.g. September 2010 in the case used for the simulations). The scenario then asks whether or not the company would be willing to "purchase" this series of cash flows for a positive price. If the answer to this valuation question is "yes, the company would pay a positive price for this series of cash flows", then the sanctions regime is not dissuasive enough – it creates positive economic incentives for foreign bribery. Subsequent sections will show that in many jurisdictions the answer to this question is indeed "yes", while in others the NPV of the investment is highly negative.

- *Uncertainty*. The second scenario incorporates the idea of imperfect enforcement – that is, not all acts of foreign bribery are detected and sanctioned. For a given sequence of cash flows (here, the bribes and benefits of the bribery scheme), lower detection and punishment probabilities result in higher expected NPVs for foreign bribery. These simulations assume that each year, the company faces a fixed probability, α, of getting caught and having to pay the sanction and $(1-\alpha)$ of not getting caught. A programme is used to calculate the expected NPV of this investment in foreign bribery for a range of α values. The simulations show that high probabilities of being caught and punished (that is, high α) can, in effect, make up for low sanctions because they lower the net present value of investment in foreign bribery. Since it is widely assumed that α is, in fact, very low in most jurisdictions, a reasonable law enforcement strategy might be to set high fines in order to compensate for consistently low probabilities of getting caught.

Further details on the simulation methodology can be found in Annex 7.A1.

The NPV of the bribery scheme under perfect certainty

The perfect certainty scenario described above can be used to benchmark sanctions regimes using the chronology of benefits and bribes associated with the actual electrical power bribe scheme. As a benchmark, it is possible to calculate the NPV of the scheme,[8] evaluated in 1997, when the scheme was initiated; that is, using the actual bribe amounts, benefits and the USD 17.1 million criminal sanction. Using these "cash flows" (including the actual monetary sanction paid at the end of the scheme) and the risk free discount rate prevailing during the bribe period (3.6%) yields a NPV for the actual bribe scheme of USD -1.6 million – thus negative and therefore somewhat punitive.[9] The simulated NPV of the bribe scheme under other sanctions regimes is shown in Figure 7.1.

The simulation results underscore the fragmented nature of jurisdictions' regimes for sanctioning foreign bribery. This fragmentation in turn creates large variations in the economic incentives (or disincentives) for engaging in foreign bribery – the range between highest and lowest NPV among the 33 countries is USD 1.7 billion if only fines are considered and about the same range if confiscation is also allowed.

Further key points about the simulation results are:

- *Scenario involving only the maximum fine*. Under this scenario, 23 countries' maximum fines would produce positive NPVs for this bribery scheme. The median NPV for all 33 countries under this scenario is positive, at almost USD 6 million. Furthermore, in one jurisdiction, which cannot sanction companies for foreign bribery, the NPV of the bribe scheme would be USD 9.6 million. This contrasts with the very large negative NPVs that are produced by other countries' fines. The largest negative NPV would have been

Figure 7.1. **Net Present Value (NPV) of the foreign bribery scheme under different sanctions regimes**

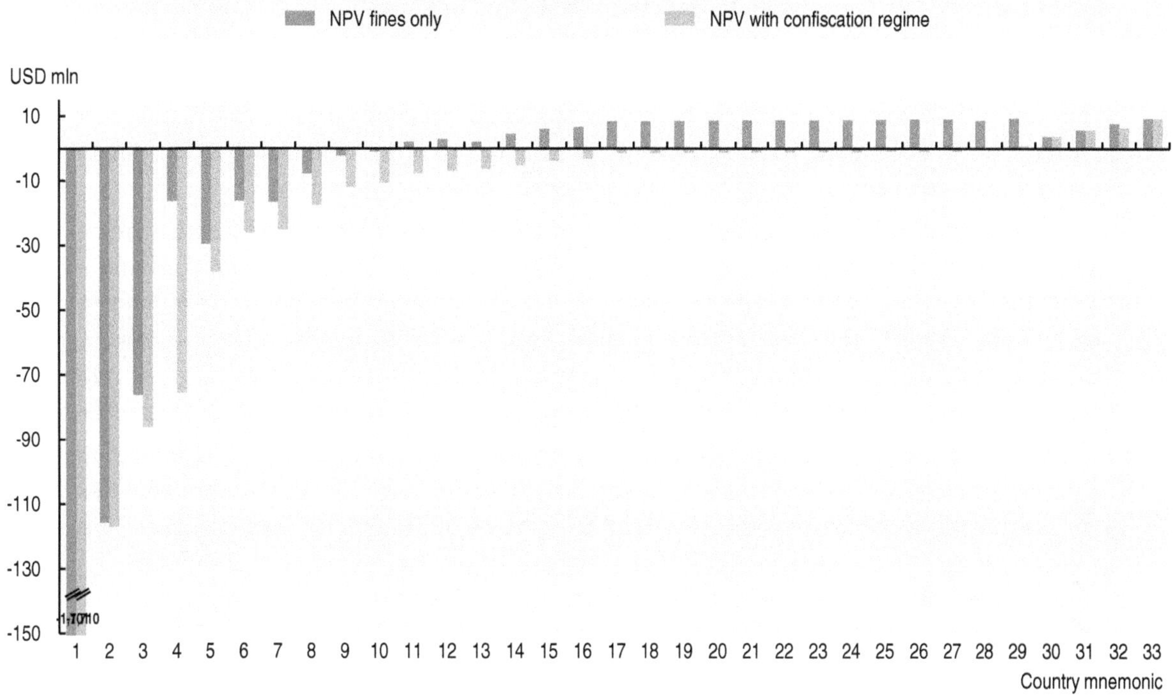

Note: One of the simulated NPVs is such a large negative that it exceeds the largest negative value on the vertical axis. Countries that have corporate fines for foreign bribery but that do not establish maximum thresholds are not included in the simulation.
Source: OECD calculations using sanctions data taken from OECD Working Group on Bribery monitoring reports (OECD, n.d.).
StatLink http://dx.doi.org/10.1787/888933362774

negative USD 1.7 billion if the maximum allowable fine were to be imposed (which is off the vertical axis in Figure 7.1). It should be noted, however, that the three countries with the most punitive fines (on paper) have never successfully prosecuted a company for foreign bribery.

- *Scenario involving a fine and/or confiscation.* Adding the possibility of confiscation along with the fine pushes many more jurisdictions into the negative NPV range. The median simulated value for the NPV with fines and confiscation falls to a negative USD 1.5 million. Whereas 23 countries had positive NPVs for the bribery scheme when only fines are involved, only six countries still have positive NPVs for the bribery scheme under the confiscation scenario. However, it should be reiterated that recourse to confiscation is rare and likely to pose major procedural hurdles in many jurisdictions.

The NPV of the bribery scheme when detection and punishment is uncertain

The second simulation explores how a company might evaluate a bribe opportunity when faced with uncertainty over whether the bribery scheme will be detected, successfully prosecuted and sanctioned. That is, unlike under simulation one, where the timing and level of the cash flows associated with the bribe (bribe payments plus benefits accrued) and the fines were assumed to be known with certainty in advance, simulation two examines the financial logic underpinning the decision to bribe when there is a non-zero probability of getting caught and punished.

In other words, this second simulation scenario combines monetary sanctions and non-zero probabilities of punishment. Both sanctions and enforcement influence the financial logic of bribery. The two variables – sanctions levels and probabilities of getting caught and sanctioned – constitute separate but related variables in any deterrence strategy. Governments can influence probabilities of detection and punishment by, for example, investing in enforcement capacity or by improving the effectiveness of prosecution and court procedures. This simulation seeks to assess whether or not these two variables combine to create a dissuasive environment for foreign bribery in various jurisdictions.

This assessment involves the calculation of the expected NPV of the bribery scheme using the cash flows of the electrical power bribery scheme (bribes and benefits) and a simulated sanction, again under the assumption that the maximum sanction available in each of the Parties to the Convention is applied. As in the first simulation discussed above, the bribe amounts are the actual bribe amounts paid in order to obtain the tainted electrical power contracts and the benefits are what the company earned from contracts.

What differs in this second simulation is the introduction of a single parameter to account for uncertain detection and punishment. The detection/punishment probabilities are assumed to be constant every year until the statute of limitations runs out. Thus, the company is assumed to face the same risk every year of getting caught. In this scenario, the statute of limitations is assumed to be the same for each country (that is, six years since the time of the last illegal act).[10] The discount rate used in this uncertainty simulation is higher than under the perfect certainty scenario in order to account for the uncertainty of detection. Specifically, the rate used is 6.5%, which was the bribing company's actual return on total assets over the period.

The results from this simulation are again presented in two scenarios: fines only (Figure 7.2) and figures plus confiscation (Figure 7.3). The figures show the expected NPV from the electrical utilities bribe scheme under the maximum sanctions assumptions and under alternative simulated probabilities of punishment.

The simulations under uncertain detection/punishment largely reinforce those of the perfect certainty scenario. That is, as in the first simulation, the finding of "fragmented" jurisdictions is very much in evidence, with some countries showing highly negative expected NPVs for bribery and others positive NPVs for investments in foreign bribery even at fairly high detection/punishment probabilities. More specific findings are described below.

- *Some countries have high de jure maximum sanctions for foreign bribery.* A few countries have very negative NPVs in Figure 7.2 (for fines only), even at low detection probabilities (in other words, their de jure maxima are so high that the associated expected NPV is negative even if the probability of getting caught is very low). Their high, de jure maximum fines produce high negative values for investments in bribery, even at the lowest detection probability (e.g. at 1% per year) and even when only fines are taken into account. When the possibility of confiscation is taken into account (Figure 7.3), then four countries have regimes which impose losses on companies even at very low detection probabilities (the lowest probability in the simulation being a 1% probability per year of getting caught and prosecuted). In other words, under these countries' sanctions rules, bribery is a bad investment (assuming the rules are enforced), even when the probability of getting caught is extremely low.
- *Many countries show positive NPVs for investments in bribery, even when detection probabilities are high.* At a 50% annual detection rate, no country has a positive NPV for this bribery scheme. On the other hand, at a 40% detection rate, five countries show positive NPVs.

Figure 7.2. **Expected Net Present Value (NPV) of bribe scheme with fines only**

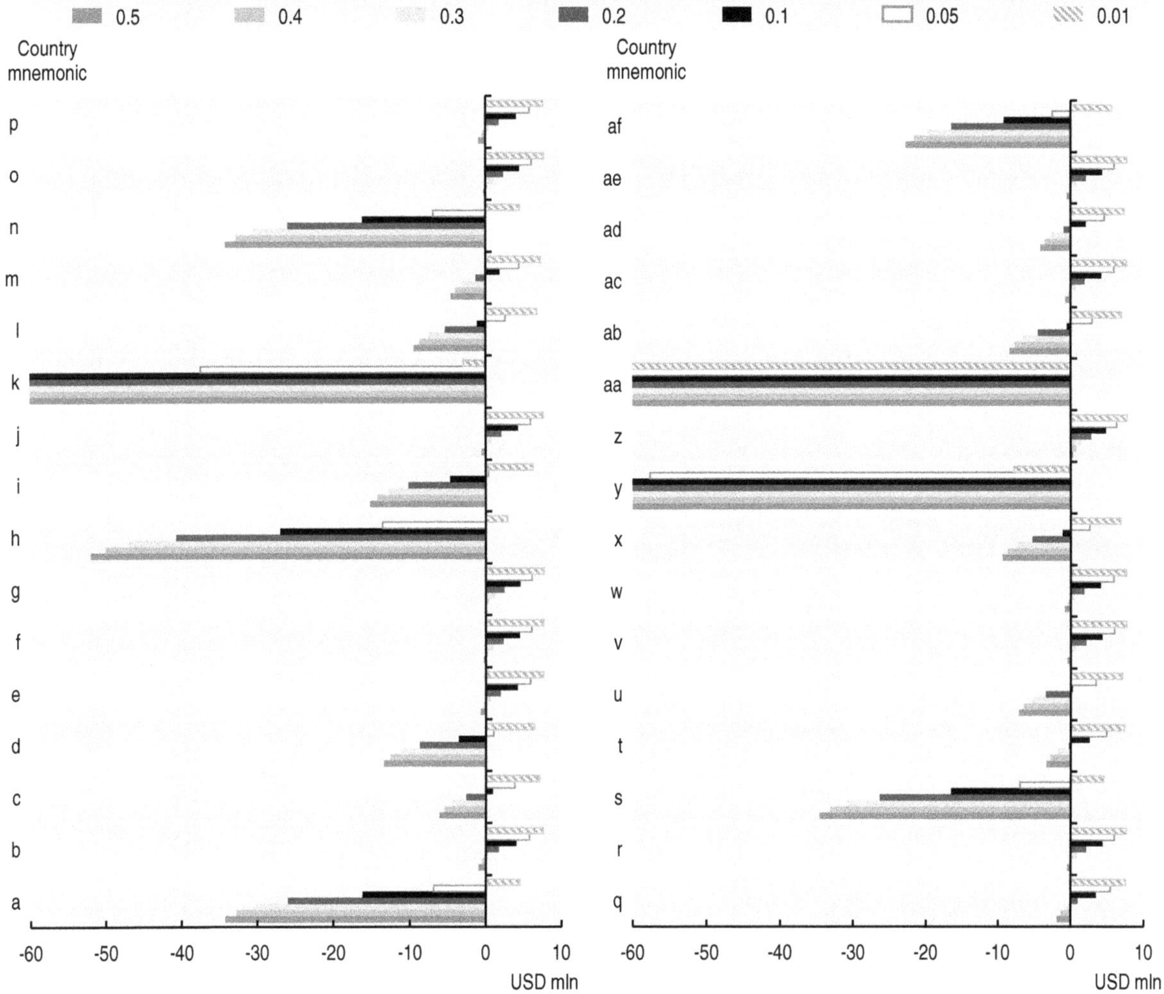

Note: Bars correspond to 7 different detection/successful prosecution probabilities, from 1% to 50% per year.
Source: OECD calculations using sanctions data taken from OECD Working Group on Bribery monitoring reports (OECD, n.d.).

StatLink http://dx.doi.org/10.1787/888933362784

The median NPV for the 33 countries turns negative (that is, the deterrence regime becomes somewhat dissuasive) at somewhere between 20% and 10% detection rates. Thus, in the absence of credible confiscation threats, many legal environments do not appear to be strongly dissuasive of foreign bribery, even with detection rates that may be quite a bit higher than those prevailing in the real world.

- *The availability of confiscation – if this tool is in fact used – weakens the finding of fragmentation.* As can be seen in Figure 7.3, the availability of confiscation weakens the finding of fragmentation in sanctions regimes for foreign bribery. Thus, putting in place credible confiscation policies would go a long way towards eliminating positive incentives for foreign bribery. This finding mirrors that of the perfect certainty simulations and, as already noted, most countries (including many of those whose rules for fines are shown to be not dissuasive) do not have operative confiscation systems. Thus, while, in theory, confiscation could help to harmonise sanctions regimes across the Parties to the Convention, in practice it does not yet play this role.

Figure 7.3. **Expected Net Present Value (NPV) of bribe scheme with fines and confiscation**

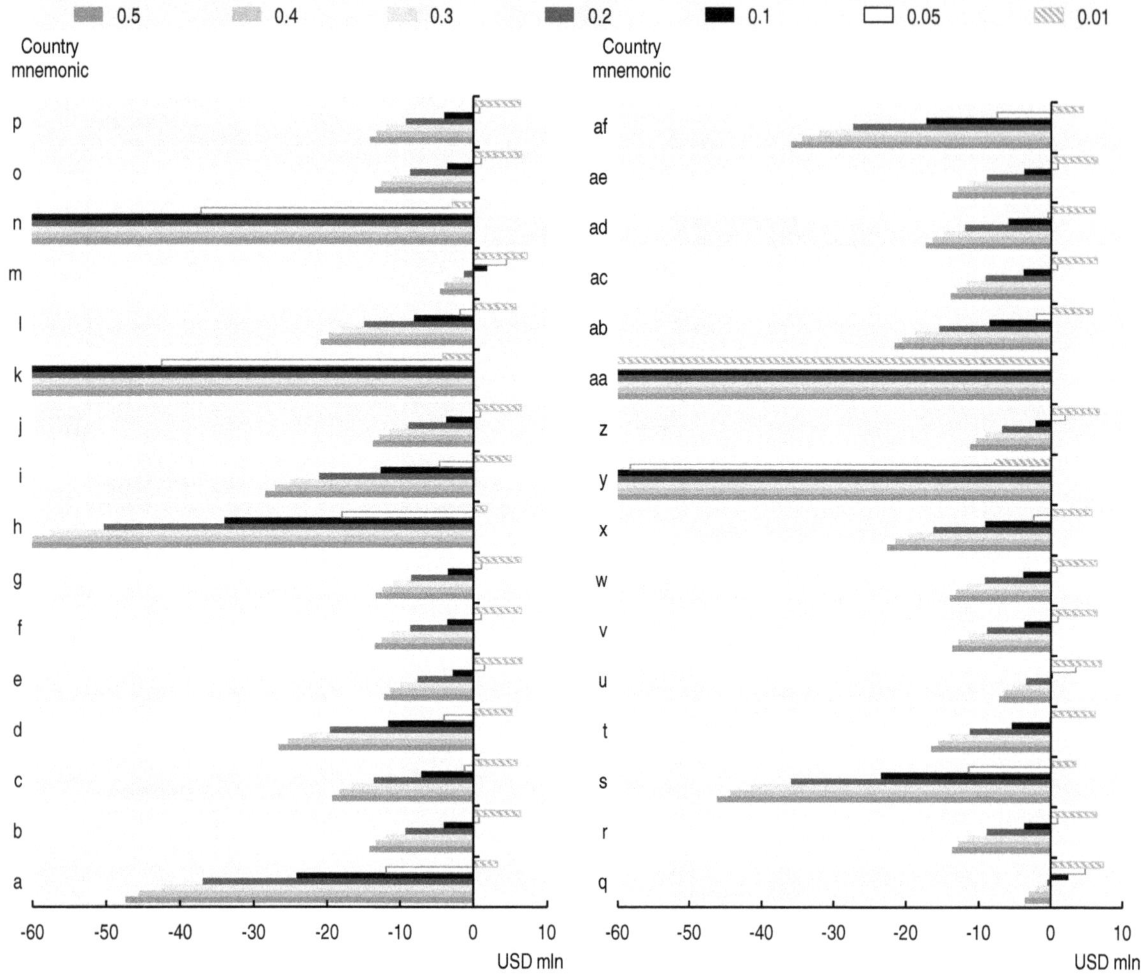

Note: Bars correspond to seven different detection/successful prosecution probabilities, from 1% to 50% per year.
Source: OECD calculations using sanctions data taken from OECD Working Group on Bribery monitoring reports (OECD, n.d.).
StatLink http://dx.doi.org/10.1787/888933362792

- *Sanctions and detection probabilities need to combine to create effective deterrence.* The uncertainty simulations clearly show that countries wishing to increase deterrence can act on two policy instruments – detection/punishment (which can be raised inter alia by investing in enforcement capacity) and on the level of sanctions. The two act as complements in determining the dissuasiveness of the enforcement system. This can be seen in Figure 7.4, which maps detection probabilities against the expected NPV of the scheme for three countries selected to illustrate different policy mixes. Figure 7.4 shows that the first country's very high nominal fines produce a positive expected NPV for the bribe scheme only at very low probabilities of punishment (between 0 and 1% per year). At the other extreme is the permissive country (which represents the many countries that have low nominal fines). Under this permissive regime, the expected NPV is positive even at quite high detection probabilities – it enters the negative expected NPV zone at an annual probability of punishment of about 36-37%. Between these two extremes is the "middle sanctions" country, where the expected NPV for the bribe scheme becomes negative at an annual detection rate in the 2-3% range.

Figure 7.4. **Expected Net Present Value (NPV) of bribe as a function of detection probabilities**

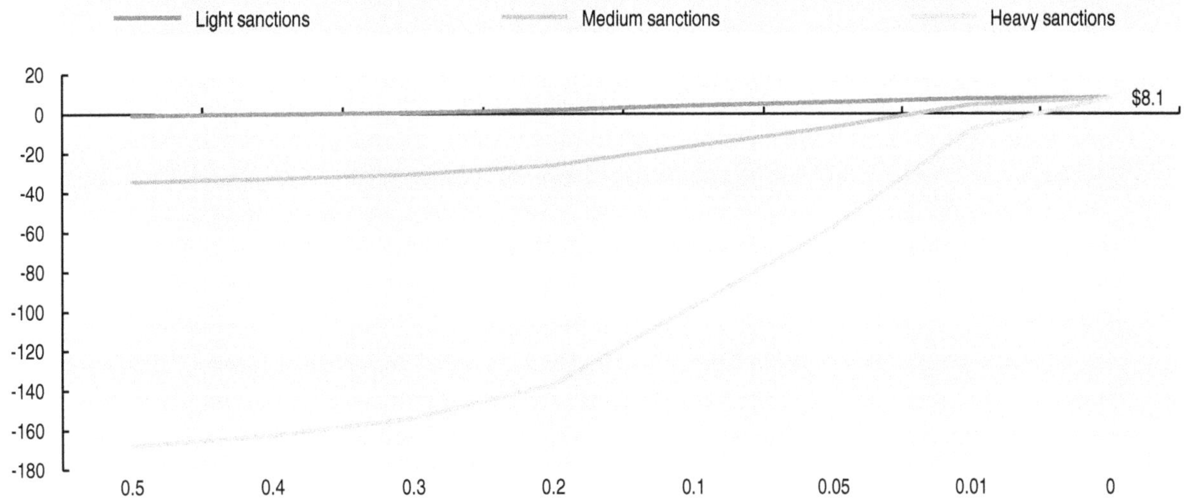

Note: Vertical axis is expected net present value in USD millions; horizontal axis is annual detection probability and is not to scale.
Source: OECD calculations using sanctions data taken from OECD Working Group on Bribery monitoring reports (OECD, n.d.).

StatLink http://dx.doi.org/10.1787/888933362808

Conclusions

At the present time, the playing field established by foreign bribery laws is highly uneven for companies operating out of different jurisdictions. Rules on sanctions create environments of heavy sanctions in some jurisdictions, while other sanctions regimes are quite permissive of foreign bribery.

These findings are subject to a number of caveats. This analysis, like all simulations, presents a simplified version of reality. Several particular simplifications should be noted. First, the analysis assumes that companies' bribery is only potentially detected and prosecuted by the authorities of that company's country. In reality, companies' malfeasance may end up being prosecuted by the authorities of another country. Indeed, this is the situation in many non-United States foreign bribery cases. Also, the model does not capture the value of intangibles, such as reputational damage, and for other forms of punishment, such as incarceration.

The evolution of foreign bribery law in the 41 Parties to the Convention is marked by processes of both convergence and divergence.

Convergence. Prior to the signing of the Anti-Bribery Convention in 1997, foreign bribery was legal in nearly all Parties to the Convention and was tax deductible in most. In addition, many of the 41 countries could not sanction companies (as opposed to individuals) for foreign bribery. In less than two decades, the vast majority of Parties have built sanctions regimes for foreign bribery by companies where none existed before. Thus, under the Convention, there has been considerable harmonisation and convergence of law and practice in three crucial areas of law: making foreign bribery a criminal offence; making companies (not just individuals) liable for foreign bribery and eliminating the tax deductibility of bribes.

Divergence. But, as shown by these simulations, major differences persist in the sanctions regimes of the 41 Parties. Without further reforms to raise sanctions for companies or increase punishment probabilities, foreign bribery will remain an attractive investment opportunity in many jurisdictions. An additional element of divergence is introduced by large differences in enforcement efforts among the 41 Parties as well as the uneven application of confiscation provisions. According to OECD enforcement data,[11] 24 of the 41 Parties to the Convention have never successfully sanctioned an individual or a company for foreign bribery since the Convention entered into force in 1999. Thus, most of these sanctions regimes exist more on paper than in practice. For example, three of the countries with the heaviest *de jure* sanctions under these simulations have never successfully concluded a foreign bribery enforcement action – thus, while their regimes look dissuasive on paper, they are not used in practice. In contrast, a few countries are active enforcers of foreign bribery law, including several countries that have stepped up enforcement activity in recent years.

Sanctions and detection probabilities jointly influence incentives to bribe. For foreign bribery – where detection probabilities are thought to be low – it is important to maintain sanctions at high enough levels to compensate for low detection probabilities. In this way, the two policy variables combine to create an environment of effective deterrence. Since it is probably easier in the short run to raise sanctions levels than to increase detection rates, countries that wish to enhance anti-bribery deterrence may wish to raise sanctions levels as a rapid way of enhancing disincentives for foreign bribery.

Sanctions need to account for lengthy investigation and resolution of cases. Another point highlighted by the NPV simulations is that, investigations and resolution (via court proceedings or negotiated settlements or both) can take a long time. The electrical power bribery scheme used in the simulations took place over a period of 14 years, starting from the first bribe payments in 1997 to the final settlement in September 2010. At a discount rate of 6.5%, one dollar of fine paid in 2010 had a present value of 41 cents at the beginning of 1997. Thus, when investigations and resolutions take many years, sanctions will be heavily discounted by companies simply because of the time value of money. Sanctions regimes need to account for this if they are to succeed in lowering incentives to bribe.

Sanctions need to be set at higher levels in many countries. Some countries' sanctions rules appear to be permissive of foreign bribery by companies – they encourage foreign bribery by helping to make it a profitable activity. Policy makers should be aware of the economic implications of sanctioning practices. Many will no doubt be surprised at how high sanctions must be if they are to be genuinely dissuasive for foreign bribery. This is especially true in situations where the probability of getting caught and sanctioned is low, where investigations and resolutions take a long time and where the business advantages obtained are important.

Higher sanctions are not always better sanctions. Appropriate sanctions regimes have a floor, the level of which is determined by not systematically letting bribery be an attractive investment opportunity. This floor can be established through a judicious combination of sanctions, detection probabilities and reliability in resolution/prosecution. However, this does not imply that higher sanctions are always better.

In a real world of deterrence, a portfolio of tools is needed to address the myriad considerations raised by sanctioning companies. For example, very high levels of sanctions could create the possibility of "liquidating sanctions" – that is, a company might be forced into bankruptcy by monetary sanctions. Although such an outcome may be acceptable (indeed, some Parties provide for dissolution of companies as a sanction), societies may wish to retain the possibility of applying sanctions that are both dissuasive and that avoid bankruptcies.

In addition, there is the difference between incentives facing companies and incentives facing their employees and business partners. It may well be the case that the various individuals within the company (e.g. officers, employees) may not see monetary sanctions paid by the company as a whole as a deterrent for their own individual decisions to bribe. Their individual incentive systems might be quite detached from the incentive systems created by law enforcement for the company as a whole. Much depends on whether and how the company's governance framework translates company interests into incentives for individual units and employees.

This highlights the importance of designing sanctions regimes with a portfolio of tools – including monetary fines for companies, but also sanctions for individuals such as possible jail terms – in order to obtain an effective overall framework of deterrence. It also suggests that countries may wish to integrate incentives for implementing effective compliance programmes into company sanctions regimes. The issue of what policy mixes create effective sanctions for foreign bribery is one of ongoing experimentation among the 41 Parties to the Convention. Possibilities include civil and criminal actions against individuals, restitution of victims, imposing interest payments on monetary sanctions in order to account for the time value of money and disqualification from government programmes such as public procurement and export credits. The WGB provides a platform in which Parties can learn from each other's experiences and improve their policies in these areas.

Notes

1. The purpose of this chapter is to explore, using standard financial analysis techniques, how fines and confiscation policies influence financial incentives and disincentives for foreign bribery. For this reason, other behavioural influences affecting the decision to bribe are not accounted for. This analysis does not include other types of sanctions than fines and confiscation (e.g. bars to companies' eligibility to participate in public procurement processes or from export credit programmes). It also abstracts from other sanctions such as reputation effects, prison sentences, executive liability and disqualifications to engage in certain types of businesses.
2. Foreign currency amounts are converted into USD using exchange rates prevailing in early November2015.
3. *Commentaries on the Convention on Combating Bribery* (adopted by the Negotiating Conference on 21 November 1997), comment 22.
4. OECD (2012).
5. See Chapter 2.A.1 of OECD (2012).
6. See Page 12 of OECD (2012). This monograph states: "Some countries still lack legislation to address the confiscation of the proceeds of bribery, considering such calculations too complicated. Other countries may have legislation in place but have never tested it in practice."
7. One of the Parties to the Convention cannot hold companies responsible in any way for the crime of foreign bribery. The simulations therefore assume that this country's maximum fine is zero.
8. Since the would-be briber under this scenario knows with certainty the future cash flows associated with the bribe, a risk free discount rate is used. This is calculated as the average over the bribe period (1997-2010) of annual interest rate on 6-month T-bills as published by the US Federal Reserve Board. For the company involved in the electrical power bribe scheme, this discount rate is 3.55%.
9. This amount does not include books and records violations imposed for this bribe scheme and others undertaken by the same multinational enterprises under a separate proceeding.
10. The assumption that the statute of limitations is the same for all countries influences the results. In particular, it means that countries that have a relatively short statute of limitations would have a "real" expected NPV for the bribery scheme that is more than the simulated value (because, in reality under such a statute of limitations, the company is at risk of getting caught for a shorter period of

time). Analogously, countries that have a relatively long statute of limitations would have a "real" expected NPV for the bribe scheme that is less than the simulated value because the company would be at risk of detection/prosecution for a longer period of time. The reason that the simulations make this limiting assumption is that, in practice, rules of statutes of limitations are exceedingly complex. For example, the events that "start the clock ticking" are defined differently in different countries (e.g. last illegal act, the start of an investigation). Moreover, in some countries, the "count" can be restarted once the procedures reach particular milestones.

11. OECD (2014).

References

OECD (2014), "Working Group on Bribery: 2014 Data on Enforcement of the Anti-Bribery Convention", *www.oecd.org/daf/anti-bribery/dataonenforcementoftheanti-briberyconvention.htm*.

OECD (2012), *Identification and Quantification of the Proceeds of Bribery: Revised edition, February 2012*, OECD Publishing, Paris, *http://dx.doi.org/10.1787/9789264174801-en*.

OECD (n.d), OECD Working Group on Bribery in International Business Transactions monitoring reports on the implementation of the Anti-Bribery Convention, *www.oecd.org/daf/anti-bribery/countryreportsontheimplementationoftheoecdanti-briberyconvention.htm*.

ANNEX 7.A1

Methodology for simulation scenarios

Using information taken from the WGB's Phase 1-Phase 3 reports, this chapter examines the type and level monetary sanctions (fines) and other property-based sanctions (confiscation) adopted by the 41 Parties to the Anti-Bribery Convention on Combating Bribery. The simulation methodology uses readily available information to in order to establish internationally comparable metrics that support the contention that fines are too low in many of the 41 Parties and to shed light on the meaning of the term "dissuasive" in the reference in Article 3 of the Anti-Bribery Convention to "effective, dissuasive and proportionate" sanctions

Key characteristics of the simulation scenarios are:

- *Scenario 1. Perfect certainty:* Assume that the company deciding whether to engage in foreign bribery knows in advance and with certainty all of the cash flows associated with the bribe. The question explored in the first simulation is whether the Parties' sanction regimes for companies make it economically rational to engage in bribery if one knows in advance what the cash flows from the bribery scheme will be. That is, will the present value of the total benefits from the bribe minus the present value of the bribe amounts paid (both of which are known with certainty under this scenario) exceed the present value of the sanctions imposed (also known with certainty)?
  - For timing of benefits from the bribe and costs of the bribe (that is, the amount of bribe paid) assume that "best case" for company: receive profits (as of Day 1) and sanctions (day of settlement – here 29 September 2010).
  - For type and level of sanctions: the simulations incorporate the "worst case" scenario for the company. That is, they assume that each country imposes the highest possible amount of fines and confiscation available.
  - The discount rate is the average yearly return on 6-month T-bills published by the Federal Reserve Bank for the period over which the bribe scheme occurred.
- *Scenario 2. Uncertain detection and punishment*: This scenario incorporates the possibility that the firm will not get caught and punished for its act of bribery. The scenario uses the same cash flow assumptions as for the perfect certainty scenario (on the cost and chronology of the bribe and of the cash flows associated as well as the "simulated" maximum sanctions for each jurisdiction). It also assumes that each year, the company faces a fixed probability, α, of getting caught and having to pay the sanction (the same simulated maximum sanction as in scenario 1) and (1-α) of not getting caught. A programme is used to calculate the value of this real option for a range of α values. The

discount rate used is the average total return on assets for the company for the period over which the bribery scheme occurred. The model will show that high deterrence (that is, α is high) can, as a means of ensuring that crime does not pay, make up for low sanctions because high probabilities of getting caught lower the net present value of the investment in foreign bribery.

The model further assumes:

- *Statute of limitations.* The statute of limitation creates time limits for enforcement procedures. Once this time limit has expired, the court lacks jurisdiction to try or punish a defendant. For the perfect certainty scenario, this statute of limitations is assumed to not come into play before the final year of the net present value calculation (that is, when the sanction/confiscation amount is paid). For the uncertainty scenarios, the statute of limitation determines when the simulation scenario ends (that is, the company no longer has legal risks because the statute of limitations has expired).
- *Discount rates.* The discount rate used to calculate present values under the two simulation scenarios are: 1) the 6 month T-bill annual yield for the risk-free scenario and the company's actual return on total assets over the bribe period for the non-zero enforcement risk scenario (3.55%); 2) the return on total assets for the company over the bribe scheme period (6.5% for the 1997-2010 period.)
- *No procedural hurdles or uncertainties regarding assets to be confiscated.* All property subject to confiscation will in fact be found and confiscated.

OECD Business and Finance Outlook 2016

Chapter 8

The impact of investment treaties on companies, shareholders and creditors

Investment treaties are concluded between two or more governments and typically offer covered foreign investors protection for their investments from host government conduct in violation of the treaty such as expropriation without compensation, discrimination or treatment that is not "fair and equitable". This chapter identifies the unique combination of rules applied under many investment treaties which includes rules about the types of loss recoverable by shareholders covered by treaties and about the availability of damages for covered investors in claims against governments. The chapter considers the incentives created by these rules and how they may affect companies, shareholders, creditors and capital markets. It also considers how those incentives may affect corporate structuring of investment.

Main findings

- Investment treaties are concluded between two or more governments. They typically offer covered foreign investors protection for their investments from host government conduct in violation of the treaty such as expropriation without compensation, discrimination or treatment that is not in accordance with "fair and equitable treatment" obligations. They include both stand-alone investment treaties (often referred to as bilateral investment treaties or BITs) and investment chapters in broader trade and investment agreements such as the North American Free Trade Agreement (NAFTA), the Transpacific Partnership agreement (TPP) or the Energy Charter Treaty (ECT).
- Investment treaties were developed to protect investors of one country when investing in another country, to lower non-commercial risk for such investors, and overall to promote a sound investment climate. A mostly-older generation of investment treaties provides little detail on the applicable substantive and procedural rules, while a number of modern agreements provide significantly greater detail on these and other issues.
- Investment treaties create economic incentives and disincentives. As treaties become better known to investors and lawyers, and apply to more investments between advanced economies, their economic impact is likely to increase. At least 70 investment claims against governments were filed last year, many against developed countries, far outstripping the 14 requests for consultations at the World Trade Organization (WTO).
- As interpreted by arbitral tribunals in claims brought by covered investors against governments, many of the over 3 000 existing investment treaties establish a unique combination of rules. Some of those rules significantly modify widely-applied corporate law and corporate governance principles, and can result in fragmentation of companies. The unique combination includes i) the acceptance of claims by covered shareholders for losses incurred by companies in which they own shares (claims for reflective loss); and ii) the general availability of damages, including lost profits, as a remedy for government misconduct in breach of a treaty, subject to adequate proof.
- The general acceptance of covered shareholder claims against governments for damages for reflective losses under many investment treaties is unique because such claims are generally barred under national corporate law and other systems of law. The injured company, not its shareholders, owns the claim for redress and recovers any damages. The impact of the unique treaty rules in fragmenting recovery of corporate loss is amplified because frequently indirect shareholders higher up the corporate ownership chain have also been permitted to recover reflective loss.
- Because the unique rules can allow covered shareholders to bring claims that could be perceived as stripping assets from the company to the detriment of company creditors and other shareholders, they could affect the availability, pricing and other conditions of debt and equity financing for investment that is subject to regulatory risk. The unique rules provide greater rights to covered foreign shareholders than those of non-covered domestic shareholders which is likely to affect the ratio of foreign and domestic share ownership.

The unique rules can also fragment corporate governance because they shift power on key issues from the centralised corporate board of directors to covered shareholders.

- By allowing a wide range of claims by direct and indirect shareholders of a corporation injured by a government, the unique rules may also encourage the complex structuring of investment through multi-tiered corporate structures. Each covered shareholder can be a potential claimant under a different treaty. Governments and others should carefully analyse and evaluate the impact of treaty incentives on companies and stakeholders as part of their investment treaty policy.

Introduction

Companies carry out practically all large-scale investment today. Throughout all sectors of the economy, companies are used to gather financial and human resources for investment and to organise the production of goods and services. The company as an institution – as a set of legal rules and incentives – is thus of central importance to contemporary society. Some describe it as the most important organisation in the world, besting governments and rivalled only by the family. Others recognise that the company is the central institution of economics that has produced remarkable benefits and prosperity for society, but have decried its recent evolution and failings. Recent comparative corporate law scholarship has underlined that the worldwide success of the company has led to its introduction in remarkably similar form in many different national legal systems.

Investment treaties play a growing role in company life. Concluded between two or more governments, investment treaties protect covered foreign investors from certain host government conduct and abuse. Treaties typically provide protection from expropriation, discrimination or treatment that is not "fair and equitable". They can provide additional protection to covered foreign investors beyond that provided in national legal frameworks, including constitutions, laws and regulations.

Today, there are over 3 000 investment treaties, including many stand-alone investment treaties (often referred to as bilateral investment treaties or BITs) and a much smaller but growing number of investment chapters in broader trade and investment agreements, such as the North American Free Trade Agreement (NAFTA) or the Energy Charter Treaty (ECT). Investment treaties have become a high-profile issue in recent years in a growing number of countries. Claims under investment treaties involving the regulation of tobacco marketing, fracking, nuclear power and health care have attracted intense public interest. An ad hoc investment arbitration tribunal recently awarded USD 50 billion to shareholders in Yukos. A public consultation in the European Union on proposed investment provisions in the Transatlantic Trade and Investment Partnership (TTIP) with the United States generated a record 150 000 comments. G20 and OECD governments have been considering investment treaty policy issues on an on-going basis since 2010 at the OECD-hosted Freedom of Investment (FOI) Roundtable and many governments are actively engaged in reform of their treaty policies.

The vast majority of existing investment treaties are short bilateral treaties, providing little detail. They may simply require the government to provide covered foreign investors with "fair and equitable treatment", for example, without further specification as to the nature or breadth of the obligation or the consequences of its breach. Arbitrators in ad hoc arbitration tribunals have broad discretion to interpret such treaties in individual cases. This approach dominated in early treaty-making and is reflected in the majority of treaties in force today. While some treaties of this type are still being concluded, this class of treaties is referred to herein for convenience as "first-generation" investment treaties.

Recent OECD analysis has identified a unique combination of rules generally applied under many investment treaties that are of particular importance to the company. First, investor-state dispute settlement (ISDS) arbitral tribunals have found that covered shareholders are entitled to recover for reflective loss under many first-generation investment treaties. (Shareholders' reflective loss is incurred as a result of injury to "their" company, typically a loss in value of the shares.) In contrast, courts in advanced systems of national corporate law generally reject shareholder claims for reflective loss – largely for explicit policy reasons. Shareholders are permitted to bring cases for direct injury – for example to their voting rights as shareholders – but not where they suffer reflective loss due to an injury to the company. Only the directly-injured company can bring the claim.[1]

Second, these treaties make money damages generally available as redress against government breaches of investment treaties. Subject to appropriate proof, treaty claimants can generally recover past and future lost profits as well as interest. In contrast, only non-monetary remedies (such as annulment of improper government action) are generally available for investors against governments under domestic law in advanced economies, except for expropriation.

This combination of rules creates incentives that may have a number of consequences for corporations with significant relations with governments. They may include both "*ex post*" and "*ex ante*" consequences as investors and others learn about and react to the new rules. This chapter explores these potential incentives and consequences.

Some treaties, recent model treaties and proposed treaties have provisions or have introduced reforms that may exclude or affect the application of these rules in different ways. These approaches are found for example in NAFTA-style treaties and many of the treaties of the NAFTA parties with other countries, the US model BIT, the Transpacific Partnership agreement (TPP), recent European Union treaties and proposals and the recent Indian model BIT. These approaches are discussed briefly below, but many are recent and not yet in force. The main focus of analysis here is the impact on companies of the many existing first-generation treaties that are in force and are likely to be interpreted as establishing the unique combination of rules. Analysis of the full range of incentives created by these existing treaties can assist in understanding their possible effects and can also help inform possible reform efforts.

The remainder of this chapter is structured as follows. It first provides an overview of investment treaties and outlines the unique combination of rules applicable under many treaties. It then examines the impact of those rules on the corporation and on corporate stakeholders including shareholders and creditors. A subsequent section examines how the rules may create incentives for the creation of complex corporate structures for investment. The chapter ends with conclusions.

Overview of investment treaties

Investment treaties entered into between two or more countries can offer covered foreign investors substantive and procedural protection for their investments in host states; assist with the liberalisation of restrictions on investment flows; and provide for dispute resolution mechanisms. Substantive protections under treaties generally include protection against expropriation without compensation and against discrimination. They may, for example, guarantee that covered foreign investors will be treated no less favourably than investors from the host state (national treatment) or third states (most-favoured nation). Fair and equitable treatment (FET) clauses have been the provision most frequently invoked by foreign investors in recent years. Additional treaty clauses can facilitate the transfer of profits, or limit or exclude certain performance requirements, such as local content rules.

Foreign investors are sometimes subject to disadvantages such as discrimination based on nationality. Most investment treaties give covered investors the right to bring claims against the host state in investor-state dispute settlement (ISDS). Many treaties do not require claimants to exhaust domestic remedies; under such treaties, covered investors are given an alternative of proceeding directly to international arbitration without being required to have recourse to domestic courts.

Under most treaties, practically all types of national law and government action can be the subject of a claim by a covered investor. The range of measures under review or at issue can include relevant provisions of national constitutions, legislation adopted by parliaments, legislation adopted by federal states or provinces, regulations of many kinds, as well as the application of the law in individual cases. A growing range of treaty provisions in recent treaties provide greater protection for regulation in particular areas such as tax or financial services through exceptions or more precise drafting.

Treaties have been subject to increasing scrutiny, debate and reform

Investment treaties have come under increasing scrutiny and the balance of their benefits and costs is the subject of intense interest and debate. An original purpose of most investment treaties was to create economic incentives and to reduce risks in order to attract foreign investment and its associated economic development.

ISDS has been an important innovation to remedy what is often lacking in international treaties: a strong enforcement mechanism. Advocates for ISDS see it as a depoliticised system in which foreign investors and host states may resolve disputes without the need for the investor's home state to become involved as under systems of state-to-state dispute resolution (SSDS). However, the ISDS system itself is now a major political issue in a number of jurisdictions and some have rejected investor-state arbitration.

The issue of the balance between investor protection and the right to regulate is another key issue both in the current public debate about investment treaties and for governments' treaty policy. Much of the current criticism of treaties focuses on their alleged impact on the right to regulate. A number of jurisdictions have taken action to reduce the risk of successful ISDS claims. In contrast, defenders of treaties contend that treaties protect covered investors from government misrule. While it has been contended that investment treaties advance the rule of law in host states by holding governments accountable, critics argue that opaque legal proceedings and conflicts of interest in the arbitration system are contrary to rule of law standards (Van Harten, 2008). Many governments are recognising the importance of the issue of balance while adopting varying policy responses (OECD, 2016).

Policy analysis of investment treaties has often been focused on the impact of treaties as a whole. There is, for example, a substantial amount of analysis about whether treaties encourage foreign direct investment (FDI). Today, however, there is increasing interest in legal, institutional and economic analysis of individual rules. Large awards and claims based on specific rules obviously draw significant attention, particularly where the rules are developed through interpretation and are not expressly set out in the treaty text. Increasing comparison of rules applied under treaties to domestic law rules also leads to greater attention to individual rules, especially where it is contended that they provide greater benefits to covered investors than those available under domestic law.

Investor claims and dispute settlement

The number of ISDS claims against governments has increased significantly in recent years, but the number of claims and damages paid by most governments remain modest when viewed against the volumes of covered investment. Disputes in ISDS now significantly outnumber those in the WTO with 70 known ISDS claims filed in 2015, compared to 13 claims initiated under the SSDS system at the WTO (UNCTAD, 2016a; WTO, 2016). Precise numbers of ISDS cases are unknown because some proceedings are confidential, but the number of publicly-known claims is now approaching 700 (See Figure 8.1).

Figure 8.1. **Claims in ISDS and at the WTO**

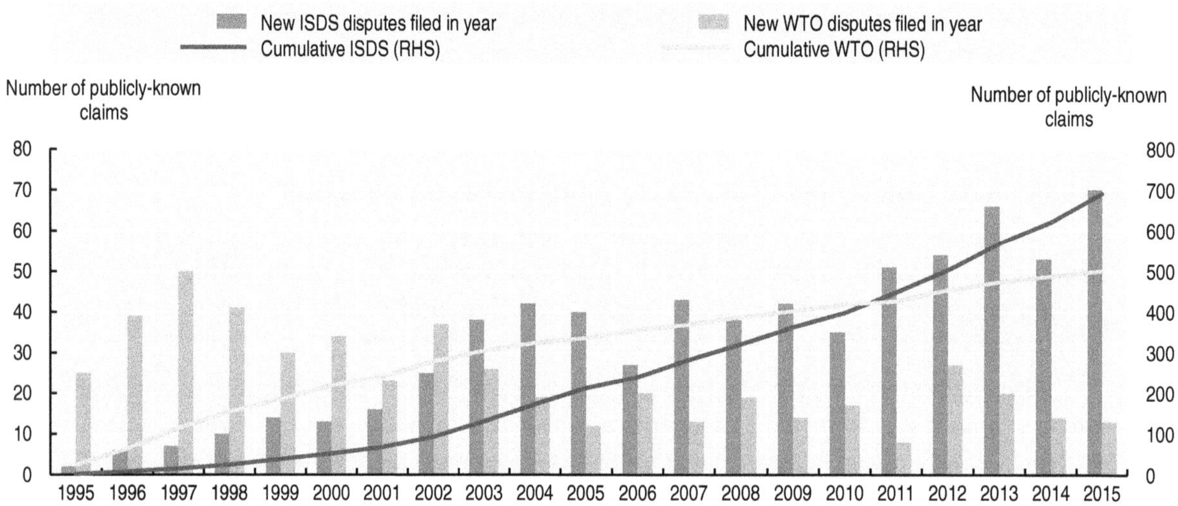

Note: ISDS: investor-state dispute settlement; World Trade Organization: (WTO).
Source: UNCTAD; WTO. WTO disputes filed are based on requests for consultations.

StatLink http://dx.doi.org/10.1787/888933362814

The average claim in all publicly-available ISDS cases resolved as of 2012 reportedly exceeded USD 620 million, almost doubling from five years earlier (Franck, 2015: 488). According to recent statistics, claimants have succeeded in establishing liability and obtaining damages in 26% of cases, respondent governments have prevailed in 36% of cases and the parties settled in 26% of cases. The remainder were discontinued or found liability but no damages (UNCTAD, 2016b). Claimants that succeed in establishing liability generally recover only a fraction of the claimed amount, but damages are still very significant, especially compared to government liability under other law, as discussed below.

The number of claims against advanced economy governments, in particular in Western Europe, has noticeably increased in recent years despite still limited treaty coverage for relations between advanced economies. Western European countries have been respondents in numerous recent energy-related claims under the ECT since 2009. There is generally little public information about these claims, in part because the ECT lacks provisions on transparency found in some other treaties.

Much of world investment, which occurs in and between the largest developed economies (such as the European Union, Japan or the United States), is not covered by treaties today. However, major trade and investment treaties under negotiation or in the process of ratification, such the TPP, TTIP or the Comprehensive Economic and Trade Agreement between the European Union and Canada (CETA), are expected to expand the application of investment treaties to much of the investment between developed countries. Treaties will interact more frequently with sophisticated capital markets and advanced corporate law and finance systems. The nature of applicable treaty rules on claims for reflective loss and damages will be of greater practical importance in many economies.

Many investment treaties, as interpreted by arbitral tribunals, create a unique combination of rules

As described below, many treaties uniquely combine allowing reflective loss claims and a broad scope for recovery of damages against governments. In many treaties, neither of these rules is expressly addressed in the text. The only reference to shares in many investment treaties is usually a clarification in general terms that shares are assets that can qualify as a covered investment.[2] Similarly, many treaties are also silent on the remedies available to investor claimants. Government obligations to provide national treatment or fair and equitable treatment to covered investors are set forth, but the consequences of breach are not addressed[3] (Pohl, Mashigo and Nolen, 2012: 31).

Permitting covered shareholders to claim for recovery of reflective loss as a general rule

The first rule applicable under many treaties expands the range of potential treaty claimants when a company is injured. Instead of the company owning the claim as under domestic law, covered shareholders of the company can recover directly for reflective losses they incur as a result of injury to the company.[4] Numerous ISDS tribunals have found that direct or indirect shareholders can claim for reflective loss.[5] Tribunals have in effect found that covered shareholder claimants can disregard the corporate entity in which they have invested for purposes of their treaty claims.[6]

Covered shareholders under these treaties are thus in the enviable position of having the best of both worlds: limited liability for debts incurred in the corporate name and direct compensation for corporate losses due to government misconduct in violation of the treaty. This "cushy position" for covered shareholders is unique to treaties and is not available under other law.[7]

OECD analysis and inter-governmental discussions have demonstrated that domestic corporate law and other bodies of law generally apply exactly the opposite principle – what has been called a general "no reflective loss" principle. Following analysis of both common law (United States; Canada; United Kingdom; Australia; Hong Kong, China) and civil law (Germany; France) systems, the findings were confirmed in inter-governmental discussions at the OECD-hosted FOI Roundtable:

> "The Roundtable recognised that all of the advanced national law systems surveyed to date, including both leading common law and civil law systems, generally bar shareholder claims for reflective loss due notably to concerns about consistency raised by such claims. Some participants from countries with legal systems not surveyed in the background paper confirmed that their national law also generally bars shareholder claims for reflective loss. Additional government input in this area was encouraged,

but there was a consensus about the widely-applied prohibition under domestic law. The general no reflective loss principle is also applied in customary international law and under the European Convention on Human Rights."[8]

Except under investment treaties, shareholders are generally permitted to recover only direct losses, but not reflective losses (Ferran, 2001). This widely recognised distinction arises because shareholders in companies can be harmed in two broadly different ways. First, they can suffer direct loss as a result of injury to their rights as a shareholder, such as the right to attend and vote at general meetings. Such injury is relatively rare and shareholder recovery for it is uncontroversial. Second, shareholders (and others) can suffer reflective loss through an injury to the company: the market value of the company's shares and/or bonds may fall.[9] Shareholders' reflective loss is incurred as a result of injury to "their" company. Reflective loss is generally suffered by all shareholders in proportion to their shareholding. Shareholder recovery of reflective loss is generally barred because the claim belongs to the company.

The differences between many treaties and national corporate law are accentuated by i) the acceptance of reflective loss claims by indirect shareholders higher up the corporate chain; and ii) the wide variety of covered direct and indirect shareholders allowed to recover reflective loss under many treaties, including 100% parent companies, majority shareholders and minority shareholders.[10]

The no reflective loss principle in domestic law is based on the assumption that the company has the power to recover the loss (although it may not do so for a variety of reasons) and is better placed to do so. In some investment cases, recourse by the company may not be feasible including due to host government interference. International protection through ISDS or SSDS may in some case be the only realistic chance for protection of the company, its creditors and its shareholders. However, the scope of shareholder reflective loss claims available under many treaties is general and extends beyond cases where the company's recourse is blocked. Shareholders are considered to have autonomous rights and can claim without showing that the company lacks an effective remedy.[11]

Awarding recovery of money damages including lost profits rather than primary (non-pecuniary) remedies for breach of investment treaties

Other than under investment treaties, damages remedies for investors are rare. National legal systems rarely award damages to investors in claims against the government other than in cases of expropriation. Instead, they use so-called "primary", "judicial review" remedies which do not involve an award of money.[12] The FOI Roundtable note took note of this fundamental difference in its 2012 report on ISDS:

> "Except for cases of expropriation, advanced national systems strongly emphasise so-called 'primary', 'judicial review' remedies which are non-pecuniary (annulling illegal action, prohibiting or requiring specified government action, etc.); these remedies (but only these remedies) are often available in specialised proceedings. In contrast, damages remedies for investors are rare. The Roundtable noted that the legal doctrines, rules and approaches that have the effect of favouring primary remedies and making damages difficult to obtain for investors vary between the countries surveyed, but the outcome in terms of remedies is uniform in all countries surveyed."[13]

The WTO system similarly excludes money remedies against governments. WTO adjudicators can recommend that a government modify or withdraw a measure they find to contravene the WTO treaty, but cannot award damages.

In contrast, money damages are routinely awarded for breach of investment treaties. Remedies under treaties generally take the form of money damages and can include lost profits where adequate proof exists (Ripinsky and Williams, 2008: § 7.3.1). Investment treaties can thus transform many types of investor claims against government action and regulation into claims for damages.

The consequences of the new potential government damages liability to some but not all investors are largely still to be seen.[14] Among other things, its impact will depend on the scope of government obligations and liability exposure under treaties, which can vary significantly depending on factors such as the nature and precision of treaty drafting or the adjudicators interpreting the treaty. It will also depend on the scope of the treaty network; this is also subject to fundamental change with both expansion, notably into relationships between advanced economies, and contraction, as governments terminate some treaties.

The prospect of being awarded monetary compensation as a result of government misconduct accentuates the financial aspects of relations between companies, stakeholders in companies, and governments. Non-pecuniary remedies against a government are generally indivisible. For example, if a government wrongly denies the renewal of a permit to a company, a court decision resulting in the renewal of the permit (perhaps after a new decision-making process) benefits the company as a whole. The benefit from the permit accrues to the company even if a shareholder were permitted to bring the claim.

In contrast, money damages are divisible. Thus, if the remedy for the permit denial is damages including lost profits, shareholder claims against governments become more attractive. Shareholders can potentially claim for reflective losses. They can argue for different evaluations of damages and lost profits. The availability of damages rather than non-pecuniary remedies under treaties increases covered shareholder interest in claims against governments.

The rules substantially increase the number of potential investor claims under investment treaties

Under normal corporate law rules, an injured company owns the claim for recovery of its loss – shareholders have no relevant legal rights. Accordingly, one proceeding can resolve the claim (Figure 8.2).

In contrast, the rules under many treaties fragment claims for government injury to a company. Instead of a single claim by or on behalf of the company, claims can be brought by different covered shareholders for reflective loss, possibly along with a claim by the company for its direct injury.

A first type of multiple shareholder claim in ISDS can be brought by unrelated foreign shareholders of the same company (Figure 8.3). The shareholders are separate entities without any common ownership. For example, CMS and Total were two unrelated minority shareholders of TGN, an Argentine gas distribution company. Each brought a separate claim in ISDS for reflective loss.[15] Subsequently the company, TGN, announced that it also intended to sue the government for alleged damages apparently arising out of the same measures; the degree of overlap with the damages awarded or at issue in the CMS and Total cases is unclear.[16]

Claims can also be brought by related entities (with common ownership). The fragmentation is amplified because indirect covered shareholders higher up the corporate chain have also frequently been permitted to recover reflective loss (Figure 8.4).

Figure 8.2. **Domestic Law: "No Reflective Loss" principle bars shareholder claims**

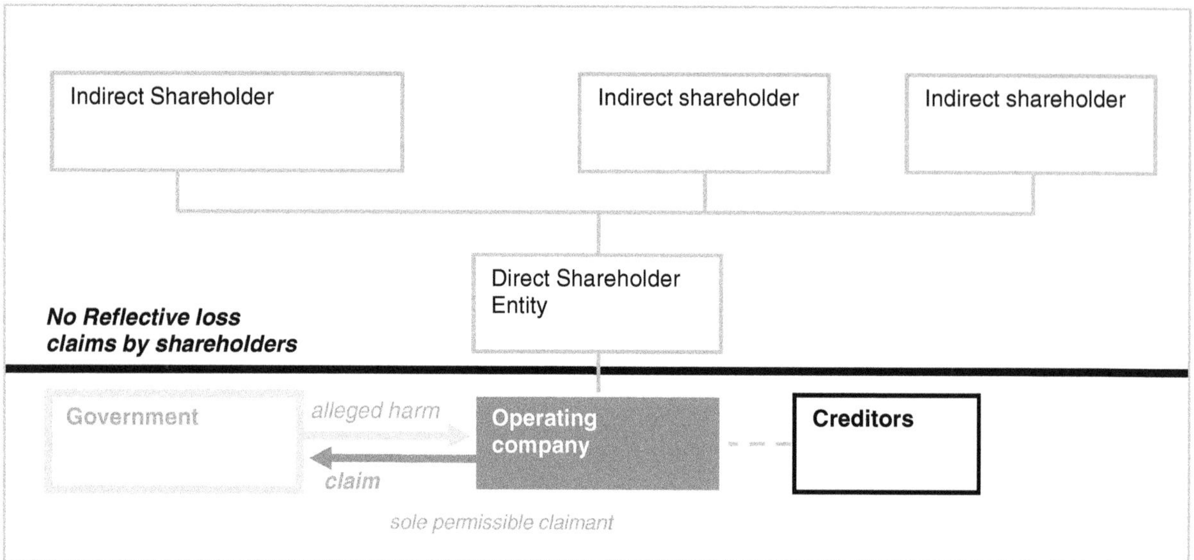

Figure 8.3. **Multiple claims for reflective loss by unrelated shareholders (domestic law claims omitted)**

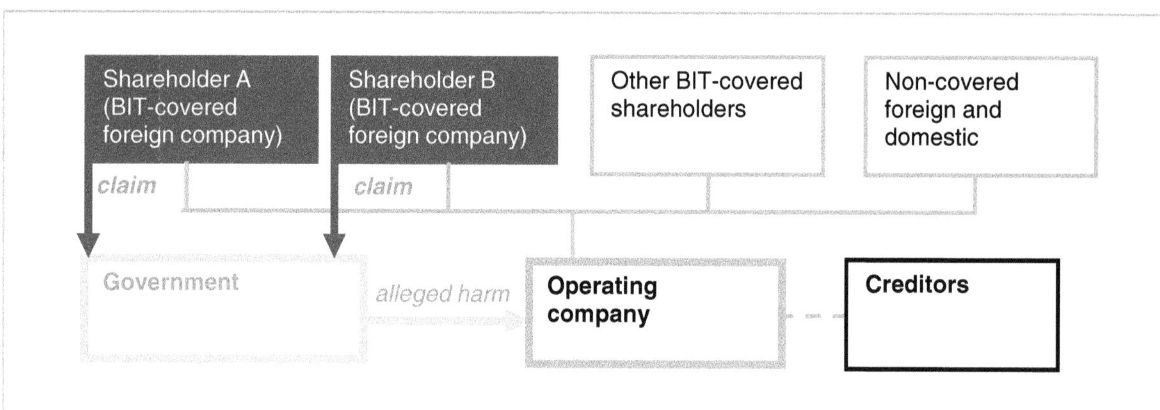

These variations can be combined. For example, claims by unrelated foreign shareholders can be accompanied by a further claim by the company (in ISDS or in the domestic courts).

Arbitral decisions on shareholder claims for reflective loss in ISDS have not demonstrated significant concern with the societal interest in "judicial economy" – reducing the number of cases needed to address the harm. In contrast, national courts have frequently underlined that the prohibition on shareholder claims for reflective loss achieves judicial economy, as illustrated by a US federal appellate court decision:

> "One rationale behind this prohibition [on shareholder claims for reflective loss] rests on principles of judicial economy. A corporation can protect its shareholder's interest by suing in the corporate name, and if the suit is successful the proceeds will inure to the benefit of the corporation; this increases the value of the individual shares in proportion to the amount of the recovery. Compare this to a situation where all

Figure 8.4. **Multiple claims for reflective loss by related entities: Two different-tier foreign shareholders both with access to ISDS (domestic law claims omitted)**

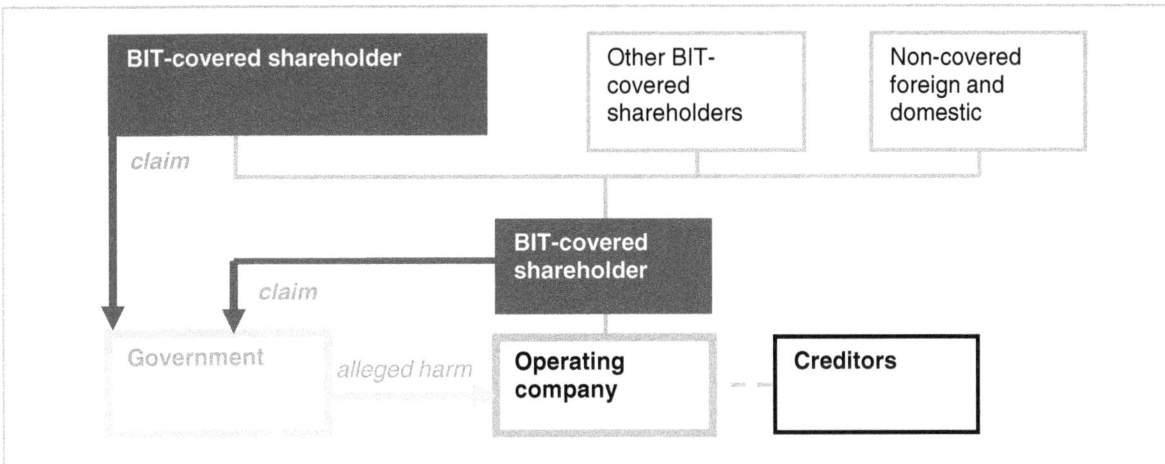

shareholders sue in their individual capacities, which achieves the same resultant recovery, but requires our legal system to process hundreds or thousands of suits, rather than one suit in the name of the corporation."[17]

As participants have noted in FOI Roundtable discussions of ISDS, high costs for the parties in ISDS constitute revenues for the arbitration bar and create economic incentives. The impact of those incentives on case outcomes, if any, is the subject of differing views (OECD, 2012: 16). High costs may also dissuade some covered investors from bringing claims, as discussed below.

Expansion of the scope of investment treaties to cover reflective loss also makes them applicable to alleged government injuries to many more companies, including major domestic companies. While domestic companies are generally excluded from treaty protection, government injury to a domestic company can give rise to treaty claims for reflective loss by foreign covered shareholders of the company which has given rise to expressions of concern. In the absence of legal barriers to covered shareholder claims for reflective loss under many treaties, high case costs for ISDS claims (averaging over USD 8 million per case as of 2011)[18] may be the principal barrier to such claims.

Some treaties adopt a different approach or address the issues in different ways

Damages as the main remedy for breach applies broadly across practically all investment treaties. A small but growing number of treaties expressly provide for damages or in effect limit final remedies to damages. The use of damages as a remedy appears to be widely accepted in current practice.

The situation with reflective loss is more complex and contested. Two additional groups of treaties are of note although they are not addressed in this chapter. First, NAFTA and NAFTA-style treaties establish more explicit regimes for covered shareholder claims. The NAFTA model in this area has been followed with minor variations in a number of other treaties including in the recently-concluded TPP and in the 2012 US model BIT. In addition to claims by covered shareholders on their own behalf, these treaties provide in particular for a form of derivative action in which a controlling covered shareholder can bring a claim on behalf of the company and with recovery that accrues to the company.

Governments party to these treaties, and in particular the United States, have stated that covered shareholders cannot bring reflective loss claims on their own behalf under these treaties; claims arising from injury to the company losses can only be brought on behalf of the company (with recovery for the company) under the derivative action-type mechanism.[19] Tribunal decisions have reached varying results. Applicable rules under NAFTA-style treaties remains somewhat uncertain (Gaukrodger, 2013: 52-56).

A second group of recent model treaties and treaties is more heterogeneous, but reflects a trend among a number of major jurisdictions to limit the potential for shareholder claims for reflective loss (or claims based on such injury in state-to-state proceedings). Several approaches have reduced protection for shareholders by excluding certain shareholdings from the definition of investment. This prevents reflective loss claims but also claims for direct loss by those types of shareholders. For example, India's new model treaty adopts an "enterprise approach" to defining covered investments that "equates investment with an enterprise incorporated in the host state".[20] South Africa's recent investment legislation also defines the investment to be protected as "enterprise-based" and does not cover short-term portfolio investments.[21] The definition of investment in Brazil's new model treaty, which is now reflected in several concluded treaties, excludes portfolio investments, i.e., those that do not allow the investor to exert a significant degree of influence in the management of the company.[22]

The CETA agreement and the European Union negotiating proposal for the investment chapter in TTIP contain a form of derivative action similar to the NAFTA model in some respects. They also contain a number of innovative provisions that would exclude or limit key aspects of reflective loss claims such as the availability of concurrent claims or overlapping claims by related entities.

A number of these approaches are recent and merit careful analysis. However, many of these new provisions are yet to take effect in treaties in force. As noted, this chapter primarily addresses the impact on companies of the many existing treaties in force which are interpreted as outlined above and which still dominate the treaty and treaty claim landscape.

The impact of the unique combination of rules under many treaties on key attributes of the corporation and on stakeholders

Corporations are created under national law. National law statutes on business organisations typically also make available other organisational options like partnerships that lack some of the attributes of corporations.[23] But market participants regularly choose companies for large-scale investment.

The corporate form that is used globally for major investments has "the same fundamental legal features around the world: legal personality, limited shareholder liability, transferable shares, centralised (and delegated) management, and investor ownership" (Davies et al., 2009: 305). The strong market preference around the world for use of the corporation for major investments over other available organisational forms suggests that it is seen as efficient.

The discussion below analyses the impact of the unique combination of rules applicable under many treaties on the corporation, on corporate stakeholders including shareholders and creditors, and on corporate governance. The analysis assumes that profit-maximising investors and others will respond to economic incentives created by treaties. A working assumption is that all treaty incentives are likely to be taken into account by informed investors and their lawyers, and that they are likely to have an impact on investor behaviour and on the legal structures proposed by lawyers to their investor clients. Treaties may not have the expected effects outlined here if there is, for example, a lack of awareness of the rules or if there are countervailing considerations. Future work can test the expected impacts identified here against available empirical evidence.

The impact on the company as a separate entity with legal personality and its own property

The establishment of a separate pool of assets that belongs to the corporation as a separate legal entity distinct from its shareholders or managers has been described as perhaps the single most important rule in corporate law (Armour, Hansmann and Kraakman, 2009a: 6-7; Blair, 2015). It is crucial to the ability of the corporation to obtain credit because corporate creditors know that they can attach (seize) corporate assets. It is also at the core of the corporation's ability to commit credibly including to contracts (Mayer, 2013). It notably facilitates contracting among the various participants in the enterprise by allowing them each to contract with the corporation itself, rather than having to create separate contracts with each of the other participants.

In addition to the pool of assets that belongs to the company, corporate law also separates out a pool of shareholders' assets. The pool of shareholders' personal assets is not available to satisfy corporate debts. Shareholders benefit from limited liability: their exposure to corporate losses is normally limited to the amount of their investment in their shares.[24]

Legal rules that provide for "entity shielding" establish and protect the company's ownership of a separate pool of assets, which is generally considered to be value-enhancing

Two key rules that establish and protect the company's ownership of a separate pool of assets have been usefully described as "entity shielding".[25] This is because the rules in effect protect or shield the corporate entity from its shareholders (and their personal creditors). Limited liability for shareholders protects them from creditors of the corporation; entity shielding protects the corporation from its shareholders and their personal creditors.

The first component of entity shielding is a priority rule that establishes the hierarchy of claims on company assets. Legal rules give company creditors a priority claim over corporate assets. The pool of assets used in the business will be available to meet the needs of the business first (including paying creditors of the company) before those assets can be distributed to shareholders. Ordinary shareholders are the lowest priority claimants (Figure 8.5).

The second component of entity shielding protects the corporation's value as a going concern by protecting it from liquidation. Legal rules make shareholders' investments in a company generally permanent and help provide the entity with stable capital. Shareholder capital is in effect "locked in" subject to limited exceptions.[26] Liquidation protection helps preserve the going concern value of the company which is important because companies are often worth more both to their creditors and their shareholders as a going concern rather than as piece-meal assets upon liquidation.

Rules that protect creditors from inappropriate shareholder diversion of corporate assets work to lower the cost of debt finance for the company, resulting in gains to both creditors and shareholders.[27] Stronger legal protection of creditors' rights is generally associated with more

Figure 8.5. **Corporate finance: repayment rank order**

Source: Ferran, Eilís, "Reflective Loss", Presentation to Freedom of Investment Roundtable 19, October 2013.

lending to corporate borrowers (Armour, Hertig and Kanda 2009: 115). A lower cost of capital for companies generally allows for increased investment (Ferran, 2009: 64).

Law and economics scholars have also suggested that the permanency of shareholder investment allows the firm to draw in other valuable resources including from other investors, and to rely on the maintenance of shareholder capital for long-term projects. It has been seen as important for the historical development of large-scale enterprises and economic growth in various jurisdictions.[28]

The rules under many treaties can undermine both components of entity shielding

The rules under many treaties can undercut both elements of entity shielding where a government injures a company in breach of an investment treaty. In the case of government injury to the company, the company has generally already incurred a loss. The reflective loss claim intervenes at a moment when the company is already weakened and the damages paid to covered shareholders reduce its capacity to reconstitute its assets. The covered shareholders are in effect permitted partially to liquidate the company to the extent of their reflective loss. Second, as discussed below, the treaty rules may upset the priority rule by giving covered shareholders, in practice or in law, a priority right to corporate assets over creditors.

If modified, corporate law rules providing for entity shielding may not be replicable by contract

As noted, corporate law typically provides investors with a choice of corporate forms. The forms typically contain a mix of default rules (that can be modified by contract) and mandatory rules (that cannot be modified). The combination of mandatory rules and the power to choose among forms helps investors to signal commitment to certain rules:

> "Mandatory rules can facilitate freedom of contract by helping corporate actors to signal the terms they offer and to bond themselves to those terms. The law accomplishes this by creating corporate forms that are to some degree inflexible (i.e. are subject to mandatory rules), but then permitting choice among different corporate forms. … Formation as a business corporation, for example, signals simply and clearly – to all who deal with the firm, whether by purchasing shares or simply by contract – that the firm is

characterised by a variety of familiar governance provisions, and that it will continue to have those characteristics unless and until it changes statutory form."[29]

Hansmann, Kraakman and Squire maintain that the mandatory law providing for entity shielding of the company is of fundamental importance in part because its enhancement of company value cannot be replicated by contract.[30] The need for law creating mandatory rules distinguishes separate legal personality from the other core characteristics of the business corporation (such as limited liability) which can be replicated by contract.[31]

The inability of market participants to recreate by contract the corporate law rules creating entity shielding would make it particularly important to analyse carefully changes to those rules by investment treaties. The uncertainties caused with regard to company assets may undermine advantages of corporate personality outlined above, including the ability of the firm to serve as a single contracting party and make credible commitments, and its ability to use its assets to obtain credit. In addition, the applicability of investment treaties only to some shareholders and not others raises additional issues.

Shareholders are impacted differentially

Policy discussion about reflective loss under national law, by courts and commentators, considers shareholders in general. Existing rules and rules under discussion, including the general rule barring reflective loss claims and any exceptions, are generally proposed and understood as a rule to apply equally (as a matter of law) to any shareholder.

In contrast, treaties create rights only for a subset of shareholders – those foreign shareholders who are covered by treaties.[32] Assuming no change in the well-established general corporate law rule barring reflective loss claims, the policy question for investment treaties is thus whether reflective loss claims should be allowed for covered shareholders but not others. This adds an additional element to the analysis and invites consideration of the impact on different shareholders.

As a practical matter, in particular in light of the high costs associated with ISDS, it appears that the unique combination of rules applicable under many treaties is likely to divide shareholders into three groups with different profiles, incentives and outcomes (Gaukrodger, 2013: 47-51).

- Category I shareholders: "Likely claimants". These covered shareholders are likely to be ready, willing and able to claim for reflective loss as shareholders under treaties. Category I shareholders first need to have a sufficient stake to make bringing a claim worthwhile. They also need to be ready to incur the cost to bring an individual claim if the company is mistreated. Such covered shareholders can decide between supporting company action or their own claim (at one or more levels as a shareholder) or both. They may be the principal beneficiaries of an expansive regime for shareholder claims.
- Category II shareholders: "Potential but unlikely claimants". This group is composed of covered shareholders but who are unlikely to claim as shareholders. This may be due to the limited size of their investment or their diversified investment strategy.[33] The fortunes of these shareholders lie primarily but not exclusively with company remedies.
- Category III shareholders: "Excluded claimants." This group includes domestic shareholders and foreign shareholders not covered by a treaty. These shareholders cannot bring an ISDS claim as a shareholder. They also cannot bring a claim under domestic law because only the company can bring the claim. The fortunes of these shareholders lie solely with company remedies.

Categories I and II are not rigid categories and the dividing line may vary depending on the facts. For most if not all shareholders, including Category I shareholders, litigation is generally undesirable. Some normally passive Category II investors might be driven to bring a personal claim as a shareholder if their losses are unusually high or if government liability appears certain. Nonetheless, the broad categories are likely to exist.[34]

Category I covered shareholders are likely the principal beneficiaries of the rules on reflective loss in ISDS. The additional rights given to such covered shareholders under many treaties should encourage investment by them. However, to some degree this may reflect transaction structuring and increased transactions costs to obtain foreign status rather than real flows.

The preferential access to corporate assets for covered shareholders as compared to non-covered shareholders, once apparent to the investing public, is likely to lead over time to decreased non-covered share ownership. Given applicable rules, a foreseeable scenario will see domestic shareholders barred from a reflective loss claim under domestic law but required, as taxpayers, to contribute to substantial damages to a fellow (covered) shareholder for the same loss.[35] Both the impact on the investment market and the political impact of such a scenario in a high-profile case may be significant. It may also affect public acceptance of investment treaties.

A variety of other reactions are possible. Some shareholders may restructure to obtain coverage, raising transaction costs for investment. New vehicles providing coverage through a foreign entity may be offered to existing domestic shareholders. Small shareholders excluded from treaty protection will have an incentive to invest through vehicles that consolidate interests and benefit from coverage through a foreign vehicle. Individual share ownership may decline if small shareholders are perceived to have lesser rights in high-profile situations.

The availability of reflective loss claims for covered shareholders but not others may give the former increased leverage within the company and affect negotiations on various issues. Most directly, it may be likely to affect negotiations and decisions about how to respond to alleged government misconduct affecting the company. More generally, Category II and III shareholders may fear that major covered shareholders will have less interest in remedies for the company than in their own individual remedies under investment treaties.

Transferability and liquidity of shares may be adversely affected

The transferability of shares is another core characteristic of the business corporation. Transferability allows the firm to continue to conduct business notwithstanding changes in the identity of shareholders. In particular, the transfer of shares by an existing shareholder to a third party generally does not significantly affect the creditworthiness of the company.[36] This enhances the liquidity of shareholders' interests:

> "Transferability permits the firm to conduct business uninterruptedly as the identity of its owners changes, thus avoiding the complications of member withdrawal that are common among, for example, partnerships, cooperatives, and mutuals. This in turn enhances the liquidity of shareholders' interests and makes it easier for shareholders to construct and maintain diversified investment portfolios." (Armour, Hansmann and Kraakman, 2009a: 11).

The existence of this transferability – share transfers that do not cause a substantial impact on the firm's creditworthiness or business – requires entity shielding. If shareholders have access to corporate assets, transfers of shares between shareholders with different financial profiles will affect the company. For example, acquisition of shares by a shareholder close to personal insolvency could generate a claim on corporate assets. The creditworthiness of the firm as a whole could change, perhaps fundamentally, as the identity of its shareholders changed. Consequently, the value of shares would be difficult for potential purchasers to judge (Armour, Hansmann and Kraakman, 2009a: 12).

The differentiation between covered and non-covered shareholders under many treaties means that a transfer of shares between covered and non-covered shareholders (as well as between different covered shareholders) may have consequences for the creditworthiness of the firm.[37] Because covered indirect shareholders can also recover reflective loss under many treaties, transfers between indirect shareholders are also at issue.

The consequences of the new rules and the incentives created are hard to determine because the treaties create a new situation and there appear to be few domestic law precedents. However, they would appear likely to interfere with transferability in part because the impact of the new rules is frequently unclear.[38] In addition, creditors and others may find it difficult to monitor share transactions that increase or decrease the likelihood of reflective loss claims including for domestic companies. The impact of the rules on creditors more broadly also deserves careful consideration.

Shareholder claims for reflective loss can injure creditors

As noted above, the entity shielding rules that help establish the corporation's legal personality protect creditors by partitioning off a separate pool of assets that belong to the company. This is achieved by i) ensuring that creditors have a priority claim on corporate assets that comes before shareholder claims; and ii) preventing partial or complete liquidation of the firm, thus protecting its going-concern value.

As noted, both rules that provide for entity shielding are undermined by the unique combination of rules under many treaties, and this has significant impact on creditors. Recovery of damages for reflective loss by a shareholder can be perceived as stripping an asset from the corporation. If recovery for a company injury does not go to the company, company creditors will suffer a detriment. For potential lenders to the company, the asset stripping permitted by the treaty rules may mean that regulatory risk for the company may be compounded by additional risks. There is liquidation risk because lenders perceive that the company is less likely to reconstitute its assets following a government injury.

The priority rule is also undermined because it is at best unclear whether ISDS arbitrators will prioritise creditor claims. As noted by a well-known practitioner and commentator, ISDS cases proceed in a "generally simplistic manner" on this issue and consider that the covered shareholder can recover its pro rata share of the company injury based on its percentage ownership of the share capital without regard for creditors.[39] Many cases do not even refer to creditors. In the recent *Micula et al. v. Romania* case, covered shareholder investors argued that these outcomes in fact reflect a legal rule that gives covered shareholders a legal right to a pro rata share of the company damages in preference to company creditors. This issue was expressly left open after significant argument on the point; in an unusual footnote, the arbitrators revealed that they would have disagreed on the issue[40] (Box 8.1).

As a practical matter, creditors will likely have reservations about the effectiveness of their protection in this context for several reasons. First, as noted, ISDS cases to date often

Box 8.1. **The issue of creditor subordination – *Micula et al. v. Romania***

In *Micula*, two individual claimant shareholders (Individual Shareholder Claimants) owned over 99% of the shares in three companies which were also claimants in the same case (Corporate Claimants). The Corporate Claimants were allegedly unable to pay their debts (accordingly to all the claimants themselves); the companies apparently had substantial tax and debt obligations although no attempt was made to quantify them.

Most of the case apparently proceeded on the basis that all five claimants would recover together without the Respondent's counsel raising the issue of reflective loss. Late in the case, however, the two Individual Shareholder Claimants sought to exclude the Corporate Claimants from the recovery and to recover all of the damages themselves on a 50/50 basis.

The Individual Shareholder Claimants argued that ISDS precedent supported finding that shareholder rights to reflective loss under the treaty trump company creditor rights. It was suggested that company creditors now understood that they have a subordinated status to shareholder treaty claims. As the tribunal's award reflects, these points were made notably in oral closing argument in response to questions from the tribunal regarding the protection of the Corporate Claimants' creditors (including Romania) in the case of an award to the Individual Shareholder Claimants:

> "[T]hose points are kind of answered in allowing shareholders to bring these kind of claims. And the reason for that in investment law is they are the real parties in interest in these matters, and creditors, including state creditors, cannot think that they have a claim to these kinds of losses because they know that shareholders have their own rights in international law. So a creditor or the taxman has no expectation that they can recover these taxes or whatever on the basis of amounts to be awarded in an ICSID arbitration. ...
>
> With respect to the position of the [C]orporate [C]laimants and their creditors and employees if the Tribunal were to make an award to the shareholders, [...] in our view strictly as a legal matter, the answer is that the BIT protects foreign investors and breaches of the foreign investors' rights entitled them to compensation, and the foreign investors are the real parties in interest, as has been decided in a number of cases. The fate of the investment vehicle doesn't come into the balance, strictly legally speaking, in our submission.
>
> As a more pragmatic matter it seems to us that if you were to make the award that we urge, then my client – Johnny Micula would have an award, and an award is not money. There would be a negotiation with the state and with the banks. Probably the banks would have to take a bit of a haircut because these are basically more or less sound businesses but crippled by debt. If the debt were relieved, things might be better. The state might have to do something as well.
>
> We see it more as an issue that arises after an award rather than in arriving at the award, as a strict matter. I suppose if the parties can't agree, it is of course plausible that the companies will go into bankruptcy. That doesn't actually mean that people will lose jobs because the businesses will presumably be sold, new investors will be found, they won't have to carry those debts; they will remain with the bankrupt entities. The banks will presumably lose money if the assets aren't sufficient to cover all the debts. We think that's the proper view."[1]

Romania argued that creditors' rights should be given priority in accordance with normal corporate law principles. The arbitrators did not resolve this question. They rejected the attempt to exclude recovery by the Corporate Claimants, but only on procedural grounds. They found that it was not possible to discontinue the three Corporate Claimants' claims so late in the case. The tribunal decided it could not allocate the damages between the five claimants and awarded the damages to them collectively.

Box 8.1. **The issue of creditor subordination – *Micula et al. v. Romania*** *(cont.)*

The tribunal thus decided not to "enter into the discussion of whether shareholder damages are equivalent to the damages suffered by the underlying company".[2] In a footnote, however, it indicated that the tribunal would have been split on that point.[3] The issue of whether treaties grant covered shareholders a priority right over company creditors as a legal matter may be somewhat uncertain and subject to future arbitral decisions.

1. *Micula*, § 1204.
2. *Micula*, § 1245.
3. *Micula*, § 1245 n.269 ("If the Tribunal had to address this point, it would not do so unanimously.")

apply a pro rata approach and provide little reason for optimism about the recognition of creditor rights in this context. Second, investment arbitration tribunals have limited powers which appear to be insufficient to engage in corporate valuation exercises. Valuation exercises that evaluate competing claims on corporate assets are time-consuming and expensive.[41] Scholars have underlined that many of the special powers of a bankruptcy court are needed to effectively recognise priorities in this context. Because the adjudicating body must be able to assess the ratio between firm assets and debts, "[t]ypically, this will require the court to exercise the broad powers associated with a bankruptcy system: the powers to stay division of firm assets and determine their aggregate value, simultaneously evaluate the validity and worth of the claims of multiple creditors, and oversee ongoing firm operations during the pendency of proceedings".[42]

ISDS arbitrators do not have these powers. Indeed, because the company is frequently not a party in a shareholder claim for reflective loss, the tribunal may not even have jurisdiction over the company. Even obtaining basic information about company finances and credit exposure may thus be difficult. Only publicly available information about the largest creditors, such as bondholders, may be available. The lack of capacity to engage in serious valuation may explain the observed tendency to use a simplistic pro rata approach that ignores creditor interests.

Third, creditors are also rarely represented in ISDS cases brought by shareholders. Creditor interests will likely only be represented at most by the government which may argue that the claimant shareholder's recovery should be reduced because creditors have suffered some of the reflective loss. The government will likely have limited information about the company. Creditors may also feel that the government is a less than ideal advocate for their interests.[43]

In advanced systems of corporate law, contracts with a corporation are drafted against the background of well-established law providing for its separate legal personality. For example, the contracting parties to a loan generally do not need to address the risks of shareholder claims in the loan contract. Because creditors do not need to worry about these issues in domestic law, their potential responses to the expected availability of such claims by covered shareholders under treaties is somewhat speculative. As discussed above, it would appear difficult to recreate the company's separate legal personality by contract.

In the absence of legal rules creating entity shielding, creditors may seek to take other actions to protect their investments.[44] Some possible reactions are outlined here. Decisions in this area are affected by creditor awareness of the issues. Most of the potential

Box 8.2. Greater opportunities for shareholder opportunism: Risks to creditors from the allocation of ISDS claims in shareholder ownership chains

The unique combination of rules under many treaties facilitate treaty shopping by shareholders because a shareholder can claim for company loss at its preferred covered level of the chain of ownership (Gaukrodger, 2013: 33). Shareholder ability to allocate claims within an ownership structure can also be used to provide benefits to covered shareholders in a fashion detrimental to creditors (Gaukrodger, 2014a: 20). National corporate law generally does not permit claims for reflective loss, but similar issues can arise from actions taken by controlling shareholders in the context of a corporate group:

> "A group structure allows controllers to set the terms of intra-group transactions, and thus to assign (and reassign) value within the group. Sometimes an intra-group transaction is designed solely in order to extract value from the creditors of a financially distressed group member or to favour the creditors of one subsidiary to the detriment of the creditors of other group members. Yet creditors may also suffer harm as a by-product of intra-group asset transfers undertaken for other reasons – for example, to secure a tax advantage."[1]

Many treaties that apply the unique combination of rules may give rise to broader scope for this type of opportunism than under national corporate law. First, any shareholder, rather than only controlling shareholders, can choose the (covered) level at which to bring its reflective loss claim. Second, the intra-group transactions described above generally involve at least some payment for the valuable asset, albeit one below its real value. In the case of a shareholder decision to locate its treaty claim, the non-claiming entities do not receive any compensation. The potential problems for creditors may be compounded by the lack of transparency in ISDS.

1. Armour, Hertig and Kanda (2009: 127); compare id. p. 116 (noting risk of shareholder opportunism vis-a-vis creditors by falsely claiming that the firm holds title to assets that actually belong to other entities or to the shareholders personally).

responses may not be meaningfully available to smaller or local creditors even if they are aware of the additional risks. Higher risks for creditors may fall in particular on them.

- *Increase the price and/or decrease the availability of credit for foreign investment.* Creditors can react to increased risk or uncertainty about the applicable rules by changing the terms on which they make credit available to the company. They can raise the price of credit or choose to lend elsewhere. The company's cost of credit and thus its overall cost of capital may be affected which may limit its perceived investment opportunities.
- *Seek contract provisions and loan covenants.* Major loan contracts with companies are frequently intensively negotiated. Lenders seek company agreement to clauses limiting creditor risk. A frequently-included covenant of relevance to the new treaty rules is a disposal of assets covenant which is "intended to prevent asset-stripping" (Ferran, 2009: 333). These covenants, however, may only address and bind the company. A contract between the lender and the company normally does not bind shareholders. A successful covered shareholder claim, however, can diminish corporate assets without any action by the borrower (the company) because it only requires a unilateral act by a covered shareholder.
- *Seek to expand use of secured credit.* For creditors with sufficient bargaining power, it may be possible to take proprietary security interests over company assets. A lender to a company could also seek security interests from shareholders over their shares. However, creditors would need to address the possibility of claims by indirect shareholders. Increased use by

dominant creditors of secured credit to respond to risks posed by covered shareholder recovery of reflective loss would likely shift additional risk to the unsecured creditors of the company. It may thus affect the terms and cost to the company for such inputs.[45] Unsecured creditors may also incur greater costs to monitor the company's financial health which may also affect the terms and cost of credit.[46]

- *Try to lend at a different level in the corporate chain.* The creditors of a bottom- or mid-tier company may be exposed if a higher tier covered shareholder makes an ISDS claim for reflective loss. Recovery for the top-tier covered shareholder would normally not benefit creditors of a lower-tier entity.[47] As outlined in Box 8.2, a shareholder may be able to choose its preferred covered level to bring its claim. One potential creditor response to this risk could be to seek to lend to a higher tier covered shareholder or even the ultimate controlling shareholder. However, this approach may not be feasible or desirable. For example, the top-tier shareholder with the power to allocate its claims in the corporate chain may not want to expose its personal assets in the event the new venture fails. It may prefer to have the lending occur at a lower level.
- *Try to recover money awarded to covered shareholders under company or insolvency law.* It has been suggested in general terms that individual shareholder recovery of reflective loss could possibly be recycled to the company or to creditors, for example in the context of company law or insolvency proceedings. The legal basis for this remains unclear. Shareholders with an award or money in hand may be unlikely to recognise creditor priority, as suggested by the *Micula v. Romania* case, discussed above. Awards of reflective loss damages to shareholders of companies in financial difficulty, however, may lead to arguments of this type.
- *Rely on shareholder reputational interests and commercial considerations.* Some larger institutional creditors may rely on shareholder reputational interests and commercial considerations. Because reflective loss claims are generally barred in advanced systems of national law, use of such a claim in ISDS to obtain a preference over creditors could be perceived as opportunistic behaviour that could affect the ability of the relevant beneficial owner to return to the credit markets in the future. Some covered shareholders with the legal ability to engage in opportunistic behaviour in ISDS may choose not to do so in light of these commercial considerations.
- *Bring treaty claims for reflective loss.* Creditors may respond to the availability of recovery of reflective loss in ISDS by seeking to bring their own claims for reflective loss.[48] This would further disaggregate the company loss and lead to a larger number of arbitration claims arising out of the same injury. The ratio of legal costs to recovery would likely rise.

The impact on centralised management by the board of directors

Centralised management is a core characteristic of the business corporation. Shareholder investors who form a company or invest in one know that absent special agreement to the contrary, almost all business decisions will be taken by the board of directors (or by management subject to monitoring by the board) rather than shareholders directly. Corporate law identifies a small number of fundamental changes or issues for which shareholder approval is required, but otherwise leaves most decisions to the board.[49]

Investors choose the corporation with centralised management because it can promote both efficiency and fairness. It streamlines corporate decision-making because most decisions can be taken without the need to inform or obtain the consent of shareholders. It can also help protect vulnerable corporate constituencies – and thus encourage their investment and participation in corporate enterprises (Armour, Hansmann and Kraakman, 2009a: 14).

Different corporate constituencies frequently have very different views about appropriate corporate policy. Among shareholders, views frequently differ between those with a relatively short time horizon and longer-term investors. Corporate decisions about government relations and litigation can be some of the most sensitive decisions taken by the board of directors.

The treaty rules release covered shareholders to act individually on key issues of corporate interest. Covered shareholders with divergent interests no longer need to convince the board or management to act. Moreover, unlike the board, covered shareholders may be able to act solely in their own interest.[50] Individual covered shareholders such as hedge funds may have interests that diverge significantly from those of the company or other stakeholders with regard to maintaining the value of a brand or the importance of maintaining a constructive long-term investment relationship in the host jurisdiction.

The new rules can also hinder the ability of the corporation to take decisions about settlement of a claim and reduce the value of settlement. Under the usual corporate law rules, the injured company's board or senior management can decide about settlement with a party that has injured the company. In contrast, under the unique combination of rules under many treaties, a settlement with the injured company is both less attractive and more complicated. It is less attractive because the company is unable to deliver "real peace"; one or more covered shareholders can still bring claims arising out of the same events.[51] The settlement value to the government, and thus to the company, will be lower. They are more complicated because obtaining a full settlement requires the agreement of more parties including indirect shareholders.[52]

Settlement discussions are rarely public. However, recent press reports pointed to a major role of likely covered shareholders and unusually complicated settlement negotiations in a recent ISDS case.[53] Shareholder approval was reportedly a condition of the settlement agreement alongside company approval through its board.[54] As lawyers and covered shareholders learn about their new rights, the rules may encourage greater covered shareholder involvement in discussions between companies and governments about government policies affecting companies.

The potential impact on corporate structuring of the unique combination of rules under many treaties

As discussed above in the section addressing the transferability of shares, the shareholder ownership structure of a company normally has no impact on claims following an injury to the company. Consequently, there is no incentive to engage in corporate structuring to maximise shareholder returns from an injury to the company. In contrast, under many investment treaties complex corporate structures can maximise shareholder returns in the event of injury to a company.

The two unique treaty rules on recovery of reflective loss and recovery of damages in themselves create an incentive for complex corporate structuring. Maximising treaty coverage for reflective loss claims would appear to require spreading ownership at different shareholder tiers across different jurisdictions so that a larger number of investment treaties can potentially be used. However, there is no definitive study of which we are aware that addresses the role these considerations play in corporate structuring.

Additional rules applicable under many treaties as interpreted may further encourage advance structuring of investments using multiple shareholder tiers. First, many treaties allow a corporation to claim as a national based only on its place of incorporation. Under this approach, no real economic link to the home jurisdiction is required and holding (or "shell") company claimants are accepted.[55] This rule makes the nationality of the corporation easy to identify, but it also makes it easy to set up complex structures with many levels of treaty protection.[56] Holding companies are easy to set up and many jurisdictions compete to attract the creation of such companies under their law.

Second, claims by shareholder entities inserted relatively late into the chain of ownership of an operating company (after a dispute or potential dispute has emerged to some degree) have been rejected in some cases on the basis that the restructuring was "abusive".[57] Risks associated with a "late" transfer of ownership to a covered shareholder make it attractive to do corporate structuring in advance as a routine matter for significant investments.[58] Multiple potential shareholder claimants will then exist under different treaties without the need for a possibly "late" transfer.

While many treaties allow claims by holding companies, an increasing number of treaties include provisions that can exclude or limit the use of holding or shell company claimants without an economic connection to their state of incorporation. For example, treaties can require that claimants have a substantial business connection to their home state or can allow respondent governments to deny benefits to companies without such a connection.

A policy question is whether investment treaties should encourage the routine use of complex structures. Such complex structures create costs both for investors and for law enforcement. Complex structures increase transaction costs and can raise the costs of mergers and insolvency proceedings. They can also obscure the beneficial owner of the investment. At the same time, corporate vehicles have legitimate uses. For example, they can be used to facilitate certain mergers or joint ventures. A multinational joint-venture company may be incorporated in a neutral jurisdiction in an effort to ensure equal treatment of participants in the venture.

Conclusions

Evaluation of the impact of investment treaties on companies is increasingly important. Formerly largely limited to the protection of the investments of developed-county investors in developing countries, investment treaties are rapidly expanding their scope of application. They are being extended to include the vast amounts of investment in and between the largest economies in the world. They are expected to apply in the near future to many more companies and to much more of their activity. The rapid growth of foreign share ownership means that major domestic companies will frequently have covered foreign shareholders.

Treaty rights applicable in more situations involving more governments will cause treaty incentives to have greater impact on the company and its stakeholders. Of course, treaty impact on the company will remain limited by their application to the government-investor relationship and to difficult situations in that context. Companies that are little affected by government regulation are likely to be little affected by treaties. But treaties will have little impact in encouraging investment in those areas. Where treaties are relevant, they will affect investment in part through their impact on the company. The areas where massive investment is most needed – whether to address climate change or to improve infrastructure – are often closely related to governments. Public-private partnerships and many other models of development involve intensive and long-term interaction between governments and companies on major projects. Achieving investment in these areas may need to harness the full power of the company idea.

There would not appear to have been any demonstration to date of a strong policy need for the current general availability of reflective loss claims under many treaties as interpreted. At the October 2013 FOI Roundtable, governments noted that no strong policy basis had been put forward for the general acceptance of reflective loss claims under investment treaties. The importance of finding a countervailing strong policy basis was identified due to the many policy issues raised by allowing such claims as a general matter.[59] The current interpretation of many treaties as creating a general rule allowing reflective loss may impede more specific thinking, at least in the context of cases and case commentary, about particular circumstances in which such claims should be permitted as a policy matter.

In many jurisdictions, investment treaties are being subjected to intensive policy analysis and political debate for the first time. The investment treaty system itself has been criticised for excessive fragmentation and some have called for broad reform. The impact of treaties on investment and governments will rightly remain the core focus of such debates. But given the increasingly-recognised critical role of the company in fostering investment and economic development, ensuring that treaties optimally harness the company should be a key consideration in treaty reform.

Notes

1. Although groups other than shareholders, such as company creditors, also suffer reflective loss when a company is injured and may be able to bring claims for reflective loss, the discussion below focuses on shareholder claims because they have been far more numerous to date.
2. Gaukrodger (2014b: 12). For example, the Netherlands-Malawi BIT, art. 1 provides that "'investments' means every kind of asset invested in accordance with the national laws and regulations of the Contracting Party in the territory of which the investment is made and in particular, though not exclusively, includes: ... ii. rights derived from shares, bonds and other kinds of interest in companies". The Energy Charter Treaty (ECT) expressly includes "shares, stock, or other forms of equity participation in a company or business enterprise". ECT art. I(6)(b).

   Corporate debt is also frequently expressly included as a covered investment, as also illustrated by the Netherlands-Malawi treaty. The ECT similarly supplements its "all assets" definition of covered investment with a specific reference (in art. I(6)(b)) to "bonds and other debt of a company or business enterprise". Many treaties are also summary in their treatment of creditors and do not address whether they can recover reflective loss.
3. The one exception is expropriation, for which a monetary remedy and valuation metric are generally specified.
4. See, e.g., *Suez, Sociedad General de Aguas de Barcelona S.A. and Interagua Servicios Integrales de Agua S.A. v. Argentine Republic* (ICSID Case No. ARB/03/17), Decision on Jurisdiction (16 May 2006) § 49.
5. See *Impregilo S.p.A. v. Argentina*, Award (2011), § 138 ("It follows from Article 1(1)(b) of the Argentina-Italy BIT that Impregilo's shares in AGBA were protected under the BIT. If AGBA was subjected to expropriation or unfair treatment with respect to its concession – an issue to be determined on the merits of the case – such action must also be considered to have affected Impregilo's rights as an investor, rights that were protected under the BIT.").
6. Alexandrov (2005: 45) (finding that ISDS tribunals considering shareholder claims "all considered it to be beyond doubt that a shareholder's interest in a company includes an interest in the assets of that company, including its licenses, contractual rights, rights under law, claims to money or economic performance, etc.") ICSID refers to the International Centre for Settlement of Investment Disputes which is the leading administrator of investment arbitrations.

7. See *Kagan v. Edison Bros. Stores Inc.*, 907 F.2d 690, 693 (7th Cir. 1990) ("The [shareholder and company creditor] investors are asking us to disregard [the company's] corporate form.... Although the [shareholder] plaintiffs want us to allow them to recover for injuries mediated through [the company], they most assuredly do not want us to hold them liable for [the company's] debts. They seek the best of both worlds: limited liability for debts incurred in the corporate name, and direct compensation for its losses. That cushy position is not one the law affords. Investors who created the corporate form cannot rend the veil they wove."); *Alford v. Frontier Enterprises, Inc.*, 599 F.2d 483 (1st. Cir. 1979) ([the shareholder] "is attempting to use the corporate form both as shield and sword at his will. [T]he corporate form effectively shielded [him] from liability" but the shareholder contended that he "can disregard the corporate entity and recover damages for himself. Of course, this is impermissible."); see generally Gaukrodger (2013: 15-24) (surveying advanced corporate law systems; shareholders generally benefit from limited liability but cannot claim for reflective loss).
8. OECD (2013a: 5); Gaukrodger (2013); *Day v. Cook*, [2001] EWCA Civ. 592 (Ct. App. 2001) § 1.
9. Reflective loss is also referred to as derivative loss or injury particularly in common law legal systems.
10. For a recent survey of shareholder cases of these various types, see, e.g., Valasek and Dumberry (2011: 73 et seq.).
11. See, e.g., *Total S.A. v. Argentina*, Decision on Objections to Jurisdiction (2006) § 80 ("Having found, however, that the assets and rights that Total claims have been injured in breach of the BIT fall under the definition of investments under the BIT, it is immaterial that they belong to Argentine companies in accordance with the law of Argentina. Total asserts its own treaty rights for their protection, regardless of any right, contractual or non-contractual that the various companies [in which it owns shares] might assert in respect of such assets and rights under local law before the courts of other authorities of Argentina, in order to seek redress or indemnification for damages suffered as a consequence of actions taken by those authorities."); Gaukrodger (2013: 27-29). Some commentators have suggested that reflective loss claims should be restricted to, *inter alia*, cases where the company's recourse in the domestic courts is impaired. Douglas (2009: 397) (suggesting that the availability of reflective loss claims in ISDS should be restricted, but that, under certain conditions, they should be available where the company has been deprived of a remedy to redress its injury or of the capacity to sue, or has been subjected to a denial of justice in the domestic courts).
12. Such non-pecuniary primary or judicial review remedies include i) the annulling of a governmental measure or decision; ii) injunctions (requiring a party to do or to refrain from doing something); and iii) declarations of the rights and obligations of the parties, or a declaration that a particular administrative decision was illegal without otherwise stating any consequences.
13. OECD (2012: 10); Gaukrodger and Gordon (2012: 24-27 & Annex 4).
14. There are many manifestations of the increasingly financial nature of investor-government relations under these rules. Claimants and governments now routinely hire financial experts to support or oppose claims for damages and lost profits. A new Journal of Damages in International Arbitration was launched in 2014 and devotes substantial attention to treaty claims against governments. Third-party financing by institutional investors of investment treaty claims against governments on a contingency basis has become common.
15. See *CMS Gas Transmission Company v. Argentina*, Award (2005); *Total, S.A. v. Argentina*, Award (2010).
16. See El Economista (2012).
17. *Gaubert v. United States*, 855 F.2d 1284, 1291 (5th Cir. 1989).
18. Gaukrodger and Gordon (2012: 19).
19. For examples relating to NAFTA-style treaties, see, e.g., *Renco Group, Inc. v. Peru*, Peru's Reply on Waiver §§ 22-24 (17 Aug. 2015); *Renco Group, Inc. v. Peru*, Second Submission of United States of America (non-disputing party), § 12 (1 Sept. 2015); *GAMI v. Mexico*, Submission of the United States (non-disputing party) (30 June 2003); *GAMI v. Mexico*, Escrito de Contestación of Mexico, §§ 166-67, pp. 61-64 (24 Nov. 2003) (agreeing with and quoting US submission); *Pope & Talbot v. Canada*, Canada Statement of Defence (Phase 3 – Damages) (18 Aug. 2002) §§ 49-54.
20. See Garg et al. (2016: 78).
21. See Carim (2016: 63).
22. See Cooperation and Facilitation Investment Agreement Between _____ and the Federative Republic of Brazil, § 1.4 (Version 2.3.1, 3 March 2016) (on file with the OECD Secretariat). It also allows only for state-to-state claims and excludes ISDS. Shareholders have no power to bring claims.

23. For example, laws in some jurisdictions also provide for entities such as certain types of partnerships that do not require the same practically irrevocable commitment of capital to the enterprise as is provided by shareholders. Partners have the power to dissolve the partnership.

24. See Blair (2003: 391) ("Partitioning has two aspects: Individual participants in the business are not held personally responsible for the debts or liabilities of the business (this aspect is commonly referred to as limited liability in the context of business corporations), *and* participants and third parties are assured that the pool of assets used in the business will be available to meet the needs of the business first (such as, to pay the claims of the business's creditors) before these assets can be distributed to shareholders") (footnotes omitted; emphasis in original).

25. The term "entity shielding" was formulated in Hansmann et al. (2006) and is used in Kraakman et al. (2009). Entity shielding is sometimes referred to as affirmative asset partitioning. See Armour, Hansmann and Kraakman (2009a: 6, n.12); Mayer (2013: 184-85) (noting use of both terms).

26. See Gaukrodger (2013: 17) (noting emphasis in German case law and scholarship on the principle that the company's assets are bound for the purpose of the business [*Zweckwidmung des Gesellschaftsvermögens*]); see also Clark (1986: § 1.2.3) (noting that because any partner can dissolve a partnership by express will at any time and withdraw its investment, "[t]he partnership's life is thus a precarious one, and this fact will give pause to those wanting to launch a large enterprise with large start-up costs"; contrasting the corporate entity in which individual shareholders cannot withdraw their investment, leading to a more stable existence that is "more likely to preserve the going concern value of large projects"); Blair (2003).

27. See Armour, Hertig and Kanda (2009: 118) ("both creditors *and* shareholders can benefit from appropriate restrictions on the ability [of shareholders] to divert ... assets, because such restrictions are likely to reduce a firm's costs of debt finance") (emphasis in original).

28. Blair (2003) ("[O]nce the funds paid to purchase those shares had been committed, limits were imposed – sometimes severe ones – on the ability of investors to withdraw funds from the business. The commitment of capital by shareholders ... helped protect the at-risk investments made by other corporate participants. ... [T]he capital contributed or pledged in the form of equity shares helped secure a pool of 'bonding assets', which made it easier to draw in other risky contributions to the enterprise."). See generally Hansmann et al. (2006) (broad historical survey); Lamoreaux and Rosenthal (2006) (impact in Europe).

    Lock-in of shareholder capital is not without costs. For example, it can allow those in control of the firm to behave opportunistically toward minority shareholders because the latter are generally unable to withdraw their investment. However, as noted, in all advanced systems of corporate law, lock-in is made available in the business corporation and is widely chosen by market participants. Corporate and other law seeks to manage the potential costs of lock-in through many devices such as the imposition of fiduciary duties on directors or constraints on transactions by the company with related parties.

29. Armour, Hansmann and Kraakman (2009a: 22).

30. Hansmann et al. (2006: 1340-41) ("It would be practically impossible in most types of firm to create effective entity shielding without special rules of law."; efforts to do so would suffer from high transactions costs and likely insuperable moral hazard) (footnotes omitted); see also Armour, Hansmann and Kraakman (2009a: 8) ("Entity shielding doctrine [imposed by law] is needed to create common expectations, among a firm and its various present and potential creditors, concerning the effect that a contract between a firm and one of its creditors will have on the security available to the firm's other creditors.").

31. See Hansmann et al. (2006: 1338) ("[E]ntity shielding, unlike [limited liability], can be achieved only through the special property rules of entity law. For this reason, we believe that entity shielding is the sine qua non of the legal entity ...") (footnotes omitted); Armour, Hansmann and Kraakman (2009b: 37).

32. The percentage of foreign shareholders in listed companies has increased significantly in recent years. See Gaukrodger (2013: 49) (citing research showing that half of the listed companies in the United Kingdom and Belgium, 40% of the companies in France and Germany and around 30% of the companies in Spain and Italy have a large foreign shareholder); The Economist (2016b) ("the proportion of shares in Britain's firms owned by foreigners zoomed passed the 50% mark in 2015").

33. Category II may include some institutional investors who prefer to diversify their risk across many companies and incur a loss in some companies rather than bring high cost claims as a shareholder.

34. If it is assumed that creditors can also claim for reflective loss in ISDS, they could be categorised into similar categories. Likely reflective loss claimants among creditors may be fewer because, as noted

above, creditors generally suffer less reflective loss than shareholders (providing the company is solvent); creditor interests and losses may also be dispersed if, for example, the company's bonds are widely held. If it is assumed that creditors cannot claim for reflective loss in ISDS, they would all be "excluded claimants" whose fortunes would lie solely with company recourse.

35. Claims arising out of the Fortis bailout and sale by the Belgian government appeared to involve a potential scenario of this type although there is little public information about the claims. Claims by Belgian shareholders in the Belgian bank against the Belgian government were reportedly rejected by the Belgian courts applying the no reflective loss principle; only the company could bring the claim (L'avenir (2011); Le Soir (2011)). A major Chinese shareholder in Fortis brought a treaty claim. Under the unique combination of rules outlined above, the claim would not be subject to a similar defence. The issue was not raised in preliminary proceedings and the treaty claim was rejected at that stage based on the timing of key events and the date of entry into force of the relevant treaty. *Ping An Life Insurance Co. of China Ltd. v. Belgium*, ICSID, Award (30 April 2015).

36. In some exceptional situations, such as where it is expected that an existing important shareholder would support the company, a transfer of shares to a third party may affect the creditworthiness of the company even under national law.

37. Compare Alexandrov (2005: 45) (finding that ISDS tribunals considering shareholder claims "all considered it to be beyond doubt that a shareholder's interest in a company includes an interest in the assets of that company, including its licenses, contractual rights, rights under law, claims to money or economic performance, etc.") *with* Ferran (2009: 147) (Under UK law, "[t]he shareholder's financial interest is in the company itself and it does not amount to a direct interest in the company's assets.").

38. See Gaukrodger (2014a: 24-25) (discussing uncertainties about transfer or retention of rights to bring an ISDS claim in connection with a transfer of shares).

39. See Gaillard (2015: 226-27) ("C'est en effet de manière généralement simpliste qu[e] [la jurisprudence en vertu de traités d'investissement] considère que l'actionnaire doit être traité comme la société elle-même, au pro rata de sa participation. En d'autres termes, un actionnaire à 80% aurait subi 80% du dommage de la société et un actionnaire à 3%, 3% de ce dommage. Sur ce point, une appréciation plus fine serait bienvenue. ... [L]a situation des créanciers de la société concernée doit également être prise en compte.") [It is in effect in a generally simplistic manner that ISDS arbitral cases have considered that a shareholder must be treated like the company itself, using its pro rata share ownership. In other words, an 80% shareholder is found to suffer 80% of the company injury and a 3% shareholder, 3% of the company injury. On this issue, a more refined analysis would be welcome. ... [T]he situation of the creditors of the company at issue must also be taken into consideration.") [Author's translation]

40. *Ioan Micula et al. v. Romania*, ICSID, Award (11 Dec. 2013).

41. See, e.g., *Mid-State Fertilizer Co. v. Exchange National Bank of Chicago*, 877 F.2d 1333, 1335-36 (7th Cir. 1989) (trying to apportion the recovery after a corporate injury according to who bears the effects between equity investors, debt investors, employees and others "would be a nightmare").

42. Hansmann et al. (2006: 1352 53).

43. The issue of damages will often arise only if the tribunal has already found that the government caused the injury to the company. The tribunal may hesitate to reduce shareholder recovery for the benefit of the government on the basis of creditor injury.

44. This section is adapted from Gaukrodger (2014a).

45. See Ferran (2009: 349) ("unsecured creditors may demand higher interest to compensate them for the risk of being postponed to the secured debt in the event of the borrowing company's insolvency").

46. Id. ("the existence of security raises the expected cost of default for unsecured creditors by reducing the available asset pool and thus creates incentives for these parties to monitor more extensively"), quoting Schwartz (1981).

47. See Gaukrodger (2013: 49-50, 42, Figure 5).

48. No view is expressed about the likelihood of success of such claims at any stage.

49. The discussion focuses on companies with a single board. Some corporate law systems, such as in Germany, provide for two separate boards with different responsibilities. These differences do not affect the basic delegation of management responsibility by shareholders addressed here.

50. See Strine (2012) ("in the American corporate law tradition, stockholders who are not directly controlling board action are entitled to pursue only their own self-interest, without owing any fiduciary duties to other stockholders or the corporation itself").

51. See, e.g., Ferran (2001: 245-247) ("Secondary policy considerations also come into play to explain the absolute nature of the rule that [a shareholder] cannot sue for reflective loss where the company also has a cause of action. If a company agrees a compromise settlement with a defendant, principles of certainty and fairness dictate that shareholders should not then be able to re-open the case by seeking to pursue the defendant in a personal capacity. Shareholder complaints about the terms of a compromise should properly be directed at those who agreed the compromise on the company's behalf, not the original wrongdoer.")

52. As outlined by US appellate courts, this hindrance of amicable settlement is one of the reasons why shareholder claims for reflective loss are generally barred under national law. See, e.g., *Potthoff v. Morin*, 245 F.3d 710, 717 (8th Cir. 2001) ("The rule is a salutary one: if a shareholder, dissatisfied with the dealings entered into between his corporation and a third party, automatically possessed a personal right of action against the third party, then corporations would be paralyzed."; dismissing shareholder suit arising out of termination of license to company by local government port authority; only the company could claim) (quoting *In re Dein Host*, Inc., 835 F.2d 402, 406 [1st Cir.1987]).

53. See Johnson (2013) (quoting former senior executive noting that "it is strange that shareholders are negotiating an issue such as this around the side of [Repsol's CEO]").

54. See Buck (2014) ("Negotiators from the company and the Argentine government signed off on the complex settlement in Buenos Aires on Friday, but the deal still needs the approval of the Repsol board and shareholders ...").

55. See Voon et al. (2014: 58) ("A central uncertainty has been whether ownership requires some form of active participation or beneficial ownership or includes merely passive ownership of an investment by a corporate subsidiary or shell company. Several tribunals have dismissed the argument that an investor must have a beneficial or active ownership interest in order to 'own' an investment. In the absence of any such requirement in the text of the relevant [investment treaty], most tribunals have taken a broad view of ownership that extends to passive and formal legal ownership. This would cover formal legal ownership by shell companies or corporate subsidiaries to whom ownership in the investment has been transferred to gain the protection of an [investment treaty]."); see also, e.g., *ADC Affiliate Limited and ADC & ADMC Management Limited v. Republic of Hungary*, ICSID, Award § 359 (2 Oct. 2006) ("the [Cyprus-Hungary] BIT is governing, and in its Article 1(3)(b) Cyprus and Hungary have agreed that a Cypriot "investor" protected by that treaty includes a "legal person constituted or incorporated in compliance with the law" of Cyprus, which each Claimant is conceded to be. ... [I]nquiry stops upon establishment of the State of incorporation"); *Saluka Investments B.V. v. Czech Republic*, UNCITRAL, Partial Award, 17 March 2006 §§ 240-41 ("The Tribunal has some sympathy for the argument that a company which has no real connection with a State party to a BIT, and which is in reality a mere shell company controlled by another company which is not constituted under the laws of that State, should not be entitled to invoke the provisions of that treaty. Such a possibility lends itself to abuses of the arbitral procedure, and to practices of "treaty shopping" which can share many of the disadvantages of the widely criticised practice of "forum shopping."; finding, however, that the BIT reference only to the state of incorporation governs.)

    Note by Turkey:
    The information in this document with reference to "Cyprus" relates to the southern part of the Island. There is no single authority representing both Turkish and Greek Cypriot people on the Island. Turkey recognises the Turkish Republic of Northern Cyprus (TRNC). Until a lasting and equitable solution is found within the context of the United Nations, Turkey shall preserve its position concerning the "Cyprus issue".

    Note by all the European Union Member States of the OECD and the European Union:
    The Republic of Cyprus is recognised by all members of the United Nations with the exception of Turkey. The information in this document relates to the area under the effective control of the Government of the Republic of Cyprus.

56. Some treaties also make it easy to obtain treaty coverage for entities incorporated in other jurisdictions as well. The Netherlands Model BIT provides that Dutch-incorporated companies are Dutch nationals for treaty purposes and also provides that any company controlled by a Netherlands holding company has Netherlands nationality for purposes of bringing treaty claims. Under this model, holding companies in any jurisdiction can benefit from treaty coverage provided they are directly or indirectly controlled by a Dutch holding company. The Netherlands and other EU Member States are reviewing their model investment treaties.

57. The exact moment when such a shift will be found to be abusive is unclear, but the existence of a risk is sufficient to encourage structuring in advance.

58. See, e.g., *Phoenix Action, Ltd. v. Czech Republic*, ICSID, Award (15 April 2009) ("international investors can of course structure *upstream* [i.e., in advance] their investments, which meet the requirement of participating in the economy of the host State, in a manner that best fits their need for international protection, in choosing freely the vehicle through which they perform their investment").

59. OECD (2013b: 18-19) ("Given the policy issues raised by claims for reflective loss, it is important to identify countervailing policy arguments that would support the availability of shareholder claims for reflective loss because they are widely available under current law. The Chair invited the group to identify the reasons that could explain the allowance of such claims in ISDS. Discussing the issue, no strong arguments were put forward to explain the differences taken in investment treaties versus the approach taken by the same countries in their corporate law systems. The lack of an identifiable policy rationale for existing law was an important finding and merited further attention.")

References

Alexandrov, S. (2005), "The 'Baby Boom' of Treaty-Based Arbitrations and the Jurisdiction of ICSID Tribunals: Shareholders as 'Investors' and Jurisdiction *Ratione* Temporis", *The Law and Practice of International Courts and Tribunals*, Vol. 4., Issue 1, pp. 19-59.

Armour, J., H. Hansmann and R. Kraakman (2009a), "What is Corporate Law?", ch. 1 in Kraakman, R. et al., *The Anatomy of Corporate Law*, 2d ed., Oxford.

Armour, J., H. Hansmann and R. Kraakman (2009b), "Agency Problems and Legal Strategies", ch. 2 in Kraakman, R. et al., *The Anatomy of Corporate Law*, 2d ed., Oxford.

Armour, J., G. Hertig and H. Kanda (2009), "Transactions with Creditors", ch. 5 in Kraakman, R. et al., *The Anatomy of Corporate Law*, 2d ed., Oxford.

Blair, M. (2015), "What must corporate directors do? Maximizing shareholder value versus creating value through team production.", *The Initiative on 21st Century Capitalism*, No. 23, *www.brookings.edu/~/media/research/files/papers/2015/06/maximizing-shareholder-value-team-production-blair/blairrevised-61115.pdf.*

Blair, M. (2003), "Locking in Capital: What Corporate Law Achieved for Business Organizers in the Nineteenth Century", *UCLA Law Review*, Vol. 51, No. 2, pp. 387-455.

Buck, T. (2014), "Repsol to Vote on $5bn Argentina settlement", *Financial Times*, 23 February 2014.

Carim, X. (2016), "International Investment Agreements and Africa's Structural Transformation: A Perspective from South Africa", in K. Singh and B. Ilge (eds.), *Rethinking Bilateral Investment Treaties: Critical Issues and Policy Choices*, Both ENDS, Madhyam and SOMO, *www.madhyam.org.in/wp-content/themes/madhyan/books/rethinking-bilateral/R ethinking-BIT-Book.epub.*

Clark, R.C. (1986), *Corporate Law*, Little, Brown.

Davies, P. et al. (2009), "Convergence in Corporate Law", ch. 10 in Kraakman, R. et al., *The Anatomy of Corporate Law*, 2d ed., Oxford.

Douglas, Z. (2009), *The International Law of Investment Claims*, Cambridge.

El Economista (Mexico) (2012), "TGN demandará a gobierno de Argentina", 10 October 2012, *http://eleconomista.com.mx/industria-global/2012/10/10/tgn-demandara-gobierno-argentinahttp:/eleconomista.com.mx/industria-global/2012/10/10/tgn-demandara-gobierno-argentina.*

Ferran, E. (2013), "Reflective Loss", Presentation to Freedom of Investment Roundtable 19, October 2013.

Ferran, E. (2009), *Principles of Corporate Finance Law*, Oxford.

Ferran, E. (2001), "Litigation by Shareholders and Reflective Loss", *The Cambridge Law Journal*, Vol. 60, Issue 2, pp. 231-264.

Franck, S.D. and L.E. Wylie (2015), "Predicting Outcomes in Investment Treaty Arbitration", *Duke Law Journal*, Vol. 65, No. 3, pp. 459-526, *http://scholarship.law.duke.edu/dlj/vol65/iss3/2.*

Gaillard, E. (2015), "Le concours de procédures arbitrales dans le droit des investissements", *Mélanges en l'honneur du Professeur Pierre Mayer*, pp. 225-239, LGDJ Lextenso Editions, Paris.

Garg, S., I. Tripathy and S. Roy (2016), "The Indian Model Bilateral Investment Treaty: Continuity and Change", in K. Singh and B. Ilge (eds.), *Rethinking Bilateral Investment Treaties: Critical Issues and Policy Choices*, Both ENDS, Madhyam and SOMO, *www.madhyam.org.in/wp-content/themes/madhyan/books/rethinking-bilateral/R ethinking-BIT-Book.epub.*

Gaukrodger, D. (2014a), "Investment Treaties and Shareholder Claims for Reflective Loss: Insights from Advanced Systems of Corporate Law", *OECD Working Papers on International Investment*, No. 2014/02, OECD Publishing, Paris, *http://dx.doi.org/10.1787/5jz0xvgngmr3-en.*

Gaukrodger, D. (2014b), "Investment Treaties and Shareholder Claims: Analysis of Treaty Practice", *OECD Working Papers on International Investment*, 2014/03, OECD Publishing, *http://dx.doi.org/10.1787/5jxvk6shpvs4-en.*

Gaukrodger, D. (2013), "Investment Treaties as Corporate Law: Shareholder Claims and Issues of Consistency", *OECD Working Papers on International Investment*, No. 2013/03, OECD Publishing, Paris, *http://dx.doi.org/10.1787/5k3w9t44mt0v-en.*

Gaukrodger, D. and K. Gordon (2012), "Investor-State Dispute Settlement: A Scoping Paper for the Investment Policy Community", *OECD Working Papers on International Investment*, No. 2012/03, OECD Publishing, Paris, *http://dx.doi.org/10.1787/5k46b1r85j6f-en.*

Hansmann, H. and R. Kraakman (2000), "The Essential Role of Organizational Law", *The Yale Law Journal*, 110, pp. 387-440.

Hansmann, H., R. Kraakman and R. Squire (2006), "Law and the Rise of the Firm", *Harvard Law Review*, Vol. 119, No. 5, pp. 1333-1403.

Johnson, M. (2013), "Repsol's Big Shareholders Call the Shots in YPF Settlement", *Financial Times*, 27 November 2013.

Kraakman, R. et al. (2009), *The Anatomy of Corporate Law*, 2d ed., Oxford.

L'avenir (2011), "Des actionnaires de Fortis exhortent Ageas de se prononcer sur une affaire contre l'Etat", 14 June 2011, *www.lavenir.net/cnt/245126955.*

Lamoreaux, N. and J.-L. Rosenthal (2006), "Entity Shielding and the Development of Business Forms: A Comparative Perspective", *Harvard Law Review Forum*, 119, pp. 238-45.

Le Soir (2011), "Fortis: L'Etat obtient gain de cause face à un actionnaire 'lésé", 4 February 2011, *http://archives.lesoir.be/fortis-l-8217-etat-obtient-gain-de-cause-face-a-un-acti_t-20110204-01879Q.html.*

Mayer, C. (2013), *Firm Commitment*, Oxford.

OECD (2016), "The quest for balance between investor protection and governments' right to regulate", OECD Investment Treaty Conference, 14 March 2016, *www.oecd.org/daf/inv/investment-policy/OECD-investment-treaties-2016-agenda.pdf.*

OECD (2013a), Freedom of Investment Roundtable 18, Summary of Discussion, *www.oecd.org/investment/investment-policy/18thFOIRoundtableSummary.pdf.*

OECD (2013b), Freedom of Investment Roundtable 19, Summary of Discussion, *www.oecd.org/daf/inv/investment-policy/19thFOIroundtableSummary.pdf.*

OECD (2012), Freedom of Investment Roundtable, Government perspectives on investor-state dispute settlement: A progress report, *www.oecd.org/daf/inv/investment-policy/ISDSprogressreport.pdf.*

Pohl, J., K. Mashigo and A. Nohen (2012), "Dispute Settlement Provisions in International Investment Agreements: A Large Sample Survey", *OECD Working Papers on International Investment*, No. 2012/02, OECD Publishing, Paris, *http://dx.doi.org/10.1787/5k8xb71nf628-en.*

Ripinsky, S. and K. Williams (2008), *Damages in International Investment Law*, London.

Schwartz, A. (1981), "Security Interests and Bankruptcy Priorities: A Review of Current Theories", *The Journal of Legal Studies*, Vol. 10, No. 1, pp. 1-37.

Strine, L. (2012), "One fundamental corporate governance question we face: Can corporations be managed for the long term unless their powerful electorates also act and think long term?", *The Business Lawyer*, 2010 Issue, Vol. 66, No. 1, pp. 1-26.

The Economist (2016b), "Land ahoy", 9 April 2016, *www.economist.com/news/britain/21696516-despite-calls-protectionism-britain-remains-strikingly-comfortable-free-trade-land.*

UNCTAD (2016a), "Record Number of Investor-State Arbitrations Filed in 2015", 2 February 2016, *http://investmentpolicyhub.unctad.org/News/Hub/Home/458.*

UNCTAD (2016b), *Investment Dispute Settlement Navigator* (database), *http://investmentpolicyhub.unctad.org/ISDS?status=3* (accessed on 26 April 2016).

Valasek, M.J. and P. Dumberry (2011), "Developments in the Legal Standing of Shareholders and Holding Corporations in Investor-State Disputes", *ICSID Review*, Vol. 26, Issue 1, pp. 34-75.

Van Harten, G. (2008), *Investment Treaty Law and Public Law*, Oxford.

Voon, T., A. Mitchell and J. Munro (2014), "Legal Responses to Corporate Manoeuvring in International Investment Arbitration", *Journal of International Dispute Settlement*, 5, pp. 41-68.

WTO (2016), *Chronological List of Disputes*, *www.wto.org/english/tratop_e/dispu_e/dispu_status_e.htm*.

ORGANISATION FOR ECONOMIC CO-OPERATION AND DEVELOPMENT

The OECD is a unique forum where governments work together to address the economic, social and environmental challenges of globalisation. The OECD is also at the forefront of efforts to understand and to help governments respond to new developments and concerns, such as corporate governance, the information economy and the challenges of an ageing population. The Organisation provides a setting where governments can compare policy experiences, seek answers to common problems, identify good practice and work to co-ordinate domestic and international policies.

The OECD member countries are: Australia, Austria, Belgium, Canada, Chile, the Czech Republic, Denmark, Estonia, Finland, France, Germany, Greece, Hungary, Iceland, Ireland, Israel, Italy, Japan, Korea, Luxembourg, Mexico, the Netherlands, New Zealand, Norway, Poland, Portugal, the Slovak Republic, Slovenia, Spain, Sweden, Switzerland, Turkey, the United Kingdom and the United States. The European Union takes part in the work of the OECD.

OECD Publishing disseminates widely the results of the Organisation's statistics gathering and research on economic, social and environmental issues, as well as the conventions, guidelines and standards agreed by its members.

OECD PUBLISHING, 2, rue André-Pascal, 75775 PARIS CEDEX 16
(21 2016 02 1 P) ISBN 978-92-64-25756-6 – 2016

www.ingramcontent.com/pod-product-compliance
Ingram Content Group UK Ltd.
Pitfield, Milton Keynes, MK11 3LW, UK
UKHW051459290926
15471UKWH00008B/1303

9 789264 257566